Hamas

'A compelling account of the origins and rise of Hamas. Through a wealth of original reporting stretching back many years, the authors break new ground as they explore the characters and thinking behind this increasingly influential Palestinian Islamist movement. It is a chastening tale, expertly told.'
Rory McCarthy, Middle East correspondent, *The Guardian*

'Hamas remains one of the main Islamist organizations of the Arab world. While it is squarely located in Palestine, the power of its message and the audacity of its activities, as well as its role in the wider Arab–Israeli conflict, give it a status, voice and influence that are well beyond its currently narrow administrative base in the Gaza Strip. In this book, Milton-Edwards and Farrell not only provide a solid analysis of this organization but apply their considerable expertise to show that the rest of the world ignores it at its peril.'
Anoush Ehteshami, author of *Globalization and Geopolitics in the Middle East: Old Games, New Rules*

'This is the essential book on the Palestinian Islamist movement Hamas. Drawing on decades of experience and meetings with the founders (such as assassinated leaders Sheikh Ahmed Yassin and Abdel Aziz Rantissi) and its current leadership, the authors provide a compelling portrait of Hamas as a nationalist party and a social welfare network as well as a violent resistance organization. Engagingly written, this book makes abundantly clear why there is no solution to the Israel–Palestine conflict without Hamas.'
Eugene Rogan, Director, Middle East Centre, University of Oxford

'In this exceptional book, Beverley Milton-Edwards and Stephen Farrell examine the emergence of Hamas, its ideological underpinnings and the extent to which its very ideological basis now has to compromise with changing realities. This is an important book, ambitious both in its conceptual underpinnings and in the new material it offers us in understanding perhaps the most dynamic popular movement to have emerged out of the crucible of the Israel–Palestine conflict in the last fifty years.'
Clive Jones, University of Leeds

Hamas

The Islamic Resistance Movement

Beverley Milton-Edwards

and

Stephen Farrell

Polity

First published in 2010 by Polity Press
Reprinted 2010

Polity Press
65 Bridge Street
Cambridge CB2 1UR, UK

Polity Press
350 Main Street
Malden, MA 02148, USA

ISBN-13: 978-0-7456-4295-6
ISBN-13: 978-0-7456-4296-3 (pb)

A catalogue record for this book is available from the British Library.

Typeset in Palatino on 10/11.5pt
by Servis Filmsetting Ltd, Stockport, Cheshire
Printed and bound in Great Britain by the MPG Books Group

For further information on Polity, visit our website: www.politybooks.com

Contents

Preface and Acknowledgements

There is no middle ground with Hamas. In the two decades since the largest, most influential and deadly Islamist organization emerged from the crucible of the Palestinian–Israeli conflict it has polarized opinion, and will continue to do so.

Hamas's credo can be defined simply as 'Islam is the solution'. It offers an Islamic solution to the conflict with Israel, wrapping itself in the twin banners of religion and nationalism. Hamas's enemies define it as a terrorist organization that has killed and maimed Israelis for more than two decades, civilians and soldiers alike. They argue that it is little more than the proxy of a regional Middle East power – Iran – and shares with its patron an all-consuming desire to bring about the destruction of the state of Israel. Hamas's supporters see it through another prism entirely: for them it is an uncompromising yet clear-sighted organization founded by a leadership which spent decades in the political wilderness telling the unpopular truth that the political orthodoxies of their time were misguided, and that in Israel the Palestinian people faced an enemy that had to be resisted, not accommodated. Hamas argues that it alone is prepared to stand up to win statehood and independence for Palestinians.

But it ill behoves either enemy or friend to make simplistic generalizations about an organization that, whatever its true nature, in 2006 became the first Islamist movement to ascend to power in the Middle East by democratic means. It is neither al Qaeda nor the Taliban. It owes something to Hezbollah and much to the Muslim Brotherhood. It is Islamist, but nationalist; Sunni, yet supported by a Shi'a regional power; democratic, yet opaque; populist, yet cruel. Many see Hamas as a significant obstacle to peace with Israel and wider hopes for stability in the Middle East. Others believe that, until it is recognized as a legitimate political force and included in the accommodation of power, there can never be peace in the region.

To study is not to support. For enemies and friends – and in both camps passions often cloud reasoned debate – Hamas, the Islamic Resistance

Movement, is a phenomenon worthy of analysis. Part political, part social, part military, it has proved adaptable and resilient in the face of opposition from regional and world superpowers. It has won parliamentary, municipal, student and professional elections, and emerged as a genuine threat to long-established Palestinian political movements more than twice its age.

The purpose of this book, through hundreds of interviews conducted over three decades, is to present first-hand accounts of Hamas's fighters, social activists, victims, political supporters and opponents, and by so doing to give a glimpse into how Hamas was born, grew and thrived in the mosques, casbahs and refugee camps of the West Bank, the Gaza Strip and East Jerusalem – the Palestinian Territories occupied by Israel since the 1967 Six Day War.

Hamas cannot be understood in isolation from other Islamist actors who preceded it. There has been a history of Muslim opposition to foreign rule and occupation since the British were awarded political control of Palestine after the First World War and the Zionists sought to make their homeland there. Its roots lie in radicalism of little-known Islamist sheikhs in the 1930s who called for 'jihad' to liberate Palestine long before the word entered the Western lexicon. A generation later, refugees of the first Arab–Israeli war of 1948–9 came to believe that, through a pious adherence to Islam, they could achieve political freedom and create a state ruled according to their Islamic principles. After the 1967 war some of these early Islamists were tolerated, encouraged even, by Israel. Under the age-old principle of 'divide and rule', Israel saw in the fledgling Islamists an opportunity to undermine Yasser Arafat's long-dominant Fatah, the mainstay of the secular nationalist Palestine Liberation Organization (PLO).

Out of these antecedents the modern Hamas movement emerged in 1987 from the tumult of the first Palestinian Intifada (uprising) against Israel's twenty-year-old military occupation. Hamas claimed the Intifada in its name, and embarked on a competition to wrest Palestinian hearts and minds from the PLO. It became a formidable foe, waging a murderous armed campaign of suicide bombings against Israel and, later, missile bombardment of Israeli towns.

But Hamas has won support from Palestinians, not just because of what they see as a legitimate campaign of violent resistance against Israeli military occupation, but also because Hamas is – at one and the same time – a movement with a powerful, highly motivated and well-organized social welfare network, which it used to support people during years of deprivation and enforced statelessness, earning their gratitude and trust. In this book we detail the ways in which Hamas forged these links with the Palestinian people, slowly ousting the PLO from its hitherto unchallenged position of pre-eminence.

Hamas has developed a powerful military wing and instilled in many

Palestinians the belief that only through violent armed struggle and the promise of paradise will they achieve their political goals of freedom and independence. Hamas suicide bombing campaigns encouraged hundreds of willing volunteers to sacrifice themselves, in a self-declared holy war, in attacks on Israeli targets. Hamas leaders defended its actions, coldly warning that, if Palestinian civilians continued to die at the hands of Israeli tank commanders, F16 pilots and snipers, then Israel's civilians would suffer the same fate.

In January 2006 Hamas won the Palestinian parliamentary elections, demonstrating that it could marshal its supporters – including thousands of women who turned out for rallies under the green banner of the movement. It also attracted the votes of many other Palestinians who were disillusioned by corruption in the Fatah-controlled Palestinian Authority (PA) and lack of progress in peace talks with Israel. The Western world refused to accept Hamas's victory at the ballot box, and Hamas refused to bow to the international community's demands that it recognize Israel and renounce violence. The outcome was a double deadlock – internal and external – which saw a higher death toll, higher rates of poverty and even more despair among Israelis and Palestinians about any prospect of a peace settlement.

Internally, Islamist Hamas and secular Fatah consistently refused to share power. Nor was this likely, given that each was dependent on patrons with conflicting agendas – Iran and the United States. Two armed forces sharing a tiny slice of land, each ambitious for total control, was a dynamic that could not be contained. In June 2007 – just eighteen months after it won the election – Hamas's armed forces routed Fatah in Gaza and seized full military control of the narrow coastal strip. When the dust cleared there was a two-headed Palestinian Authority – Hamas in Gaza and Fatah in the West Bank. Externally, there was also a stand-off between Hamas and Israel, with the West supporting Israel.

Israel sought to isolate Hamas with an economic and military blockade. Hamas hit back with rockets into Israel. The nearest either side came to any form of agreement was a six-month ceasefire, which ended in December 2008. Hamas immediately began firing hundreds of rockets into Israeli towns and villages, and Israel hit back with an unprecedented three-week military offensive which left more than 1,300 Palestinians and thirteen Israelis dead. Gaza was shattered, but Hamas remained in power and as defiant as ever.

Hamas can be excoriated, but it should not be underestimated. As we demonstrate throughout this book, it is one of the most important Islamic organizations in the Middle East. Its Sunni credentials mean that it is admired by Islamic groups active in North Africa, the Levant, the Gulf, Asia and Europe. For them, Hamas's brand of religious nationalism echoes their own political aspirations more than the worldwide jihad of Usama Bin Laden's al Qaeda. Thus, it represents the increasing fusion of religion and politics among Muslims in the twenty-first century. But it also highlights the consequences for the West of refusing to acknowledge the role that such movements play in shaping and governing their societies and influencing their relationship with the regional and global order. Hamas has redefined the nature of national liberation struggles by inserting its own brand of lethal violence into the equation. It has shown that Islamists can compete, and win, against weak secular regimes in power in many politically constrained regimes across the Muslim world. Even to the point that, exactly four years after Hamas's historic 2006 victory in the Palestinian parliamentary polls, its opponents balked at the military and political difficulties of ousting it electorally, and opted instead to delay the next parliamentary elections, scheduled for January 2010. Hamas's success has only been underscored by the refusal of secular, Western-backed regimes to let Islamists compete in free elections in Egypt and other neighbouring countries. Against this domestic and international context Hamas has had to come to terms with the limits of its own strength, but so have its far more powerful enemies. Hamas cannot conquer them, but they have failed to crush Hamas.

*****

We want to thank the many people who helped us in the realization and writing of this book. Particular thanks to Nabil Feidy of Jerusalem, for inspiring the collaboration and friendship that has developed during the course of this project. Nabil's emporium is a unique meeting place of calm and companionship in a tense and uneasy world. We also want to thank many colleagues and friends who have been so generous in supporting us and sharing their own work and insights, giving us advice, views and resources which it has taken many decades in the field to amass. They include, among nameless others, Hein Knegt, Franz Makkan, Tor Wennesland, Colin Smith, Jonathan McIvor, Colonel Michael Pearson, Colonel Barry Southern, Khadr Musleh, Bob and Mary Mitchell, Rema Hammami, Alex Pollock, Ray Dolphin, Aileen and Scott Martin, Mouin Rabbani, Jeff Aronson, Ilan and Galia Katsir, Don Macintyre, Rory McCarthy, James Hider, Yonit Farago, Ilan Mizrahi, Ronen Zvulun, Sarah El Deeb, Diaa Hadid and Alan Johnston.

We have been enormously lucky to benefit from the help of a unique crew of people in Gaza and the West Bank who have put themselves at risk in their attempt to bring us to some of the most illuminating and important voices in this battered and brutalized conflict zone. For years Azmi Keshawi, with his laser-sharpened vision, has been a fantastic help in squirrelling out a range of usually reticent and publicity-shy Islamist sources to tell us their stories and share their experiences in Gaza, often at great risk to himself and his wonderfully phlegmatic driver, Abu Hanafi.

Nuha Awadallah also cuts a unique figure and has been a dear friend in helping us to realize this project. Her many changes of fashion and headgear make her instantly recognizable, along with her deep passion for bringing the light of truth out of the darkness. She has gone to extraordinary lengths to introduce us to the great cast of actors that all have a place on the stage in this particular account of Hamas.

Hassan Jabr and Fares Akram in Gaza have both played an extremely important role in facilitating our research. Our thanks also to driver-bodyguard extraordinaire Ashraf al-Masri, who has accompanied us on our many visits to the Gaza Strip and made sure we didn't get kidnapped, even during the most lawless times. Without Nuha and Azmi, Ashraf, Fares Akram, Hassan Jabr, Abu Hanafi and their unflagging sense of determination and bravery, this book would not have been possible. Most of the people we have cited in the text have been identified, but there were some instances when for security reasons interviewees requested anonymity. To those interviewees – Palestinian, Israeli, Egyptian, European, Canadian, American – and to others who gave their time to listen to our questions and talk to us, we offer our profound thanks.

All the photographs in the book were taken by Stephen Farrell, apart from photo 6.2, for which we extend our thanks to Ronen Zvulun.

At Polity we would very much like to extend our deep gratitude to Louise Knight, Emma Hutchinson, Clare Ansell and Rachel Donnelly for taking the book on and having the patience and forbearance to wait for it finally to materialize when at times there were immense trials and travails. Our thanks also to Caroline Richmond for her copyediting.

We would also like to give our chocolate-flavoured thanks to Cara McNeill and Joshua McNeill for keeping the authors grounded in the real world of throwaway culture, sushi, chocolate, MIKA music, hi-energy drinks, more chocolate, mini-clips, ice cream, children's DVDs, mp3 players, more chocolate, and the everyday challenges of learning homework, taking school exams, playing rugby and refining the fine arts of debating and film-making.

Map 1   1947 UN Partition Plan

Maps

Map 2   Gaza pre-disengagement, May 2005

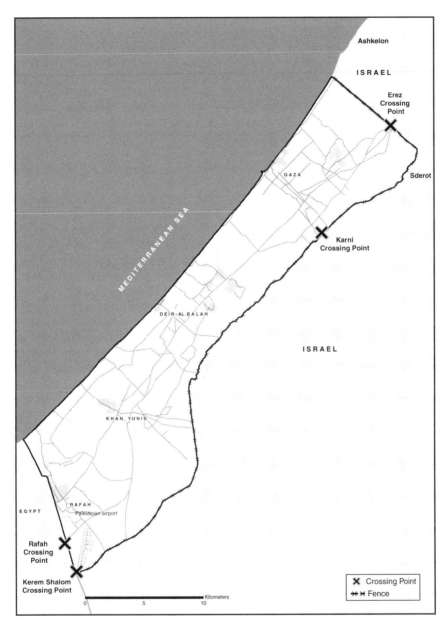

Map 3   Gaza post-disengagement, November 2005

This book is dedicated to Reem Makhoul – an extra-ordinary wedding gift to you, Reem, from the authors.

1

We Deal with Allah Directly

The world is in a hurry. We are not in a hurry.

Abu Bakr Nofal, Hamas[1]

Gaza, shortly after dawn on 26 January 2006, and a chill wind has scattered the last echoes of morning prayers down a deserted Izz ad-Din al-Qassam Street. For once, everything is quiet. In the winter skies above Gaza, Israeli spotter planes are buzzing overhead alongside huge white surveillance balloons. Both are transmitting real-time data down to fortified border posts where olive-uniformed Israeli soldiers monitor the Jewish state's Palestinian neighbours.

But this morning the electronic descendants of Gideon's spies have little to report to their commanders in Tel Aviv, only 40 miles north up the Mediterranean shoreline. No one is being killed. No one is being wounded. There are no armed men rushing their dying colleagues to hospital. There are no rallies, demonstrations or angry funerals, which are a feature of life in the sealed-off coastal strip that is home to one and a half million stateless Palestinians. Everything is normal – which is abnormal, for Gaza.

The reason is that Palestinians are in shock. And for once it has nothing to do with Israel. The day before, Palestinians in the Gaza Strip and 50 miles away in the West Bank and East Jerusalem held parliamentary elections, only for the second time ever. This morning they awoke to a new political power in the land, the radical, politically inexperienced, populist – and extremely violent – Islamist faction *Harakat al-Muqawama al-Islamiyya*, better known to the world as Hamas.

This was not supposed to happen. Hamas was running in its first-ever national elections after two decades as a pariah. In the five years leading up to the elections its armed militants had killed more than 400 people – including Israeli soldiers, settlers and civilians, foreign tourists and immigrant workers – and carried out more than fifty suicide bombings.[2] During this period Israelis from all walks of life were targeted, and treated as a monolithic mass by Hamas's enmity.

Fatah, the secular nationalist movement which had long dominated Palestinian politics, was widely expected to win. True, its iconic founder, Yasser Arafat, was gone, dead and buried more than a year earlier on a hilltop in the West Bank city of Ramallah instead of the city that he truly coveted for his capital: Jerusalem. True also, Fatah was handicapped by a decade-long reputation for mismanagement, nepotism and corruption over its stewardship of the Palestinian Authority (PA) in the West Bank and Gaza, the Palestinian-majority territories which have lived restively under Israeli military occupation since 1967. All this Fatah could probably have survived, in what until then had amounted to a one-party system. But it was also chronically disunited, having divided its own vote by allowing rejected Fatah candidates to stand as independents against the party's official nominees. This was a wholly self-inflicted failure of party discipline, symptomatic of a movement grown complacent after years in power. For decades Arafat's movement had never faced a serious challenge from its smaller rivals within the Palestine Liberation Organization (PLO), the Palestinian Authority (PA), the Palestinian Legislative Council (PLC), and the near impenetrable alphabet soup of organizations through which the same handful of Fatah leaders had long exercised control over Palestinian affairs. So when Hamas declared that it would come in from the cold and contest the 2006 parliamentary elections, Fatah's leaders remained confident to the point of complacency about an election that few of them wanted to fight, and none seriously expected to lose. Almost everyone else, including many in Hamas, also expected Fatah to win. 'In one night everything was completely reversed', said Ghazi Hamad, a Hamas official in Gaza. 'Hamas was in government and Fatah was out of power.'[3]

The result was a shock to almost everyone. Only twelve months earlier the same corrupt, bickering Fatah had confounded widespread predictions of post-Arafat chaos by uniting behind his solid but uncharismatic deputy Mahmoud Abbas – widely known by the familiar name Abu Mazen – to win the January 2005 presidential election with ease. True, Hamas had boycotted that election, deciding that it was not yet ready to enter politics, especially for a job that involved negotiating with Israel. But even so, most observers thought that Arafat's successors would simply pick up where they left off and muddle through the parliamentary sequels a year later, extending Fatah's decade-long hegemony over the executive and legislative branches of the PA. In the absence of a Palestinian state, the PA is the closest thing that the Palestinians have to a government.

So it did not come to pass. Once Hamas decided to follow the path of other armed groups – such as Lebanon's Hezbollah, the Provisional IRA, and indeed some of Israel's own founding fathers – from bomb to ballot box, the rhetoric, planning and sophistication of the political newcomer proved far superior to that of its veteran secular rival. This came as more of a surprise to Westerners than to Palestinians. In the West the name Hamas is invariably associated with the bloody legacy of its military wing: explosions in Israeli restaurants, rockets fired into Israeli border towns, the twisted wreckage of Israeli commuter buses, huge rallies of angry Palestinian mourners carrying aloft the green-shrouded corpses of their 'martyrs', and grainy propaganda videos of cold-eyed, bearded gunmen declaiming in Arabic about the bloodshed that they are either about to inflict, or have just inflicted, on the Zionist enemy.

Certainly Hamas is a military organization which has long used force against Israeli soldiers and civilians, whether inside Israel proper or in the scores of Jewish settlements which are the most visible face of Israel's forty-year plus military occupation of the West Bank, Gaza Strip and East Jerusalem.

Israel and the international community routinely denounce such attacks as 'terrorism', particularly in the post-9/11 era, which has seen successive Israeli governments argue that the threat posed to Israel by Palestinian armed groups is comparable to that facing the Western world from al-Qaeda and other jihadist organizations. 'The state of Israel is at the forefront of the world's fight against the terror threat', Israel's prime minister, Binyamin Netanyahu, told a memorial service for Israeli victims of terrorism at Jerusalem's Mount Herzl military cemetery in April 2009. 'Israel has the strength to defend itself, but we expect greater international determination in confronting the common danger we share. History has taught us the price of appeasement of bloodthirsty anti-Semitic tyrannies, which is a lesson that we will never forget.'[4]

In response, Hamas and other Palestinian militant factions argue that they have a legitimate right of resistance against an occupying military force – a right, they claim, that is recognized by United Nations General Assembly resolutions, including 3236 and 3375, as well as Article 51 of the UN Charter, and international humanitarian law. Israel, they maintain, has a far more powerful military arsenal, with which it defends its own state, enforces its occupation of nearly 4 million stateless Palestinians, and keeps millions of others stateless by refusing to recognize their right of return.

The interwoven issues of nationhood, religion, land, possession and entitlement have necessitated decades of work by negotiators and dip-lomats even to bring the two sides to the same table without offending sensibilities. In 2009 the dispute took a new twist when Prime Minister Netanyahu called upon President Abbas to recognize Israel as a Jewish state. This would be anathema for Hamas, and even Abbas, a Western-backed moderate who embraces the 'two-state solution' concept of Israeli and Palestinian states living side by side, refused to do so because of its possible implications for the future right of return of Palestinian refugees now living in enforced exile abroad. 'It is not my job to give a description of the state. Name yourself the Hebrew Socialist Republic – it is none of my business', retorted an irritated Abbas.[5] Such are the complexities of dealings even between mainstream Israeli and Palestinian leaders operating, with varying degrees of enthusiasm, within the framework of a peace process that has gone on for two decades in the hopes of resolving a century-long conflict over land and statehood.

Semantics are of immeasurable importance. 'Terrorism' versus 'resistance' is only one of the tortuous linguistic disputes characteristic of the Palestinian–Israeli conflict, in which cities, regions and neighbourhoods have different names according to religious or political perspective: Jerusalem or Al-Quds; Hebron or Al-Khalil; Judea and Samaria or the West Bank; Temple Mount or Al-Haram al-Sharif. One person's Arab terrorist murdering Jewish innocents to conquer Israel's eternal capital Jerusalem is another's Palestinian freedom fighter avenging the blood of innocents murdered by Israel to liberate occupied al-Quds from Zionist military occupation.

Of course one of the main disputes is the name of the land itself: Israel or Palestine. Israel has been a member state of the United Nations since May 1949.[6] Palestine is not a member, although it has the status of a permanent observer mission at UN headquarters.[7] Despite infinite permutations of what are, were, should have been, or should be the exact boundaries of the most disputed patch of ground on earth, in common usage both Israel and Palestine refer to some or all of the territory bounded by the Mediterranean to the west, Jordan to the east, Lebanon and Syria to the north and Egypt to the south.

Credo

Hamas, however, is unambiguous about its definitions, credo and methods. The Hamas crest depicts crossed swords against the distinctive scimitar-shaped slice of land which includes all of Israel, the West Bank and Gaza. It also bears a picture of the Dome of the Rock, the golden-topped Islamic shrine which dominates the Jerusalem skyline. These are flanked by the Islamic exhortations 'There is no God but Allah' and 'Mohammed is the messenger of Allah.'

In 2002 Dr Abdel Aziz Rantissi, Hamas's then deputy leader in Gaza, voiced the standard Hamas position on its claim to the land:

> In the name of Allah we will fight the Jews and liberate our land in the name of Islam. We will rid this land of the Jews and with Allah's strength our land will be returned to us and the Muslim peoples of the world. By God, we will not leave one Jew in Palestine. We will fight them with all the strength we have. This is our land, not the Jews' . . . We have Allah on our side, and we have the sons of the Arab and Islamic nation on our side.[8]

Photo 1.1   Hamas graffiti in Gaza, March 2008

All this plays to a hardcore base of Hamas's support – radical Islamic fundamentalists who believe that Israel and the international community have denied them a state. It also speaks to the aspirations of millions of displaced Palestinian refugees living in squalid camps who dream of returning to the Palestinian villages from which they, their parents or grandparents fled after 1948 to escape the war which erupted over the creation of the modern state of Israel.

But there is another face of Hamas that the West rarely sees, because it is a face turned inward to its own people, not outward to Israel and the rest of the world. Without seeing this face it is impossible to understand how such a violent, rejectionist Islamist group could have won the votes of so many Palestinians who were neither violent nor rejectionists. This side of the movement can be seen at work daily in the sandy dirt paths through Gaza villages and in the shoulder-width alleyways of breezeblock refugee camps. In these sinks of poverty Hamas's non-military wings provide the food, medical services, clothing, books, schooling, orphanages, kinder-gartens, summer camps and other social services which are the bedrock of its success. Hamas was formally created in December 1987, but its crea-tors – and their Islamist forerunners – had spent decades laying down this grass-roots network of benevolent charitable and social activities. It even-tually grew into a shadow state which supplemented – and in many cases rivalled – the services provided by the official PA, the United Nations and humanitarian organizations.

Hamas benefited from this grass-roots approach and its image of being intolerant of corruption, deliberately losing no opportunity to contrast this 'clean' image with the near universal perception among Palestinians that Arafat's generation of Palestinian Authority officials had siphoned off millions of dollars in foreign aid that should have gone to their people.

This powerful credo of material support, within the framework of a religious faith which champions the collective community of believers (*ummah*), begins to explain the appeal of Hamas. 'I do not believe Hamas has its base because it doesn't recognize Israel. I believe that Hamas has its base mainly because of the failures of Fatah to rule, because of the corruption and mismanagement', said Khaled Abdel Shafi, a Gaza political analyst and no natural ally of the Islamists. 'Hamas cared for the poor and provided social services. It is only the hard core of Hamas that is worried about the recognition of Israel and so on, which isn't so significant in terms of numbers.'[9] So it was that in January 2006 Hamas, which means 'zeal' in Arabic, was victorious while Fatah, which means 'conquest', was defeated. It was a surprise victory but a comprehensive and democratic one, in elections widely regarded as the freest ever held in the Arab world.

Change and reform

Over the millennia countless religious movements have raised their banners to Jerusalem and its holy places, with different gods, prophets, leaders and ideologies. But where had it come from, this latest player in a conflict fought by Pharaohs, Israelites, Philistines, Romans, Crusaders, Mamluks, Ottomans, British, Jordanians, Syrians and numerous others throughout history?

Hamas's full name, *Harakat al-Muqawama al-Islamiyya*, translates into English as the Islamic Resistance Movement. Foremost among Hamas's founding leadership was Sheikh Ahmed Yassin, the movement's wheelchair-bound spiritual leader and figurehead, who was born near the modern Israeli town of Ashkelon but fled his home with his family in 1948, never to return. He lived the rest of his life as a refugee in Gaza, until he was assassinated by Israel in a helicopter air strike in March 2004. An inspirational preacher, the bearded Yassin was an organizational genius with a single-minded devotion to returning his fellow Palestinians to what he regarded as the straight and narrow path of Islam. He understood the refugee camps from which he came.

Yassin's roots, and those of Hamas, lie in the Muslim Brotherhood, the Sunni Islamic revival movement which was founded in Egypt in 1928 by Hassan al-Banna and which has become one of the most influential religious and political organizations in the modern Islamic world. The

Muslim Brotherhood opposed the advance of Western-inspired secular political regimes across the Arab world, arguing that they were corrupting Muslim society. They believed that society, including political rule, should be inspired by the Koran and the model of the Prophet Mohammed himself. Islam's first leader had indeed ruled as a political and military leader in the 'city state' of Medina in the seventh century. Advocating a return to the fundamental precepts of Islam, the Brotherhood is the grandfather of modern political Islamism across the Middle East, and is still nominally the parent body of Hamas. 'The Islamic Resistance Movement is one of the wings of Muslim Brotherhood in Palestine', states Hamas's 1988 founding covenant, unambiguously.[10]

However, operating under Israeli occupation, Hamas is in a unique position compared with other branches of the Brotherhood. While it functions within the ideological framework of the umbrella organization, most analysts believe that it has considerable freedom to operate within those parameters. Certainly it is an organization with a very clear sense of its own identity, and of how to adapt its image without altering the underlying fundamentals. Although in the January 2006 election Hamas campaigned under the innocent-sounding platform 'Change and Reform', no one was fooled for a second about the party's real identity. Campaign workers wore Hamas's distinctive green caps and sashes. Hamas leaders addressed rallies and stared down from 'Change and Reform' posters. And everywhere the – invariably smiling – image of Sheikh Yassin adorned the party's billboards.

Furthermore, although it moderated its hard-line rhetoric during the election, Hamas had never made any secret of its bloody methods. So interwoven are politics and arms for Hamas that even on election day Ismail Haniyeh, a Yassin protégé who was about to become its first prime minister, made it clear that his movement was not about to abandon the gun, and intended to advance its cause through bomb and ballot simultaneously. 'It is premature to say that Hamas is transforming itself into a political party like those in countries that are stable and independent', he told journalists while casting his vote near his home in Gaza's Shatti refugee camp. 'We still have the questions of the Israeli occupation, refugees, Jerusalem and our prisoners. It's premature for Hamas to drop its weapons.'[11]

The problem of combining the bomb and the ballot – politics and resistance – bedevilled the Hamas leadership after it won the 2006 election and became accountable not just to the Hamas membership but to the entire Palestinian electorate. 'For me this is the main problem', said one of Hamas's most publicly self-critical thinkers, Ghazi Hamad. 'In the past Hamas fired missiles, but now it has to be responsible to the people . . . [the people] look to Hamas for a solution.'[12]

Hamas remains frank about its ultimate goal – the establishment of Islamic rule across historic Palestine. However, in recent years it has modified this to offer Israel a long-term *hudna* (truce), in return for the establishment of an independent state in the West Bank, Gaza Strip and East Jerusalem, which Israel has occupied since the 1967 war. This offer was first made by Sheikh Yassin in the mid-1990s, and is regularly repeated by Hamas leaders in an effort to demonstrate that the movement can adapt to circumstances. 'We are with a state on the 1967 borders, based on a long-term truce', said Khaled Meshaal, the head of Hamas's Political Bureau, in Damascus in May 2009. Meshaal assumed leadership of the movement after Israel assassinated Sheikh Yassin, but steadfastly refused to recognize Israel and loaded his offer with conditions. Defining 'long-term' as ten years, he said the proposed state must include 'East Jerusalem, the dismantling of settlements and the right of return of the Palestinian refugees'.[13]

The offer is consistently dismissed by Israeli leaders, who refuse to countenance the return of millions of Palestinian refugees because they want to maintain Israel's Jewish majority. They also fear that Hamas will merely use the breathing space of a ceasefire to prepare for the next stage of its long-term plan: to regain all the land of Palestine from which their people were dispossessed after 1948, including Jaffa, Ashkelon, Haifa and other towns which now lie within Israel. 'There won't even be a tempo-rary political agreement between Israel and Hamas, maybe a temporary cooling-down period but no more than that. I don't believe in Hamas's intentions in the long run', said Yuval Diskin, head of Israel's internal security service Shin Bet in March 2007. 'Hamas say they will give us ten to 20 years of quiet but we know what they want to do in this period: build up their military.'[14]

Power and politics

Amid the unnatural silence on the Gaza streets after Hamas's election victory in January 2006, the immediate question was: what now? Post mortems and blame games would keep analysts busy for months to come, but in Gaza, Jerusalem, Ramallah and Tel Aviv Palestinians and Israelis were far more concerned about the future now that the pro-negotiation Palestinians were out and the rejectionists were in power.

While the Palestinian domestic reaction was shock, the Israeli one was immediate, and overwhelmingly negative. Israel's acting prime minis-ter, Ehud Olmert, held emergency talks with his inner security cabinet before emerging to deliver his government's response: 'Hamas has been declared to be a terrorist organisation by most of the international com-munity . . . Israel will demand that the entire international community compel the Palestinian Authority and its Chairman to implement the commitment to eliminate Hamas as a terrorist organisation that calls for Israel's destruction.'[15] Within the wider body politic of Israel there were leaders who were not so pessimistic. They argued that Hamas did not necessarily represent the majority of Palestinians. As an architect of the Oslo peace deal, Dr Ron Pundak, director general of the Peres Centre for Peace, contended, 'I don't see today a Palestinian Hamas constituency which is bigger than the moderate secular constituency, which would like to see a peace process.'[16] Yossi Beilin, a former government minister, also opined that, although he considered Hamas to be a 'religiously fanatical organization that has used the worst kind of terrorist violence against Israelis', the bitter reality was that Israel had to deal with Hamas rule in Gaza. 'Israel cannot afford to pretend that Hamas does not exist . . . The only option that I see serving the cause of peace is to enter into a dialogue with Hamas through a third party in order to reach a cease-fire.'[17] Binyamin Netanyahu – a right-winger then serving as opposition leader between two spells as prime minister a decade apart – was more succinct: 'Today Hamastan has been formed, a proxy of Iran in the image of the Taliban.'[18]

Many in the West also simply could not understand how the Palestinians could elect an armed extremist faction that made no secret of one of its main goals – the end of a Jewish state in Palestine – or its means: violence. The answer lies in the profoundly different perceptions of the Palestinian–Israeli conflict. Where Israel's supporters see a small, vulnerable Jewish state surrounded by Arab enemies, Palestinians see a nuclear regional superpower backed by the US which seeks to control, or even expel, them. Hamas's Western critics see it as a vanguard for Islamist fanatics such as al-Qaeda or Iran, intent on establishing Islamic rule across first the Middle East, and then the world. However Hamas's supporters see it as a beacon of hope for Islam's majority Sunni population: a Sunni model for the overthrow of despised authoritarian regimes and foreign occupiers, so that they no longer have to look to Lebanon's Shi'a Hezbollah or the Ayatollahs of Tehran. In summary, where the world saw a vote for Hamas as a setback for the peace process, many Palestinians saw no evidence of a peace process, so voted for Hamas.

Those Palestinians had come to believe that, after years of negotiations with Israel without any deal that would offer them hope of statehood and independence, there was little point in investing further political will in a process that was making their living conditions worse, not better. From the Palestinians' perspective Hamas's rivals, such as President Mahmoud Abbas, had nothing to show for their partnership in peace negotiations with Israel.

Grass roots

There was also another wellspring of support for Hamas. Sheikh Yassin and his creation are forever associated with Hamas's deadly bombing and shooting campaigns against Israel during the 1990s and after the outbreak of the second Palestinian Intifada in September 2000. Yet in the early days of the movement it was precisely Yassin's decision not to fight Israel which laid the foundations for its future success. In the 1970s Yassin made the strategic calculation that he would need time to Islamize Palestinian society from the grass roots up. So he decided not to jeopardize his fledgling network by risking immediate conflict with Israel. Instead he focused on setting up a grass-roots network of social, preaching and cultural organizations to act as the spearhead of his Islamic revivalism. At first his network was overlooked, or even tacitly encouraged, by Israel, which was seemingly content to see the emergence of any internal threat to its main Palestinian foe, Yasser Arafat's then dominant PLO.

Throughout the 1970s and 1980s Yassin and his followers assiduously set about building ever expanding networks of mosques, charitable institutions, schools, kindergartens and other social welfare projects – seeds planted early with a view to later harvesting hearts, minds and souls. It was not until the eruption of the first Palestinian Intifada in December 1987 that Yassin formed Hamas, to capitalize on the spontaneous outburst of street-level protest against Israeli occupation.

Arafat's PLO immediately recognized the nationalist-religious Hamas for what it was: a rival threatening its hitherto unchallenged leadership of the Palestinian street. 'When Hamas laid out its charter, it made it an alternative to the secular PLO charter', said Ibrahim Ibrach, a Gaza political analyst. 'Right from the start it considered itself an alternative to the PLO, but it didn't declare it because both parties were busy with the first intifada, fighting the Israelis.'[19]

Later, as Israel and the PLO were edging towards a peace process, Yassin formed his own military wing to continue fighting without the PLO. Through the soon to be infamous Izz ad-Din al-Qassam Brigades, Hamas launched armed attacks on Israeli targets in the West Bank and Gaza Strip, later escalating to suicide bombings inside Israel itself. It was not the only Palestinian faction to do so, but the name Hamas soon became synonymous with suicide bombers, as it remained resolutely outside the Palestinian political mainstream, refusing to participate in any political process with its Zionist enemy.

No, no, no

Throughout the early 1990s it was Arafat who led the PLO into the Madrid and Oslo peace negotiations with Israel, and it was he who stood on the White House lawn with the US president, Bill Clinton, and the Israeli prime minister, Yitzhak Rabin, to sign the Declaration of Principles in September 1993, the undoubted high point of Israeli–Palestinian relations. It was the PLO and its dominant faction Fatah which benefited from that era of hope with the return from exile of Arafat and thousands of his apparatchiks in 1994. And it was the PLO which, however many doubts were harboured by Israelis, presented to Palestinians the hope that the path of negotiations with Israel would one day lead to their own Palestinian state. During that optimistic era Hamas stood marginalized on the sidelines, killing Israelis in their bomb attacks while trumpeting from minaret and loudspeaker that Israel could not be trusted and that armed resistance, as they term it, was the only way to achieve Palestinian ends.

But gradually through the 1990s the era of optimism came to an end; Israeli troop redeployments did not occur according to previously agreed timetables, elections were delayed, and Yitzhak Rabin was assassinated by a far-right fellow Israeli. Israeli settlements continued to grow in contravention of international law, and as new ones were established Palestinians took it as a sign that Israelis could not be trusted. Israel meanwhile accused Palestinian leaders of failing to meet their obligations under security agreements by multiplying their armed forces and failing to stop Hamas setting off suicide bombs on Israeli streets. Peace talks were deadlocked, or produced little that was tangible for either Israelis or Palestinians. In such conditions Hamas's implacable world view found more supporters than during the era of peace and optimism.

But relations with Israel were not the only factor, although they dominated the headlines. Less attention was paid to the growing disillusionment among even moderate Palestinians about the increasingly unpopular Fatah leadership, whose efforts had produced no Palestinian state, no control over their own borders, and no free access to the outside world and its markets for Palestinian goods but, apparently, sizeable homes, limousines and fortunes for themselves.

This proved crucial to the Islamists' appeal. When a new round of Palestinian municipal elections loomed in 2004–5, Hamas mobilized thousands of loyal and zealous followers to present it as the vanguard of 'resistance' against Israel and to highlight corruption within the Fatah-controlled PA. With brilliant populist instincts, it even managed to turn its own pariah status into an electoral asset, portraying the West's criticisms as unwarranted interference in Palestinian affairs. 'The Israelis deal with America directly, but we deal with Allah directly', read one election slogan, shrewdly playing to religious and Arab nationalist sentiment in a conservative society where both are powerful factors.

Victory

Whatever claims of prescience its leaders later made, it is clear that Hamas never imagined it would win the January 2006 parliamentary elections which followed the local polls. It expected to gain some seats and spend a few years languishing on the opposition benches, gradually preparing the movement for the evolution from bullet to ballot. But there was to be no such transitional phase: it was propelled straight from political wilderness to political power.

While Hamas pointed out that it had fought by the rules and won fairly, it was quickly introduced to the realpolitik of international diplomacy as its domestic and external enemies frustrated it by using all the weapons available to them – political, economic and military. Israel halted the transfer of all funds to the PA and urged other countries to follow suit. The international Quartet of the United Nations, the European Union, the United States and Russia withdrew direct aid to the Hamas-controlled PA and imposed three conditions on Hamas before it would resume payments: renounce violence, recognize Israel, and abide by all agreements signed by previous Palestinian governments.

Hamas refused. Foreign aid dried up, and so did the salaries of thousands of PA employees. Hamas formed a government alone as Fatah refused to taint itself by association. Citing fears of terrorism from the new 'Hamastan', Israel also tightened control of goods and passenger crossings into Hamas's Gaza stronghold. The Islamists' internal Palestinian rivals looked on delightedly as Israel rounded up Hamas's new MPs and senior figures in the West Bank and threw them in jail. Immediately after Hamas's election victory Fatah sabotaged its rule by fomenting disorder, just as Hamas had systematically undermined Fatah in the 1990s by wrecking peace initiatives.

The political bickering spilled onto the streets, and Palestinians watched, appalled, as their leadership became a two-headed monster, tearing itself apart. The separation became near absolute in June 2007, when in a lightning military operation Hamas fighters swept through the Gaza Strip, seizing Fatah-controlled security headquarters and government offices and killing – in some cases publicly executing – Fatah loyalists. Hamas presented the takeover as a drastic measure to restore law and order after months of internecine warfare. But it drew worldwide condemnation and led President Abbas to dissolve the Hamas-led government and swear in another administration in the West Bank.

Hamas, by contrast, believed that, if it could ride out the immediate crisis and bypass the embargo, it could prove to Palestinians that it was steadfast and force the world to deal with it as the real power on the ground in Gaza. With the external battle lines drawn, it was also increasingly apparent that an internal debate was raging within Hamas, between 'pragmatists', who believed the movement should evolve into a truly political and social force, and 'hardliners', who argued that force alone would achieve Hamas's ends against Israel. It was not the first such debate within Hamas – whose ruling *shura* council and other decision-making bodies constantly reflect the tug of pragmatists versus radicals within the main pillars of the movement: Gaza, the West Bank, the 'outside' leadership abroad, the military wing and Hamas's prisoners.

Religious or nationalist?

The crucial question is whether Hamas is at root a nationalist movement – that is, one motivated by a calculation of Palestinian political and national interests – or a religious one, driven by a wider Islamic agenda. Certainly it is firmly rooted in Islam, but it has always confined its military activities to Israel and the occupied Palestinian territories. It has also had repeated verbal disagreements with worldwide jihadi organizations such as al-Qaeda, which castigated its decision to enter politics, arguing that holy war is the only path. Indeed, in August 2009 in the Gaza Strip, Hamas was involved in armed clashes with al-Qaeda-influenced jihadi militants, who challenged them on their Islamic credentials. In protesting that Hamas was betraying the wider ideals of militant Islamism, it was a significant if little-noticed development, because it was the first challenge to Hamas's hitherto unassailable military position in Gaza since it had ousted Fatah. Hamas has subsequently found itself between a hammer and an anvil – on one side demands from the international community that it moderate its positions, and on the radical side an increasingly vociferous complaint that it is not hard-line or Islamic enough.

Veteran analysts of Hamas see a development of the movement in stages: from the 1970s and early 1980s, when the focus was a religious one, to Islamize Palestinian society; a second stage of militarization in the build-up to the outbreak of the First Intifada; and an evolution into a military/political movement, culminating in the 2006 election.

'Hamas is a very, very pragmatic political institution. Very pragmatic', said Professor Ali al-Jarbawi, of Birzeit University in the West Bank. He argues that the Islamist group's success lies in its appeal to many different categories of voter: its bedrock membership; religious Palestinians naturally more inclined to vote for an Islamic party than a secular one; pessimists sceptical of the 'negotiate forever' policy of Fatah in dealing with Israel; protest voters angry at Fatah for enriching itself during its decades in power; and the countless thousands who benefited from Hamas's social and charitable services over the years. Where Hamas went wrong, he said, was in trying to be both a political party and a resistance movement after the 2006 election. 'They made mistakes because they got entangled with ruling. They couldn't understand that rule ruined Fatah, it ruined Abu Ammar [Arafat]. So why are they different?' he said.

> You cannot be an 'in-between' about having a state, quasi-state or whatever, and being a liberation movement. It is a conflict of terms, and duties, being

a liberation movement but also having a structure under occupation called a quasi-state . . . Either you want to remain a liberation movement struggling against occupation, or you want a quasi-state and accept the limitations that this will put on you, either by the international community or by your opponent, Israel, that you reached agreement with to establish this authority.[20]

Thousand year plan

It is an article of faith in Israel, and correctly so, that Hamas is dedicated to the end of a Jewish state. But this is to misunderstand its ultimate goal by mistaking milestone for destination. For Hamas the removal of the Zionist occupation is a necessary condition for the realization of its ultimate goal, but not a sufficient one. That final goal is an independent state in Palestine governed in accordance with Islam. Hamas regards Israel as an aggressor and an occupier which seeks the eradication of the rights of the Palestinians to statehood. The implications of this are that secular and leftist Palestinian movements such as Fatah, the Popular Front for the Liberation of Palestine (PFLP), the Popular Front for the Liberation of Palestine–General Command (PFLP–GC) and the Democratic Front for the Liberation of Palestine (DFLP) are just as much of a threat, if not more so, in many ways, to the realization of Hamas's goal. Whereas the Jewish state is a military obstacle, these rival factions are competing with Hamas for the hearts, minds and souls of Palestinians.

Nevertheless, Hamas's own 1988 founding covenant contains passages which have for more than two decades left the movement with little answer to the charge that as a movement it formally advocates a poisonous and murderous strain of anti-Semitism. Article 20 of the covenant states: 'In their Nazi treatment, the Jews made no exception for women or children. Their policy of striking fear in the heart is meant for all . . . They deal with people as if they were the worst war criminals.'[21] The rest of the covenant develops the theme, citing the anti-Semitic propaganda forgery *The Protocols of the Elders of Zion* and talking, in Article 22, of how the 'enemy' was behind 'the French Revolution, the Communist revolution and most of the revolutions we heard and hear about, here and there. With their money they formed secret societies, such as Freemasons, Rotary Clubs, the Lions and others in different parts of the world for the purpose of sabotaging societies and achieving Zionist interests.'[22]

Hamas also blames the Jews for turning the conflict into a religious one. Dr Mahmoud Zahar, one of Yassin's earliest followers, asserted: 'The Jews made their religion their nation and their state. They have declared war on Muslims and our faith system of Islam. They have closed our mosques and massacred defenceless worshippers at Al Aqsa and in Hebron. They are the Muslim-killers and under these circumstances we are obliged by our religion to defend ourselves.'[23] Some within Hamas concede that they are uncomfortable with such language, and say its subsequent evolution into a political organization has made the covenant a relic. 'You will find there is a huge difference between that and Hamas now. It has become part of history. It is part of the literature of Hamas, but it doesn't orchestrate the movement's thinking. In practical terms it is out of practice but it is not political to abandon it in public. The political programme of Hamas overpasses the covenant', said Yehya Moussa Abbadsa, a Gaza MP and one of the most prominent of Hamas's 'pragmatic' wing.[24]

Shifting uncomfortably in his chair when challenged by the authors about the covenant, Dr Omar Abdel Razeq, the Western-educated economist who briefly served as Hamas's finance minister in 2006, acknowledged the damage done to his movement by such sentiments. 'That is why Hamas has been looking into changing or modifying this charter', he said. However, he called upon the West to give the newly political incarnation of Hamas time to evolve, instead of turning it into a pariah. 'You don't get changes in Hamas's platform or charter through pressuring the government, or pressuring the Palestinian people economically. We need time to adjust.'[25] Others within Hamas insist that, despite its proclamation of jihad, it is not engaged in a war against Jews or Christians as such. 'For us as Muslims it is not a religious war because we lived together here before 1948', said Sheikh Saleh al-Arouri, a leader of the military wing who had emerged from fifteen years in an Israeli jail.

> Christians have been living here since the start of the ages. If it were a religious war the Jews and Christians would not have lasted 1,400 years. Religious war means what happened in Europe in the Middle Ages where they didn't accept anyone who wasn't a Christian. In our area there was never a genocide based on religion. This is only a nationalistic issue and a nationalistic war because of occupation.[26]

Israelis see it very differently. Some believe Hamas is an implacable enemy with which no long-term accommodation can be reached. 'Hamas: their hatred of the Jews is in their blood and they raise their children on the same blood libel', stated Colonel Yossi, a recently retired Israeli officer, as he sat drinking coffee in the lobby of Jerusalem's King David Hotel after four bloody years of the Second Intifada. 'I've looked them in the eye and I know what's in it. They'll use their bombers against us until we are gone. Peace is not in their vocabulary.'[27] But other Israelis believe that with Hamas, unlike the unpredictable Yasser Arafat, Israel at least knows where its stands.

In December 2008 Israel launched an unprecedented air and land offensive against Gaza, killing more than 1,300 Palestinians – many of them women and children – in an effort to deter Hamas from firing rockets into Israeli towns and communities bordering Gaza. Israel and Hamas would later be condemned by the UN Human Rights Council for their conduct during the offensive, which led to both parties being accused of war crimes and crimes against humanity. It was not the first, although it was by far the deadliest, Israeli strike into Hamas-controlled Gaza. Standing outside his office just 4 miles from the Gaza border, Haim Jelin, the Israeli mayor of Eshkol Regional Council, said that, while before 2006 there was some cooperation between Israelis and Palestinians, 'from the moment Hamas came in' to power in Gaza in 2006, 'there was no chance at all'. But Mr Jelin then continued:

> Arafat used to tell us that he wanted peace, but terror used to continue. And I did not like that. I also don't like Hamas, but at least they tell me that they don't want me. They wage war against me; they do not pretend to want to make peace with me. Therefore we know that we are dealing with an enemy that does not recognize us. We, the people in the council, know that they need their own country. But they do not recognize us. As long as they do not recognize us, it seems like the situation will continue to be that they fire on us and we enter Gaza every few years, until someone makes a decision that we need something else. This something else will be us sitting together and talking. The question is when this will happen, and how many people will die until then and how much each side will suffer.[28]

There is evidence to suggest that this is not an isolated point of view. A joint Israeli–Palestinian opinion poll carried out in March 2009 found that '50% of the Israelis support and 48% oppose talks with Hamas if needed to reach a compromise agreement with the Palestinians.' It found that an even larger number (69 per cent) would support talks with a Palestinian national unity government in which Hamas sat with Fatah, with only 27 per cent opposing.[29] However, there was also a despair factor. Nearly three-quarters (73 per cent) of Palestinians and two-thirds (60 per cent) of Israelis believed there was little or no chance of an independent Palestinian state being established alongside Israel in the next five years, a pessimism upon which extremist factions thrive.

Explaining the deep-seated nature of the Islamists' appeal to Palestinians, Dr Eyad Sarraj, a Gaza-based psychiatrist, said that, unlike its secular rivals, Hamas gave its followers 'a new identity of victory and belonging to God. Hamas people are ideologues and they have a project, to resurrect the Islamic *ummah* [nation]. They believe this is their mission and what they do on the way is to transform Muslims to be good Muslims.' Inevitably, he added, such an appeal draws on powerful cultural and historical sentiments. 'Of course we sympathize as Palestinians and Arabs and Muslims with this. We Arabs and Muslims have suffered from chronic failure for the last 1,000 years. Since we lost Andalusia we have been defeated. This has gone deep into the collective unconscious of the Arabs.'[30]

It is instructive that military reverses suffered by the Moors on the Iberian peninsula between the eleventh and the fifteenth century – an era as historically remote as the Domesday Book or Tudor period is for most Britons – are still active causes for lamentation among twenty-first-century Arabs living 2,000 miles and more than 500 years from medieval Granada and Cordoba. It is instructive because, fortified by religious certitude and in a region where all sides share an acute sense of historical grievances and entitlement, Hamas is nothing if not patient. Sometimes, indeed, its leaders draw on surprising historical models to illustrate the length of the time they are prepared to wait. 'In such matters we should look to how the Jews conduct their affairs', said Dr Abdel Aziz Rantissi during one discussion of the protracted nature of the Middle East conflict in 2002, two years before he was assassinated by Israel. 'King David had a state in this area 3,000 years ago. For 3,000 years until now did they ever once say that it wasn't their land, although they didn't have it? But through 3,000 years they lived by adapting and living with what was the reality there.'[31]

The same message is put more bluntly by Abu Bakr Nofal, a Hamas negotiator in Gaza. 'The world is in a hurry. We are not in a hurry.'[32]

2

In the Path of al-Qassam

If the Arabs despair of justice then every soul and family will become an Izz ad-Din al-Qassam.

Al-Jamia'a al-Islamiyya, editorial[1]

His name meant 'Might of the Faith', and he was an early prototype of the Islamist radical leader and fugitive, nearly a century before Usama bin Laden. Bearded, white-robed and ascetic, Sheikh Izz ad-Din al-Qassam relied on a small band of armed followers to survive for years in the 1930s as an outlaw among the valleys and jagged hilltop ridges of British colonial-governed Palestine, using the inhospitable terrain to evade capture by one of the world's mightiest military powers. Preaching Islamic revivalism and resistance through jihad – the radical creed of faith and firearms that would serve as a model for future generations of Islamists – the Syrian-born preacher urged his fellow Arabs to rise up against their 'infidel' British overlords, against the plan to create a Jewish homeland in Palestine, and against the successive waves of Jewish Zionist immigrants in the 1920s and 1930s. The influx of these new arrivals was transforming the political and social fabric of the land, leading to the dispossession of the Palestinian peasantry from a way of life it had known for centuries.

When Qassam was finally hunted down and killed by British police in a shoot-out in Ya'bad near the northern town of Jenin on 19 November 1935, thousands attended his funeral to pay tribute to the 53-year-old cleric who was scorned by his British pursuers as the 'Brigand Sheikh', a derogatory epithet that was a colonial forerunner of the 'terrorist' label applied to Hamas in the modern era. After his death Qassam's armed followers, bands of self-styled Islamic mujahidin (holy warriors), went on to instigate the 1936–1939 Arab revolt against British rule. But while Qassam was certainly an obstacle to the British, he failed both to overthrow them and to stop mass Jewish immigration, and as a historical figure he remains virtually unknown outside the Arab and Muslim world – marginal certainly by comparison with his younger Egyptian contemporary Hassan al-Banna, a fellow teacher and Islamic revivalist who founded the Muslim Brotherhood. Indeed the extent to which Qassam failed during his own lifetime is epitomized by the fact that his grave now lies in Israel, the Jewish homeland whose very creation he fought in vain to prevent. The grave is to be found in a dilapidated Islamic cemetery at Nesher, near the northern Israeli port city of Haifa. Here Qassam's tall, whitewashed headstone is one of the few that has not been broken by time, neglect or vandalism – no doubt because it alone is protected by high, green railings, and is kept clean and well ordered by his twenty-first-century admirers. Inscribed in Islamist green lettering, the ornate Arabic script on a Syrian's headstone in an Israeli graveyard reads: 'This martyr, learned and generous, who was the best at teaching the way of God. He is our Sheikh, al-Qassam, the first to raise the flag of jihad with us to support the faith.'

Lying beside the grave is an older, damaged, headstone replaced some years ago, which is smaller and bears a Koranic verse and the exhortation: 'Together in the path of al-Qassam'. This message is the key to Qassam's enduring appeal for later generations of Islamists – not the destination he reached, but the path he laid down, and the example of personal sacrifice – martyrdom – which he set in doing so.

Within the Middle East the impact of the 'Brigand Sheikh' has far outlasted the events of his lifetime. Indeed the word Qassam has passed into the Israeli lexicon. For years Israeli motorists have unknowingly driven within a few yards of Qassam's grave beside the Haifa to Nazareth highway, tuning in to Hebrew-language radio bulletins to hear Israeli politicians denouncing the latest outrage of Hamas's military wing, the Izz ad-Din al-Qassam Brigades, or to be updated on the latest 'Qassam' rocket fired by Hamas from Gaza into Israeli towns.

It is no accident that Hamas chose the name of a man who died more than fifty years before it was founded, when it could easily have selected that of any number of the group's own 'martyred' fighters or leaders. Although he was Syrian, not Palestinian, Qassam's narrative has endured in the imagination of Palestinian Arabs from all communities, whether religious, secular, Muslim or Christian, whether citizens of Israel, residents of the West Bank and Gaza, or refugees living in Lebanon, Syria and Jordan. 'He was known to be an Arab nationalist, one who fought for the Palestinian cause', recalls one elderly Palestinian veteran of the Mandate era. 'Everybody knew of him, he was in all the Arab newspapers and was considered to be a hero and a nationalist.'[2]

For Hamas the particular appeal of the 'Brigand Sheikh' was that Qassam provided the template of how to build a populist grass-roots movement founded on faith, social and political works and, eventually, arms. These are fundamental elements of Hamas's own agenda – as evident from the three pillars of its full name in Arabic: *Harakat* ('movement'), *al-Muqawama* ('resistance') and *al-Islamiyya* ('Islamic'). In its founding 1988 covenant Hamas pays direct tribute to Qassam,

proclaiming that it is 'one of the links in the chain of the struggle' against
Zionism, dating back 'to the emergence of the martyr Izz ad-Din al-
Qassam and his brethren the fighters, members of Muslim Brotherhood'.[3]

Upheaval

Mohammed Izz ad-Din bin Abdul Qadar bin Mustafa al-Qassam was
born in the village of Jablah, near the Syrian coastal town of Latakia, in
1882, into a family of prominent Sufi Muslim leaders and scholars. After
he showed early signs of being a promising pupil his parents sent him to
study in the Egyptian city of Cairo, the seat of the Islamic world's most
prestigious centre of learning: al-Azhar University. Its sanctified cloisters
had changed little over the centuries, but the young Syrian arrived at a time
of political turmoil in Egypt as it entered the twentieth century. In 1882 the
British had occupied Egypt and were busy remaking Cairo according to
the European model. Tensions ran high as Egyptian nationalists agitated
against the British and their puppet Ottoman ruler, the Khedive.

At al-Azhar a new generation of radical reformist and fundamentalist Muslim scholars such as Mohammed Abduh and Rashid Rida had
been preaching that Muslims had strayed from the true practice of Islam.
Calling for the faith to be cleansed of superstitions and rituals that had
accrued in the 1,200 years since the time of the Prophet Mohammed,
they argued that such purification would strengthen the Islamic world
and ensure that it would no longer be subject to humiliations such as
the subjugation of the once great Muslim nation of Egypt to European,
and in particular British, military might. Citing Islam's golden history
of achievement in science and technology between the tenth and twelfth
centuries, the reformers argued that Islamic revivalism would help the
faith respond to an era of economic, technological and scientific challenges at the end of the nineteenth century, an era thus far dominated by
the Western imperial powers.

But for some of these scholars an integral part of the revivalist
movement was anti-colonial hostility towards the foreigners who had
conquered them. Qassam became one of the advocates of reform, and
sought to put his ideas into practice first in his home country of French-
dominated Syria, and then in British-ruled Palestine. In Syria, after he
returned from his studies in Cairo and took up a post as a preacher,
Qassam promoted the reform of Islam as a means of resistance. During
the First World War the French had coveted Syria, and like the British in
Palestine had secured the mandate to administer the country as part of
the post-war peace settlements and territorial acquisition of the Middle
East by the European colonial powers. Syria was restive, and opposed
its colonial presence even before trouble broke out in Palestine. During
the war Arab armies had fought alongside Britain and the victorious

Allied Powers, and helped to bring about the final demise of the Ottoman Empire by driving the Turkish army out of Damascus. Throughout the war Arab leaders had made clear their aspirations for independence after living for four centuries under Turkish rule. But the Arabs' plans proved short-lived. In April 1920, the victorious Allies met at a peace conference in San Remo in Italy to divide up the former Ottoman territories. France was awarded the mandate for the area that is now Syria and Lebanon, and in July 1920 in Damascus promptly deposed the newly crowned monarch King Faisal, the Arab leader who, with Lawrence of Arabia at his side, had led the Arab revolt and captured the city during the First World War.

Now back in Syria experiencing first-hand his fellow Syrians' disillusionment and frustration, Qassam was already hard at work teaching and preaching. He had served as a preacher in the Ottoman army, tried to organize a local jihadist force and agitated against the French. In his home town he built a school and ran a campaign to encourage Muslim piety, urging his townspeople to return to the mosque and commit themselves to fasting for Ramadan. At the same time he was directing his energies against the colonial power, organizing fund-raising drives and preparing small companies of fighters. His hostility towards the French derived from his deeply held belief that all Muslims should strive to maintain the fundamental precepts of their faith, free from non-Muslim or foreign rule. This striving was articulated as a 'jihad' or holy war, directed both at making his community a better model of faith and at organizing armed struggle against foreign interlopers who, he believed, would threaten the practice of Islam. He had every cause to fear the potent secular drive behind France's practice of rule and government. In Algeria, which the French had occupied since 1830, their 'civilizing mission' and colonial occupation had led to the demise of Ottoman Islamic power. The Muslim majority was then subjugated to more than a hundred years of French domination and colonial rule. Qassam wanted to resist any such prospect in Syria. Although his efforts gained him widespread support, they also brought him to the attention of the French, who put him on trial in absentia and condemned him to death for leading an uprising.

Realizing he was unlikely to survive long in the French sphere of influence, Qassam fled south to preach the message of jihad in Palestine, where the capture of Jerusalem and the surrounding territories by British forces during the First World War had put the Holy Land back in Christian hands for the first time since the Crusades.

At the San Remo peace conference the victorious powers had granted Britain the mandate for Palestine. At first the British appeared intent on being seen as benign administrators, in comparison with the often brutal Ottomans. But even before its forces captured Jerusalem in December 1917 the British government had already made separate agreements about Palestine's fate with the Arabs, the French and the Zionist movement that the Arabs, in particular, later considered duplicitous. Throughout 1915–16

the British entered into discussions – the Hussein–McMahon correspond-
ence – with the Arab leadership and promised territorial independence
(including, the Arabs would argue, Palestine) in return for their support
against the Ottoman Turks on the desert battlefields of Arabia. However,
the British had also entered into a secret agreement with the French in
1916 (the Sykes–Picot agreement) in which they agreed in any post-war
scenario to divide the Middle East into spheres of control and influence.
Britain had also issued a declaration to Jewish Zionists that it would help
bring about their dream of a homeland for the Jewish people. The British
commitment to the Jews was enshrined in the Balfour Declaration of 2
November 1917, named after Britain's then foreign secretary, which read:

> His Majesty's Government view with favour the establishment in Palestine
> of a national home for the Jewish people, and will use their best endeavours
> to facilitate the achievement of this object, it being clearly understood that
> nothing shall be done which may prejudice the civil and religious rights of
> existing non-Jewish communities in Palestine, or the rights and political
> status enjoyed by Jews in any other country.[4]

When the British intentions became public they immediately set
Zionist ambitions on a collision course with Palestinian interests. In that
era those Palestinian interests were traditionally articulated through the
aristocratic classes and prominent clans, the so-called notable Palestinian
families which provided administrators, judges and governing functionaries to the Ottomans. These wealthy families – such as the al-Husseinis,
Nashashibis and al-Alamis – owned considerable property in rural areas
and such important towns as Jerusalem, Haifa, Hebron, Bethlehem and
Nablus. They constituted the Palestinian establishment, which in the years
after the First World War found its vested interests directly threatened by
Britain's policies and the growing numbers of Zionist immigrants. These
families also formed the cradle of the Palestinian nationalist movement.

It was into this atmosphere of social and political upheaval that Qassam
arrived in Haifa in the early 1920s with a French price already on his head.
He was to become the figurehead of a very different and highly politicized model of religious opposition to British rule, for he carried with
him the scent of rebel, the precepts of jihad and the lessons learnt from his
previous encounters with foreign occupiers in his native Syria.

Fertile soil

Haifa was a city in flux. On the steeply sloped terraces around Mount
Carmel, newly built villas and apartment blocks housed recently settled
Jewish residents, while down in the Muslim quarter and beside the docks
and railway yards, unpaved roads and squat single-storey dwellings

offered only the most basic of shelter to thousands of poor Arab labourers. It was here, around the docks area and the neighbourhood of Wadi Salib, that Qassam came to preach at the *Istiqlal* (Independence) Mosque. A man who devoted his energies to the practical rather than the theoretical, his strength lay in harnessing the energies of the poorest among Palestinian society. As a self-declared enemy of colonialism and Zionism, he certainly found in Haifa and the surrounding villages of northern Palestine an audience receptive to his ideas about the need to reform Islam and organize armed resistance in defence of the Palestinian 'homeland'.

Palestinian Arab leaders were increasingly alarmed by the escalating rate of Jewish immigration and land settlement and by the bloodshed caused by the upheaval. By the early to mid-1920s Jewish immigration to Palestine was causing an accelerated and unprecedented rate of land dispossession among the Palestinian peasant classes. Palestine, as a predominantly peasant society, was being forcibly altered by Zionist land settlement. As absentee Arab landowners sold out to Jewish immigrants, poor Palestinian Arab villagers were being displaced and were pouring into cities such as Haifa. There they joined the ranks of the urban underprivileged and swelled the audiences for Friday prayers at Qassam's mosque, where they heard a message of Muslim resurgence and identity.

Believing that, through the framework of Islam, Palestinian opposition could be translated into direct action, Qassam began literacy programmes for the poor, taught the Koran, ran evening classes and became heavily involved in the Muslim Young Men's Association (MYMA). He also established agricultural cooperatives for the rural poor. By 1929 he had assumed leadership of the MYMA and was getting audiences of thousands at the mosque. Crucially, he was also appointed marriage registrar by the Muslim court in Haifa. This position gave him the perfect cover to travel around the countryside on official business, allowing him to forge relationships with Palestinian leaders in villages and hamlets across the region, while he officiated at some of the most important social events in their annual calendar.

In the 1920s and 1930s marriages were an opportunity for whole villages to come together in celebration of a union that would perpetuate old alliances and forge new ones. Families, clans and tribes defined Palestinian society and allowed for alliances of power and influence. Marriages were one symbol of how the family was pre-eminent during this period. The male members of the family, the patriarchs, would use the occasion to demonstrate how rich they were. The rituals associated with the marriage, the dowry, the trousseau of the bride, the ceremony and the celebration and feast were more often about power than love.

Amid the celebrations Qassam would have the opportunity to meet with the most influential figures of the village and discuss his ideas. One of the most significant issues raised by the sheikh on such occasions was the preaching of jihad against both the British and the Zionist settlers.

As one British police official observed, 'during his tours Qassam would bring together the more religiously minded of the villagers and preach to them the doctrines of Islam, cleverly interpolating such passages from the Koran as were calculated to stimulate a spirit of religious fanaticism.'[5]

Both in his official positions and his unofficial role as social activist, Qassam promoted his fundamentalist beliefs, which led him to criticize the dissipation of the faith through what he termed 'folkish practices'. In 1925 he wrote a newspaper article spelling out the practices which he regarded as a deviation from true Islam:

> As for holding funeral processions, with wailing, and praying loudly and making noise and visiting graves of the prophets and leading men in the known procedure of touching and rubbing the tombs and committing sins and the blatant mingling of men and women and spending money in not the right and proper manner . . . this is not how it was devised or performed by the Prophet.[6]

His Islamic fundamentalist strictures were apparent in every aspect of his life. As the British police commissioner in Palestine at the time reported, 'his interpretation of the parts of the Qur'an which sanction the use of physical violence, was unorthodox . . . but . . . his policy . . . selected from among the poor, ignorant and the more violently dispossessed of the pious.'[7]

Qassam was different from establishment Muslim leaders because he led a lifestyle similar to that of the people among whom he worked. This was quite different from the studied aloofness of Hajj Amin al-Husseini, the British-appointed mufti of Jerusalem and leader of the Supreme Muslim Council, who, as a leading member of a notable family and senior official in the British Mandate authority, had a status which dictated distance rather than familiarity. Qassam – although himself from a notable clerical family – was renowned for living plainly and for striving to achieve the purest practice of Islam alongside the Palestinians. He was far from aloof, but trod a common path. This was a path that his spiritual and political descendants in Hamas would also strive to follow. From his experiences in Syria he was convinced that foreign occupation and settlement would not deliver Arabs their rights, but would instead deny them. This was the message which he brought to Palestine, and which he proclaimed in the sermons and public speeches which rapidly brought him to the attention of the British governing authorities and his Zionist foes.

Black Hand gang

By the late 1920s and early 1930s Qassam was spending more and more time with the stevedores, the urban poor of Haifa and peasants from surrounding villages. These workers lived, according to contemporary accounts, in hovels made out of old petrol tins, without a water supply or the most rudimentary sanitary arrangements. The high cost of living meant that, for thousands of these people, life was nothing more than subsistence, while Jewish workers were paid double the wage rates by the British Mandate authorities. Qassam began to identify select groups of followers to train as mujahidin, believing occupation and Zionism had to be opposed by force of arms. His attraction was revealed by one of Qassam's followers who was captured and put on trial by the British authorities:

> According to the statement of Assad el-Muflah, one of the accused, he had been a vendor of eggs in Haifa but his income was not sufficient to support his wife and four children. After prayers at the mosque he would ask for charity and one day a man took him to see Sheikh Izz-ad-Din Qassam. The accused joined the gang voluntarily, he told police, in order to escape from his miserable existence.[8]

It was easy for Qassam to highlight the growing disparities between the Arab workers' situation and that of the British authorities and the new Jewish immigrants. Yet this was no ordinary workers' struggle similar to the strikes and labour chaos that prevailed in Haifa in the 1920s and early 1930s. For Qassam there was always an Islamic agenda, and his meetings took an increasingly strident political tone. At one meeting he asked his listeners whether they knew about Jewish plans to 'take the country by force', including the smuggling of arms into Palestine and military drills in Haifa. To this he added bitterly: 'Jews and Arabs are subject to the same laws . . . Jews do not have to take the country by force as the Arabs are selling it to them.'[9] Such statements were also a challenge to the Palestinian notables and national leaders, whom he often attacked for their inability to mount an effective challenge to what he considered the calculated British policy to turn Palestine from a Muslim land held in perpetual trust for future generations into a Jewish state.

News reports, memoirs, memorandums and accounts from the period indicate that at some point in 1930 Qassam decided to escalate his arguments and sermons into armed action. With a small group of supporters he took to the hills and villages of northern Palestine in readiness to launch a series of armed attacks on their enemies. His secretive group became known as the Black Hand gang, and they engaged in fund-raising, military training, and preparations to launch jihad. The poorest peasants who joined his call to jihad even donated part of the compensation for their forfeited lands to the Sheikh for 'the purchase of arms'.[10]

For five years they carried out attacks on Jewish settlements, Jewish settlers and the British in northern Palestine. The British established that it was based in and around Haifa, was closely connected to the Muslim Young Men's Association, was well armed and included 'men wearing the Sheikh's gabardine and occupying pulpits in important mosques'.[11]

Among other attacks, they were held responsible for the murder on 6 November 1935 of a British Mandate policeman, Sergeant Moshe Rosenfeld, for an attack on Zionist pioneers, and for inspiring numerous conspiracies and murder plots. Certainly those who remember that era recall the ruthlessness of Qassam and his followers. 'Everybody who dared to say anything bad about him used to be killed by his people. He had many supporters and they used to protect him. Even policemen were killed because they said bad things', recalled one nonagenarian Palestinian in the Galilee.[12]

This armed struggle, which many claimed sparked the Arab revolt of 1936, was portrayed by Qassam as an act of jihad, so that his followers would see not just a national struggle on behalf of the Palestinian people, but a religious war against the occupation of Muslim lands. As early as 1930 Qassam had secured a *fatwa* (religious edict) from a religious cleric in Damascus which declared that jihad against the British and the Zionist settlers was permissible. Qassam proclaimed the *fatwa* in his sermons in the mosques and at secret meetings with his Muslim compatriots.

Many young Palestinian preachers were also receptive to his call for jihad. Among their number were Sheikh Farhan Sa'adi, Sheikh Hussein Hamadi, Sheikh Attiyeh Ahmad and Sheikh Khalil Issa. Sheikh Sa'adi, a devoted follower of Qassam and his ideals, would later become a 'notorious gang leader' during the Palestinian revolt. He was captured by the British in November 1937, sent to trial and executed by hanging in Haifa, all within the space of five days. His execution was the first by the British-instituted military court in Palestine. Described as 'bronzed and grey bearded,' the sheikh was executed in Acre prison where, on British orders, 'the prisoner was taken from his cell . . . he showed no agitation and received religious consolation before his death.'[13] Following Qassam's death it was also reported that the 'HQ of the terrorist gang' had been moved from Palestine to Syria, 'where a meeting took place to discuss the renewal of the gang's activities'. Today Qassam's ideological descendants, including Khaled Meshaal, also have their headquarters in the Syrian capital, Damascus.[14]

Qassam called for a jihad, arguing that the strategy of appeals to the British relied upon by the leaders of institutional Islam and the notable families was completely ineffective in dealing with the dual challenge of British colonial might and the Zionist drive to settle the land. Hence the call was also a challenge to Palestine's Muslim elite, some of whom strongly disapproved of the sheikh and his colleagues. Qassam had met with Hajj Amin al-Husseini, the mufti of Jerusalem, and asked him to support the jihad. The mufti declined, arguing that a political solution could still be found to give the Palestinians freedom – much as nearly a century later Qassam's rejectionist Islamist descendants and the pro-negotiation Palestinian establishment represented by President Mahmoud Abbas would differ over the means to achieve their ends. The mufti believed that Qassam was not allowing enough time for a negotiated political solution to emerge. In time he changed his perspective, but only after Qassam was already dead and his disciples had triggered the Palestinian revolt. But Qassam also symbolized the break with high politics led by notables and elites and channelled the hitherto unheard voice of the ordinary Palestinian people.

Qassam's campaign came to an abrupt end in a fatal gunfight with British police in November 1935. As news of his death was reported, demonstrations and protests broke out across Palestine. The British complained of a 'tendency in the Arab press to regard these gangsters as "martyrs" to the cause' and noted bitterly that, 'as was to be expected, the Sheikh . . . and [his] fellow conspirators are now being canonised.'[15] Later British news reports observed that the editor of one Arabic newspaper was 'insisting upon regarding the gangster as a hero'. One local newspaper editorial appearing in the wake of Qassam's death declared:

> If these men, our martyrs and heroes, are regarded by the government as brigands, then the whole Arab nation are brigands . . . Although we differ from the dead martyr as to the means we are partners with him in the attainment of the ultimate objective. If the Arabs despair of justice then every soul and family will become an Izz ad-Din al-Qassam.[16]

In true colonial style it was difficult for the British to conceive of Palestinian demands as legitimate or to see beyond their own hostile stereotypes of the Arab 'other', demonized as they were so comprehensively in the Western imagination. There were, of course, a few exceptions – individual British officials and administrators who urged a more attenuated approach to the Arabs – but they did not occupy senior positions in Jerusalem or London.

At his funeral in Haifa thousands of people mourned Qassam's loss and proclaimed him as a new leader and symbol of Palestinian resistance. At a meeting held by the British high commissioner, Sir Arthur Wauchope, it was remarked that: 'One day it might be that every Palestinian would become as one of those who were killed a few days ago near Jenin. A sense of hopelessness was widespread throughout the country and this feeling has been expressed by different symptoms.'[17] As the printing presses rolled with hurriedly produced eulogies, poems and letters addressed to the 'martyr' sheikh, thousands of ordinary working people came to the mosque in Haifa where his funeral was to take place. At one point the planned procession was delayed because the buses bringing mourners from outlying towns and villages had not yet arrived. Schoolchildren, scouts with flags and the members of the MYMA led the funeral cortege, amid the wails and cries of veiled women and anti-British slogan-shouting from the assembled crowd. Hours later the cortege arrived at Qassam's final resting place in the cemetery of Balad el-Sheikh.[18]

Palestine's 'notables' and national leaders were initially unsure about how to respond to the sheikh's death. Rawiya Shawwa remembers her father, Rashad Shawwa, a prominent Palestinian figure, recounting the events of that day to her when she was a child. 'He told me that he was in Haifa to act as one of the bearers of the dead sheikh's body.'[19] Other notables, however, steered clear of this and other public events. This absence symbolized one aspect of the divide between the masses and their leaders. Qassam's death epitomized a form of self-sacrifice that many ordinary Palestinians suspected would never be found among the leaders of the establishment. The strength of feeling among working-class protesters in the wake of his death, however, alerted some notables to the increasing sense of desperation pervading Palestinian society, and at a private meeting with British officials they expressed fear that their influence might be waning. As public subscriptions for the families of the 'martyrs' poured in from Palestinian factory workers, and memorial meetings were planned in cities, towns and villages across Palestine, the only remedy that the leaders could commend was 'a suggestion that the government should change its present policy'.[20]

The British, however, tarred the notable leadership with the same brush as the slain sheikh. A lengthy editorial was published in the English-language daily of the Zionist movement, the *Palestine Post*, entitled 'A new orientation needed':

> Whether they were all common bandits or whether some of them were mistaken idealists urged by a perverse impulse who decided to join these lawless elements in the illusion that they would thereby serve their people's cause, what is important, we believe, for the Government, and the population at large in Palestine, is the attitude taken up by the official and recognised representatives of the Arab political parties to the persons who fought with the police in Jenin last week.
>
> For it is one thing if a number of extremists, prompted by religious hysteria, or possibly by more material stimulus, attempt to intimidate the Jewish settlers, and perhaps hope to influence Government also, by murder in ambush. It is quite another when people who parley with the same Government and presume to speak on behalf of a community, . . . allow themselves to appear to condone and applaud those methods.

In effect, the writer accused Palestinian leaders of failing to keep figures such as Sheikh Izz ad-Din al-Qassam under control. 'It is inconceivable', he continued, 'that the British – of all Governments – will allow itself to be deflected from the course it thinks right, by attempts to determine law and order.'[21]

The parallels are unavoidable. Eighty years later, as Hamas set Jerusalem and Tel Aviv afire, the Israelis were to demand – in very similar terms – that Yasser Arafat and his successors rein in their own extremists.

But the British were to discover that in Palestine, as in Ireland and

India, they were not to have it all their own way. It became apparent that in the face of growing Palestinian opposition to British and Zionist policies, something would have to give.

Fury and retribution

In Zohar el-Kokhab, a café in Haifa's working-class district, 4,000 men from the MYMA met under a black-draped portrait of the slain sheikh to hear speeches lauding him as a 'hero', a 'martyr', and a champion of the Palestinian cause. One speaker after another condemned British imperialism and deplored a legislative council, which the British had proposed for the territory, as a catastrophe for Arabs. All assembled 'rose to the cries of "Death to the Legislative Council"'. At other meetings in the Arab workers' clubs speeches were made declaring Izz ad-Din al-Qassam a 'great nationalist who fell for the cause'. Eager to stem the public swell of opinion against them, Palestinian Arab notables sent messages of support to such meetings. One such from Jamal Effendi Husseini reportedly pointed to 'the immortality of the Sheikh as a symbol of Arab protest against the English rule'.[22]

Sensing the tide in favour of the slain sheikh, journalists, prominent nationalists and religious figures began to vie with each other in calling upon the masses to throw off their British yoke and demand freedom and independence. Sheikh Ibrahim Shanti, a popular religious figure and newspaper editor, called upon Palestinians to launch jihad in Palestine. Shanti, whose own family was of peasant origin, ensured that his newspaper represented strong Muslim and anti-British sentiments.

At another meeting in Haifa at the MYMA, which was held at the end of the traditional forty-day mourning period, more than a thousand people lamented the late sheikh. Rejecting statements in the Hebrew press denouncing him as a 'brigand', instead they declared that Qassam should be commemorated as a hero, a symbol of struggle to inspire the Palestinian people to rise up and reject British subordination. His death was described as an act of martyrdom in 'defence of his country against the British'. He was also declared a 'great nationalist who fell in the cause'.[23]

In death Qassam became a symbol of national resistance for all Palestinians – irrespective of their ideological hue. In later decades his story would be retold by nationalists in the PLO as homage to the armed resistance against the Zionists and the British. The Islamists in Hamas would also claim ownership of Qassam.

Qassam had reached out to the poor, the untutored and the recently dispossessed peasant classes who had been forced to scrape a living by working in some of the hardest and most unpopular industries of Haifa. In so doing he challenged the traditional leadership of Palestine, preaching resistance and steadfastness at a time when they were often squabbling among themselves. His legacy found almost instant expression in the outbreak of the Palestinian revolt in 1936. The revolt and general strike – which lasted for three years – paralysed the country and forced Britain to introduce harsh measures as it sought to restore law and order among the increasingly divided Palestinian Arab and Jewish communities.

In April 1936 a band of Qassam's armed followers launched an ambush and killed two Jews. In retaliation the Jewish resistance attacked and killed two Palestinian Arabs. In the coastal city of Jaffa tensions rose as sporadic violence broke out between Palestinian Arabs and Jews. The British, struggling to maintain control, declared a state of emergency. Later that month Palestinian leaders called for a general strike, and all sectors of Arab society banded together in solidarity to protest against what they saw as draconian British measures and Zionist encroachment. Political impulses were quickly harnessed by the local elite through the establishment of the Arab Higher Committee (AHC), led by the mufti, 'who although appointed and beholden to the British authorities, had no alternative but to join the militants.'[24] The AHC issued a series of well-rehearsed demands: cessation of Jewish immigration to Palestine, an end to land sales to the Zionists and the foundation of a Palestinian Arab government.

None of these demands was new, but the context in which they were made was. It appeared that the ordinary Palestinian Arabs had had enough. Their livelihoods, their society, their structures of power, their sense of place, space and dimension were all under threat, and a collective sense of despair now propelled people towards rebellion. The Qassamites and the resort to an armed resistance signalled a popular uprising that took Palestinian leaders as much by surprise as it did the British authorities. The Qassamites targeted mandate officials and those accused of land sales, arms trading or collaboration with the Zionist cause. Unlike many of the roving rebel peasant bands which engaged in wanton destruction, the Qassamites had a cause. According to official British reports the Qassamites organized meetings in which 'the peasants were called to join the revolt . . . and also in acts of terror against those Arabs who were not considered nationalistic enough or disregarded the strike.'[25]

The Qassamites, however, never succeeded in transforming the revolt into a full-scale jihad with the goal of establishing an Islamic state in Palestine. Ultimately their revolt was to fail. Within a decade the Zionists had their state and, amid the bloodshed which accompanied the end of the British Mandate, hundreds of thousands of Palestinians had fled to become refugees, stateless, homeless and dispossessed in foreign lands and refugee camps in Gaza and the West Bank. But it was in these very camps, among the children and grandchildren of the refugees, that later generations of Islamists would emerge to pick up from where Qassam left off and begin rallying the poor, the angry and the dispossessed to the call of Islam. For them Qassam had shown the path.

3

Sowing

None of the political organizations paid it any attention. It was apolitical and was not perceived as a threat.

Dr Haider Abdel Shafi[1]

The British eventually succeeded in putting down the 1936–9 revolt that was in large part inspired by Sheikh Izz ad-Din al-Qassam. Some of those who took part were believed to be 'Izz ad-Din's followers' and 'disciples of the Holy Martyr',[2] but the spirit of Islam as a political force appeared to be spent, along with much of the energy that had propelled the Islamists' nationalist counterparts.

The British Mandate authorities punished the Palestinian leadership: they were deported, exiled, put in prison camps and even executed, and their followers were subjected to severe law and order measures. Many of the sheikhs who had risen up against the British during the revolt to protest against land sales and Jewish immigration to the country were arrested, tried and imprisoned by the British military courts.

The religious leadership, personified by the mufti, Hajj Amin al-Husseini, embarked on a collision course with the very British authorities which had installed him at the head of the Muslim institutions of Palestine. Increasingly, however, the *ulama* (religious elite) of this vast institutionalized network of mosques, courts and schools had become too tainted by its association with the British to enjoy widespread support among ordinary Muslims, who were agitating against colonial rule. Forced to assert himself, al-Husseini tried to direct the Palestinian general strike and 1936 revolt. The British decided that the mufti was working against their interests and should be dismissed, and when he gained advance intelligence of their plans al-Husseini fled into exile.

During the Second World War al-Husseini based himself in Berlin, where he cooperated with Hitler's propaganda machine in the vain hope that the Germans, once victorious, would drive the British out of Palestine. This was a blunder of historic proportions, not only because he picked the losing side, but because his readiness to further his people's national interests – even to the extent of allying with a Nazi regime which dragged the world into war and perpetrated the Holocaust – has ever since been held up by Israelis as evidence of the Palestinian leadership's cynicism, anti-Semitism and amorality.

Unprepared

The movement of political Islam, which made such an impact on Palestinian destiny during the British Mandate, simply failed to rise to the subsequent challenge of losing Palestine in 1948. It had certainly tried. The Muslim Brotherhood opened new branches in Palestine in the late 1940s: more than 1,000 people attended the opening of its Jerusalem branch in Said al-Husseini's garden in the Muslim quarter of the Old City in May 1946. Contemporary accounts report that 'several fiery speeches were made and broadcast' and that the band of the Muslim orphanage played during the intervals. The speeches were made by figures drawn from many well-known Jerusalem families, including Jamal al-Husseini, Sheikh Abdel Hamid al-Sayegh, Nasri Nashashibi, and the poet Seif el Din Kailani. A declaration was made that 'the Muslim Brotherhood considers the infringement of the rights of Palestine's Arabs as a threat to all Muslims'.[3]

West of Jerusalem in the coastal region of Gaza, long a neglected backwater of the British Mandate, some heads of the notable Palestinian families had been imprisoned or deported during the 1936–9 revolt. But afterwards many were allowed to return because the British no longer considered them a threat. Islam had its place in Gaza, through the formal offices held by these families during the Ottoman era. But revivalist Islam was also becoming a factor with the steady arrival of Muslim Brotherhood representatives from Egypt. In such a provincial outpost these envoys would have appeared to many Gazans as sophisticated emissaries from cosmopolitan Cairo, then the centre of the Middle East.

Throughout the 1940s the Muslim Brotherhood's branches in the Gaza area largely mirrored the structures and activities of the rapidly expanding Egyptian Brotherhood. The Gaza City branch was located in one of its wealthiest neighbourhoods, and two Gaza members – Mohammed Taha and Abd al-Fatah al-Dukhan – were appointed to the Brotherhood's regional committees. Such was its importance that in 1947 the Brotherhood's founder and supreme leader, Hassan al-Banna, visited Gaza.

But even as the Brotherhood was laying its roots, the region was shaken by the announcement in 1947 that Britain would terminate its mandate the following year, and that the United Nations planned to partition Palestine into separate Jewish and Palestinian Arab states. Worse, the

Palestinians and neighbouring Arab countries were outraged that the UN partition resolution proposed to award about 56 per cent of the land between the Mediterranean and Jordan River to the Jews, who represented 32 per cent of the population, leaving 44 per cent for the majority Palestinians. Although they had their own concerns, including the presence of a sizeable Arab population within their proposed state, and that this state was broken into fragments, the majority of the Jewish leadership accepted the United Nations partition plan. The Arab sides refused, but lost the vote at the UN. In the ensuing months, as Zionist armed groups readied for statehood, Arab leaders simply reassured the Palestinians that they would protect them and that they should not panic or flee their homes. The Muslim Brotherhood, however, began to organize for jihad. Mujahidin from Egypt began to arrive in Gaza in the early months of 1948 to 'fight with the Palestinians in the war as a serious attempt to support the Palestinian issue'.[4]

The mujahidin proved inadequate to the challenge, and were overwhelmed. The combined Arab armies lost a significant amount of territory and at the end of the fighting the Arabs – that is to say the armies of neighbouring Jordan and Egypt rather than the Palestinians themselves – controlled only the West Bank and Gaza. It was half what the Arabs would have received had they accepted partition, and, in addition to losing half their allotted land, they had also lost half the Palestinian population: by the end of 1949 726,000 refugees had fled or been driven out.[5]

After the war it was clear that the small number of Islamists could do little to support the huge new refugee population that had flooded into Gaza and the West Bank. 'There were no big mosques, just small buildings which we call mosques. We were penniless and we didn't have the means to build our movement', recalls one Brotherhood activist.[6] Faced with thousands of young students ripe for education and indoctrination, the Brotherhood 'tried to gather the students and the teachers and labourers to remind them of the two most important things – restoring the lost land and the religion'.[7] But there was nowhere for them to go and there were not enough members to lead the now homeless and stateless population. Among the arrivals was Ahmed Yassin, a young refugee from the village of al-Jura, near what is now the Israeli port city of Ashkelon. 'Our lands and homes were taken from us and we had to fight. From this early age I dreamt of martyrdom if it would bring freedom',[8] recalled the man who would later go on to become the founder and spiritual leader of Hamas.

For Palestinians living in the West Bank and Gaza Strip, the disruption of the war was followed by a period of adjustment to the new realities. The British were gone, the new state of Israel was on their doorstep, and the Egyptians and Jordanians were now in charge in the West Bank and Gaza. In the wake of Israel's victories against the combined Arab armies many Arabs still asked how Jerusalem, the third most holy site in Islam, could have fallen into the hands of Jewish nationalists. The dispossession convinced some god-fearing Muslims that only through faith, patience and arms would they ever return to the homes and villages they had been forced to abandon. 'I always thought about my village of al-Jura, and when I became involved with the Brotherhood I knew we would be in a war to restore Palestine and return to my village', recalled one Muslim Brotherhood veteran of that era.[9]

Ferment

Such hopes were, however, to go into temporary abeyance. The Islamic trend was soon to be overwhelmed by the dominant ideology of Arab nationalism that, by 1952, had taken hold in Egyptian-administered Gaza and was also popular in the Jordanian-controlled West Bank, where a young British-supported monarch now sat on the Hashemite throne. Both President Gamal Abdel Nasser of Egypt and King Hussein of Jordan sought to ensure that Islam would not be the sole solution for the Palestinian issue, or any other dimension of Arab politics. King Hussein, however, was not above employing his declaration of Prophetic lineage to lay claim to the right to protect Jerusalem's Muslim holy sites, rather than let them stay in Palestinian hands.

Thus the years immediately following the war of 1948 would prove crucial in establishing a collective sense among Palestinians of being a nation denied a state, of forging a national identity, and of pursuing the struggle for liberation and self-determination. Growing consciousness of an identity shaped through turmoil, statelessness and the experience of becoming refugees bound the people together through nationalism, not religion, and in ways which transcended the newly created borders which kept them apart from their lands, families and livelihoods.

The political message of Islam – liberation through jihad – was lost in the drumbeat of Arab nationalism and the promises of radical new Arab leaders that Palestine would be recovered by their armies. These forces were not armed, as Izz ad-Din al-Qassam's mujahidin had been, merely with a few rifles and bullets, but with the kind of heavy weaponry that had the whole region believing that the new state of Israel would soon be defeated on the battlefield and the lost land would be regained. The Arab nationalist military coups in Western-backed countries such as Egypt and Iraq in the 1950s also fuelled a sense that the Arab failures of 1948 were being purged.

By the late 1950s and early 1960s the Palestinian refugees became politically restive in places such as the Egyptian-controlled Gaza Strip. The Egyptian regime placed Gaza under military administration and implemented the same crackdowns on Islamists there as inside Egypt itself. Gaza's shanty-tented refugee camps had been a fertile recruiting ground for the Islamists, and the Brotherhood's adherents were rounded up and sent to prison, forcing the movement underground. It responded by establishing military cells with grandiose names such as the Young Men of Vengeance (*Shabab al-Tha'r*) and the Battalion of Justice. New recruits gained only the most rudimentary training in paramilitary activities, along with assurances by their instructors that Islam would provide the solution to their miserable existence as refugees. 'We believed in Allah and our faith to turn us to the jihad against the Jewish state', recalled Abu Mohammed, a young recruit to the *Shabab al-Tha'r*. 'I was not afraid to go to war because I was now armed with God's power and faith in him. I understood that if I died I would go to paradise and therefore alive or dead it didn't matter.'[10]

Some of the leading lights of the Muslim Brotherhood's military cells at this time were young men such as Salah Khalaf (Abu Iyad) and Khalil al-Wazir (Abu Jihad), who later left to play a central role in the Fatah movement headed by Yasser Arafat. The Brotherhood's members were bound together as refugees and potential mujahidin who believed that only Islam could deliver them from their daily ordeals. But after the 1952 Free Officers' coup deposed the monarchy in Egypt, the Islamists were confronted with a powerful new rival: Arab nationalism.

The Egyptian figurehead of that movement, Nasser, endured a fractious relationship with the Brotherhood. It had played a part in the coup that brought his Revolutionary Command Council to power, but only two years later in 1954 a gunman tried to assassinate Nasser at a mass meeting in Alexandria, and later confessed that he did so at the behest of the Muslim Brotherhood. Thousands of Egyptian and Palestinian members of the Brotherhood were arrested, branch offices were closed down and activists were executed. Even today the memory of those times is seared in the collective consciousness of the Islamists, and there is an enduring mistrust of Egyptian motives. 'We felt it was bad enough to be dispossessed by the Jews, but then to have no control over our lives in Gaza because our Arab brothers were ruling us . . . it was too much', declared Sheikh Yassin in 2002.[11]

With Nasser unwilling to tolerate any protest, Gaza's Islamists found unlikely bedfellows: the communists. Led by Fathi Bilawi, the Brotherhood held joint demonstrations with the leftists. Abu Zaki, a member of the Communist Party at the time, ended up in jail in Cairo along with fellow Palestinians from the Palestinian Muslim Brotherhood. 'In prison both sides had their own points of views and differences, but we managed to live together as we were all in the same boat and had to deal with the problem together', recalled Abu Zaki. 'We received encouragement and support from the Egyptian *Ikhwan* [Brotherhood] because we were all Palestinians, and Arafat, who was head of the student's movement in Cairo, gathered clothes and money for all of us in prison.'[12] However, such solidarity dissipated once the Palestinians were released from jail and returned to Gaza. In the late 1950s there was 'no affection for the *Ikhwan*', noted Abu Zaki. 'Most of the *Ikhwan* changed their political orientation or went to the Gulf countries, and thus they vanished completely from Gaza and the minds of the people.'[13]

The members of the Brotherhood who settled in Gulf countries such as Saudi Arabia and Kuwait would later serve as an important ideological and financial conduit for a revived Islamic movement in Gaza and the West Bank. But for the moment Nasser's brand of Arab nationalism was the dominant ideology. 'At the time I fully supported Nasser's system – just as everyone else did. He taught us how to dismiss Israel and work towards the creation of one Arab state . . . we were amazed by the personality of Abdel Nasser',[14] recalls Mahmoud Zahar, a senior Hamas leader who studied medicine in Egypt during this era, and who began his political life as a nationalist. Yet, for Zahar and other conservative young Gazan refugees, the heady populism of the 1960s, decadence and further victories by the Israelis in wars against the Arabs would prove to be a turning point in the revival of Islam as a political force for change among certain sections of Palestinian society.

Between 1948 and 1967 new Palestinian political organizations began to emerge, and often they were patronized by the Egyptian authorities. But increasingly the Muslim Brotherhood was greeted with mistrust and suspicion by the Egyptians, and support eroded in favour of the new Palestinian nationalists arising in their midst.

Gaza too began to change. Under Egypt's influence it became more urban, less conservative, and traditional. Popular pastimes of cafés, beach picnics, parties and cinema-going preoccupied the free time of the growing ranks of the refugees. Dreams of liberation centred on a new generation of charismatic young personalities such as Yasser Arafat. In this popularity contest the traditional stalwarts of the Muslim Brotherhood represented a defunct and bygone age.

Swinging sixties: the wilderness years

As Gaza began to turn to Nasser's way of seeing the world, Palestinians enjoyed some political benefits under the new dispensation. More young people turned to the ideas of liberation associated with the Arab Ba'ath, Nasserist, nationalist and leftist movements. The social conservatism of Gaza's traditional families and structures was challenged by a new generation. Young men swapped the tarbush of an earlier generation for Elvis-like quiffs, sunglasses and skinny-Mod ties. Their traditional galabaya were replaced with shirts and trousers. Women wore pencil skirts and mini-skirts and sported beehive hairstyles. 'To us during this time . . . living well in Gaza was as normal in the 1960s as Beirut or Cairo. It was a decent society',[15] recalled Rawiya Shawwa, a member of a wealthy and influential Gaza family. Gaza City developed and became a leisure destination for Egyptians seeking tax-free shopping, beach-side restaurants, and cinemas showing the latest Egyptian movies.

Egyptian universities were opened up to hundreds of Gazan students, and the experience of studying in Cairo and exposure to the wider currents of Arab political thought proved to be a seminal factor in the development of Palestinian political movements, for Islamists and nationalists alike. Dr Mariam Abu Dagga, a teenage radical and member of the Guevara faction of the Popular Front for the Liberation of Palestine (PFLP) in the 1960s, also remembers the changed atmosphere: 'Gaza then was totally different from now . . . I found all the women now have put on scarf and Shari'a *hijab*, but in the past even my mother didn't wear such things.'[16] Mariam, like so many others, came to believe in the Arab socialist solution to the refugees' predicament. Gaza fell under the Nasserist spell.

In the West Bank the Islamic movement endured a different experience under Jordanian Hashemite rule. Most West Bank branches of the Muslim Brotherhood were closed directly after the 1948 war, so Jerusalem became marginalized, and its leaders made regular pilgrimages to the movement's office in the Jordanian capital, Amman. There the movement judiciously sought a more harmonious relationship with the conservative monarchy than its Gaza colleagues endured with the more radical ideas of Nasser's regime. As a result the Brotherhood had not only survived the Jordanian political crackdown of the 1950s, which banned other political movements, but by the 1960s was the only significant political opposition in the country. Nevertheless, although identified as pro-Hashemite and conservative, the Brotherhood knew that it was under constant scrutiny by the ubiquitous Jordanian secret services – the *mukhabarat*. 'We supported the regime and its national aims even at times when we were accused of supporting a pro-Western king', explained Yousef al-Athm, a senior figure from that era.[17]

In the West Bank the Brotherhood maintained close ties with preachers and acted as a religious institution rather than a political party. It celebrated popular festivals, offered sports activities and classes in the study of the Koran, and put on theatre performances, all reflecting the values of a Muslim, as opposed to a Western, way of life.

The enforced geographical separation of the Gaza Strip and the West Bank – with Israel between them – meant that the path of Palestinian Islamism had a dual character. It was Gaza which emerged as the heart of a particularly Palestinian interpretation of political Islam. In Gaza progressive politics and radicalism would eventually inspire Islamists to react to the changes around them and formulate their own vision of liberation. In the West Bank Islamism remained conservative and traditional, tied to elite power structures associated with preserving the power of the Hashemite monarchy and traditional family and clan structures.

The 1967 war and Israeli occupation

The Six Day War of June 1967, in which Israel comprehensively defeated the combined Arab armies of Egypt, Jordan and Syria, led to another period of profound upheaval for the Palestinian people. The war led to the Israeli occupation of the Palestinian territories of the West Bank and Gaza Strip, Syria's Golan Heights and Egypt's Sinai peninsula. Israel not only defeated the Arab armies of the largest countries in the region but captured and occupied East Jerusalem, which it subsequently annexed.

It quickly became clear that Arab nationalism had failed in its promises. For Palestinians the experience was more intensely personal. Thousands had become refugees for a second time, and, shattered by yet another defeat, it took years for the nationalists to regroup. But they did so, this time under the leadership of Yasser Arafat, Nayef Hawatmeh, George Habash, Khalil Wazir (Abu Jihad) and Salah Khalaf (Abu Iyad), through the umbrella group of the Palestine Liberation Organization (PLO). As Arafat and his *fedayeen* fighters grew in stature across the region, the socially conservative and anti-nationalist Muslim Brotherhood was, yet again, perceived as badly out of step with the revolutionary ethos of the time.

The Brotherhood initially put its jihad on hold, arguing that it was not ready for such a step. Instead it became convinced that it should first launch a social jihad to Islamize its own society. A leading Islamist figure, Abdullah Azzam, who went on to become a mentor to Usama Bin Laden, later admitted that this was a mistake that 'allowed revolutionary organisations to outstrip [us], organisations which the Brotherhood berates for their leftist leanings, their deviation, their bungling and for brainwashing the youth'.[18]

In Israeli-occupied Palestinian cities such as Gaza City, Nablus and Ramallah, radical young Palestinians threw off their parents' conservative social and religious mores. Rejecting Islam as the solution to the problem of Israeli occupation, they turned instead to the theories of secular Arab nationalists, socialists and Marxists. It was not until the late 1970s, the second decade under Israeli rule, that there was an Islamic renaissance.

For all their fervour, Arafat's *fedayeen* forces were waging a losing battle. By 1971 Israel had deported as many as 15,000 guerrillas and activists to prison camps in the Sinai desert, and in 1973 Israel once again inflicted further humiliation on its Arab enemies, repulsing the Egyptian and Syrian armies who attacked on the Jewish holy day of Yom Kippur.

Some Islamists had long regretted the Brotherhood's early decision to lie low and cede the initiative to the nationalists. These Muslim opposition forces sought to capitalize on the return to Islam which Dr Mahmoud Zahar and other prominent Islamists believed they had begun to notice in the mid- to late 1970s. 'The people', Zahar claimed, 'returned to their religion [and] started to study Islam thoroughly, and began to live Islam as a system governing their way of life.'[19] The people to whom Zahar referred were mostly young graduates of Egyptian universities, whose experience of student politics at the time had led them to the radical sermons and writings of Egyptian fundamentalists such as Sayyed Qutb.

Qutb, a leading figure in the Muslim Brotherhood, was an inspiration for Islamist radical movements such as al-Qaeda, the Afghan mujahidin and *Gamma Islammiya* in Egypt. He was imprisoned and executed by the Egyptian authorities in the late 1960s for his seditionist views, but his execution only inspired other young Muslim radicals to read his works, debate his arguments and wear the mantle of jihad. Qutb had declared Westernized Muslim societies to be infidel, led by leaders unfit to stand under the banner of Islam. He called on Muslims to return to their faith and to lead a jihad against societies which he believed were intoxicated by corrupt Western morals and values.

The 1970s: Yassin and the rise of the Islamists

In the 1970s the predecessors of Hamas set about remaking Palestinian society in the image of Islam, prepared if necessary to impose their vision by force. The chief architect of this revival project was the educator and preacher Sheikh Ahmed Yassin. Yassin was a young child when he and his widowed mother became refugees in Gaza in 1948. After breaking his spine in his early teens – different accounts have been given of how he suffered the damage – he was left wheelchair-bound for the rest of his life. Nevertheless, he completed his elementary and secondary education and went to Cairo in the early 1950s to earn his teaching qualifications. Attracted to the ideas of the Muslim Brotherhood on his return to Gaza, he began to work as a teacher, community worker and preacher at a mosque and became a prominent figure in the refugee neighbourhood of al-Sabra in Gaza City where he lived. But his Muslim Brotherhood affiliation was well known, which led to his brief imprisonment in 1966 by the Egyptians during one of their regular anti-Brotherhood purges.

Increasingly Yassin came to believe that his role as an activist in Gaza's Muslim community was to bring Islam to the secularized youth, to get them to commit to the fundamental tenets of the faith: to pray five times a day, to fast during Ramadan – in essence, to be pious and exemplary Muslims in all aspects of life. Yassin devoted himself to promoting Islamic revivalism through preaching and education. As he himself later asserted, 'our faith is tied to the future of this society and the command to make Islam flourish again.'[20]

Yassin proved to be an inspirational educator among his natural con-stituency: stateless refugees like himself. 'His experience was a shared experience', said his biographer Dr Atef Adwan. 'This is part of his appeal to so many in Gaza.'[21] Yassin's vision advocated individual change as

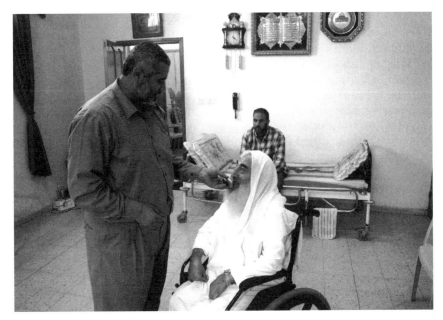

Photo 3.1   Hamas's founder Sheikh Ahmed Yassin in his Gaza City home before his assassination in 2004; with him is the future prime minister Ismail Haniyeh.

the instrument to bring about the overhaul of society. In 1973 he and a group of followers established *al-Mujamma' al-Islami* (The Islamic Centre), an organization whose prominent figures would later win international notoriety as the leaders of Hamas: Dr Mahmour Zahar, Dr Abdel Aziz Rantissi, Ibrahim Yazouri, Abd al-Fattah Dukhan, Issa al-Najjar and Salah Shehadeh.

Yassin's role was pivotal. He engendered formidable loyalty and devotion in his followers, upon whom he was completely dependent because of his physical disability. Seated in front of the television mounted high up on the wall, he would follow the screen with his eyes until he saw something which prompted him to whisper instructions to lieutenants in his distinctive thin, high voice. He had to be lifted in and out of cars and at mealtimes would have to be spoon-fed, with a napkin around his neck. His only means of communication with the outside world – beyond the pulpit – was when aides held up a telephone handset to his ear. Despite his physical frailty there was strength of spirit apparent in any encounter with Yassin. He would make firm, well-articulated pronouncements on the serious questions of the day.

Those with whom Yassin surrounded himself seemed to absorb from him a confidence not only to make their mark on society, but to take on their enemies, apparently without fear. 'No one can deny that the resurgence of Islam depends on such people . . . he was the creator of the new Islamic movement in Gaza',[22] was the later assessment of Mahmoud Zahar. As ideological descendants of the Muslim Brotherhood and thinkers such as Qutb, his followers were concerned, first and foremost, to return society and politics to the true path of Islam. Therefore their first targets were their fellow Palestinians, specifically the secular nationalists and leftists of the PLO. Only later would they turn their attention to Israel. 'We have to be patient because Islam will spread sooner or later and will have control over the world. Patience will shorten the journey of Islam', Yassin declared.[23] They directed their energies at every aspect of society and demanded that their rivals relinquish political control. They objected to the new world view promoted by the secular nationalists. On university campuses they shouted down lecturers teaching Darwin's theory of evolution, spreading conspiracy theories that Darwin's thinking was inspired by Jews.[24]

The Islamists organized demonstrations to protest against leftist or secular institutions. They began to target professional associations and other groupings, demanding a hearing for their Islamist agenda. However, the Israeli authorities did not, at that time, appear to believe that the Islamists' agitation against their fellow Palestinians was something to worry about. 'The Israelis turned a blind eye to all the harmful activities that the Mujamma undertook against the people . . . ambushes against individuals on the streets, raids on houses of leaders of nationalist groups', recalled one Palestinian official. 'They sent to me about 500 armed Mujamma supporters and threatened me, telling me to leave . . . the national groups were paralysed . . . therefore the Israeli strategy . . . paid off',[25] said Dr Riad al-Agha, a former president of the Islamic University of Gaza.

Other Palestinian analysts believe that Israel was merely opportunistic about the Mujamma's growth. 'I don't go as far as to say that Israel created Hamas or the Islamic movement, but Israel of course used all the existing Palestinian mosaic to its advantage', said Professor Ali al-Jarbawi. 'They were not as harsh on Hamas or the Islamic movement as on the nationalist factions, because of what they were standing for. If you were not for resisting the occupation, then why should Israel at that time crack down on them?'[26]

In these early days there was little indication to suggest that this group of Islamic activists would become one of the most formidable resistance movements in the Middle East. They were barely tolerated in Palestinian secular and leftist circles, and were largely dismissed by the cosmopolitan leadership of the PLO, which was now living in exile after the rout of the Arab forces in the 1967 war. Nevertheless, the increased religiosity that the Mujamma promoted began to have an impact, as did the building of mosques and libraries and the work of *zakat* (charity) committees and the encouragement of Islamic dress, regular prayer and fasting. 'They began to repair old mosques and enlarge others. They also planned to build a new mosque in each camp, each lane and at each institution in the Gaza Strip and began the slow process of enacting these plans',[27] recalled one Gazan.

While Israeli officials deny that Israel went so far as to arm or actively encourage the Islamists, some concede that governments at the time regarded them as a useful tool to use against secular nationalists in the PLO. 'At the beginning I think some elements within the Israeli government – not the government, some elements within the Israeli government – were thinking that by strengthening Mujamma they could put some more pressure on Fatah in the Gaza Strip, back in the mid-eighties', said Brigadier General Yossi Kuperwasser, a former director of intelligence analysis for the Israeli military. 'I think it was a mistake, yes.'[28]

Brigadier General Itshak Segev served as the Israeli military governor of Gaza from 1979 to 1981, just after he returned from a posting to Iran. Having just seen the 1979 Iranian Revolution and the opening weeks of Ayatollah Ruhollah Khomeini's regime up close, he had no illusions about the dangers posed by Islamist fundamentalists. But during his time in charge, he said, Sheikh Yassin's people presented him with 'zero, zero, zero' problems. Segev remarked that he even arranged for Yassin to be taken to hospital in Tel Aviv to see if the best surgeons in Israel could operate on his spine, but they pronounced the damage too severe to be corrected by surgery. Nevertheless, although the Mujamma was ostensibly religious and social in its intent, Segev warned his superiors in 1980 that they faced a 'catastrophe' if they stayed in Gaza, because its population was growing so fast and was likely to be affected by the wave of Islamic fundamentalism apparent across the region, not just in the Palestinian territories. 'There was a demographic atom bomb that was going on', he said. 'I didn't think about Yassin or Islamic Jihad, but I saw this society was going in the direction of fundamentalism, and this phenomenon was all over – Algeria, Egypt, Iran. This phenomenon had come about because of the failure of the regimes in these countries to satisfy their people.'

Even then, according to Segev, it was apparent that the Islamists in Gaza were exploiting the failings of the PLO.

> The people in the refugee camps were very poor. If money went to Arafat's people they took it and put it in their pockets, but when Yassin got money he gave it to the people. . . . If he took money from Saudi Arabia he built a mosque, he gave education to children, or started ping pong for them. He did a lot of things, really, to help the people.[29]

Indeed, Sheikh Yassin founded a small sporting club and youth association on some waste ground at the back of his humble home in the al-Sabra neighbourhood of Gaza City. His ambitions, however, could not be enclosed by the dusty football pitch, dilapidated chairs and decrepit hut which acted as a changing room for the bearded players of the Mujamma football, volleyball and ping pong teams.

The first obstacles in their way were secular Palestinian nationalists and the PLO. Sheikh Yassin and his associates were appalled at what they considered to be pernicious leftist and infidel tendencies among Gaza's youth. By targeting the youth, they targeted the heart of Palestinian society. Gaza's refugee community had one of the highest birth rates in the Middle East and its population was young. Many of these young people had accessed the opportunities offered by an education from the Egyptians and had encountered more liberal and cosmopolitan societies in cities such as Cairo and Alexandria. These young men had been attracted to the nationalist fervour that swept the region, and particularly communist and leftist ideologies that had inspired revolutions such as that in Algeria against the French in 1962, or the coup in Iraq in 1958. As one Gazan recalled of those years, 'we felt we had the cause and the people on our side. We wanted to liberate Gaza and enjoy our lives in the same way that our brothers were in Cairo, Baghdad or Damascus.'[30]

There was also a sense that the PLO, while reviled as a terrorist organization in Israel, had captured the imagination of the wider world. Even as Yassin was an unknown teacher labouring among Gaza's refugee community to set up an Islamic framework, Yasser Arafat was becoming one of the most famous and instantly recognizable figures in the world. In an era of revolutionary politics, international socialism, liberation movements and anti-colonial movements rising in Africa, Latin America and the Middle East, the PLO and its guerrillas were regarded as populist icons. Arafat headed a movement which could count on hundreds of thousands of supporters spread across the Middle East. By the mid-1970s the PLO had grown in stature and was identified as a state within a state, first in Jordan and then in Lebanon.

Confrontation

The message of Sheikh Yassin's Mujamma inevitably led to internal strife. There was nothing unusual about this. The Palestinians had always engaged in robust debate. However, internal acts of violence were rare. Communal clashes had played their part in the collapse of the first Palestinian revolt against British occupation and Zionist settlement in the 1930s, and Palestinians recalled that historical lesson.

But rivalries were common, and often the splits were along political, family and clan lines. The Mujamma ran into all sorts of confrontations as it sought to challenge from within. Although many denied that they had political ambitions, it was clear from their rivalry with the nationalist-secularists that power was on their minds. 'They emphasized that the only path to liberation was through the realization of an Islamic state.

Even at this stage they were voicing political ideas – they belittled fighting the occupation', declared Dr Haider Abdel Shafi, a Gaza notable and nationalist leader.[31] Before long Abdel Shafi was forced to confront Muslim hoods who attacked and burned the office of the Palestine Red Crescent Society, of which he was director.

The Mujamma received a boost in 1978, when it was granted official status by the Israeli authorities ruling Gaza, at a time when it was nigh impossible for secular groups to get the same recognition. Officials in the office of the Israeli prime minister, Menachem Begin, gave approval to the registration. Many Palestinians believe, and some former Israeli officials concede, that this happened against the background of an Israeli strategy to produce a counterbalance to the PLO, and to divide secular nationalists by encouraging them to turn to this Islamic alternative.

Some Palestinians have long accused Israel of giving both direct and indirect support to the Islamists at this period, through the Mujamma. 'They were given permission from the Israeli authorities to form', said a former president of the Islamic University of Gaza. 'The [Israeli] authorities kept their eyes closed to the realities of what they were allowing to be created, to the preaching of Islam that was spreading all over the Gaza Strip, because at that time the PLO factions had power . . . and the Israelis wanted an adversary to fight them.'[32] Thirty years later the same Islamic University of Gaza stood as one of the most potent symbols of Hamas power, a place from which many of the Islamist movement's senior leadership had graduated. In December 2008 it was among the first places to be bombed by Israel's warplanes striking against Hamas's power centres during the 22-long offensive codenamed Operation Cast Lead.

By the early 1980s the Mujamma had acquired a reputation for campaigning against the PLO and the institutions that supported it, not against the Israelis. Local health-care institutions, universities, and professional associations and other movements which traditionally bore allegiance to the PLO and its leftist factions were targeted by the Mujamma, and such places quickly became battlegrounds. The Israeli authorities and their soldiers allegedly stood by as blood was spilt on Gaza's streets by Mujamma supporters, who denounced 'atheists' and 'communists' in sermons, leaflets and speeches. After Friday prayers burning torches were held aloft as Mujamma thugs set fire to libraries, newspaper offices, billiard halls and bars. They burned cinemas and cafés, closed liquor stores, and ran intimidation campaigns in the community and on the university campus. The apparent indifference of the Israeli authorities to such violence was noted by PLO supporters.

'Israel turned a blind eye to distribution of Mujamma leaflets, and it appears that the authorities also ignored its stockpiling of crude weapons',[33] said Dr Haider Abdel Shafi, a decade later. Danny Rubinstein, a left-wing Israeli journalist, also perceived an extension of Israeli support for the Islamists in the West Bank:

As a young journalist in the early 1970s, I joined Israel's deputy prime minister, Yigal Allon, at the dedication ceremony of the Islamic Academy in Hebron, which the Israeli military authorities even funded for more than seven years. Many graduates of this very institution became the most vicious enemies of the State of Israel. Ever since, many have accused Israel of providing the raison d'être for the Islamic religious movement – a phenomenon identical to American support for the Mujahedin in Afghanistan during the Soviet occupation.[34]

Seizing control

Dr Eyad Sarraj, one of Gaza's most prominent figures, remembers the day in January 1980 when the Mujamma attacked the offices of the Palestine Red Crescent Society (PRCS), a humanitarian health-care service that is the Muslim equivalent of the Red Cross. The leaders of the Mujamma had failed to get control of the PRCS through recently contested elections to its administrative council and were incensed by rumours that the nationalists were also planning to found their own university:

> I heard shouting in the street, so I went out into the road, and it was a big Islamist demonstration, [thousands of] people with beards shouting their slogans. At the end of the demonstration was an Israeli military jeep which did not interfere. That day the Mujamma went to the Red Crescent, shouting slogans 'Liberation of Afghanistan'. I confronted one of them one day and said, 'Why the liberation of Afghanistan when Jerusalem is closer? We should liberate Jerusalem.' He said, 'No no, you don't understand. Our problem is not with the people of the book. Jews are the people of the Book. Our problem is with the infidels – people who don't believe in God. These are the real enemy.'

Sarraj said he later saw Brigadier General Segev, the Israeli governor, and told him: 'You are playing with fire, this could really come back to you in a violent way.' Sarraj claimed the Israeli governor reassured him: 'He said: "Don't worry, we know how to handle things. Our enemy today is the PLO".'[35]

The Mujamma mob proceeded that day to the offices of the PRCS, attacking cafés and video stores along the way. When they arrived they set fire to the building, including its library and offices. Palestinians were left shocked at the fury behind the attack and the destruction in its wake. Social control was an important dimension of the Islamists' agenda, and they came close, on occasion, to consolidating control through coercion.

At the secular-oriented al-Azhar college, Fatah fought successfully to keep the institution affiliated to the PLO, through its students and faculty. But it was relatively easy for the Mujamma to establish a monopoly of power at the neighbouring Islamic University of Gaza (IUG). The ways in which the university would become Islamic were soon apparent; segregation between men and women was enforced throughout the university, in its classrooms, cafés, and library and campus areas. Strict Islamic dress codes were introduced for men and women. Opponents of the Mujamma accused it of suppressing political diversity through a climate of fear. Nationalist students and lecturers were regularly targeted for humiliation by their fellow students, the university administration and even the university's doormen and guards, who were bearded Mujamma members with a reputation for meting out violent beatings to dissenters. Activist supporters of the PLO were singled out for attack and denunciation and were publicly condemned as atheists and infidels, accused of elevating the PLO leader Yasser Arafat above Islam.

It also became common knowledge that the Mujamma had a cache of crude weapons at the university that it used in its attacks against the secularists and nationalists. For women in particular, Islamic dress implied a stricture to wear the *hijab* (headscarf) as well as a long *thobe* (coat). The Islamic movement established wings in the university, first for its male adherents and then later for women. Money for such dress was often made available to poor students, the cost met by pledges from overseas donors.

By 1981 the Mujamma and its supporters had succeeded in having seven out of the thirteen members of the university senate ejected or forced to tender their resignations when called to a meeting at the headquarters of the Israeli civil administration in Gaza. Many questioned why such a meeting was being held under Israeli auspices at all. One critic who alleged that the Israelis were tacitly backing the Islamists, and denounced the latter as 'collaborators and a danger to us all', was attacked and severely beaten.[36]

From the highest to the lowest employee in the university, the Mujamma's influence was increasingly apparent. Gazan journalists wrote that faith appeared to matter more than qualifications to those appointing university lecturers, and one caustic observer accused the university authorities of filling the staff 'with sheikhs rather than PhDs'. Students were often singled out for denunciation campaigns and attacks culminating in ostracism on campus and at home. 'It reached a point where friends would stay at my house to protect me and certain members of my family would not even speak to me because they believed what Mujamma were saying about me',[37] one student recalls. In 1983 alone more than eighteen people, including staff, student council members and Fatah activists, were beaten by Mujamma hoodlums. Men and women students were severely beaten or had acid thrown at them for speaking out against the Mujamma.[38]

The Islamists forced compliance by demanding that 'bad Muslims' and 'PLO agitators' return to the mosque and submit to their faith in front of the congregation. Mujamma slogans proclaimed 'An uncovered woman and Beatle-haired men will never liberate our holy places.' Every year thousands of IUG students graduated with degrees born out of a pedagogic mindset that was strictly Islamic in character. These graduates would go on to form the backbone of the Mujamma and, later, Hamas.

Mujamma activists had also joined, and attempted to dominate, many of the professional associations that substituted for formal political parties in the Gaza Strip during an era when Israel's occupation authorities denied Palestinians the right to form their own political parties. Free assembly was also strictly prohibited, unless the Mujamma was taking to the streets. The Medical Association, the Engineering Association and the Bar Association were all identified by the Mujamma as important institutions to control.

Open era

While the welfare and charity arms of Israel's public enemy number one, the PLO, were compelled to remain clandestine in Gaza and the West Bank throughout the 1970s and 1980s, the Mujamma was able to operate openly and freely. From its legally registered offices in Gaza it set up kindergartens charging reduced fees, and offered free food and clothing donations. It established clinics offering primary health care and free or subsidized medicines.

Mujamma leaders, most without any formal religious training, led prayers and preached to their followers on the need to return to the path of Islam. Their lack of theological expertise or training was never perceived as hindering the Mujamma. The manual for change was inspired by the teachings and practice of the Muslim Brotherhood. Dr Abdel Aziz Rantissi, an active member of the Mujamma and a later founder of Hamas, explained the motives of the movement at the time: 'The situation had reached terrible levels of desperation and humiliation to our people. We were a pioneering movement with an influential role in the Gaza Strip.' He was always prepared to point out the differences between the Islamic goals of his group and those of the PLO. 'The most important point of difference between us', he argued shortly after his release from Israeli detention in 1990, 'is that we deal with this issue of Palestine in accordance with Islamic law . . . and it is not permissible to us to cede to our enemies on this issue.'[39]

The majority of supporters appeared to be drawn to the Mujamma more in a social and organic way than for strictly fundamentalist, theological reasons. Pious youngsters were recruited to the movement in the mosques, which had become the focus of life in many deprived neighbourhoods, camps and villages. Hamdi, a refugee who had grown up in a camp, tells the story of his journey into the arms of the Mujamma:

It started in 1979. I was thirteen years old. I used to go to the mosque and an *Ikhwanji* asked me, 'Are you a Muslim?' And when I replied that I was he said I need to read Koran and Sunna. He taught me to pray and also encouraged me to go to other people and try and lead them away from their bad and wicked lives and come and work for Islam instead. And, let me tell you, the people were bad, drinking, having love children – all the people were not good. The man then told me that the time had come to build an Islamic society and that I should help him . . .

By then I was sixteen years old. The second stage was to learn about the Mujamma and to kill all the bad people, finish them off . . . I then went to many people in their homes in the camp and told them about the *Ikhwan* . . . Then I went to my family and told them I loved the Mujamma and I said to my brothers, 'Go to them, they are a very good group, you must go to the *Ikhwan*.'[40]

There was never a strict theological clique that was the Muslim engine of Mujamma thought. No Ayman al-Zawahiri, no Hassan al-Banna, no Sayyed Qutb, no Sheikh Yusuf Qaradawi would spring from the group as an expression of the Mujamma generation. Sheikh Yassin was there to provide spiritual guidance and inspiration, but this was no movement that promoted a theology of liberation in the way that the Roman Catholic Church in Latin America encouraged its faithful to use faith to overthrow dictators and authoritarian rulers. Indeed, many Mujamma and Hamas supporters have acknowledged that they rarely open religious tracts or attend seminaries to explore the finer points of theology. 'I read Koran, pray and attend the mosque', attests one life-long member. 'It is not a complicated relationship.'[41]

Avner Cohen, a former Israeli government adviser on religious affairs in Gaza from the mid-1970s on, said that even other Palestinian religious figures shared with him their contempt for Sheikh Yassin's religious credentials. 'To talk of Ahmed Yassin as a sheikh is like talking about me as a priest', said the Tunisian-born Israeli, who speaks fluent Arabic and met Yassin many times during his two decades in Gaza. 'He had no religious intelligence. In my time he was a very junior teacher, no one had heard of him.'[42]

Indeed, the title 'Sheikh' was always an honorary one. Unlike other Islamist movements of the time, or elsewhere in the region, the leaders of the Mujamma were the epitome of lay preachers, largely bereft of the theological training offered by world famous Muslim seminaries such as al-Azhar in Cairo. Mujamma priorities lay with the restitution of the Muslim family, Muslim religious practice, Muslim education and Muslim welfare support, not the overthrow of the Israeli occupation. Its other priority was to defeat the secular national forces. From its mosques it ran classes in the reading of the Koran, set up small libraries and study circles, distributed Islamic literature, and ran sporting activities such as judo clubs and other forms of popular martial arts and football matches.

From these bases in the community the Mujamma had a foothold on every aspect of life in the impoverished Gaza Strip. It was there to make sure that life was regulated the Islamic way, even if this meant banning the broadcast of popular Egyptian films because they were deemed offensive to Muslim sensibilities (although those determined to get their Friday fix of Abdel-Fattah el-Qasri as 'Ibn al-Balad' (Son of the Country), or Zeinat Sidqi as the 'Spinster', devised ways to get around the Mujamma censorship in towns such as Deir el-Balah and Rafah).

The mosque became the place where marriages were arranged, where family disputes were mediated and resolved, where clan clashes were reconciled, where pupils and students studied to improve their chances of good exam results, where news of work opportunities in Israel and further abroad were shared, where children were immersed in a world of Muslim scholarship and where a sense of security was established. However, as the years went on the Israelis, including Avner Cohen, became increasingly suspicious that the Mujamma was also using mosques to store weapons, train fighters and incite hatred against Jews. 'I warned the military authorities that they were using mosques for incitement and as storage room for weapons and that one day it would come back on us', Cohen recalls. But, he said, his superiors told him: 'as long as they aren't doing anything we can't stop them.'[43]

In these conditions it was inevitable that radical fundamentalist factions would emerge. Such elements included the Palestinian Islamic Jihad (PIJ). However the PIJ was too small to carry the masses and, unlike the Mujamma, had no desire to transform its narrow campaign of jihad against Israel into a wider social movement. Nevertheless PIJ remain an important component of the Palestinian Islamist landscape.

By the mid- to late 1980s a number of fundamentalist elements had also emerged in southern Gaza in the towns of Rafah and Khan Younis. These *salafi* – fundamentalists – were inspired by Saudi Wahhabi-style Islamic teachings which demanded that Muslims should adhere – strictly and without deviation – to the original principles of seventh-century Islam. The *salafi* in Rafah and Khan Younis vowed to eradicate from Palestinian society all vestiges of the West and forms of secular living. They organized sustained attacks on cinemas, video shops, cafés and stores serving or selling alcohol. They argued that jewellery, make-up and elaborate hairdos were not traditional Islamic forms of adornment. They even considered those who ate with their left hand worthy of a beating, deeming it to be un-Islamic. At weddings and parties the *salafi* sent their thugs to enforce segregation and to ensure that no Western music was played. They even presented themselves for recitation of the Koran. Musicians playing tabala drums and trumpets, gypsy singers and dancers were all subject to their wrath. Decades later the *salafi* would emerge as opponents to Hamas rule in Gaza. They were critics who complained that Hamas were simply not Islamic enough.

Growth

As with any other Islamic organization, it was difficult for the Mujamma to pretend that it maintained a strict separation between politics and religion. From his own home and the nearby mosque, Sheikh Yassin developed the political power base to undermine the PLO-dominated power structures of Gaza.

In the years before the outbreak of the First Intifada in 1987, thousands of people had started returning to the mosque, and the Mujamma built more than a hundred new mosques in Gaza to accommodate the new Muslim generation. It created an infrastructure that not only rivalled the PLO, with its reputation for building 'states within states', but often surpassed it. Moreover, as Israel continued its occupation, the Mujamma provided a form of religious solidarity and comfort.

The Mujamma controlled the allocation of welfare to thousands of needy families; it granted loans and allocated scholarships, book allowances and clothing coupons to hundreds of young students hoping to attend school or go to university; it had doctors and pharmacists to help the sick for free; and it had lawyers for people detained in Israeli jails. If Israel bulldozed a home or a field, uprooted trees or damaged other property, Mujamma activists would organize some form of compensation.

This is how Rafat Najar, a senior PFLP leader in the Gaza Strip in the 1980s, perceived the Mujamma's strategy. 'We [in the PFLP] were on the Mujamma list of enemies because we were considered atheists, and they incited their supporters against us to attack us with the reward of paradise . . . They had been encouraged by the Israelis . . . [who] turned their heads away from the Mujamma actions.'[44] But he also believed at the time that, 'even in a worst-case scenario, the Islamic movement will never succeed because Palestine is not like Iran. Democracy is the most favoured solution, and the Arab states surrounding us will not allow for the existence of an Islamic state here.'[45]

Indeed, many in the PLO, both inside Palestine and in exile, did not take the Mujamma seriously. Even Yasser Arafat's most senior lieutenants, Khalil Wazir (Abu Jihad) and Salah Khalaf (Abu Iyad), both former members of the Brotherhood, did not consider it a major threat. They and others overlooked the fact that by 1987 the Mujamma had gained a reputation for clean and honest leadership, even if – thus far – it had held back from confronting Israel.

Other Palestinians, however, regarded the Mujamma as a danger to their long-cherished moderate ideals. Rafat Abu Shaban, the director of Gaza's Muslim Endowments programme (*Waqf*), had warned the Israeli authorities against registering – and thereby legitimizing – the Mujamma. Avner Cohen recalls meeting the Palestinian religious establishment, including Shaban, around this time. 'They told me: be careful, there is nothing religious in this body at all. They are a political body who want to delegitimize the Islamic authorities and to use autonomy for other, political purposes under the cover of religious affairs.'[46]

By the late 1980s the Israelis themselves were beginning to realize the danger posed by the new Islamic force, fearing that the Islamists might turn their sights on Israeli targets. In 1984 they issued orders to arrest Sheikh Yassin and some of his associates. Yassin was accused of founding a military cell calling for an end to Israel's occupation. The Israeli charge sheet alleged that he had amassed weapons and explosives. Yassin was sentenced to thirteen years in prison but was released a year later as part of a prisoner exchange deal that also secured the release of PFLP–GC detainees held by Israel.

Yassin was not allowed to return to his position as the chairman of the Mujamma. But this did not mean that he would desist from his activities. In 1986 he set up a group called *al-Majd* (Glory) to threaten and expose drug-dealers. Military wings were being grafted onto the social, and an embryonic Hamas was taking shape. But, as the proto-Hamas activists prepared their lengthy campaign to Islamize Palestinian society, little did they know that their long-term planning was about to be overtaken by events, in the form of a spontaneous civil rebellion.

4

The First Intifada

We defend ourselves with nothing but stones while Israel rains bullets and missiles on us . . . and still the West calls our resistance unjustified violence.

Sheikh Ahmed Yassin[1]

In December 1987 the rains fell and a sense of gloom pervaded Palestinian towns and cities across the West Bank and Gaza Strip. Every day thousands of Palestinian workers congregated long before daybreak to begin a commute in battered and overcrowded vans and cars to their menial jobs in Israel. Thousands of men with nothing more than a packet of cigarettes and a black plastic bag with pitta bread and olives would travel to service Israel's booming economy, while at home their wives and mothers would try and make meagre earnings stretch through yet another week of unrelenting poverty, hardship and occupation.

On 9 December some of these workers from Gaza's Jabalia refugee camp ended up in a fatal car crash when an Israeli driver struck their cars as they returned home from a day's work. The deaths would trigger the uprising. When their bodies were returned to Gaza, rumours and angry rhetoric swirled around their funerals. Protests broke out in the refugee camps.

Preachers, many of them Mujamma loyalists, joined the fray, insisting that it was a religious duty to avenge the men's deaths. From funeral to funeral the prayers of mourners and imams contained calls for revenge on Israeli soldiers.

This was the birth of the Intifada, the Arabic word for 'uprising' which was soon to enter the international lexicon. The marches, protests, demonstrations, petrol bombs and stones were all directed at one target: the Israeli occupation. Within ten days of the accident, thousands of Palestinians had taken to the streets from refugee camps, cities, towns and the smallest hamlets to protest at the occupation.

Thousands of men and women, young and old, grabbed the rocks and stones that came naturally to hand, hurling them at Israeli soldiers and border guards. Tyres were set on fire, their black acrid smoke a pall in the sky. The crowds used anything to build barricades – rubbish skips, old bicycles, boulders and oil drums – to stop Israeli soldiers breaking up demonstrations. It appeared as if one mighty force was uniting the Palestinians, their desire to bring the Israeli occupation to an end through an unprecedented campaign of mass rebellion and civil disobedience. Thousands took to the streets, closed their shops, stayed away from work and scrawled graffiti condemning the 'Zionists' and urging the people to join in the Intifada.

Initially taken by surprise, the exiled PLO leadership hundreds of miles away in Tunis quickly moved to harness that anger. Yasser Arafat and his lieutenants supported the creation of the PLO-led United National Leadership of the Uprising (UNLU). Early in the uprising, at a press conference convened in East Jerusalem's National Palace Hotel, the UNLU's fourteen demands were outlined to attending journalists who had crammed into the meeting room and spilled over into the corridor outside. The speakers included well-known nationalist figures such as Sari Nusseibeh and Mubarak Awad, but there were no Islamist personalities present when the demands were made in the name of the nationalists of the West Bank and Gaza. Among this urbane, mostly Western-educated and secular nationalist elite, the Islamists would have appeared incongruous.

Hamas

The Islamists also reorganized – by creating Hamas. In Arabic, Hamas means 'zeal', and is also an acronym for *Harakat al-Muqawama al-Islamiyya* (the Islamic Resistance Movement). The founders included Sheikh Yassin, Dr Abdel Aziz Rantissi, Dr Mahmoud Zahar, Musa Abu Marzouq, Ismail Abu Shanab, Salah Shehadeh, Ibrahim al-Yazuri, Issa al-Nashar and Abdel Fattah al-Dukhan.

By 23 December, twenty-one Palestinians had been killed and 158 wounded, while according to Israeli officials thirty-one Israeli soldiers and border guards had been wounded.[2] The Israelis admitted that they were taken by surprise. 'I think the situation has come as an unexpected flood. I don't think someone organized it, and predicted it, and wrote – as they say – a scenario: You'll do this, and I'll do that. I think that most of the difficulties encountered were due to the uncontrolled and unexpected nature of this event',[3] said Shimon Peres, the vice premier and foreign minister in an Israeli national unity government that was an uneasy blend of the right-wing pro-settler Likud Party of the prime minister, Yitzhak Shamir, and the two future Israeli architects of the Oslo Peace Accords – Peres and the defence minister, Yitzhak Rabin.

Rabin was visiting the United States and returned to deal with the crisis. He provoked international controversy with what became known as his 'iron fist'[4] policy, saying in the opening weeks of the uprising that 'the first priority is to use force, might, beatings' to restore order.[5] Rabin accused Yasser Arafat of exploiting it for his own ends, highlighting again the Israeli government's tendency to emphasize the role of the PLO, then its main Palestinian enemy. 'The PLO terrorist organisations and activists in the territories seized on this wave of events and did everything they could, both inside and outside the territories, in order to heighten and intensify the events', he told members of the Israeli parliament – the Knesset.[6]

The Israeli cabinet moved to counter the worldwide criticism which provoked domestic and international headlines such as 'The week of the sticks', 'Israel's new violent tactic takes toll on both sides' and 'Israelis worry about their image.'[7] Yitzhak Shamir's government insisted, in terms similar to those Israeli governments have used many times since when reacting to allegations of excessive force, that 'Israel is acting in a way that is more restrained than any other government in the world in similar circumstances, and is certain of its moral strength and its security forces.'[8] Rabin defended the conduct of Israeli soldiers, saying that Israel had to protect its 'military rule' in Gaza and the West Bank 'with all the means at our disposal within the framework of the law', including curfews, closures, 'deportation and administrative detention against the inciters and the organizers', tear gas and rubber bullets. Soldiers were permitted 'to fire with the intention of wounding those leading the riots and throwing petrol bombs, initially at their legs, as far as this is possible, and this only after shots in the air have also failed to disperse the rioters.'[9] Some of the legislation relied on defence emergency regulations left over from the British Mandate.

Avner Cohen, then an adviser to the Israeli military authorities on Palestinian religious affairs, recalls the urgency of the mood at the time: 'Rabin was in the States and was called back. He gathered everyone together for a meeting and said: "This Intifada, what tanks and warplanes couldn't do to us, women demonstrating and stones did, because the world cannot tolerate seeing these demonstrations".'[10]

Divisions within the Intifada

The establishment of Hamas came at a time of unprecedented national unity in Palestinian ranks against Israel's then twenty-year-old occupation of Gaza and the West Bank, including East Jerusalem. But still the Islamists refused to subsume their organization into Yasser Arafat's PLO. This would have meant working alongside the secularists and communists they despised. Instead Hamas's leaders sought from the very beginning to battle the secular nationalists for control of Palestinian society. It was the opening move in a power struggle that was to continue for more than two decades.

At the time, however, Hamas was preoccupied not with long-term issues of statehood but with challenging the PLO's UNLU for control of the Intifada by issuing rival communiqués, calling rival strikes, demonstrations and marches, and appealing for money to support the families of martyrs and prisoners and for food and medicines to give to the residents of camps and towns under curfew. It made it clear almost from the outset that it saw itself as the embodiment of the Muslim Brotherhood in Palestinian form, and first and foremost as an Islamic organization. Communiqué number 3 issued by Hamas also stated the objectives of the new group:

> Here is the voice of Islam, the voice of the Palestinian people in the West Bank, Gaza Strip and the rest of the Palestinian land. Here is the voice of an erupting volcano . . . Objectives (short-term) – liberate the prisoners, reject colonialism, political exile and administrative detention, the barbaric practices against our civilian population and prisoners, the political ban on travel and harassment, the disgraceful expansionism, the corruption, subordination . . . end to all the taxes to the abominable occupation and all their supporters.
>
> Objectives (long-term) – reject negotiated solutions, break with the deviations of Camp David, reject proposals for autonomy, reject the idea of an international conference, open the way for a permanent end to the occupation and liberate the homeland and the places of our holy saints which have been sullied and subject to profanity . . . To achieve these efforts the people must redouble their activity.[11]

This linkage alarmed many in the nationalist camp, who saw such a move as undermining the Palestinian cause and provoking fissures. 'They may call themselves a wing of the Muslim Brotherhood, but this is Palestine, and this is about ending the occupation', argued one UNLU leftist.[12]

Some nationalists, regarding Hamas as little more than the Mujamma in a new guise, predicted that the old internal divisions would stall the Intifada and distract global attention from the cause at hand. Many in UNLU saw Hamas's rival activities as placing an untenable burden on a society engaged in a mass rebellion against a state and its well-armed military forces. There was debate about whether Hamas-imposed strike days should be adhered to, whether they should be ignored, and whether its demands applied to all or some within the Palestinian community.

Hamas quickly established an organizational framework of activists that made it difficult for the UNLU to challenge it. Drawing on the grass roots prepared during the years of charitable and welfare work, it established a credible profile for itself in the early months of the Intifada. But it was also careful to insist that it regarded the Intifada as a Muslim rebellion against the occupiers: 'The Islamic Resistance Movement is the Palestinian national resistance movement, and we fight for Palestinian rights . . . our resistance is against the occupation of our country . . . Hamas also extends into the Muslim world', said one of its early prominent figures, Musa Abu Marzouq.[13] And one of its early communiqués declared: 'At this time the Islamic uprising has been intensified in the occupied territories. In all the villages, all the refugee camps our martyrs have fallen . . . But they have died in the name of Allah and their cries are those of victory . . . In the name of Allah, Allah is Great . . . Death to the occupation.'[14]

In addition to its pre-existing foundations, Hamas was relatively free from Israeli interference in the early days of the Intifada. Its leaders and members were largely untroubled by Israeli prohibitions, arrest campaigns, deportation or imprisonment without trial. Israeli soldiers did not at first raid its secret printing presses or committee offices or break up its political, military and intelligence cells, so Hamas continued to grow, and to define its Islamic message to the Palestinian people. Mahmoud Musleh was one of the organizers of the Hamas communiqués in the West Bank. 'I used to write the communiqué and then, through an underground network of people throughout the West Bank, we would print and distributed it once a month', he said. He claims that poor Israeli intelligence meant that they avoided arrest and detention: 'It was difficult for the Israelis to find us, and it was only through later security breaches that they then made arrests.'[15]

By the summer of 1988 Hamas had issued its covenant – a charter to rival that of the PLO – and claimed the Intifada as an Islamic possession in leaflets which were clandestinely distributed on the streets: 'We are with every person who truly works for the liberation of Palestine, the whole of Palestine. We will continue to have faith in Allah and his power. Every Muslim around the globe is our asset, this is our strength, this is our base and these are our beliefs and victory is ours with Allah's will.'[16]

Secular national activists regarded Hamas and its agenda with suspicion, despite some close personal friendships. Bashir Barghouti, a West Bank Intifada organizer, argued that the Islamist leaders 'were strong characters, charismatic and good orators', but he dismissed them as having 'no history of addressing Palestinian issues'.[17] Others perceived Hamas's stand to be a direct provocation, not to Israel but to the PLO. 'Their ideology is a full rejection of the PLO', stated Dr Riad al-Agha, a prominent Gazan leader.[18]

By August 1988 there were disputes between Hamas and the secular nationalists. Israel's policy of mass arrests to quell the Intifada resulted in tens of thousands of Palestinians ending up in prisons or in hastily erected 'prison camps', such as Ansar III in the Negev desert. There Palestinian nationalists and Islamists were held alongside each other, and thrown together into overcrowded jails, often without trial or due process, as the

Israelis swept through the occupied territories, hoping that by detaining enough Palestinians they could end the Intifada.

Once inside jail the Palestinians organized themselves into the same structures as on the outside. Tensions erupted over Hamas leaflets, which called for separate strike days. Matters worsened when Hamas published its covenant in August 1988. 'In it we read statements against the PLO . . . The nationalist factions decided to take a unilateral action against Hamas in the [prison] camp and stop all coordination with them', recalls one ex-prisoner.[19] As more Hamas prisoners began to arrive in the 1990s, fights often broke out between the different factions, with the Israeli prison authorities calling on other Palestinians to mediate.

It was significant that Hamas's first clash with the PLO came over strikes, which had been a key protest activity undertaken by Palestinians since the British Mandate. For a disempowered people the withdrawal of labour and the closure of shops, offices, factories, schools and universities were acts of mass defiance that symbolized Palestinian unity. Strikes were a defining feature of the First Intifada; they regulated the uprising, punctuating the months and years of protest with 'days of rage', 'days of mourning', 'solidarity with the prisoners', and the commemoration of key events in Palestinian history, such the *nakbah* (dispossession of 1948), the founding of the PLO, May Day, Women's Day and later dates commemorating the death of key Palestinian figures killed in the Intifada.

Although they often hurt Palestinians more than the Israelis against whom they were directed, the strikes assumed a potent symbolism in the Intifada. They were non-violent protests and involved everyone: schoolchildren, farmers, merchants, shopkeepers, public and private sector employees and students. The images of shuttered shops and deserted Palestinian streets were often broadcast by the international media as an indication of the strength of feeling that permeated Palestinian society about Israel's occupation of its towns and cities. The leaders of the UNLU were careful to time the strikes so that they did not unduly burden Palestinians. Hamas understood that leadership of the Intifada lay in organizing and enforcing strikes, and by the late summer of 1988 was calling its own stoppages. Hamas supporters enforced them by attacking shops that remained open, beating up drivers who broke the traffic embargo and throwing Molotov cocktails at political rivals, leading to clashes in PLO strongholds such as Ramallah.[20]

Nationalists appealed to Hamas leaders to avoid an escalation of internal conflict and urged it to 'place national interest above their factional concerns . . . and to correct negative attitudes which, whether intended or not, serve only the interests of the enemy.'[21] However, Hamas had other ideas, spelled out in its covenant. This criticized the PLO for accepting UN resolutions 181, 242 and 338, which in effect accepted a two-state solution to the conflict with Israel and in so doing abandoned the goal still proposed by Hamas: liberating all of Palestine. Tension grew between

Hamas and the UNLU, and by 1990 the two factions were operating on parallel lines.

Friend or foe?

As the Intifada wore on through 1988 and 1989, Hamas's popular support base grew in both the Gaza Strip and the West Bank. Its penetration in the latter, which had long been a heartland for secular nationalists, was unprecedented and disturbing for many nationalists. One key factor was Israel. Initially the Hamas–Israel connection was a legacy of the relationship that had developed between the Israeli authorities and the Mujamma in the late 1970s and the 1980s. Even pro-Islamic newspapers complained about Hamas's links to Israel. 'For all the anti-Israeli rhetoric', opined one editorial, 'its [Hamas's] efforts were dissipated in infighting rather than against the common enemy.'[22] The Intifada and the formation of Hamas – with its open declaration of intent to wage jihad against Israel – should have severed this relationship immediately, but it did not. As one source asserted: 'The Israelis essentially followed the same policy towards Hamas as they followed against the Mujamma earlier: not suppressing it in the hope that it would distract young Palestinians from supporting more dangerous groups.'[23]

Hamas's leaders publicly identified Israel and its occupation of the West Bank and Gaza as a primary cause of Palestinian woes. Yet they were also finding it difficult to break their ties with the Israeli authorities which had, at a minimum, benignly supported them during the Islamists' early revivalist campaigns in Gaza. Early on Israel also extended legitimacy and, therefore, a form of recognition to Hamas by meeting with its leadership, including founding members such as Dr Mahmoud Zahar. Hamas leaders reciprocated by remaining in communication with the Israeli political leadership – in turn extending a form of recognition to the Jewish state at a time when their secular nationalist rivals were refusing to recognize it.

During this early period, from 1987 to the early 1990s, Hamas held back from launching attacks on targets in Israel proper, limiting itself largely to military targets or Jewish settlers in the occupied territories. However, in its public rhetoric it continued to complain bitterly about the 'Zionist' entity and called on its supporters to wage jihad for Palestinian freedom.

By the second year of the Intifada Hamas's leadership recognized that its links to Israel were becoming a hindrance to the movement. By this point, however, the relationship was at its strongest. Israel regarded Hamas as a convenient foil to the PLO, and Hamas exploited this. The large amounts of money that were flowing into Hamas's coffers from Muslim supporters abroad were ignored by the Israeli authorities, while those same authorities did everything they could to stem the dollars heading to the PLO. Israeli officials involved in the administration of the West Bank and Gaza Strip still maintained contacts with the Islamic activists of the Mujamma who were now heading Hamas. In the Gaza Strip Hamas leaders were able to keep Palestinian schools open when the Israeli authorities were closing them in the West Bank.

In March 1988, three months into the uprising, Dr Mahmoud Zahar was meeting with Israel's political establishment and speaking the language of negotiations. As he said in an interview two years later:

> When I met with Shimon Peres on 23 March 1988 we put our proposal to him. It consisted of the following: a call for Israeli withdrawal from the 1967 territories, put the occupied territories under a neutral side, choose our representatives by our own methods, elected by us. Everything should be on the agenda, and we should even discuss Israel's existence and the right of return.

Zahar insisted that Hamas had nothing against Jews as such, but saw for them only a politically subservient role in Palestine. 'We are not anti-Jewish . . . we accept Jews under the Islamic umbrella. But never a secular state. We want an Islamic state.'[24]

The same year that Zahar met Peres he was also widely reported to have met Rabin to discuss a solution to the conflict. Sheikh Yassin also indicated at this stage that Hamas was not averse to entering into dialogue with Israel so long as Israel was prepared to recognize Hamas and its demand for Palestinian rights. Rabin confirmed that both he and Shamir had met with Palestinians from 'the territories'. He defended the contacts, saying they provided a promising alternative 'address' for future negotiations, giving Israel other options from the neighbouring Arab countries which had long sought to control Palestinian affairs, and the exiled Arafat-led PLO leadership which was still – at that point – anathema to Israel. Rabin told Israeli television in 1989:

> I have met with figures spanning the entire conceptual spectrum existing in the territories, from Islamic fundamentalists to very moderate individuals, all shades of the spectrum were present at the talks, including those who had been detained for many months. I still believe that it is indeed possible to realize the peace initiative directed at one address: the Palestinian residents in the territories. . . . For the first time since 15 May 1948 the Palestinians in the territories are the ones leading the struggle for the fate and future of the territories and the Palestinians.[25]

Israel and Hamas both calculated that their enemy's enemy was their friend. Raanan Gissin, a former media adviser to Ariel Sharon, is frank about the Israeli political establishment's pursuit of what he terms a 'divide and conquer' strategy during this era:

The broad consensus was that here is a religious movement that has great sway among the public and could actually, because of its animosity to Fatah, because of its policy of opposing the corruption of Fatah and all those manifestations of Fatah people taking money for their pocket, could serve a useful purpose in weakening the strength of Fatah on the street. That would benefit Israel in its struggle against Fatah. We are talking about before Oslo. The major leading terrorist group was Fatah. Statistically speaking, or in any way you look at it, they were responsible for the major terrorist attacks, they had the most sophisticated and largest terrorist organization. [Hamas] at that time was not involved in terrorist activity, didn't even have a military arm . . . Later, when they started developing their military arm, I think the Shabak [Shin Bet] was the first one to point out the change in their policy, or the fact that they were actually now becoming a terrorist organization.[26]

The difference in emphasis is significant. While Yitzhak Rabin, the future Labour architect of the Oslo Accords, talked of political progress by encouraging those who 'desire to transfer the solution from the conflict in the street to the negotiations table', the Israeli right viewed it in security terms, stressing the need to neutralize Arafat. However, there were warning voices cautioning that Israel could one day suffer from its tacit – at best – encouragement of the Islamists. This was a phenomenon that the Americans were later to term 'blowback', when the CIA channelled money and weapons to Usama bin Laden and other mujahidin fighting the Soviet Union in Afghanistan, only to see their former proxies turn against them.

Avner Cohen, the former Israeli adviser on Palestinian religious affairs in the 1980s and early 1990s, said that in June 1984 – a full three years before the Mujamma metastasized into Hamas – he was already becoming concerned about reports that Yassin's Islamists were using mosques to store weapons, train fighters and incite against Jews. Mr Cohen says he sent a letter to the then head of the Israeli Civil Administration and security forces headlined 'A survey of mosques in the Gaza Strip area'. One copy, which he has kept at his home in a small Israeli *moshav* which now lies within Hamas missile-firing range of Gaza, reads: 'If we keep covering our eyes or continue with our forgiving attitude to *al-Mujamma' al-Islami* it might go against us in the future, therefore I recommend that we focus our efforts on looking for ways to break up this golem before reality blows up in our faces.' He said that he was made even more nervous ahead of the Intifada by a meeting with prominent Palestinians in Gaza, including one former director of the Islamic University of Gaza who, he recalls,

earned huge applause from the Palestinian audience when he stood up and told the meeting: 'The Jewish ruler who is living among us, he is the last to know what is happening in his own kingdom. He is behaving like a deaf man at a wedding.' We were so innocent, most of the Mujamma were refugees and we thought that we could create an alternative leadership to the PLO. They warned us, the hard days are coming, and this was before the Intifada. A week later I received a telephone call from Ahmed Yassin's gang. They told me, 'If you don't stop causing trouble for Sheikh Yassin, you will be killing yourself.'[27]

However, other veteran Israeli officials have different perceptions and different analyses of events. Brigadier General Shalom Harari, a former senior adviser on Palestinian affairs for Israel's Defence Ministry, insisted in 2007 that Israel 'never backed' Hamas. 'The only thing that you can accuse it of is that it started to treat it too late', said Harari, who long warned that the Islamists' underlying popular support was greater than showed up in opinion polls and political studies. 'The rise of the Muslim Brotherhood here and there, in Syria and Jordan, is an overall Middle East process', he said.

> I am not saying that Israel hasn't influenced it here and there in the margins. But generally this is an overall rise, after the fall of Arab Nasserism and other dreams that the Arab world had. And every country around us fights the Muslim Brotherhood in their own way. Jordan in its own way, hot and cold. Egypt in its own way, hot and cold. Israel in its own way.[28]

The Israelis' relationship with Hamas changed abruptly when in 1989 Hamas murdered two Israeli soldiers, Avi Sasportas and Ilan Saadon. Sasportas was kidnapped in February 1989 and his body lay undiscovered for several months. Saadon was kidnapped and murdered in May 1989 by the same Hamas cell, and his remains were not recovered until seven years later, when the Israelis received information from Yasser Arafat's security officials in the newly created Palestinian Authority. The killings were a turning point for Israel. It rounded up more than 300 Hamas supporters, Sheikh Yassin and Zahar among them, and declared that the Israeli authorities which administered the West Bank and Gaza would cease all contacts with the organization. By the end of the year Israel had declared membership of Hamas a punishable offence.

In January 1990 Sheikh Yassin was put on trial in Israel charged with fifteen offences, including 'the organisation of attacks on civilians and causing the deaths of two soldiers'. In court Yassin denied the charge, while the mother of Saadon, whose remains were then still missing, cursed him, saying, 'God will pay him back . . . He knows where my boy is. I don't even have a grave to weep at.'[29] The arrest, imprisonment and deportation of the Hamas leadership was designed to have a deterrent effect, to demoralize Hamas's supporters and to weaken its chain of command. But while Sheikh Yassin remained in prison awaiting trial, other senior cadres in the movement were released by the Israelis, allowing them to play a part in organizing against their rivals in the PLO. As support for the movement increased, Hamas strengthened its activities on university campuses among the students, in professional associations, among the educated middle classes and in its charitable activities.

Still the secular nationalists remained disparaging and failed to take the Hamas threat seriously. As one PLO official, Abu Issa, noted: 'This movement is not really a part of the people but pulling the people apart . . . the last thing we need is division in the name of Islam.'[30] Another prominent figure in Gaza offered the following perspective: 'I don't feel threatened by these fanatics [Hamas]. They are like a small cloud passing through a summer sky.'[31]

Hamas, well aware of the hostility, countered by stepping up its campaign against Fatah and by seeking alliances with its old enemies on the Palestinian left. It also tried to exploit internal PLO disputes. In April 1990, after local tensions between Fatah and the leftist Popular Front for the Liberation of Palestine (PFLP), Hamas sought to form an alliance with the PFLP and announced the 'consolidation of the internal front and appreciation of the perceptive position of the Popular Front'.[32] This first alliance was short-lived. Within days Fatah and the PFLP issued a communiqué announcing that their differences had been resolved.

By contrast, the tension between Hamas and Fatah was far more deep-seated. Throughout the spring of 1991 the two regularly engaged in clashes – some armed – in major West Bank cities such as Nablus. Newspaper headlines carried daily reports of Fatah activists being attacked and wounded by 'masked fundamentalists . . . motivated by political and personal grudges'. The next day's news would then carry details of a new communiqué from both sides calling for a halt to violence and reconciliation, but within days the newspapers were back to reporting more clashes between the masked youth of Fatah and Hamas. At the same time both Hamas and the nationalist leadership were still mobilizing their supporters on the ground in strike actions, campaigns, boycotts and other activities designed to consolidate the Intifada and maintain its momentum.

The relationship went from bad to worse over the following years as Hamas and secular nationalist leaders clashed over the direction of the Intifada, its organization, the demands being placed on the Palestinian people and whether there should be negotiations with Israel. The two organizations were diametrically opposed, with growing mutual mistrust. In private Hamas leaders regaled listeners with tales of PLO excesses, their disgust palpable despite the public rhetoric of being 'brothers' in the national struggle. The PLO, for its part, saw Hamas as lackeys of Israel, or as a passing phenomenon.

In 1990 Saddam Hussein's invasion and occupation of the oil-rich state of Kuwait had far-reaching consequences for the Palestinians. Yasser Arafat supported the Iraqi dictator, while Hamas condemned the invasion. It quickly became evident that the PLO leader had made a major strategic blunder, delighting the Palestinian street at the cost of alienating much of the Gulf, where the PLO had enjoyed the generosity of wealthy Arab rulers sympathetic to the Palestinian cause. Hamas was far more attuned to the mood of its Gulf donors, who funded many of its social and welfare projects, and who were greatly alarmed by Saddam's expansionism. To balance its position Hamas also issued communiqués denouncing the presence of American troops in Kuwait and Saudi Arabia.

With the Gulf War looming, intra-Palestinian clashes intensified between what were now perceived to be pro-Saddam and anti-Saddam factions. After one episode of violence a local reconciliation agreement between Hamas and Fatah was announced. The agreement detailed a plan that would give Hamas a role in a number of bodies that were organizing the Intifada. Although this was a good outcome for Hamas, the tensions with Fatah continued.

The reverberations of the Gulf War also had a significant impact on the Intifada. After the war the US president, George Bush, announced a new peace initiative for the Middle East, which brought Israel and the Arabs to the negotiating table in October 1990 in the Spanish capital of Madrid. The talks were the first in which Israel negotiated with Syria, Jordan and a delegation of Palestinian representatives who were the PLO in all but name. The PLO, having chosen the wrong side during the war, was also losing its superpower patron with the collapse of the Soviet Union, so it had little choice but to go with the emerging international consensus on the need for a peace process. The Bush administration, in its strategic rethink and vision for a New World Order, considered the resolution of the Arab–Israeli conflict key to the stability of the Middle East.

Hamas was not as constrained as the PLO. It denounced the Madrid process and the eleven rounds of multilateral peace negotiations which subsequently took place. When the rounds of talks hit the inevitable obstacles, Hamas railed from the sidelines, launched attacks on Israeli targets and employed other strategies to derail the peace process.

Some secular nationalists believed that a policy of coopting Hamas into Palestinian national political institutions might dissuade them from attacking the Madrid process, and in August 1991 Hamas's leadership was offered the chance to be integrated into the Palestine National Council, the 'legislative' body that elects members to the PLO's all-powerful central committee. Hamas consented, but then imposed conditions which it knew the PLO could not accept. 'We told them that the price for entry would be at least 40 per cent of the seats of the PNC and that recognition of Israel would not occur', stated Dr Mahmoud Zahar, reversing the position he had taken four years earlier when he told Shimon Peres that Israel's right to exist was on the table. Unable to neutralize Hamas by absorbing it into the political mainstream, Palestinian secular nationalists felt they were left with no choice but to continue confronting it on the street.

This caused no little satisfaction to Hamas. 'There have been years of success for us . . . we came as kittens and now we have emerged as lions', said Zahar. 'We are bringing the message of jihad to the people here and winning the war against our enemies in Israel too.'[33] The lion's 'roar' came from the newly created armed wing of Hamas – the Izz ad-Din al-Qassam Brigades. Formed in 1991, the Qassam Brigades were named after the sheikh who had inspired the Palestinian revolt against the British, and would develop into one of the most potent wings of the Hamas movement. However, they would also, in later years, prove to be a polarizing force within the movement, tending to pull it in a violent direction.

Kidnap and deportation

Late in 1992 Hamas tried to seize the initiative with Israel. In December that year it kidnapped a border officer from an Israeli town across the Green Line that divides Israel from the Palestinian territories it occupied in 1967. A ransom note demanded the release of Sheikh Yassin from prison: 'We announce to the occupation authorities and the leadership of the Zionist entity to release Sheikh Yassin [*sic*] and in return for the release of this officer . . . We pledge from our side to release the officer once the Sheikh is released in a way we deem fit.'[34]

Israel refused, and when the body of the kidnapped officer was discovered a few days later there was widespread outrage across Israel. Many Israelis, particularly those on the right wing and within the settler movement, demanded definitive action against Hamas. Retribution was swift. Israeli troops stormed Hamas and Islamic Jihad offices, homes and institutions throughout the West Bank and Gaza Strip, and rounded up some 400 men. The detainees were unceremoniously deported and dumped on a snowy hillside in south Lebanon, which was then under Israeli occupation. Human rights organizations condemned the act as a mass deportation and a major violation of international law. One of those deportees recounted the events:

> It was very late at night. They took us on a bus and then another, but we were blindfolded and had no idea of our journey's end. Of course our hands and feet were in plastic cuffs and there no was possibility of escape. After some hours they told us that our fate would soon be decided on the order of the Israeli court. There was more than one bus and we realized that there were many hundreds of us. It felt like a *nakbah* all over again. The soldiers were jeering and shouting at us and then when we crossed the border they put us on open trucks and through the Lebanese checkpoint at Marj al-Zahour ['Meadow of Flowers']. It was very cold, and then we had to walk and they started firing their guns to make us go faster. When we arrived it was like the destination of nothing and no return. It was snowing and there were just some tents with water coming in from many holes in them. We

lived like natives, walking to find wood for our fires and only getting food from people in the villages nearby.[35]

Amid international censure over the illegal deportations, Yitzhak Rabin, by then elevated to prime minister, remained defiant. 'This government will fight any manifestation of violence and terror, and will not permit, and will not allow either Hamas or Islamic Jihad to harm citizens of the State of Israel, and it will take all . . . steps at its disposal to battle murderous terrorist organisations', he said. The statement was tantamount to a declaration of war on Hamas: 'to battle to the end against terror . . . to temporarily remove from the occupied territories Hamas . . . who nourish the flames of terror.'[36]

Israel by now knew what it was dealing with. But Hamas was unrepentant. In the wake of the deportations it enjoyed unprecedented popularity and recognition among Palestinians and across the Middle East, and it became the new cause célèbre of the international Islamist movement. The PLO was forced, as the official representatives of all Palestinians, to halt peace talks with Israel in protest, and to champion the cause of the Hamas leaders on the hilltop. Thousands of Palestinians protested at the deportations, while Hamas leaders held television audiences in thrall as they declared their unbending dedication to jihad against Israel.

Dr Abdel Aziz Rantissi, one of the movement's co-founders, acted as the deportees' spokesman. As they were filmed huddled around the campfires outside their tents he declared that Hamas had only been strengthened. 'The movement has achieved great benefits after the deportation. It emerged from being a local and regional movement into an international movement . . . Therefore we now find that public opinion in Palestine is in full harmony with the stand of Hamas', he proclaimed.[37]

The deportations did not stop Hamas attacks or eradicate the movement. By the spring of 1993 Israel was in the midst of a wave of Hamas-inspired violence. Settlers, soldiers and civilians alike were all targeted in lethal attacks. Far from deterring such attacks, the deportations exposed Israel's inability to capture Hamas's armed men, rather than their political leaders, and left Israel exposed to a barrage of international criticism. The Israeli approach had backfired; there was no deterrence, and no end in sight to what now appeared to be the inexorable rise of Hamas. The possibility of friendship – even in alliance against a common enemy in the PLO – was now impossible.

Peace and politics

However, the area in which Hamas appeared to be out of step with the very Palestinians that it claimed to represent was the issue of peace negotiations and settlement of the conflict with Israel. Although they were not initially a declared goal of the Intifada, the logic of the Palestinian demands for statehood and an end to occupation was negotiations. The PLO leadership had quickly determined that the Intifada created a unique opportunity to press for the realization of Palestinian demands for freedom – the international community was increasingly sympathetic and the resolution of the conflict through an unarmed uprising appeared to be the way to achieve their ends. This meant that the PLO's historic pledge to liberate Palestine through armed struggle would have to be abandoned in favour of negotiation. Yasser Arafat, the 'guerrilla-diplomat', had always kept his options open when faced with a choice between armed struggle and peace. In 1974 he famously addressed the United Nations General Assembly while wearing an empty holster and telling them: 'Today I have come bearing an olive branch and a freedom fighter's gun. Do not let the olive branch fall from my hand.'[38]

The PLO – now bereft of its wealthy Gulf patrons – was nearing financial collapse, Hamas was gaining a foothold among Palestinians in the West Bank and Gaza Strip, and pressure was building for some kind of tangible reward for the huge sacrifices they were making in the daily confrontations, campaigns of civil disobedience and demonstrations against Israel. Palestinian public opinion, and many on the Israeli side favoured peace negotiations that could be based upon the formula of a two-state solution.

When the PLO bowed to the inevitable and entered peace talks with Israel, Hamas reacted with fury. It condemned the PLO as traitors to the cause, opening up a public rift. Hamas issued countless leaflets denouncing the 1991 Madrid talks and the subsequent rounds of negotiations. It urged instead an escalation of the Intifada and continuation of the armed struggle against Israel. As pro-peace rallies in the Palestinian city of Ramallah featured Palestinians and Israelis standing beneath banners reading 'TWO PEOPLES SPEAK PEACE', a few miles down the road in Nablus Hamas organized an even bigger rally against Madrid. In leaflets, speeches and Friday sermons Hamas leaders assailed the talks as 'a heresy that will lead to the surrender of Muslim lands to Jews'. When Palestinian negotiators returned to address public meetings and rallies, Hamas activists pelted them with stones and bottles and broke up the meetings.

Hanan Ashrawi, one of the Palestinian negotiators, was declared unfit to represent the people by Hamas leader Dr Mahmoud Zahar because, in his own words, 'she is a woman, she is a Christian and she smokes'. A thyroid surgeon by profession – and Sheikh Yassin's personal physician – the pugnacious Zahar will often use medical metaphors to make political points: Israel is referred to as a cancer, the 'illness' of Palestinian society can only be treated by inoculation according to Islamic prescription, and 'radical surgery' is often the prescribed Zahar remedy for political problems. Gazan-born and Egyptian-educated, Zahar is one of the most formidable leaders of the Palestinian Islamic movement. He has survived Israeli assassination attempts which killed and wounded members of his immediate family. A co-founder of Hamas, he was vehemently opposed to peace negotiations with Israel, but has never been confounded by the high art of pragmatic politics. He is also a veteran of the clashes between the Islamists and secular nationalists. In 1995 he complained that, while the attention of the world was focused on the peace talks, the PLO was taking the opportunity to launch attacks and 'make provocations' in Hamas strongholds such as Rafah to weaken the movement at a time when it, like everyone else, faced increased curfews, arrests and other collective punishments. 'But we'll defend ourselves against Israel and the PLO', Zahar declared. 'We will stand strong and not weak.'[39]

Frustrated and increasingly marginalized by the peace process, Hamas set about trying to derail it.

5

Oslo and 'Vain Endeavours'

> The problem is that we have reduced the issue from one of sacred liberation
> to merely a dream of independence, a dream that a Palestinian policeman
> will organize traffic.
>
> Musa Abu Marzouq[1]

'The Peace of the Brave', proclaimed newspaper headlines across the
world, as two old enemies stood on the White House lawn shaking hands.
The outcome of secret negotiations in Norway, the Oslo Accords were
hailed as the curtain-raiser for a final peace agreement between Israel and
the Palestinians which would come into force by the far-distant deadline
of February 1999, by which time all things seemed possible.

While Israel's prime minister, Yitzhak Rabin, and the PLO leader,
Yasser Arafat, stood before cheering crowds in Washington on 13
September 1993, their host, President Bill Clinton, told the assembled dig-
nitaries: 'A peace of the brave is within our reach. Throughout the Middle
East there is a great yearning for the quiet miracle of a normal life. We
know a difficult road lies ahead. Every peace has its enemies, those who
still prefer the easy habits of hatred to the hard labors of reconciliation.'[2]

The signing ceremony, unquestionably the high point of Israeli–
Palestinian relations in more than sixty years of conflict, had been
preceded by secret negotiations in Norway between the PLO and the
government of Israel. In a move that completely outflanked Hamas and
other radical Palestinian factions, the PLO promised to recognize Israel,
renounce violence, amend its charter, and recognize Israeli sovereignty
over the parts of historic Palestine which Israel had gained in the 1948
war. In return Israel would grant Palestinian autonomy in the West Bank
and Gaza Strip and redeploy Israeli troops from some Palestinian areas.
The most difficult issues, including Jewish settlements in the West Bank
and Gaza Strip, borders, Jerusalem, and the return of Palestinian refugees,
would be left for final status negotiations.

With the signing of the Oslo Accords it appeared that peace-making would deliver real dividends: freedom, prosperity and eventual state-hood for the Palestinians; recognition, security and prosperity for Israel. The horizons were further expanded when King Hussein of Jordan signed a peace treaty with Israel in 1994. Even *Sesame Street* was illuminated in the glow of improving Israeli–Palestinian relations, with special episodes of the children's programme featuring Big Bird and other multi-coloured puppet characters promoting peace, education and fun. Hundreds of young people from both sides of the conflict were invited to encounter groups, and to attend joint theatre productions of *Romeo and Juliet* by Israeli and Palestinian actors. Despite the difficulties, such events revealed a sizeable pro-peace constituency: business executives were encouraged to rethink economic cooperation and contractual relationships. Humanitarian activists met on issues that mattered to both sides: the environment, agriculture, promoting consciousness of women's rights.

Within a year of the agreement Arafat and his Tunis-based PLO functionaries staged a 'triumphant' return to Gaza to begin building a Palestinian state in the overcrowded coastal strip. Gaza, in a cold dose of reality for the optimists, was dominated by more than a million 1948 refugees and their descendants who for decades had dreamed not of building a state there, but of returning to their homes in Jaffa, Majdal (Ashkelon) and Beersheba – all of which now lay within the modern state of Israel.

One of Arafat's greatest challenges would be to unite his own movement and deal with critics who were already condemning the deal before the ink was dry. Throughout 1993, as the two-year-old Madrid peace talks soured, Arafat faced internal criticism. Munir Miqdar, a refugee who commanded Fatah forces in Lebanon, was among the Fatah commanders who called upon Arafat to resign. Senior PLO officials spoke of an 'organizational crisis' and blamed Arafat for the PLO's predicament arising from Arafat's backing for Saddam Hussein in 1990 at the expense of wealthy Gulf donors such as Kuwait and Saudi Arabia. By late August 1993 the PLO had been forced to introduce austerity measures to try and avert a financial meltdown that was depriving its followers of vital welfare support. The secret talks in Norway with the Israelis would produce an agreement that could save the PLO and allow it to continue to represent the Palestinian people at the negotiation table.

Furthermore, there were aspects of the agreement which, upon closer scrutiny, caused concerns not just among the usual fanatics and rejectionists. On the Palestinian side, respected secular figures such as the writer and academic Edward Said publicly complained that Arafat had capitulated by signing up to the Palestinian equivalent of the 1919 Treaty of Versailles, a surrender that a defeated party had no choice but to accept. Moreover, critics argued that the agreement would store up dangerous levels of resentment for the future, as Versailles had with the defeated Germans.

The most vocal of the Palestinian detractors – the 'enemies' referred to by President Clinton – was Hamas. 'Proceeding from our aware-ness of our enemy's nature and in accordance with the teachings of our great Islam, we have declared a relentless war', said a Hamas statement released after the agreement.[3] Hamas insists that its opposition was not based on its desire to be declared a 'partner for peace', or because it wanted to enjoy American support and Israeli recognition, but because it believed the deal was a poor one for Palestinians living under occupation or those denied statehood and living in the Palestinian diaspora across the globe. 'We need a peace process not a security arrangement', complained Dr Mahmoud Zahar in 1995. Pointing to a map of the Gaza Strip, he ful-minated: 'They are still controlling the crossings, preventing pilgrimage. Every day they harass people who search for work . . . This is not a peace process . . . this is still occupation.'

Hamas leaders believed that the PLO had sold out the Palestinians, particularly those who had made huge sacrifices during the Intifada. 'We suffered under occupation', opined Zahar. 'We lost hundreds of our youth . . . as a movement we've spent billions of years in Israeli jails and as deportees, and financially the Gaza Strip is still suffering from the occupation. We do not enjoy this occupation and so we are still looking to eliminate it.'[4]

Aside from its publicly enunciated reasons, the Hamas leadership was angered at being excluded from the Oslo process. It was also immediately apparent that the PLO had immeasurably strengthened its own domestic position, just two years after its financial and diplomatic nadir. The PLO, now the official 'partner for peace', was enjoying American support and recognition and was at the helm of a project that would attract hundreds of millions of dollars in foreign aid and support. This was an unprece-dented turn of events for the nationalist liberation movement. It appeared to have undertaken the transition from armed struggle to resolution of the conflict with Israel through internationally sponsored negotiation. Yasser Arafat acquired the status of an international leader on the global stage. In 1994, along with Shimon Peres and Yitzhak Rabin, he was awarded the Nobel Peace Prize.

Nevertheless, Hamas leaders complained that Oslo was a chimera. 'This agreement is just a different face of the occupation', alleged one of its com-muniqués. 'It will be a weak autonomous administration over just two percent of Palestine. Jerusalem and the settlements are left under the control of the Zionist entity.'[5] The split over Oslo clarified the internal Palestinian battle lines, pitting Hamas and Fatah against each other again with two very different visions of the future. Such actions only deepened the hostil-ity between the two Palestinian movements, and exacerbated what were becoming endless rounds of internecine strife in the West Bank and Gaza Strip. 'We and the Tunis group [PLO]', announced one Hamas leader, 'are now competing for the hearts and minds of the average Palestinian.'[6]

But, for once, Hamas was badly out of kilter with popular sentiment, which favoured a peace settlement. The Palestinian street was growing weary of the daily struggle of life under occupation and the demands of waging a populist uprising. The energy that had propelled the Intifada in its early years and driven people from almost every level of Palestinian society to acts of civil disobedience had dissipated by the early 1990s. Palestinians demanded self-determination and independence. The Oslo Accords, with the promise of initial autonomy and negotiations for a final peace settlement, was what the majority of Palestinians had hoped their struggle would deliver.

Determined to act as spoiler, Hamas launched coordinated attacks against Israeli targets on the eve of the White House signing ceremony. It also called on all Palestinians in the West Bank and Gaza Strip to participate in a comprehensive strike to 'protest the signing of the accord of humiliation and disgrace', and tried to organize protest marches and demonstrations in solidarity with the deportees who had been exiled to Lebanon in 1992. While the PLO was agreeing to end the Intifada, Hamas responded by calling for a 'day of Intifada escalation . . . days of writing nationalist slogans on walls and raising banners expressing our people's rejection of the accord'.[7] The Hamas leadership was not prepared to negotiate with its enemy. It continued to maintain that only through armed struggle, resistance and jihad could the goal of liberating all of historic Palestine be achieved.

Rejecting Oslo

Hamas also rejected Oslo because it involved a negotiated settlement, international intervention and recognition of Israel and appeared to set the parameters of any future Palestinian state. 'The problem is that we have reduced the issue from one of sacred liberation to merely a dream of independence, a dream that a Palestinian policeman will organize traffic', said Musa Abu Marzouq, then head of Hamas's Political Bureau. 'We have diminished the Palestinian cause to a very simple thing.'[8]

Musa Abu Marzouq's opinion counts in Hamas. Born in Rafah refugee camp in southern Gaza in 1951, he was a follower of the Muslim Brotherhood. He studied engineering in Egypt, where he was actively involved in student politics, and completed his studies in the US, where he lived for more than a decade until the early 1990s. Urbane, cosmopolitan and a fluent English speaker, he played a pivotal role in the movement almost from its inception and was a lynchpin in the development of Hamas outside the Palestinian Territories, believing that its leadership needed both an internal and an external dimension. Veteran Hamas leaders in Gaza say it was Abu Marzouq who travelled to Gaza in 1989 to oversee the reorganization of Hamas when Sheikh Yassin and hundreds of other members were jailed. He headed the Political Bureau for much of the 1990s, promoting Hamas throughout the Middle East and further afield.

Abu Marzouq was arrested in New York in 1995 when he tried to return to the US and spent nearly two years in jail. The US courts accused him of helping to finance and organize Hamas attacks in Israel. Israel requested extradition. Abu Marzouq admitted heading Hamas's politburo but denied claims that he raised money for Hamas weapons, maintaining that his fund-raising activities in the US were for the movement's social and charitable projects.

Israel dropped the extradition request in 1997, apparently fearing it would disrupt the peace process. The US expelled Abu Marzouq to Jordan, and he later moved to Syria, where he served as deputy to Khaled Meshaal, who had by then already taken over as leader. In 2004 a US court finally indicted him in absentia on allegations of conspiracy to finance terrorist attacks against Israel. A year later Abu Marzouq was a key interlocutor with former CIA chiefs at a secret meeting in Lebanon to discuss Hamas and the political process. At this meeting, held in Beirut's luxurious Albergo Hotel, he was described by one former CIA senior official as the 'face of Hamas that wants to talk with Israel and progress to statehood through negotiation'.[9] He has never forgotten his roots. Moving among a group of former Western diplomats and intelligence agents in the hotel, he suddenly broke off to ask one guest to stop by his family home in Rafah and call on his sister for him.

Two years later Abu Marzouq underscored his call for negotiations with Israel in an article he wrote for *The Guardian*, emphasizing Hamas's breadth as a movement. 'Talking to Hamas is a prerequisite for any sustainable solution', he wrote. 'If the international community is serious about peace in the Middle East, there need to be non-partisan efforts to achieve it. It is not sufficient for Israel or its allies to continue to dismiss Hamas as "extremist", as we are made up of every part of Palestinian society.'[10]

Such overtures from Hamas's exiled leadership lay far in the future. From the very outset Hamas insisted that it remained opposed to negotiations with Israel or to third-party mediation because it believed that such talks would 'suit the unbelievers'. For Hamas, jihad was the only means of delivering the Palestinians to freedom and independence. 'There is no solution to the Palestinian question except by jihad. Initiatives, proposals and international conferences are all a waste of time and vain endeavours', reads Article 13 of its covenant.[11]

Hamas's mistrust of Western intervention stems from its interpretation of centuries of Palestinian history. 'Palestine', the covenant laments, 'is the navel of the globe and the crossroad of the continents. Since the dawn of history, it has been the target of expansionists.'[12] The litany of wrongs cited by its leaders stretches from the Crusaders to the Balfour Declaration of 1917. For Hamas, only unity beneath the banner of Islam will liberate Palestine from foreign rule, whether Crusader, British or Zionist. Still less, it argued then, as now, is it likely to come about through negotiations pursued by Palestinian leaders whom the Islamists considered to be morally bankrupt and intent only upon enriching themselves and gaining American and Israeli favour. Again from the covenant: 'Nothing can overcome iron except iron. Their false futile creed can only be defeated by the righteous Islamic creed.'[13]

Hamas also questioned the sincerity of Fatah's motives for choosing the path of Oslo, as it had done since 1991 during its public campaigns to condemn earlier PLO dialogue with Israel. A consistent message of rejection came from mosques, university lecturers and newspaper editorials, wherever Hamas could get its articles printed. It denounced every aspect of the negotiated process with Israel and the role of the international community: the meeting place, the date of the first meeting, the choice of Palestinian representatives, the hotels and the nature of negotiations. Hamas discerned the hand of externally imposed humiliation in every aspect from the minute that the first Palestinian representatives put their feet over the threshold of the palace in Madrid in 1991 to the Arafat/Rabin signing ceremony in 1993.

From the perspective of Hamas, Oslo was not a peace agreement: it was questionable whether armed conflict would come to an end, and it failed to guarantee the legitimate and internationally recognized rights of the Palestinian people. They argued that Oslo was not about establishing a Palestinian economy independent of Israel or about the promotion of democracy (there was no Palestinian referendum on the agreement). Hamas lost no opportunity to point out that it contained no agreement on the continuing presence and expansion of Israeli settlements in the West Bank, Gaza and East Jerusalem, in contravention of international law, no right of return for Palestinian refugees, and did not establish Jerusalem as a capital city for the Palestinians. Hamas complained that there was no land exchange and that Israeli redeployments were delayed.

Marginalized from mainstream Palestinian opinion, Hamas joined with secular Marxists within the Damascus-based Palestinian Alliance Force to promote themselves as the alternative to Oslo: 'We must mobilize all our efforts to confront the occupation', read one contemporary Hamas communiqué. 'We must remain steadfast until liberation. We must struggle against Zionist occupation and continue our blessed Intifada and join in popular action. There must be a withdrawal from all negotiations and an end to the rejection of our rights, cause and future of our homeland.'[14]

By and large the call was ignored, as Palestinians attempted to enjoy the fruits of the Oslo peace and celebrated the return of their deported leaders, the release of their prisoners from Israeli jails, the reunification of families, and the return of the national leadership of the PLO, including

Yasser Arafat's triumphal homecoming to Gaza in 1994. Palestinians were also encouraged by the sense of protection afforded by the newly established Palestinian security forces and Palestinian Authority (PA), which was created to administer Palestinian affairs in parts of the West Bank and Gaza and, in the absence of a Palestinian state, was the closest thing they had ever had to a government. After years of death, suffering, sacrifice and occupation, the simple pleasures of life were a relief: children returned to the streets to play football and fly kites, and families flocked to parks, municipal gardens and the beach to picnic. These brief escapes from the reality of their squalid lives were seen as a respite delivered by Fatah, not Hamas. As one young resident from a refugee camp in the West Bank put it, 'Fatah are here to help us share the peace and the good time. When we need Islam is that point when our suffering returns to us from Israel's hands and to our hearts and heads.'[15]

Turning points

Yasser Arafat chose to ignore the advice of his Arab neighbours and decided against competing with Hamas in the realm of faith and politics. He feared that taking the route of the 'pious president' would play Hamas at its own game[16] and, rightly or wrongly, believed that simply demonstrating his own personal attachment to Islam would satisfy his critics in Hamas. Arafat never hid his attachment to Islam. 'There is one thing bigger than the Palestinian people', he said shortly before his death, 'one thing that also unites us all and reminds us of our attachment to this land, and that is Islam.'[17] But Arafat, unlike many of his contemporaries in Fatah, had never been a member of the Muslim Brotherhood. He always maintained a strict secular nationalist line when it came to politics, his faith largely part of his private realm. He had tried to bring Hamas in under the PLO umbrella in 1993, meeting with its leaders in the Sudanese capital of Khartoum to try and hammer out an agreement.

The PA also acknowledged the reality on the ground that it would simply be impossible to eject Hamas from the mosques. Nevertheless, in August 1994 its police, security forces and intelligences agencies began a crackdown, calling upon members of Hamas's Izz ad-Din al-Qassam Brigades to surrender and hand over their weapons. Hamas activists were arrested by the Palestinian police and told that they must sign a pledge promising not to engage in any more clashes with the PA. Throughout 1994 and 1995 tensions grew and clashes erupted regularly.

Finding itself confronted by the PA, Hamas's leadership settled for other strategies, following the cautious approach advocated by Sheikh Yassin. Even hardliners such as Dr Abdel Aziz Rantissi understood the benefits of playing the long game at this critical stage in the movement's development.

As it faced the mass of Palestinian opinion in support of the political process, Hamas sought to craft a critique of the PA institutions based on religion as well as politics. 'You can't compare the institutions of the PLO and Islam', asserted Dr Mahmoud Zahar, shortly before PA forces arrested him in 1995. 'In one there is corruption, bad management, violation of human rights, destruction of integrity and a failure to meet promises made to the people. In one there are representatives debauching themselves, drinking, singing, carrying on like they did in Jordan, Lebanon and Tunis. But what they forget is that this is Gaza.'[18] Nevertheless, in the period directly following the signing of the Oslo Accords Hamas leaders publicly announced that they would try and avoid internal or civil conflict with the PA – but only if the latter met certain conditions in return.

The PLO and Islamists formed conciliation committees in the West Bank and Gaza Strip to avoid armed clashes. Sometimes these agreements resembled mutual deterrence more than conciliation. From Jordan, Hamas's spokesman Mohammed Nazzal warned that, if there was a proven intent by the PLO and Fatah to destroy Hamas, it would respond. He also made clear Hamas's concerns about Israeli and Palestinian security forces working together against it.[19]

Until 1993 both Hamas and Fatah had controlled their own armed wings: Hamas's Izz ad-Din al-Qassam Brigades, and the PLO's Fatah Hawks, Black Panthers and Red Eagles. But under the Oslo Accords Arafat formally disbanded the Fatah militias, and rewarded many of their members with jobs in the newly formed official PA security services that were now at his disposal. Additionally Arafat was allowed to bring in 7,000 members of the Palestine Liberation Army (PLA) from their bases in Jordan, Yemen and Sudan. Each was armed, and by the summer of 1995 Palestinian security forces in the PA's areas of control numbered in the tens of thousands.

Hamas now found itself outnumbered and outgunned by the new PA forces. Many in Hamas were outraged and publicly critical of a recruitment process which, they believed, was based on 'jobs for the boys' and blatantly discriminated against Hamas and its supporters. They claimed the PA was recruiting Fatah partisans to man the forces of what was supposed to be a national authority.

The same patronage extended to other Palestinian Authority ministries. There was scarcely a PA office, from the Ministry of Tourism to the Ministry of the Interior, that made a secret of its pro-Fatah and PLO affiliations. With hindsight, some senior PLO officials from that era now concede that it made a grave error from the outset by allowing Fatah to become so identified with the newly created Palestinian Authority that the PA effectively became the executive and legislative branches of the party. 'Before 1994 the PLO in exile had a certain glow to its image, lustre. But they weren't made to build institutions. They were *fedayeen*, not statesmen', conceded Ambassador Dr Abdelrahman Bsaiso:

Fatah let its membership slip, people in the party felt left behind. They were disenfranchised. It neglected its basic institutions and concentrated on government. Fatah's big problem was that, when it came time to retaliate, the people wanted to punish Fatah the party, but it was interchangeable with the government. The people couldn't distinguish between Fatah the party and Fatah the government.[20]

Hamas lost no time in criticizing Fatah for its partisan approach to recruitment, convinced that the latter's intent was to exclude Hamas and others from the funds that were now flowing into PLO coffers from the international community – what became known as the 'peace dividend'. It told its supporters to be patient, to return to the mosque, their studies and jobs, and to continue the work of Islamizing Palestinian society. As one senior leader, Ismail Abu Shanab, remarked, 'Our youth spent too long during the years of the Intifada throwing stones, making demonstrations and missing school. Now the Intifada in Gaza is over and it's time for the youth to return to the mosque, be educated and prepared for their role in society – there must be social reform along Islamic lines.'[21]

Abu Shanab represented what became known as the 'pragmatic' wing of the Hamas leadership, moderating the influence of 'hardliners' such as Dr Rantissi. Though neither was a parallel to Israel's 'hawks' and 'doves' in political terms, the pragmatists always tried to signal that the organization was the repository of differing political perspectives and approaches. Abu Shanab was a refugee, born in a village near Ashkelon in 1940, and had been one of the founders of Hamas. Like Musa Abu Marzouq, he had studied in the US, qualifying in civil engineering. A 'bridge builder' politically, he promoted dialogue with Arafat's deputy Mahmoud Abbas (Abu Mazen) and spearheaded various rounds of intra-Palestinian dialogue. He was the first Hamas leader to promote internal debate on the possibility of a ceasefire, holding secret meetings at his home with Western interlocutors. Quietly spoken and bearded, he would engage in debate while his children played around the legs of the important visitors to his home. He was assassinated by Israel on 21 August 2003.

Fatah was more circumspect in its public criticisms of Hamas. It ensured that the official face of Islam within the Palestinian Authority was represented by senior Sunni clerics from Jerusalem's Al Aqsa mosque and the religious courts. It also ensured that religious affairs, including *waqf* (endowments) and courts as well as the salaries of official clergy, were removed from Jordanian hands and placed in the new Ministry of Religious Affairs. This was the official Islamic establishment of the PA.

In the contest for the political support of the Palestinian people both Hamas and the PLO used Islam and nationalism. Both sides also sought to promote their ideology of liberation – nationalist or Islamist and to fit political changes on the ground to the new balance of power. This brought the two sides into a relationship which emphasized difference, not commonality.

As the PA consolidated its security forces, Hamas began building up its own arsenal by smuggling weapons into Gaza through tunnels. This was to facilitate its twin-pronged strategy of carrying out armed attacks against Israel, and building up parallel structures of authority in the Gaza Strip to rival those of the Fatah-controlled PA. Hamas also began infiltrating the myriad PA security forces, including the police, national security forces and Preventive Security. As early as 1995 Abu Islam, a leader of the Izz ad-Din al-Qassam Brigades, said: 'We are everywhere, but not in public, only in the shadows. And we are even inside the *sulta*'s [PA's] security.'[22] Years later these infiltrators would apply their knowledge both to help break Fatah in Gaza and to create a Hamas police force and other paramilitary units.

Wreckers

However, the presence of Palestinian security forces did not deter Hamas from organizing attacks on Israeli targets. Even after Israel carried out the first stage of withdrawing its troops – from Gaza's major Palestinian towns and from Jericho in the West Bank – Hamas continued its attacks. The Izz ad-Din al-Qassam Brigades and Hamas's internal intelligence apparatus also continued punishment attacks against Palestinians accused of collaborating with Israel. The PA proved unable to stop the extra-judicial killings, and bodies of Palestinians began to turn up bearing the marks of summary execution. Hamas also became increasingly convinced that its weapons would prove just as useful protecting itself from the PA as from Israel.

Then suddenly the whole post-Oslo situation changed because of the actions of one Jewish settler: Baruch Goldstein. On 25 February 1994 Brooklyn-born Goldstein walked into the Ibrahimi mosque in the West Bank town of Hebron wearing an Israeli soldier's uniform, and opened fire on Palestinian worshippers as they knelt in prayer during the holy month of Ramadan, killing twenty-nine people. The mosque stood on the Tomb of the Patriarchs, reputed to be the burial site of the Old Testament Prophet Abraham, and is a site revered by Jews and Muslims alike.

In the furore that ensued Israeli soldiers killed more Palestinians and imposed curfews. Palestinian Muslims, and Hamas in particular, questioned how such a 'massacre' – as the attack was universally described across the West Bank and Gaza – could be perpetrated by an Israeli settler while Israeli guards and soldiers were protecting the area. Israeli politicians were compelled to admit that the act revealed a disturbing level of extremism within their own society. Yitzhak Rabin, the Israeli prime minister, launched a crackdown on extremist Jewish groups and gave a powerful speech to the Israeli parliament three days later condemning the massacre. 'I am shamed over the disgrace imposed upon us by a degenerate murderer', he told the Knesset. 'This murderer came out of a small and marginal political context. He grew in a swamp whose murderous sources are found here, and across the sea; they are foreign to Judaism . . . To him and to those like him we say: You are not part of the community of Israel.'[23]

Less than two years later Rabin himself was assassinated by a right-wing Israeli fanatic as he attended a peace rally in Tel Aviv. Although he was replaced by Shimon Peres, another principal architect of the Oslo peace process, the Hebron massacre and Hamas's reaction to it were landmark events in the unravelling of that process over the next half-decade.

Hamas, not content with verbal condemnations, vowed that it would seek revenge for the Hebron killings. In a communiqué entitled 'The settlers will pay for the massacre with the blood of their hearts', it said that, if Israel was indiscriminate in distinguishing between 'fighters and unarmed civilians', then Hamas would be 'forced . . . to treat the Zionists in the same manner. Treating like with like is a universal principle.'[24] After the traditional forty days of Muslim mourning, it struck – but not at settlers. The target was Afula, an Israeli town a few miles north of the West Bank, founded by an American Zionist group in 1925. On 6 April 1994 a nineteen-year-old Palestinian, Raed Zakarneh, carried out a suicide bombing there, killing eight Israelis and wounding thirty-four. At one stroke, Hamas forever altered the Israeli–Palestinian conflict.

Hamas's bombing outraged Israelis, just as Palestinians had been appalled by the Goldstein massacre forty days earlier. But it was not only Hamas which drew the Israelis' wrath. The PLO, and Yasser Arafat personally, were caught up in a wave of Israeli revulsion over a statement from PLO headquarters in Tunis, the wording of which – that the PLO 'expresses its regrets for the incident' – was widely seen to be weak and wholly insufficient. Shimon Shetreet, Israel's economics minister, urged a suspension of peace talks with the PLO until Arafat condemned the bombing more forcefully, and some right-wingers called for negotiations to be called off altogether. The very next day Hamas shot dead an Israeli hitch-hiking near Ashdod, and a week later, on April 13 – in the midst of Israel's Memorial Day and Independence Day holidays – another Hamas suicide bomber from a village near Jenin killed five Israelis on a bus in Hadera.

Although right-wing Israelis gathered at the bus station chanting 'Death to the Arabs', Prime Minister Rabin insisted that he would not let Hamas derail the seven-month-old peace deal. 'There are those who say the peace talks have to be stopped', he said. 'What this will lead to is more elements joining in the terror. Even on Memorial Day, Jewish lives are being sacrificed in the quest for peace, a quest which we shall not abandon no matter what.'[25]

The change in strategy signalled by the suicide attacks on Afula and Hadera was an ominous sign of things to come. Nothing would ever be the same again. Exploding suicide bombs inside Israel and against Israeli civilians, on a scale designed to kill as many as possible, was a deliberate assault by Hamas on the Israeli psyche. From this point onwards the wider dynamic of the Palestinian–Israeli conflict would be irrevocably altered, for the worse. 'We were against targeting civilians', said Musa Abu Marzouq several years later, 'but no one asked about Palestinian civilian deaths . . . no one cared . . . After the Hebron massacre we determined that it was time to kill Israel's civilians . . . we offered to stop if Israel would, but they rejected that offer.'[26]

Many of Hamas's leaders sought to justify suicide bombings in religious terms, as 'an eye for an eye'. Dr Rantissi argued that, 'if the other side has done this, we find ourselves obligated to do the same. We are mandated by Islam – in a war situation – to do unto others as they have done unto us.'[27] Other Hamas leaders offer not religion, but tactical necessity and reciprocation as justification. 'We have done our best to target the military not civilians', argued Usama Hamdan in Beirut, 'but the talk of suicide bombers in Israel misses the major point – which is the occupation. All other channels have been closed to us, so we use violence.'[28]

Rabin ordered a major crackdown on Hamas and the closure of the crossing points into Israel. His government arrested more than 1,600 Islamists in the West Bank and Gaza Strip in an effort to halt the suicide attacks, and turned to the fledgling Palestinian Authority, demanding that Arafat use his new security forces to tackle Hamas. Arafat's forces duly rounded up thousands of Islamists and threw them into prison, prompting Hamas to react to the dual crackdown with bluster and defiance: 'The latest insane arrests will not affect Hamas strength one bit. Rabin must understand that only when he is able to make the sun rise in the West will he be able to affect the strength of Hamas', said one communiqué.[29]

In the eight months after the Ibrahimi mosque attack Hamas organized five suicide bombing missions, killing nearly forty Israelis and injuring hundreds. It demonstrated that it had the technical and operational ability to pull off such attacks, and discovered that there was no shortage of Palestinian 'martyrs' offering themselves for such missions. Palestinians had grown used to the idea of their young people being willing to die in the name of the struggle for freedom and liberation, but the notion that such people would strap explosives to their bodies and throw themselves at Israeli civilians was a new development. Israel's security services also grew frustrated, as they were, at least initially, unable to infiltrate the secret cells which were organizing the bombings.

Although many were imprisoned, the attacks continued. Israeli soldiers were shot at and ambushed. In October 1994 Hamas kidnapped an Israeli soldier near Gaza, demanding the release of imprisoned Hamas leaders in return, and in October 1994 a Hamas suicide bomber killed twenty-two people aboard a busy commuter bus in Tel Aviv. The bomber, Salah Abdel Rahim Sawi, appeared in a posthumous video, declaring, 'We will continue our brave martyrdom operations. There are many young men who long to die for the sake of God.'[30]

The Israelis responded by arresting hundreds of Hamas people in raids on homes, institutions and mosques throughout the West Bank. Once again the Israelis applied intense pressure on Yasser Arafat to bring his own house to order. Israel reminded him of his obligations under the Oslo Accords to preserve Israel's security from Palestinian threats, and from Hamas and Islamic Jihad in particular. Hamas thus found itself as much at war with Arafat and his forces as with its Zionist enemy. As one senior Palestinian security official put it: 'We play Hamas at their own game, but, because we make the rules and there is only one law, they will have to realize we'll win this one.'[31]

Gaza's PA security chief, Mohammed Dahlan, had hundreds of Hamas leaders and members arrested and interrogated. At one point Hamas leaders such as Dr Mahmoud Zahar had their beards forcibly shaved off by their Palestinian interrogators. Speaking from his headquarters in Gaza's Saraya security compound – its name a legacy from the Turkish Ottoman era – another of Arafat's security chiefs, Nasr Yusuf, declared, 'This is not a popularity contest. The people of Hamas have to understand that they can't end the peace process with their bombs and we won't let them.'[32]

The security chiefs, however, also complained of Israeli foot-dragging over the implementation of Oslo, particularly on issues such as settlements, security coordination and troop redeployment. Jibril Rajoub, head of the PA's intelligence services in the West Bank, was clearly a man under pressure. At his Jericho headquarters, an appointment to meet him would begin with a lengthy series of security checks and the unlocking of steel security doors. Sitting, early one morning, in his office, Rajoub argued that, while the PA could contain the threat from Hamas within its jurisdiction, Israel was making it difficult to 'build a bridge of trust over a river of blood'.[33]

Dual purpose

Hamas claimed that it carried out bombings in revenge for Israeli attacks which killed Palestinian civilians, but it was also motivated by a determination to undermine negotiations between Israel and the PA. For this it was made to pay a heavy price by Arafat's forces. Firstly the PA demanded that it disarm. Hamas's spokesman replied in July 1994 that 'We will not hand over our fighters' weapons and jihad will continue.'[34] When it was announced that only PA security forces would be legally permitted to carry arms, Hamas's Ibrahim Ghosheh retorted: 'As far as we are concerned we tell the self-rule authority to go to hell. We are keeping the arms to carry out the jihad.'[35]

The situation deteriorated further after Yitzhak Rabin was assassinated in November 1995, to be replaced by Shimon Peres until elections six months later. In those elections Peres, the veteran Nobel Laureate faced a resurgent right wing led by one of the principal opponents to the Oslo process, the young and telegenic hard-line Likud Party leader Binyamin Netanyahu.

On both sides of the conflict there was growing disillusionment about Oslo. Palestinians saw Jewish settlements continuing to grow every year in Israeli-occupied Gaza, the West Bank and East Jerusalem, hemming in their villages and confiscating their farmland. Within their own society they also saw disturbing evidence that corrupt Palestinian Authority political and security officials were siphoning off money at the expense of the Palestinian people. Israelis, meanwhile, saw Palestinian bombers and gunmen on their high streets, many wondering what was the point of Oslo if it gave autonomy to a Palestinian Authority with tens of thousands of security officials who either would not, or could not, deliver safety for Israelis.

With the Israeli elections set for May, Hamas mounted a bombing campaign in early 1996. The deadliest was a suicide bombing on a bus in Jerusalem in February, in which twenty-six people were killed. Three more bombings by Hamas and other factions brought the death toll to more than sixty, fast eroding support for Mr Peres's fragile government. Hamas claimed the attacks were revenge for Israel's assassination in January 1996 of Hamas's most notorious bomb-maker, known as Yahya 'the Engineer' Ayyash. But two months later, in March, Palestinian television ran an interview with a jailed Hamas suspect, Mohammed Abu Warda, who had been arrested in Ramallah accused of recruiting three of the suicide bombers. On television Abu Warda said the leaders of Hamas's military wing had told him that they wanted an escalation in bombings to ensure the defeat of Mr Peres's moderate Labour party at the hands of Mr Netanyahu's right-wing Likud. 'They thought that the military operations would work to the benefit of the Likud and against the left', he told the watching Palestinian public. 'They wanted to destroy the political process, and they thought that, if the right succeeded, the political process would stop.'[36]

The broadcast was clearly designed to show Hamas intent on wrecking the peace process and its advocates, Labour on the Israeli side and Fatah on the Palestinian. The Israeli right was furious, accusing Arafat of stage-managing the 'confession' to boost Peres. From his own prison in America, where he was being held in detention awaiting possible extradition to Israel, the jailed Hamas leader Musa Abu Marzouq rejected the substance of Abu Warda's statement, saying that it had been coerced. He repeated Hamas's consistent line throughout the years that its military and political leaderships were 'completely separate', and dismissed the linkage between Hamas's bombs and the Israeli elections, saying: 'We can't tie our future, you see, with Labor party or Likud party or who wins the elections.'[37]

In March 1996, at an anti-terrorism summit convened in Egypt as part of the international response to the Hamas suicide bombing campaign, it was clear that both Israel and the PA were being given encouragement to close Hamas down and to employ extreme measures, if necessary, to end the violence.

Mr Netanyahu went on to win the elections, narrowly, and became Israel's new prime minister. His premiership was marked only by the most limited steps on the road to peace, and these came largely as a result of intense US pressure.

Palestinian elections

As the Palestinians' own January 1996 presidential and legislative elections neared – with Yasser Arafat of course the Fatah candidate and overwhelming favourite for president – Hamas leaders viewed Fatah's promotion of the ballot with suspicion. The issue of elections had become a dilemma for Hamas. In 1995 it had declared that it approved the idea of elections in principle, as a 'right of the people', but it rejected the idea of participating in elections for the parliament – the Palestinian Legislative Council – or the presidency. Some, such as Ismail Haniyeh and Ghazi Hamad, were in favour of participating but others, including West Bank-based Bassam Jarrar, were opposed, arguing that 'participation in self-rule gives legitimacy to the peace process.'[38]

Believing that Arafat's every move had more to do with Fatah's compliance with Israeli demands than a genuine desire to bring democracy to Palestinian society, many in Hamas dismissed the elections as tainted by association with Israel. Countering this, Fatah supporters sneered that if Hamas had contested the elections it would have discovered the true measure of its support: 'They knew that even Sheikh Yassin would never be voted by the Palestinian people as the president, and they knew that they would never form a majority in the parliament, so they prefer to sit on the side and moan while we get on with the really difficult stuff', said one Fatah supporter.[39]

Although in prison, Sheikh Yassin remained a hugely influential figure within the movement. In a series of 'letters from the cell' he urged his supporters to consider participating in elections to the PA to create an 'opposition from within' the Oslo institutions they hated so much. He also addressed the issue of peace with Israel. Yassin claimed there was a precedent for Hamas's participation in Palestinian self-rule but also made it clear that Hamas was only offering a fixed-term *hudna* (truce), during which it could participate in elections.

Haniyeh and his supporters decided to stand in the polls but were quickly persuaded by hardliners in the movement to withdraw their candidacy. Public opinion polls from this period also illustrated how little popular support there was for Hamas. Only 3.2 per cent trusted Sheikh Yassin in 1996, compared with 41 per cent for Yasser Arafat.

Palestinians ignored Hamas's pleas for an election boycott and turned out in unprecedented numbers to vote. The elections were held on 20 January under Article III of the Oslo Accords, with the Palestinian territories divided into sixteen electoral districts – eleven in the West Bank and five in the Gaza Strip. Of 1,028,280 registered voters, turnout was 736,825, or 71.66 per cent. The presidential race was a foregone conclusion: Mr Arafat won 88.2 per cent of the vote and was opposed by only one other candidate, Ms Samha Khalil. In the elections to the Palestinian Legislative Council, Fatah won or controlled sixty-eight of the eighty-eight seats, giving it an insurmountable majority. Within the assembly thirty-seven seats were from Gaza and fifty-one from the West Bank. Only five women were elected, representing 5.7 per cent of the members.

Hamas had signally failed to win the argument at a political level, and prepared for several years in the wilderness, to wait – and push – for events to turn against the Oslo peace process.

Symbol and threat

As they waited, Hamas's supporters continued to rely on its leadership to guide the movement politically and strategically. One of the most influential was Yassin, who had been imprisoned by Israel in 1991. The circumstances of his release in October 1997 were so bizarre that they could have been taken from a bad movie script.

The chain of events began with a bungled operation by Israel's Institute for Intelligence and Special Operations, better known as Mossad, to assassinate the exiled Hamas leader Khaled Meshaal by poisoning him. Born in a village near Ramallah, Meshaal has been an exile ever since 1967 when his family left for Kuwait. He rose through the ranks of the movement, first as a student leader in Kuwait and then later through the political echelons. Astute, and famed for his calm demeanour, he was a leading light among the younger generation of Hamas leaders.

In 1997 two Mossad agents with false Canadian passports were sent to Amman in Jordan on the orders of the newly elected Netanyahu, with orders to kill Meshaal. Although they succeeded in getting close enough to spray poison on him, they were caught and taken into custody. Meshaal was rushed, critically ill, to hospital in Amman. King Hussein intervened personally, telling Netanyahu that he would get Israel's agents back only if he provided the antidote and if Yassin were freed. Humiliated, the Israelis agreed, releasing Yassin among other Palestinian and Jordanian prisoners. King Hussein was reportedly infuriated that Israel had been prepared to jeopardize their relationship in pursuit of Hamas.

The episode emphasized Netanyahu's growing preoccupation with the threat that he considered Hamas now posed. It also infuriated Arafat, who was reportedly enraged at being excluded from the deal to release Yassin. When the Hamas leader arrived at hospital in Amman he was feted by both King Hussein and Arafat. A few days later he returned by helicopter to a tumultuous welcome in Gaza, greeted by banners welcoming back the 'sheikh of the Intifada' and pictures of Yassin alongside the assassinated bomb-making hero Yahya Ayyash.

The drama surrounding the assassination attempt and the release of Yassin temporarily strengthened popular support for Hamas. At a press conference Yassin declared: 'There will be no halt to armed operations until the end of the occupation . . . I would address the whole world and say that we are peace-seekers. We love peace. And we call on them [the Israelis] to maintain peace with us and to help us in order to restore our rights by means of peace.' But, forthright as ever, he added: 'If these means are not available, we will never accept the occupation to remain on our shoulders.'[40]

Politically weakened, Hamas relied increasingly on its religious credentials to wage its jihad against Israel at a time when its secular counterparts in the Palestine Liberation Organization had embarked on peacemaking through negotiation. This reflected a divide within the Palestinian house that would have significant consequences in succeeding years.

6

The Second Intifada

The first intifada was the stone-throwing intifada. Now, who now believes
in stones?

Jamila al-Shanti, Hamas MP[1]

Look left just before you enter the Palestinian parliament in Gaza and there
is a mosaic of a Palestinian boy confronting an Israeli soldier. The youth is
upright, defiant and armed only with a catapult. The soldier is crouching
behind a wall, and aiming an M16 automatic rifle straight at the boy's heart.
Fading beneath the Levantine sun, the chiselled stone fragments proclaim:
'We will not bow.' In icon and slogan there is no better insight into how the
Palestinians see themselves. The stonework simultaneously distils a thousand newspaper front pages and inverts the biblical legend of David and
Goliath. For Jewish boy-king David and his sling, read Palestinian and cat-
apult. For Goliath and his javelin of bronze, read Israeli soldier and M16.

Much to Israel's frustration, this was the defining worldwide image
of the First Intifada in the late 1980s: overmatched Palestinian youths
hurling rocks at Israeli tanks and heavily armed soldiers. The abiding
image of the Second Intifada was altogether different. Seared into the
world's consciousness was the near daily sight of bloodstained Israeli
buses and restaurants blown apart by Palestinian suicide bombers.

In fact the Palestinian death toll was far higher in both uprisings.
What accounted for the shift in perceptions was the different nature of
the Palestinians' weapons: a difference summarized by Hamas's most
prominent woman politician, Jamila al-Shanti: 'The First Intifada was the
stone-throwing intifada. Now, who now believes in stones?'

The Second Intifada

The immediate events which led to the outbreak of the Second Intifada
– or Al Aqsa Intifada, as it also came to be known – are not in question.

Photo 6.1 Mosaic outside the Palestinian parliament building in Gaza City of a Palestinian boy with a catapult confronting an Israeli soldier

On 28 September 2000, two months after US President Bill Clinton failed to broker a peace agreement between Israel and the Palestinians at Camp David, Israel's right-wing opposition leader, Ariel Sharon, went for a highly publicized walkabout in Jerusalem's Old City. He visited the site revered by Jews as Har Ha-Bayit (Temple Mount) and by Muslims as *Al-Haram al-Sharif* (the Noble Sanctuary).

Sharon, nicknamed 'the Bulldozer', was a hate figure like no other across the Arab world. A former general and veteran of successive Israeli–Arab wars, he was also a long-time champion of Jewish settlers. He acquired particular notoriety when, as Israel's defence minister in 1982, he masterminded the invasion of Lebanon, only for Israel's Christian Phalangist allies to massacre Palestinian refugees in Beirut's Sabra and Shatila refugee camps.

The site of Sharon's walkabout was probably the most sensitive political and religious fault-line in the world. Once home to the Jewish Temples of antiquity, it was where Jesus drove away the moneylenders, according to the New Testament, and was later to become the third holiest site in Islam, revered as the first *qibla* (direction of prayer) for Muslims and for the fabled night journey of the Prophet Mohammed to heaven. Its hilltop plateau is today dominated by two huge shrines built by the early Muslim conquerors of Jerusalem: the Al Aqsa Mosque and the golden Dome of the Rock. The site's recapture from the Crusaders by the Muslim commander Salah ad-Din in 1187 is an epochal event in Islamic history, signifying Muslim victory over the Judeo-Christian West. Directly beneath these is the Western or Wailing Wall, which is the most sacred site in the world for Jews. The plateau's capture by Israeli troops during the Six Day War is equally a defining moment in Zionist history, immortalized by the battlefield radio transmission on 7 June 1967 by the Israeli paratroop commander Colonel Motta Gur: 'The Temple Mount is in our hands.'

When Ariel Sharon appeared there, Palestinians were infuriated, seeing it as an attempt to assert Israeli control over the long-disputed site. As Palestinians demonstrated, Israeli police fired tear gas and bullets coated with rubber. Four Palestinians were killed, and riots and protests spread across Jerusalem and beyond into the West Bank, Gaza and even Israeli Arab towns such as Nazareth. The violence escalated into deadly clashes between Palestinians and Israeli forces.

In the first week of the Second Intifada at least fifty-five people were killed: forty-two Palestinians, nine Israeli Arabs and four Israelis. Emotions were heightened even further by two polarizing events which shocked the world. On 30 September, just two days into the Intifada, a twelve-year-old Palestinian boy named Mohammed al-Dura was shot dead in Gaza after being caught in crossfire between Palestinian militants and Israeli soldiers while he huddled defenceless behind his father. His last moments were captured by a Palestinian cameraman working for a French television station, and he became an instant martyr across the Arab and Islamic world. Less than two weeks later, on October 12, two Israeli reserve soldiers, Yosef Avrahami and Vadim Norzhich, were lynched and mutilated by a Palestinian mob after they took a wrong turning in the West Bank and drove into Ramallah. Their brutal deaths were broadcast across the globe.

As the casualties rose, any prospect of a peace settlement faded. The centre-left government of the Israeli prime minister, Ehud Barak, collapsed, and barely four months after his Temple Mount walkabout Ariel Sharon was elected prime minister.

Israeli intelligence officials argue that the Intifada was not spontaneous, claiming that the Palestinian leadership began planning for violence months earlier and that they detected an increase in Palestinian attacks around the time of Israel's unilateral pullout from Lebanon in May 2000. 'We as an intelligence service failed a little bit to recognize the time and the day when the Palestinian Authority, which was supposed to be backing counter-terrorism, started to carry out terror activities', said one of Israel's most senior intelligence officials.

> It started in April 2000 when we had some tough events, some terror activities, in the Gaza Strip. It was around seven or eight events that until mid-August or the end of August we didn't know who was behind them. After the fourth or fifth one we thought maybe some combatants of Hezbollah had come into the Gaza Strip and were behind the terror activities. It took four months before we learnt that behind these terror activities were people from the Preventive Security Organization, the Palestinian Authority's equivalent of Shin Bet, or MI5.[2]

Looking back from the post-2006 era in which Hamas has become Israel's *idée fixe*, it is remarkable to note how little focus Israel placed on the Islamists during this period, only five years before they became the elected Palestinian government. Instead the Israeli political and military establishment's public rhetoric was almost entirely devoted to Yasser Arafat and the Fatah-dominated Palestinian Authority. In speech after speech, Israeli officials from the very top down hammered home their main talking point in the Second Intifada – that, while Hamas posed a danger, the main threat to Israel's security was the Fatah-led apparatus of the PA, which Israel had allowed to be created under the Oslo Accords, but which it now regarded as a terrorist quasi-state. Before long Israeli leaders would be equating Yasser Arafat with al-Qaeda's Usama Bin Laden.

Methods

For the first month of the Second Intifada the vast majority of the fatal attacks on Israelis were from gunshots, through ambushes, sniper fire or drive-by killings. The first car bomb came on 2 November 2000, an Islamic Jihad blast which killed two Israelis near Jerusalem's Mahane Yehuda market. Hamas then perpetrated a series of suicide bombings which greatly escalated the toll. One of the deadliest was on 1 June 2001, when a suicide bomber killed twenty-one youths outside a disco in Tel Aviv. Two months later, on 9 August 2001, a similarly deadly Hamas blast killed fifteen at the Sbarro Pizzeria in Jerusalem's city centre. Hamas said the restaurant bombing was in revenge for the assassination of Hamas leaders.

But more Palestinians were dying from Israeli missile attacks, tank incursions and bombing raids. Twelve months into the Second Intifada, 564 Palestinians and 181 Israelis were dead, according to figures from the Palestinian Human Rights Monitoring Group[3] and the Israeli Foreign Ministry.[4] The death tolls on both sides were far higher than in the first year of the 1987–8 Intifada, which saw around 300 Palestinians and fifteen Israelis killed. But Hamas was playing a far more cynical numbers game. Its leaders pointed out that, while the early stone-throwing Palestinians may have enjoyed the world's sympathy, the Palestinian to Israeli death rate was around 25:1 during the opening phase of the First Intifada, compared with a much closer ratio in the same period of the second. 'It's much better than the past', said Sheikh Nizar Rayan, one of the hardest of the Hamas hardliners, in 2002. 'Now, if one Israeli is killed, it equals only three Palestinians.'[5]

During the height of the Intifada, when challenged about whether Hamas would end its campaign, another of its *mutatarrifeen* (hardliners), Dr Abdel Aziz Rantissi, used his customary rhetorical device of turning defence into attack: 'We are talking about a high casualty rate on our side', he replied angrily, 'and everyone wants the victim to change his method.'[6]

Whatever Hamas's rationale for its suicide bombings, the international context changed utterly on 11 September 2001, when al-Qaeda hijacked four airliners in the US, crashing two of them into New York's Twin Towers and one into the Pentagon. In that era-defining moment, Yasser Arafat condemned the attacks and moved quickly to stop impromptu Palestinian street celebrations at the reverse suffered by Israel's chief ally, although not quickly enough in East Jerusalem. Hamas's Sheikh Yassin also insisted that his movement had no intention of joining al-Qaeda in a jihad against the West, emphasizing his movement's narrow, geographically focused struggle. 'We in Hamas: our battle is on the Palestinian land. We are not ready to move our battle out of the occupied Palestinian territories', he said.[7]

What concerned Palestinians most in the aftermath of 9/11 was that, amid the inevitable fear and confusion gripping US policy-makers and intelligence agencies, there would be little interest within the world's only remaining superpower in making fine distinctions between Muslim armed groups with Arab names in far-off places defining their cause as a nationalist war of independence against one of America's leading allies and, on the other, Muslim armed groups with Arab names in far-off places defining their cause as worldwide jihad against America and its allies.

Israeli leaders were quick to make the parallels. Two days after 9/11 Prime Minister Ariel Sharon told the US secretary of state, Colin Powell: 'Arafat is our bin Laden.'[8] Sharon also warned the US about the consequences of appearing soft: 'I call on the Western democracies, and primarily the leader of the free world, the United States: Do not repeat the dreadful mistake of 1938 when enlightened European democracies decided to sacrifice Czechoslovakia for a convenient temporary solution. Do not try to appease the Arabs at our expense . . . Israel will not be Czechoslovakia. Israel will fight terrorism.'[9]

During the very first days of an era which gave birth to the polarizing certainties and simplicity of rallying cries such as 'War on Terror' and 'Islamofascism', Sharon's was by no means the only attempt to link Palestinians and al-Qaeda. Israelis were not alone in blurring the lines, although Fatah – not Hamas – was the focus of one of the first attempts. On 13 September the US Republican senator Charles Grassley, after receiving a briefing from his country's law enforcement officials, said of the evidence: 'Most of it today points to Usama bin Laden, but the speculation is that he and his network were very much involved with Hezbollah, Fatah and other terrorist organisations.'[10]

However, even amid the heightened emotions, some Israeli intelligence analysts outside the political hierarchy were more restrained, reserving judgement until more evidence emerged. Yoram Schweitzer, an expert on international terrorism and Islamic fundamentalism, claimed that in February 2000 two Palestinians from Gaza and the West Bank had been arrested after returning from one of bin Laden's training camps in Afghanistan, but cautioned: 'I don't think Hezbollah or Fatah were involved. Not because they are not capable of doing this, but because all the information I have implies it's not true.' Professor Ehud Sprinzak, an Israeli expert on terrorism and religious radicalism, and a former adviser to Yitzhak Rabin, also said that he did not see 'any serious or significant' organizational link with Palestinian groups. 'From what I know Israel has been using the Usama bin Laden analogy to draw US support', he said, 'and they will probably do so more. But in reality I think the contacts are minimal.'[11]

The initial concern of the Bush administration in Washington, as it sought a response that would meet the demands of a devastated people and a sense of national insecurity, was to ensure that the all too apparent crisis between Israel and the Palestinians did not undermine US efforts to keep Arab states such as Saudi Arabia on board as it prepared to launch its 'War on Terror'. But would Hamas change its methods and halt the suicide attacks on Israel?

Chasing Hamas

As 2001 drew to a close, the death rate accelerated. On 23 November Israel assassinated Mahmoud Abu Hanoud, a senior Hamas military leader in the West Bank, and Hamas struck back by killing thirty-seven Israelis in December, including eleven in a double suicide bombing on Jerusalem's Ben Yehuda pedestrian mall, fifteen in a bus bomb in Haifa the next day, and eleven Jewish settlers in a bomb, gun and grenade attack on a bus at the ultra-orthodox settlement of Immanuel. It was the deadliest attack in the West Bank since the start of the Second Intifada, and the international opprobrium forced Arafat to act. President George W. Bush's envoy, retired Marine General Anthony Zinni, said: 'Chairman Arafat and the PA must move immediately to arrest those responsible . . . coexistence with these organizations or acquiescence in their activities is simply not acceptable.'[12]

Now finding itself for the second time in a decade in the uncomfortable position of being unwilling gamekeeper to Hamas's poacher – perhaps more accurately poacher/gamekeeper to Hamas's poacher – Fatah became nervous at the increasing popularity of the Islamists. Arafat's and Fatah's popularity fell, but support for Hamas increased. The Palestinian leader ordered the closure of all Hamas and Islamic Jihad offices, but it was not enough for Israel, which focused not primarily on Hamas – an organization whose hostility it took for granted – but on Yasser Arafat, whose PA security apparatus was supposed to be a partner in the Oslo peace process but was, in Israel's eyes, either refusing or failing to rein in the violence.

During a rare and lengthy interview with foreign journalists in 2002, the Israeli prime minister, Ariel Sharon, barely mentioned Hamas except as an afterthought, reserving his venom for Yasser Arafat, his old enemy, whom he had tried and failed to kill in Beirut twenty years earlier. Pointing out that 646 Israelis had been killed during the violence of the previous two years – a figure which he said would be the equivalent of 6,460 deaths for a country of Britain's size – he said that Arafat could continue as a 'symbol' but could no longer be permitted to oversee Palestinian affairs: 'He must be disconnected completely from the security/terror organization, and of course he should be fully disconnected from the control of the financial side because, as long as he controls the financial side and the security organization controlling terror, it's very hard to expect that there will be reforms.' Specifically, Sharon reiterated Israel's long-standing demand that Arafat's security chiefs close down the Islamists and other violent factions. 'They have to arrest terrorists, their leaders, interrogate them and sue them . . . they have to dismantle terrorist organizations like the Hamas', he said at Israel's fortress-like prime ministerial residency in Jerusalem. Significantly, he also cited the country that was to feature increasingly large in Israel's list of enemies over the next decade: Iran. Already identified by President George W. Bush in

Photo 6.2 A bus 'graveyard' in Kiryat Ata, where the Israeli public carrier Egged stored the remains of buses blown up by Hamas and other factions during the Second Intifada. Photo: Ronen Zvulun, August 2002

January 2002, alongside Iraq and North Korea, as a member of the 'Axis of Evil', the Iranian regime was referred to by Sharon as 'a danger to the Middle East, to Israel and a danger to Europe', and he called upon the Americans to target it 'the day after' they finished in Iraq.[13] It is unlikely that he foresaw the Iraq war outlasting both his own political career and that of President Bush.

The 74-year-old Sharon gave a detailed list of accusations against the Iranians, citing its alleged efforts to acquire weapons of mass destruction and ballistic missiles, providing Hezbollah with up to 10,000 short-range missiles along Israel's northern border with Lebanon, its efforts to smuggle weapons to the PA and, he claimed, its attempts to get 'more and more involved' among Israel's minority Arab population, mostly through the northern-based Islamic Movement.

The specifics of Iran's alleged links to Hamas were dealt with by one of Sharon's most senior intelligence chiefs. Armed with colour flip charts and flow diagrams, the senior official claimed that 'something changed' with Hamas in the twelve months following 9/11. Hamas, he admitted, had initially 'kept its independence since being established in 1987, but during the last year we could see how it has been changed, and Hamas became more dependent on Iran. The leadership of Hamas sits in Damascus, and they travel every three or four weeks to Tehran.'[14]

Palestinian security officials protested that Sharon's demands were impossible because there would be zero public support for cracking down on their fellow Palestinians at a time when Israel was attacking Palestinian towns, cities and refugee camps. 'They want us to do the job that their own "most sophisticated" army in the Middle East has been unable to do themselves', said one senior Palestinian intelligence officer.[15] As he picked among the rubble of his buildings recently bombed by Israel, a senior National Security Force officer in Gaza said: 'They tie our hands behind our backs, take our weapons, uniforms, communications, equipment, destroy our HQs and prisons, allow the prisoners and wanted to go free, shoot at us if we move from one area to the next, and then say we have to destroy the terrorists among us . . . but how?'[16]

The Israelis and their Western backers also found themselves hampered. Arafat, the man they installed to implement Oslo, was now seen as a grievous liability but, partly through his own machinations and partly because of the radicalization of the Palestinian street, there was a fear that replacing him could lead to more chaos. One poll had already shown Sheikh Yassin and Fatah's Marwan Barghouti, a talented rabble-rouser, to be the next most popular figures after Arafat.[17] Another poll carried out eight months later by Birzeit University in the West Bank found that 74 per cent of Palestinians rated the ability to 'confront Israel' as the most important factor in choosing their leader, with 'commitment to Islamic values' close behind at 70 per cent.[18] Both findings were good news for Hamas.

By this stage, after more than a year of violence, the mutual trust integral to the Oslo peace process had evaporated almost entirely. Israel protested that Palestinian suicide bombers had blown the peace process off course, and insisted that any state had a right to defend itself. The Palestinians were angered at the civilian deaths caused by Israeli raids into Palestinian towns and villages and the continued construction of Jewish settlements in the West Bank and Gaza.

Arafat was under huge domestic and international pressure to stop the violence. But he found himself trapped between Hamas and Israel: an unwilling middleman trying to reconcile irreconcilable agendas. Israel wanted Palestinian shootings, bombings and mortar attacks to stop, while Hamas demanded an end to Israeli raids and assassinations. For Israelis a similar hardening of political attitudes was taking place in relation to the Palestinians. Pro-peace leaders and politicians saw support collapse, and the diversity of opinion in Israel regarding the peace process increasingly narrowed. People-to-people peace efforts funded by the international community started to weaken, and there was a growing sense of insecurity for Israelis as Hamas and others mounted their deadly and apparently random bomb attacks.

When Arafat did try to satisfy Israel's demands to place Sheikh Yassin and Dr Abdel Aziz Rantissi under arrest and shut down Hamas offices in the Gaza Strip, Islamist supporters rioted. On 16 December 2001 Arafat managed to forge a partial ceasefire after calling for a 'complete and immediate halt of all armed operations', but he obtained a promise from Hamas only that it would stop suicide bombings and mortar attacks within pre-1967 Israel, if and only if the PA stopped arresting its members. The cessation was to prove short-lived. Israel was not satisfied, demanding a complete halt to violence and the arrest of Islamist ringleaders. Hamas was openly scornful from the outset, saying its cessation was only a temporary 'tactic' and sneering that Arafat was now a collaborator. 'Arafat says one thing to our faces and another behind our back when it comes to any political threat that we might pose', said Hamas leader Ismail Abu Shanab.[19] Dr Mahmoud Zahar was more scathing, turning to anger at the suggestion that the Hamas movement ought to heed Arafat's call to desist from suicide operations against Israel and allow the PLO to continue with peace talks:

> For how long is Mr Arafat going to negotiate? What is the alternative? Even when there are talks, Israel still kills us. Give me one wise man in this world that can convince us that Israel really is ready to leave our soil and enter negotiation. No one believes negotiation is possible. Everyone is calling for continuation of the Intifada. And sooner rather than later Israel will realize the price of their existence here . . . We need our liberty and sovereignty.[20]

Polarization

By 2002 continuing violence was eroding Ariel Sharon's authority, with his rightist rival and the former prime minister Binyamin Netanyahu waiting in the wings. The year had begun well for Sharon, when on 3 January Israeli naval commandos in the Red Sea captured the 4,000 ton cargo freighter *Karine A* laden with 50 tons of Iranian-supplied weapons destined, Israel said, for the Palestinian Authority. Yasser Arafat denied PA involvement, but the discovery of the *Karine A* at a time when Arafat was meant to be abiding by a ceasefire helped Sharon to convince President George W. Bush that he was not a man to be trusted. But marginalizing Arafat, while appealing to the hawks, further emasculated the PLO once it became apparent that Arafat was an irrelevance in Washington. Shrewdly aware of the Palestinians' deep mistrust of all things to do with Washington, Hamas was quick to spin Arafat's fall from grace as yet another example of how the perfidious West builds regional leaders up, only to knock them down once they have outlived their usefulness.

Sharon's problem was that, for more than half a century as general and politician, his role as a 'Warrior' – the title of his autobiography – was to make Israelis feel safe. But, now that he had risen to the highest office, he was failing at that primary task. Matters disintegrated still further on 14 January 2002 when Israel – during the ceasefire – assassinated Raed al-Karmi, a prominent Al Aqsa Martyrs' Brigades leader from Tulkarem. Karmi's death took an extraordinary posthumous hold on the collective imagination of Palestinians, no matter what faction. From the most north-ernmost olive farmer in the West Bank to the southernmost tunnel-digger in the Gaza Strip, it became an unshakeable article of faith that Karmi's assassination during a ceasefire proved that Israelis could not be trusted.

Israeli officials rebutted the allegation. One senior Israeli military officer later claimed that they had intelligence that Karmi was about to carry out attacks on Israelis: 'We thought that maybe it was the right thing to do to try and stop him.' He also dismissed the notion that it was a significant factor in the ensuing violence. 'Even if we didn't do what we did at that time, sooner or later the violence would have erupted again.'[21]

The Al Aqsa Martyrs' Brigades immediately resumed hostilities, killing three Israelis within twenty-four hours of Karmi's death. Another eleven Israeli deaths were to follow over the next month, which was to see a landmark event when the Al Aqsa Martyrs' Brigades recruited Wafa Idris, a refugee from Ramallah's al-Amari camp, to become the first ever Palestinian woman suicide bomber. Idris, a 28-year-old divorced para-medic, killed an 81-year-old man and wounded more than 150 when she blew herself up in Jerusalem's Jaffa Street on 27 January.

In the West Bank, radicalization of Palestinian public opinion was evident on the ground. Fatah leaders cautioned that their own young radicals were proving increasingly difficult to rein in. While the Israelis never missed an opportunity to blame Arafat personally, Fatah street leaders maintained that the situation was more fluid and complex. They asserted, not entirely convincingly, that the hot-headed youngsters of the Al Aqsa Martyrs' Brigades had not been let off the leash centrally by Arafat or the Fatah command, but that regional commanders were taking it upon themselves to deliver payback to Israel, even across the Green Line inside Israeli towns and cities. This meant that in practice sometimes there was no difference in methods between Hamas and the Fatah-supported Al Aqsa Martyrs' Brigades, which increasingly regarded all Israelis as targets. As the cycle renewed itself – Palestinian shootings and bombings, Israeli airstrikes and tank incursions – Sharon's popularity continued to plummet.

The number of Israelis killed rose from around forty in 2000 to 200 in 2001, and to 450 in 2002 – a total of around 700. In the same years the Palestinians lost around 320, 580 and 1,070, a total of around 1,970.[22] Israel's mood was not helped by morale-sapping setbacks such as the loss on Valentine's Day 2002 of one of its hitherto invincible Merkava battle tanks to a powerful landmine in a joint Hamas–Fatah attack near Netzarim in Gaza.

From a solid 57 per cent public support for Sharon's performance in mid-January, his rating slipped to 37 per cent in February. By mid-February Israeli newspapers reported that nearly 50 per cent of the public was losing confidence in the national leadership's handing of the security situation. By early March Israeli public opinion was in freefall, with rates of dissatisfaction with Sharon's government reaching nearly 80 per cent. These political weathervanes were being watched carefully by Palestinians. 'He [Sharon] has been scared by the recent polls that show he's losing his control. It's an indication of his failures', sneered Hussein Abu Kweik, a member of Hamas's political wing in Ramallah.[23] The Israeli left was openly, and with no little satisfaction, already writing off their right-wing prime minister. 'We are seeing the demise of Sharon', concluded Danny Ben Simon, a columnist with the liberal Israeli newspaper *Haaretz*. 'He promised total security and he provided total insecurity. It took a year to come to this conclusion.'[24]

Poised, although they did not know it, on the brink of a major escalation in the violence, Israelis found themselves divided between those on the right, such as Mr Sharon, who argued for no concessions to Palestinian 'terror', and those who raised yet again the criticism which had dogged Sharon throughout his military and political careers – that, while he was unquestionably a master short-term tactician, he lacked the necessary long-term strategic vision to look beyond his 'security-first' stance and find a political solution. It cannot be overstated how politically weak Sharon was at this point, haemorrhaging both support and credibility, and therefore, as Palestinians were about to learn to their cost, how little he had to lose.

As secular-nationalist armed factions accelerated their bombing and shooting campaign – far exceeding Hamas in the number of fatal attacks carried out in early 2002 – Sharon and his aides intensified still further their attack on Arafat, blaming him personally for Israel's woes. 'We identify him as the single obstacle to peace or any settlement. It was time for us to call a spade a spade', said Danny Ayalon, then Ariel Sharon's foreign policy adviser. 'With 60,000 troops, Arafat should be able to over-whelm any terrorist outfit of a few hundreds, such as Islamic Jihad and Hamas.'[25]

While the barricaded Arafat, whether sincerely or otherwise, was paying lip service to the notion of restraint by repeatedly calling for a Palestinian ceasefire, Hamas made no such pretence. In February 2002 Dr Rantissi told a Hamas crowd: 'I say it clearly, that Hamas will continue the martyrdom operations. Let's not care if they say that we are terrorist organizations . . . Your choice is your gun.'[26]

Squeezed

Rantissi was talking from Gaza, Hamas's stronghold. But Gaza was sealed off from Israel by a high fence, and, with rare exceptions, Hamas and the other Gaza-based factions were – until the later advent of mortars and rockets – limited to carrying out attacks on Jewish settlements and military bases inside Gaza itself.

The real wellspring of attacks against Israel came from the much larger West Bank, where Fatah was dominant. Their coexistence was uneasy – Fatah officials still recalled with bitterness Hamas's deliberate wrecking of the Oslo peace process in the mid-1990s. But differences would often be put aside for personal friendships or solidarity in death. In March 2002 an Israeli tank fired into the West Bank capital of Ramallah, killing five Palestinian children and two women on their morning school run. The Israeli army expressed regret over the death of 'innocent Palestinian civil-ians' and claimed to have hit the wrong car by mistake. But Palestinians were sceptical, as the dead included the wife and three children of the Hamas leader Hussein Abu Kweik. Hamas left little doubt that there would be retaliation. 'Don't we have the right to defend ourselves? The military wing will take the decision, but the Israeli occupation is pushing us toward responding', said Sheikh Hassan Yousef at the crowded condo-lence ceremony in al-Bireh.Yousef was careful to use the formula always employed by Hamas when its leaders are attacked. To stop cults of per-sonality, they emphasize that leaders are not important in themselves, but only because their suffering reflects that of all Palestinians. 'They are targeting the entire Palestinian people', he said, surrounded by nodding, green-capped Hamas supporters. 'This man [Abu Kweik] isn't wanted, he's not on the list put forward to the Palestinian Authority. He's not a member of the military wing. It is just an attempt by the Israelis to put the whole Palestinian people in a cycle of blood.'[27]

As the Hamas leader spoke, a short, stout figure sat beside him nodding, glad-handing and exchanging greetings with friends. This was Marwan Barghouti, officially Fatah's secretary-general in the West Bank, but a figure of far greater importance in the movement than that middle-ranking position suggested. A Fatah member of parliament and skilful orator, Barghouti had been an organizer during the First Intifada and had, during the second, achieved international fame as the face of Fatah's younger generation through his rabble-rousing rhetoric at West Bank protests and barricades. Despite their religious and political differences, Barghouti chatted amiably with Yousef at the condolence ceremony, like rival Westminster MPs socializing on the Commons terrace after a working day spent barracking each other from opposite sides of the House.

It was a rare sighting. Barghouti had drastically curtailed his public appearances since the escalation of the Israeli military operations in the West Bank, fearing arrest by Israeli snatch squads. Israelis – and his internal enemies within Fatah – claimed that Barghouti had been a key figure in Fatah's decision to escalate its campaign of violence to the point where it had carried out far more attacks and killed far more Israelis than Hamas since Karmi's assassination in early 2002. They alleged that he persuaded Arafat that the only way to counter Hamas's inexorable rise in popularity was to match its tactics by carrying out attacks inside pre-1967 Israel. Barghouti vehemently rejected the accusations, insisting that he was a political leader committed to a two-state solution. But he voiced satisfaction that Fatah's violence had strengthened the movement, giving it a stronger bargaining hand with Israel, and relegating its Islamist internal foes back to the sidelines.

A senior Israeli military official alleged that Fatah's escalation was part of an internal struggle to succeed Arafat between Fatah's political wing and its security overlords Mohammed Dahlan and Jibril Rajoub. Barghouti's aim, the Israelis said, was to use the newly created Al Aqsa Martyrs' Brigades to bring Fatah back under the control of the political party machinery – the Tanzim – thereby bypassing Dahlan and Rajoub's Fatah-dominated PA security forces. The long-term goal, they said, was also to neutralize Hamas's growing reputation on the Palestinian street as champions of the armed struggle. 'About two or three months ago the militant leaders of this organization . . . persuaded Arafat that all the restraints and limitations . . . imposed on the Tanzim should be lifted, and since his organization contained many more potential activists than Hamas or Islamic Jihad he should give them full freedom to act . . . Arafat was persuaded', said the Israeli official.[28] The Israeli intelligence establishment's view was that Arafat valued above all things keeping the reins of power in his own hands. Although evidently self-serving, the Israelis' analysis was useful, if only to give an insight into how they were tailoring their narrative. Once again their message centred on Fatah – and Arafat personally – not on Hamas.

The Israelis caught up with Marwan Barghouti on 15 April 2002, arresting him near his home in Ramallah and charging him with murder in a Tel Aviv court where he, vainly, protested his innocence and claimed immunity as an elected Palestinian MP. Barghouti's arrest – by no means his first – brought to a rapid end this phase of his career. However, his stature and the cross-factional relationships he had forged were to make him an influential figure in jail. Palestinian prisoners in Israeli jails have an exalted status within their society because of the sacrifice they are perceived to have made for the 'cause', and they remain an important decision-making wing of movements such as Hamas and Fatah. As the most high-profile of Fatah's leaders in prison, Barghouti became a totemic figure and an important point of liaison with the Hamas prison leadership. His stature continued to grow to the extent that he was soon regarded as a future contender for the Palestinian presidency, even from behind bars.

As the Intifada ground on, the rhetoric of some of Fatah's armed groups became increasingly indistinguishable from that of Hamas: rejecting Oslo, scornful of Israel's right to exist, and calling on Israelis to 'go back' to their homes in Russia and Eastern Europe. The radicalization was not just on the front lines. Speaking in a nondescript office block in Ramallah, the head of the city's Al Aqsa Martyrs' Brigades berated his own Fatah senior leadership for corruption and inefficiency: 'When Israel started the assassinations we could not be silent. That is why we went out and took revenge. The other factions were quiet. At other times we cooperated with the military wing of Islamic Jihad and Hamas.' Like Hamas, he appeared to have little time for the traditional Fatah distinction between Israelis living inside pre-1967 Israel and Israeli soldiers and settlers in the occupied territories. 'I don't know what is civilian in the matter of Israel because I believe they are a militarized people', he said.[29]

Fatah appeared to be going through an identity crisis, attempting to out-hawk Hamas by attacking Israelis on both sides of the Green Line, while simultaneously protesting that it remained a dove at heart, committed to a two-state solution. Trying to square an impossible circle often forced Fatah officials into logical absurdities. Some tried to draw a distinction between Hamas suicide bombs and Al Aqsa Martyrs' Brigades explosions by arguing that, while Hamas conducted its bombings as part of a long-term strategy which embraced attacks inside Israel, Fatah's Brigades only bombed inside Israel out of temporary tactical necessity to force it back to the negotiating table, or as a reaction to Israeli provocations, or because individual brigade leaders were out of control, or because they were controlled by nefarious outsiders dictating their own agendas. 'We don't like suicide bombings inside Israel. We see it as a reaction to the aggression we face in our daily life. We are under occupation: you can't control all the people', explained Qadura Fares, a prominent Fatah leader in the West Bank.[30]

Similar rationalizations were given by Hussein ash-Sheikh, one of Barghouti's Fatah rivals and himself a wanted man, who moved from hiding place to hiding place to avoid arrest. After slipping into the back room of a café in Ramallah where he could not be seen from the street, he insisted that suicide bombings inside Israel were 'not the strategic way of Fatah'. They were merely a short-term measure to demonstrate Fatah's strength and secure a better deal from Israel at the negotiating table, he maintained. 'Each side wants to put pressure on the other in the field', he said. 'Our aim was to show our voice to public opinion all around the world and impose more pressure on Israel to start moving.' He bridled at the suggestion that bombings meant there was now no difference between Hamas, Fatah and Islamic Jihad:

> Fatah is strategically not interested in having operations inside Israel. The big difference between Fatah and Hamas is that our political vision is totally different and the background of these attacks is different. The main reason is that the Al Aqsa Brigades are nationalist and political, not religious. What the Al Aqsa Brigades did was not a result of hatred of Israel and Jews. This was not the reason. The reason was a reaction to Israeli aggression.[31]

Fatah was trapped: rejected by Israel because it was no longer moderate, and losing relevance on the Palestinian street because it was trying to be what Hamas already was. Unsurprisingly, less than a year after 9/11, its tortuous rationalizations cut little ice with the Israelis or the Americans. On 22 March 2002 the US State Department declared the Al Aqsa Martyrs' Brigades a 'foreign terrorist organization' alongside Hamas, Islamic Jihad and al-Qaeda. By this time Israel was confidently asserting that Fatah was the main problem because Hamas was much smaller. 'We are in conflict with some dozens of very dangerous Hamas activists, but hundreds of Tanzim activists', said one senior Israeli military official. 'We are fighting against an organization that is not only formally but directly instructed by Arafat himself.' He also assessed that Hamas's military capabilities had been 'reduced dramatically' by raids against its weapons-making facilities. 'It doesn't mean that they can't carry out suicide attempts, but 70 per cent fail simply due to the fact that the military capability was affected by a series of operations – for example, against four of their experts in Nablus a month ago.'[32]

That note of caution proved more accurate than the rest of the assessment. The strikes and counter-strikes were by then coming hourly, not daily. It was not uncommon to have two or three Palestinian suicide bombings a day, and journalists became uncertain whether to cover the afternoon funeral for that morning's suicide bombing or wait for the inevitable afternoon rush-hour explosion. Television screens were filled with a montage of bloody stretchers and hospital emergency rooms, and so quickly did they segue into each other that viewers on both sides were left straining to glimpse a Jewish Star of David or an Islamic Red Crescent on speeding ambulances to tell whether the blood-masked victims were from Palestinian suicide bombs or Israeli air strikes.

8 March 2002 saw the bloodiest day of the Intifada thus far, with forty Palestinians killed in Gaza during Israeli tank and air strikes on PA targets. The very next day Hamas penetrated to within a few yards of the Israeli prime minister's office in Jerusalem, when a suicide bomber with dyed blonde hair and wearing a heavy coat walked into the fashionable Moment café in Aza Street and killed eleven Israelis. Aza is the Hebrew name for Gaza. Surveying the wreckage of the café, usually filled with journalists and Israeli intelligentsia, one Israeli onlooker named Efrat said bitterly: 'I don't want to talk politics right now, because it's not the right time. But there is a big feeling that we are helpless because we can't stay in the middle. Either you have a big war, or you give them what they want. You can't stay in the middle.'[33]

The big war was coming.

Passover

From its birth as the military wing of the Muslim Brotherhood in 1987 through to the rocket-firing which provoked Israel's December 2008 military onslaught on Gaza, Hamas operated on a working assumption: when Palestine burns, its support grows. That calculation was never more starkly illustrated than in March 2002, when its deadliest ever attack ensured that an Arab peace initiative anathema to the Hamas credo was delivered stillborn.

In mid-February Saudi Arabia's de facto ruler, Crown Prince Abdullah bin Abdul Aziz al-Saud, floated through the *New York Times* columnist Thomas Friedman the suggestion that Israel could have normalization of relations with the Arab world in exchange for its withdrawal from the occupied territories. As rulers of the wealthiest Arab state and custodians of Mecca and Medina, Saudi Arabia had long played a role in Palestinian affairs. Saudi patronage had always been important for Hamas because, as a conservative Muslim regime, it lent Sunni Arab credentials to counterbalance the latter's ties with Iran, a Shi'a country. Arafat, on the other hand, had enjoyed a tumultuous relationship with the Saudis, particularly after his ill-advised support for Saddam Hussein's 1990 invasion of Kuwait.

Many welcomed the Saudi proposal, seeing it as an imaginative move that offered a long-term solution to the intractable Middle East problem. Not Hamas: on 27 March 2002, the very day that the Arab League was gathering for a high-level summit in Beirut to discuss the Saudi proposal,

Hamas upstaged the event by killing thirty Jewish celebrants at a Passover dinner in the seaside town of Netanya. No one believed that the timing was coincidental. The Passover bomb struck to the core of Israel's religious, cultural and national identity. The victims were assembled for the most important family gathering of the year, the Passover seder, with its biblical resonances of suffering, exile, deliverance from slavery and escape from the Angel of Death. Further compounding the evil in Israeli eyes was that most of the dead were pensioners in their seventies, eighties or older, from the Holocaust generation.

Hamas's claim of responsibility showed that the message from Netanya was not only directed south along the coast to Tel Aviv but also 120 miles north to the Arab rulers gathered in Beirut, that Hamas acted inside Palestine, while all they could do was talk outside it. 'This operation comes as a response to the crimes of the Zionist enemy, the assassination of innocents and as a message to the summit convening in Lebanon that our Palestinian people's option is resistance and resistance only', Hamas declared in a communiqué.[34]

At a stroke the bombing erased whatever remaining interest Israelis had in troubling themselves with distinctions between Fatah, Hamas, the PFLP, and a bewildering array of Palestinian security forces and armed factions. It was immediately apparent that Ariel Sharon had carte blanche from his electorate to launch a massive and immediate retaliation. On the right there were calls for retaliatory strikes, and even among the left there was a sense of betrayal and incomprehension. As she stood among the incinerated ruins of her hotel's ballroom, Paulette Cohen, the Park Hotel manager who survived the blast but lost her son-in-law, said:

> I never hated the Arabs. I used to bring Arab workers here, and one of my former staff called me from Jenin after the bomb and cried and said he was sorry for what happened . . . I don't want to destroy, I don't want to kill. But if they come and destroy people who are sitting down at a party and they come on this holy holiday, they have crossed the line.[35]

Arye Mekel, an Israeli government spokesman, put it more succinctly. 'Every Jew in this country saw this as a personal attack on his Passover seder, and I don't think that the people of Israel can accept this.'[36]

At the Arab League summit in Beirut, word spread quickly among the Syrian, Saudi and other delegations about a Passover massacre. Soon the details emerged – the bomber was from Tulkarem, just 10 miles from Netanya, had worked in the Israeli seaside resort and used his knowledge to penetrate the hotel. Even in Lebanon – especially in Lebanon – everyone knew that Ariel Sharon's wrath was going to be felt.

One day after the Netanya bombing a Hamas gunman killed three Jewish settlers in Elon Moreh, near Nablus, and on 31 March Hamas unleashed another suicide bomber on the northern city of Haifa, killing fifteen in a restaurant. With the situation already aflame, the bomb appeared deliberately chosen by Hamas to strike at the city most often cited as a model of Jews and Arabs coexisting peacefully. 'This is a mixed city and, as you can see, we also suffer together', said Amram Mitzna, Haifa's mayor, while a Hamas statement in Jenin refugee camp, where the bomber came from, threatened only to 'continue the martyrdom attacks on Israel until the full withdrawal from Palestinian territory.'[37]

Significantly Sharon did not allow the Hamas affiliations of the Netanya and Haifa bombers to nudge him off message. Israeli officials remained focused laser-like on laying the blame at the door of one man – Arafat. Meir Sheetrit, an Israeli cabinet minister, listed Arafat's past sins, including rejection of the Camp David agreement, and claimed that Fatah's gunmen and bombers had since 2000 carried out 'five times the number of attacks committed by the Hamas and Islamic Jihad. Arafat is thus committing five out of every six attacks that kill Israelis.'[38]

Israel declared many Palestinian areas of the West Bank a closed military zone. Palestinian residents prepared for a siege. As thunder and lightning rolled across the skies on Good Friday – or Sad Friday, as it is known to Palestinian Christians – Israel's tanks rolled into the West Bank to carry out its largest military operation in years, what Israeli officials termed 'Operation Defensive Shield' but what Palestinians experienced as a full-scale reinvasion of West Bank cities. The Israelis' first target was Yasser Arafat's hilltop Muqata compound in Ramallah. The Israelis cut off water, telephone and electricity to the neighbourhood. Then they tore up the main roads. Then, smashing into the front wall of the Muqata, they trapped Arafat inside one wing. Here he would remain, behind the rubble and sandbags, a virtual prisoner until shortly before his death in a Paris hospital two years later.

The Israeli forces besieged cities, smashed PA ministries and security headquarters, and detained thousands of prisoners. A key target was Nablus, which had long been fertile ground for Palestinian radical movements. They found it easy to recruit volunteers from the city's 20,000 refugees, who could look into the Israeli plains from the West Bank hilltops above the city but could never return to their pre-1948 homes there. It was also renowned for its fortress-like casbah, whose dark subterranean alleyways and dungeon-like stone walls provided a perfect battleground for guerrilla fighters.

By no means all the population were hardliners. At the height of the fighting Abed Rahman, a seventy-year-old refugee from the coastal city of Haifa just 40 miles away, said he was no longer seeking to return to his pre-1948 home which now lies within Israel, but simply wanted a Palestinian state in the West Bank and Gaza. 'We only want the 1967 lands', he said. 'How can I go back to Haifa? All the people I know have gone. I could not go back alone. Twenty years ago I went to Haifa to see my home. An Iraqi walked in, a Jewish lady who was living there. She started shouting at me. I said, "This is my house." She said, "This is my house." What to do?'[39]

As a deterrent to the continuing suicide attacks, Israel pursued the controversial policy of demolishing the homes of bombers. Some were deterred. Others were not. After the departure of yet another Israeli raiding party from Nablus's Balata refugee camp one gunman, who gave his name only as Mustafa, shrugged unconcernedly at the damage, saying he didn't care how much Israel damaged it because it was never his home anyway. 'This camp is not my country. We left our home in 1948, in Deir Tarif, near Ludda [Lod]', he said. 'Where else shall I go? If we die, we die here.'[40]

Palestinian fighters and Israeli troops were the only people visible in the city, its residents hiding behind closed doors and shuttered windows. The fighters moved through the narrow alleyways of the refugee camps and underground passageways of the casbah to escape notice by the Israeli helicopter warships hovering above the biblical peaks Mount Gerizim and Mount Ebal. From his office packed with nervous aides Mahmoud al-Aloul, the Palestinian governor of Nablus, pronounced that 'All the factions are together, Fatah, Islamic Jihad and Hamas.'[41] But, even as Arafat promised to implement the latest US-backed peace plan, Israeli officials were scorning his words as too little, too late, and Hamas was delivering its own retort with actions, not words.

Over the following weeks Palestinian refugee camps and entire cities were virtually sealed off from the outside world and turned into battle-fields inside Israeli cordons. Masked Palestinian fighters fought running gun battles with Israeli units around Ramallah's central Manara Square, as Israelis rounded up young men of fighting age in the surrounding streets. Dressed in balaclavas and *keffiyehs* and wearing khaki ammu-nition pouches, Palestinian militants fought from behind the walls of mosques and spice shops within Nablus casbah and the heavily populated streets of Jenin refugee camp, the two sites of the deadliest encounters with Israeli troops. In Bethlehem, Hamas and Al Aqsa fighters took refuge in the Church of the Nativity, provoking a month-long siege around the reputed birthplace of Christ.

But even as the Palestinian gunmen fought on the streets there remained very real differences between the leaderships. There was wide-spread outrage on the street – with Hamas as cheerleader – when Fatah's West Bank security chief Jibril Rajoub surrendered half a dozen Hamas activists to Israeli troops which had surrounded his Preventive Security compound in Beitunya, on the outskirts of Ramallah. In pamphlets and across Arabic satellite networks, Hamas leaders immediately accused him of betrayal, and its military wing issued a communiqué saying: 'Rajoub sticks to treachery, hands six Hamas activists to IDF.'

Hamas was in its element. For years marginalized during the era of compromise and negotiations, it now saw an angry younger generation increasingly in despair at the twenty-four-hour Israeli curfews, tank raids and dismantling of the Palestinian Authority. In Gaza's Jabalia refugee camp Sheikh Yassin urged Arafat on, proclaiming that the resistance had reached a new level. Other leaders, such as Dr Abdel Aziz Rantissi, warned Arafat not to succumb to Israeli or US pressure to end what Hamas termed its rightful resistance against the hated occupation.

And while Hamas openly competed with Fatah for control of the street there was, behind the scenes, growing support within the Islamic movement for the opening of a second front against Fatah: for Hamas to capitalize on its growing popularity by challenging Fatah in parliament. But the paradox at the heart of Hamas's planned entry to politics was that from the very outset its embrace of the ballot was intended not to end the violence, but to ensure its continuance. Hamas feared that, if left in control, Arafat would sooner or later do a deal with Israel and the Americans, and deploy the numerically superior PA security apparatus to crush its own zealous, but much smaller, forces. 'The international community's plan was, "If we get Hamas involved in politics they will become more involved, and then it will become harder for them to do resistance"', said Jamila al-Shanti. 'But it was clear from day one that we came with the purpose of protecting the resistance.'[42] The other factor working in Hamas's favour was that, as Israel destroyed the PA's ministries, the collapse of its social and welfare institutions created more of a need for Hamas's shadow network of charitable support. Hamas organized food runs, donations, medical supplies and support across the West Bank throughout the Israeli lockdowns, providing compensation for destroyed homes and support for the families of prisoners.

The Sharon Curtain

Jenin, the northernmost city in the West Bank, proved by far the deadliest single battle for Israel throughout Operation Defensive Shield. More than twenty soldiers were killed, including thirteen in a single ambush in the refugee camp on 9 April. Around fifty Palestinians also died, most of them fighters. Although Nablus was deadlier, Jenin drew more attention because Palestinian leaders grossly exaggerated the death toll, accusing Israeli soldiers of killing hundreds during the fierce battle for control of its refugee camp. The accusations flew on both sides, Israel saying their soldiers encountered 'dozens of heavily armed terrorists shielding themselves behind Palestinian civilians',[43] and the Palestinians accusing Israel of collective punishment because it razed part of the refugee camp where some of the fiercest fighting happened.

Capitalizing on the furore, Hamas drew attention to the battle by

sending a suicide bomber from Jenin to blow himself up on a bus in
Haifa, 25 miles away, killing eight Israelis. Although it was unclear when
the bomber slipped out of the camp, it was a deliberate attempt to goad
the Israelis. Hamas wasted no time trumpeting its self-proclaimed coup,
posting a statement on its website crowing: 'To Sharon and his ministers and generals, we have shown that there is no Defensive Shield.' In
fact just such a shield was coming, but one more permanent than the
Palestinians had hitherto seen. Even as Israeli soldiers rolled through
the West Bank, confiscating weapons caches and rounding up hundreds
of youths for questioning, Israel's security planners were advocating a
physical barrier to separate Israelis from Palestinians. This was something
that Sharon the arch-Zionist had long resisted because he feared that it
could one day become a de facto border, forcing Israel to cede some of the
West Bank. But he was reluctantly having to embrace it as a security and
political inevitability.

Gaza had been fenced off from Israel since the mid-1990s, but West
Bank Palestinians who wanted to cross the invisible Green Line had only
to walk across a road or unguarded field to enter Israel. Sharon's forceful
response to the Passover bombing had reversed his popularity freefall – a
poll published by the Israeli newspaper *Maariv* in late April 2002 showed
65 per cent support.[44] But he was still coming under increasing pressure from the security services and the Israeli public to separate Israelis
from Palestinians. The result was Israel's West Bank barrier – a 500-mile
continuous stretch of razor wire and concrete snaking around the Jewish
settlements and other parts of the West Bank and East Jerusalem which
Israel wanted to keep.

Hamas and other Palestinian groups protested that it was a land grab,
pointing out that huge tracts of Palestinian land were sliced off from
farms and villages in the areas where the barrier pushed up to 13 miles
deep into the West Bank. Israel insisted it was a security fence, necessary
to cut off the gunmen and suicide bombers. The decision had a major
impact on Hamas and other factions, at a stroke making it far harder for
them to penetrate Israel. The level of suicide bombings and shootings
declined sharply as the barrier was first completed in the north, sealing
off Jenin, and slowly wound southwards through the West Bank and East
Jerusalem.

Citing dramatically reduced violence figures after 2003, the Israelis
hailed the barrier as a success. Shin Bet, Israel's domestic security agency,
says that, in the forty-two months from the outbreak of the Intifada in
September 2000 to August 2003, Hamas and other Palestinian factions
in the northern West Bank carried out seventy-three suicide attacks,
killing 293 Israelis. But in the thirty-four months after the completion of
the first, northern, section of the security fence, from Salem to Elkana in
August 2003, they managed only twelve suicide attacks, killing sixty-four
Israelis.[45]

Redirection

The Second Intifada continued after 2002, although increasingly casualties were on the Palestinian side. From 2003 to 2004 there was a 45 per cent drop in the Israeli death toll, from 214 to 117,[46] whereas Palestinian deaths rose by 35 per cent, from 637 to 866.[47] Throughout the five years after the outbreak of the uprising in September 2000 to December 2005, the Israelis lost 1,080[48] and the Palestinians 3,570.[49]

The US, in 2002, had taken the decision to intervene to try and get the peace process back on track by outlining a 'Roadmap for Peace', which would be facilitated under the framework of an International Quartet of the US, the UN, Russia and the EU. Under the terms of the 'performance-based' Roadmap it was hoped that Israelis and Palestinians might achieve a peace deal by 2005. The Roadmap required the Palestinians to stop violence against Israel and take security measures to halt armed groups. Hamas and other armed elements were furious that Palestinian Authority officials were giving commitments to Israel to halt what they believed was a legitimate right to resistance.

Hamas began a process of reorientation. When in late 2001 European Union envoys made overtures about a ceasefire, it proved receptive, a signal that it wanted to be treated differently, not to be regarded as part of a global jihad and consistently equated with al-Qaeda.

Ismail Abu Shanab, the main architect of the ceasefire, devoted all his energies to the process, believing it could bring Hamas in from the sidelines and eliminate civilian casualties from both sides. In the summer of 2002 as he sat in the salon of his home – after waiting to speak while one of his young daughters came into the room to ask when he would be finished with his visitors – the Hamas leader insisted that the movement's followers 'support resisting the occupation, developing better Palestinian life and reform and developing a Palestinian state and struggling towards the return of the refugees'. But then he paused and added: 'The *hudna* [ceasefire] should be tried, because no one should have to bury their children in the heat of this war.'[50]

The second factor, and the one that Hamas leaders will never admit in public, is that Israel's unrelenting attacks on the Hamas leadership from 2002 on did have an impact. Within two years almost the entire senior tier of Hamas leadership in Gaza was assassinated, in what Israel's former defence minister Shaul Mofaz has latterly referred to as a plan to 'liquidate the terrorists'.[51]

In 1997 Israel had tried but failed to kill Khaled Meshaal, the head of Hamas's Political Bureau, in Amman. In July 2002 Ariel Sharon's government succeeded in killing the head of its military wing, Salah Shehadeh, by dropping a 1 ton bomb on the building where he was staying in Gaza, also killing at least thirteen other people. In March 2003 it assassinated another senior military leader, Ibrahim al-Maqadmeh, and in August 2003

Ismail Abu Shanab. One Israeli attack severely wounded, but failed to kill, the new military leader, Mohammed Deif. In March and April 2004 Israel finally took the decision to assassinate the two most prominent political leaders in Gaza, the movement's founder, Sheikh Ahmed Yassin, and his hardline deputy, Dr Abdel Aziz Rantissi.

Leaders in death

Strong leaders, the cult of personality, the notion of the despot and tyrant and the omniscient ruler are common currency in the Middle East region: Muammar Ghadaffi of Libya, Hafez al-Assad of Syria, Gamal Abdel Nasser of Egypt, Saddam Hussein of Iraq and Yasser Arafat. Israel has grown used to dealing with such powerful leaders, and in turn they have produced their own men of myth. Israel believed that in the Hamas leadership, and especially with Yassin, Rantissi, Zahar and Meshaal, they were encountering the same phenomenon. In many respects they were, but in one important respect they were not. Israel believes that Hamas, like the PLO and elsewhere in the Arab world, is led through the will of one or two individuals. But this is not Hamas's style.

The death of Sheikh Yassin and other Hamas leaders had long been anticipated by the movement. Yassin himself had stated that he was ready for paradise. It was the manner of his assassination that elevated him into a symbol of martyrdom – killed by Israeli missiles as he was being pushed down the street in his wheelchair after attending dawn prayers at his local mosque. For every leader lost, Hamas declared that there were hundreds of others lining up. Hamas's diffuse process of decentralized decision-making also made it harder for Israel to destroy its core. On a strategic level, however, Israeli security chiefs believed that they could weaken their enemy by targeting its leadership. This was a view echoed in the supportive statements of Bush administration officials in the wake of Israel's attacks on Hamas leaders.

As the Second Intifada continued, the financial squeeze was also on Hamas. Israel persuaded the PA to freeze bank accounts belonging to Hamas charities in Gaza and the West Bank, and funding from some of its traditional backers began to dry up as the European Union put Hamas on its list of terrorist organizations.

The first hints of a Hamas change of direction had been noticeable both in statements made by Sheikh Yassin before his death and in the movement's unprecedented commitment in June 2003 to a formal unilateral ceasefire with Israel. Its announcement was greeted with approval from the Palestinian street that had paid the price in Israeli reprisals for Hamas suicide attacks. Popular support for the ceasefire was evidence enough to convince sceptics in the movement that their appeal would not decline if the resistance was suspended. But there were many doubters. Neither

Israel nor the US believed that Hamas was sincere, and Israel continued to target the Palestinians in a series of arrests, air strikes and assassinations, which meant that within weeks the ceasefire had, for Hamas hardliners, become untenable.

Nevertheless Yassin, before his death, indicated that Hamas would allow a *tahdiyah* (period of calm). This came ahead of Israel's planned withdrawal from Gaza – what was to prove one of Ariel Sharon's last acts on the political stage. The 2005 withdrawal was hugely controversial within Israel. Many on the left believed that Gaza – home to 1.5 million Palestinians – was no longer worth the price in blood and treasure to defend a few thousand Jewish settlers. The settlers and their supporters argued that to pull out would be an unconscionable sign of weakness and serve only to encourage Palestinian 'terror'. Sharon pushed it through against considerable opposition – those inclined to take the withdrawal at face value accepting the argument that it was an act necessary to ensure Israel's demographic survival, while sceptics suspected Sharon of sacrificing Gaza in order to secure its hold on the West Bank.

Members of the Hamas leadership continued to offer Israel the deal Sheikh Yassin had first proposed five years earlier for a lengthy truce (*hudna*) with Israel, in return for a Palestinian state in the occupied West Bank and Gaza. But it was an offer that Israel had always scorned, protesting that it could never trust an enemy whose founding covenant devoted itself to Israel's destruction.

Hamas's apparent intention was to fine-tune its campaign of 'resistance' in a way that would win it back regional and even international support. This also gave it important leverage in its discussions with the Fatah-dominated PLO and Palestinian Authority. Sheikh Yassin indicated that Hamas was prepared to participate in power-sharing in any post-withdrawal government. Details of this had been hammered out over the following months during rounds of inter-Palestinian dialogue, and were formalized in the Cairo declaration of March 2005. The new orientation, however, would lead to the greatest changes of all, not just for Hamas, but for its secular rivals and the government of Israel.

7

The Qassam Brigades

Since we don't have F16s or Apache missiles or tanks we have our own weapons to defend ourselves. Believe me, if we had F16s we would never use suicide attacks.

Dr Abdel Aziz Rantissi[1]

At Passover on 27 March 2002, 250 Jewish celebrants were packed into a ground-floor ballroom in the seaside town of Netanya to mark one of the holiest days in the Jewish calendar. The ghost at the banquet was 25-year-old Abdel Baset Odeh, who walked into the Park Hotel shortly after 7 p.m. and detonated a suicide belt which exploded with such force that it killed thirty guests, wounded 140, and drove a kitchen knife an inch deep into the concrete ceiling. Hamas's military wing, the Izz ad-Din al-Qassam Brigades, had just committed the deadliest suicide bombing in Israel's history – bloodier even than its slaughter of twenty-one mostly teenage partygoers outside the Dolphinarium in Tel Aviv nine months earlier, and reminiscent in scale and impact of the 1972 PFLP and Japanese Red Army attack on Lod Airport a generation earlier.

In timing and execution the Netanya bombing was a classic Hamas operation, striking at the core of Israelis' identity during the most important family meal of the year. It escalated the two-year-old second Intifada into a state of war in all but name, prompting Ariel Sharon to unleash his tanks onto West Bank cities and refugee camps. The Oslo peace process was dead, and within days the security apparatus of its begotten child, the Fatah-dominated Palestinian Authority, was being ground into dust by Israel's F16s and armoured bulldozers.

Although the Park Hotel was an operation carried out by Hamas, the latter's nominally secular and moderate rival Fatah had actually been responsible for many more attacks in the preceding few months. It was therefore Arafat who found himself besieged by the Israeli army in his hilltop Ramallah compound for the remaining years of his life, not

Photo 7.1   A knife embedded in the ceiling of the Park Hotel in Netanya after Hamas's Passover bombing

Hamas leaders, who remained at liberty in Gaza. Far from punishing Hamas for escalating the bloodshed to unprecedented levels, many critics said Israel's aggressive retaliatory measures actually strengthened the Islamists by weakening both its own enemy and that of Hamas: the Fatah-dominated Palestinian Authority.

And as the dust cleared half a decade later to reveal a new Palestinian regime emerging from the wreckage of the Second Intifada, it was the green banner of Hamas fluttering over the Palestinian parliament. From Passover bomb to parliament, there is no better illustration of how Hamas uses violence and politics as twin levers to advance its ends. And although Hamas has developed other armed branches before and since, the Izz ad-Din al-Qassam Brigades are the deadliest.

Allah slew them

The logo of the Izz ad-Din al-Qassam Brigades depicts a gunman, his face shrouded in a chequered Palestinian *keffiyeh*, standing in front of Jerusalem's Dome of the Rock brandishing a semi-automatic rifle in his right hand and a Koran in his left. Alongside is a banner proclaiming 'There is No God but Allah' and the Koranic verse: 'Therefore you did not slay them, but Allah slew them.'

The Qassam Brigades, Hamas's military wing, was created in the early 1990s by Sheikh Yassin. Once ultra-secretive, it now even has its own letterhead, uniformed spokesmen and English website, complete with starbursts, scrolling news, multimedia section, lists of 'Martyrs' and 'Prisoners', and 'Statements' and 'Interviews', all above the address 'Ezzedeen al-Qassam Brigades – Palestine.'[2]

Despite its relatively small size, its discipline, organization and ruthlessness soon established the Qassam Brigades as one of the principal Palestinian fighting factions. It refuses to confirm its size: 'the number of Izz ad-Din al-Qassam Brigades members is known only to the leadership of the Brigades, which adopts the principle of secrecy in organization and recruitment', the website reads. However, it claims to have lost 800 fighters since the outbreak of the Second Intifada in 2000 and is believed to have more than 10,000 men under arms – nothing like the 176,000 active personnel in Israel's armed forces. Qassam commanders are known deliberately to understate their numbers.

Because Hamas refuses to recognize Israel it has had no compunction about carrying out suicide bombings and other attacks on Israeli civilians within the Jewish state, as well as against Israeli settlers and soldiers in the occupied Palestinian Territories. Hamas leaders justify the suicide bombings by arguing that Israel's missiles, tank shells and artillery rounds make no distinction between Palestinian civilians and fighters. 'Since we don't have F16s, Apache missiles or tanks we have our own weapons to defend ourselves. Believe me, if we had F16s we would never use suicide attacks', said Hamas's deputy leader Dr Abdel Aziz Rantissi on 22 June 2002. 'If we had something which could stop the enemy from killing us without killing ourselves, it would be much, much better.' Such views are echoed by the armed men on the ground. As one Qassam Brigades commander declared, 'When we apply pressure [on Israel] we know they suffer, but we have a greater suffering.'[3]

Hamas also sought to use Israel's reprisals for such attacks – including the demolition of suicide bombers' homes – to stoke Palestinian anger and create more support for its cause. 'Here is the equation', said one camp dweller in Gaza. 'The [Israeli] army come and besiege us from one house to the next. They call for our surrender, but if we give it we still have occupation. So we say let us confront rather than surrender for life. We have no choice.'[4]

The military wing's role is to carry out armed operations within a broad framework laid down by the movement's ruling *shura* or consultative council. This *shura* includes the political leadership inside the Palestinian territories of the West Bank and Gaza Strip, Hamas's prisoners – whose exalted status is akin to that of the Provisional IRA in Northern Ireland during 'The Troubles' – and the outside leadership headed in Damascus by Khaled Meshaal, who is today widely regarded as Hamas's supreme leader. Hamas insists that its military and political wings are separate. Insiders say that, once the political leadership has authorized attacks, their location, timing and nature are left to the military leadership. 'We are just political leaders. We have nothing to do with military things', maintained Rantissi in June 2002.[5]

Israel argues the distinction is meaningless. After Israel's helicopter gunships assassinated Yassin in Gaza City on 22 March 2004, the Israeli military countered worldwide criticism by accusing the wheelchair-bound cleric of being 'personally responsible for numerous murderous terror attacks'.[6] 'The perception that Yassin was the "political" leader and left the management of terrorist activities to others is incorrect. In fact, there is no differentiation between the "political" and "military" wings of Hamas', declared an Israeli government statement, citing unnamed Israeli security sources. It said that in 1984, after being arrested by Israel's domestic intelligence agency Shin Bet, Yassin 'stated during questioning that he had founded an organization of religious activists with the goal of fighting non-religious factions in the territories, and carrying out "jihad" operations against Israel.'[7]

When the Israelis assassinated Yassin's successor Rantissi less than a month later, on 17 April 2004, it issued a similar statement defending its actions. 'Rantissi maintained contact with senior terror leaders within the Hamas and encouraged them to continue carrying out attacks. He was responsible for establishing and overseeing secret terrorist cells', it said. 'Rantissi publicly called, at every possible opportunity, to continue armed attacks and specifically to increase the suicide attacks and attempt to kidnap Israeli soldiers. These public calls were taken as operational directive of the Hamas leadership.'[8]

The Israelis claimed that, after the void caused by the loss of its two most senior Gaza leaders in quick succession, the balance of Hamas's leadership changed, and the leadership in Syria took greater control of military operations. 'The military headquarters in Damascus comes under the clear control of the politburo, with policy guidelines set by Meshaal', said an Israeli government analyst who specialized in the study of the Islamist group:

> Let's say the politburo decides it's time to carry out a terror attack against Israel because of certain political circumstances. It will give the order to Damascus military HQ. They'll say it's time to do something signifi-cant. They might say it should be in Israel, or limited to the [Palestinian] Territories. The military HQ will translate that into practical action and give orders to cells 'inside', who decide the target and location. Haniyeh and Zahar are not directly involved in attacks.[9]

Although Hamas is part of the international Muslim Brotherhood and its extensive fund-raising and propaganda activities extend much further afield, one of the few red lines which Hamas has publicly declared – thus far – is extending the conflict beyond the boundaries of Palestine. 'Hamas has a clear policy – no militant actions against anyone except the occu-pation, no militant actions outside the occupied territories', said Usama Hamdan, a senior member of the Political Bureau who is based in Beirut.[10] In this it is different from earlier Palestinian armed groups such as the PFLP, which hijacked international airliners and flew them to Jordan in 1970, or Black September's notorious massacre of the Israeli team at the Munich Olympics in 1972. Neither does Hamas publicly sanction attacks on third party nations inside Palestine.

Western governments such as the US, the UK and other European Union states have proscribed Hamas as a terrorist organization. Although Hamas rejects the label 'terrorist', it concedes that a central part of its military strategy is to create fear. 'Hamas wanted to make [the Israelis] fear every Arab who passed in front of their eyes, to make them fear us as much as we fear them', said Mohammed, a veteran Qassam Brigades fighter in Gaza.[11] Whether resistance or terrorism, the impact of Hamas's armed attacks on Israeli targets is an important part of how the rest of the world perceives it. While Hamas leaders claim the legitimacy of its violence as part of resistance against a foreign occupier, the rest of the world views it in a variety of often contradictory ways and draws its own conclusions. In this respect Hamas's words matter far less than the images of destruction, portrayed in an ever expanding propaganda war between the organization and its Israeli enemy.

Early days

The origins of the Izz ad-Din al-Qassam Brigades were in the 1980s, before the outbreak of the First Palestinian Intifada, when Sheikh Yassin was laying foundations for the Islamic movement. Yassin argued that a greater jihad would lead the Palestinians to freedom, but in the early days the priority and the most immediate task at hand was that of Islamizing Palestinian society. In many respects the early Islamists who joined Sheikh Yassin in his endeavours viewed their work as a form of jihad that would set the foundations for what would later be an armed conflict against Israel and Palestinian nationalist-secular opponents.

In 1984 Yassin founded an embryonic military group known as *al-Mujahidoun al-Filistinioun* (the Palestinian Fighters) to launch attacks on Israeli targets. As a fledgling group it had few weapons. Abu Khalil, a veteran Gaza militant, said the group was 'personally supervised' by Yassin and his close aides Salah Shehadeh and Ibrahim al-Maqadmeh, and that its first recruits made clumsy efforts to obtain guns through the Israeli black market. 'They managed to collect some weapons. But because the eyes of Shin Bet were so open to our activities at this time the Israeli authorities arrested everybody involved, including Sheikh Yassin. There were twenty-three of us and the Israelis caught seven', he said during a meeting at a prearranged hiding place in Gaza City in 2007. Abu Khalil said they tried to obtain weapons from Israeli criminal networks and Bedouin smugglers in Beersheva – 'pistols, M16s, whatever. Each M16 cost us $10,000. They were very expensive then.'[12] His colleague, Mohammed, also recalled the amateurishness of the early days, paying middlemen for weapons that either did not work or had been sabotaged by the Israelis. 'We only had one bazooka and we bought it for $24,000 from a Bedouin officer in the border police', he said. 'We didn't know how to use it or even how to inspect it, and it was broken.'[13]

Much of the early weaponry was employed not against Israeli targets but against internal targets: on nationalist and leftist Palestinians in Gaza. These attempts to acquire weapons led to Sheikh Yassin's arrest on various charges, including membership of a Muslim fundamentalist organization, promoting jihad to destroy Israel, possession of sixty rifles and receiving 12,000 Jordanian dinars (about US$30,000) from a Jordanian member of parliament to purchase weapons in Israel. In April 1984 Yassin was sentenced to thirteen years in prison, and he and five others were jailed by an Israeli military court. Qassam Brigades veterans concede that his arrest was a 'severe blow' to the movement.[14]

Turning point

Sheikh Yassin, however, was released just eleven months later in a prisoner exchange deal between Israel and Ahmed Jibril's Popular Front for the Liberation of Palestine – General Command. After his release he went straight back to work, in 1985 setting up a new armed organization called *al-Majd* (Glory) – an acronym for *Munazamat al-Jihad wa al-Da'wa* (the Organization of Holy War and Preaching). Headed by Yihyeh Sinwar and Rawhi Mushtaha, the first cell started operations in 1986 and 1987, leading up to the outbreak of the First Intifada in December 1987. Veterans say *al-Majd* was more of an intelligence and security apparatus than a military wing, devoted mainly to collecting information about collaborators and fighting corruption, principally in Gaza. According to Mohammed:

> In 1987 there were individual cells doing individual work and taking action on their own. One of these groups found some weapons left over from the Egyptians in a village close to Gaza. There were six Carl Gustav machine guns. They killed collaborators and one Shin Bet officer, but this was freelancing. The *Ikhwan* did not count this as a proper attempt to form a military wing because they considered the guys doing it to be too impatient. Hamas and the *Ikhwan* always lay down a structure first before they do anything.[15]

Al-Majd was distinct from *al-Mujahidoun al-Filistinioun*, which continued its activities throughout 1987 to 1989, by which time Hamas had been formally established. Like the PLO, Yassin and his fellow Islamists were not prepared for the spontaneous outbreak of the First Palestinian Intifada in December 1987. This marked a turning point. The outbreak of anti-Israel violence on the streets gave the Islamists of Hamas a chance to put into practice what they had been preaching from the pulpits for years.

Initially Hamas units were not deployed against Israeli military targets, instead spending much of the first year of the Intifada training and acquiring strategic and military knowledge of Gaza and the West Bank. Meanwhile senior Hamas officials in Jordan undertook fund-raising tours of the Gulf Arab states to raise millions of dollars. Then, on 16 February 1989, in an operation that had far-reaching consequences for both Israel and Hamas, a Hamas cell kidnapped and killed 21-year-old Sergeant Avi Sasportas, an Israeli paratrooper, while he was hitch-hiking near Gaza. The Israeli authorities immediately suspected the Palestinians. The trail quickly led to Sheikh Yassin, who was arrested, along with hundreds of other Hamas activists. Yassin, then aged fifty-four, went on trial in an Israeli military court in January 1990 accused of fifteen offences, including organizing attacks on civilians and causing the deaths of two soldiers. Although Yassin denied all the charges, his lawyer, Abdul Malik Bahanshe, admitted that Yassin had founded Hamas and had helped transfer funds to build the organization. 'My client says it is not just his right but his obligation to establish this organization to battle the occupation', Mr Bahanshe told the court. 'He is not sorry for what he did.'[16] Yassin was found guilty and sentenced to two life terms in prison. But pressure was growing from within the movement to hasten the jihad against Israel. The result was the formation of a new military wing.

Izz ad-Din al-Qassam Brigades

The creation of the Qassam Brigades came about because Hamas activists wanted to restart their armed activities under a new organization to avoid being compromised by those already under arrest and in jail alongside Yassin. Veterans said the first Qassam cell was set up in 1990 in Rafah, and its first fatality – in Israel's terms a 'terrorist', in Hamas's a 'martyr' – was Mohammed Abu Naqira. 'For security reasons we changed the name so people would not connect us with the old cases', said Abu Khalil. 'After Sheikh Yassin was arrested we started to form groups, all in the Gaza Strip, but we lacked weapons. The Rafah group was the only one which managed to get their hands on guns because they were closer to the Egyptian border. They mainly targeted collaborators.' The other Hamas armed cells were devoted to intelligence, gathering arms, 'collecting information about collaborators and Israeli intelligence and getting ready in case we managed to obtain weapons. But we didn't.'[17]

In 1991 the entire military structure was overhauled and formally given its new name: the Izz ad-Din al-Qassam Brigades. Its first leader was Sheikh Salah Shehadeh, an Egyptian-educated former Muslim Brotherhood activist from Beit Hanoun in northern Gaza, whose family were refugees from Jaffa. Shehadeh studied at the Higher Institute for Social Service in Alexandria, where he showed early Islamist inclinations and earned a brown belt in Japanese wrestling. In his late thirties he was already behind Israeli bars, and was no stranger to Israeli prisons. Detained with Sheikh Yassin in 1984, he had been released with the cleric in the 1985 PFLP–GC prisoner swap before being arrested again in a crackdown in 1988. Israeli intelligence claims that in 1989 Shehadeh 'admitted during questioning by the ISA [Shin Bet] to the establishment of a terrorist element within Hamas'.[18] He was chosen as the leader of the Qassam, according to Abu Khalil, because he was well educated, had 'great charisma' and was 'a military man to the core'. Abu Khalil's colleague Mohammed concurs: 'He was the type of person who is your father, your uncle or your brother. He was well loved by everyone, which helped him to recruit and operate. Also his degree was in social studies so he knew about people. He knew how to find them and how to recruit them.' Shehadeh's followers also saw humility in their leader. 'He knew when he made a mistake and was prepared to admit it and correct it, so he was always raising the level of performance.'[19]

The name Izz ad-Din al-Qassam Brigades is thought to have been the idea of one of Shehadeh's senior lieutenants, Mohammed Deif, an early member in southern Gaza who wanted to honour the cleric who had stood up against the British and Zionist settlers in Palestine in the 1930s. The organization's official website refers to the him as a 'pioneer mujahid' and says the Brigades 'considers its effort as part of the resistance movement against the Zionist occupation of Palestinian lands, which has been ongoing since the British occupation . . . and restoring the rights of the Palestinian people under the sacred Islamic teachings.'[20]

Other significant early figures included Yahya Ayyash, from the village of Rafat, near Nablus in the West Bank. Ayyash held a degree in electrical engineering from Bir Zeit University, and his skill in fashioning bombs from the limited materials available in the Palestinian Territories earned him the soubriquet 'the Engineer'. He was credited with assembling the first bombs that Hamas used on its suicide attacks against Israel between 1994 and 1996, and his success in eluding capture by Israel turned him into a hero for many young Palestinians. He was idolized by some children with the same fervour that Western youngsters revere sports stars such as David Beckham or pop singers such as Britney Spears.

One Hamas military wing veteran, Abu Khalil, said that once the explosives were serviceable Qassam cell members developed a code word to deceive Israel's telephone and radio surveillance teams while discussing how, where and when the completed materials were to be delivered. 'I don't know what the explosives were made of, but we gave them a nickname: Umm al-Abed [Abed's Mother]', he said. 'We would call each other and say "Umm al-Abed is coming to you, she's going here, she is going there".'[21]

Perhaps inevitably, Ayyash the master bomber was himself killed by an Israeli bomb, on 5 January 1996 in Beit Lahiya, northern Gaza. The device was hidden inside a booby-trapped mobile telephone supplied by Israeli intelligence agents to a Palestinian collaborator. His funeral was the largest that Gaza has ever seen, with hundreds of thousands pouring onto the streets. The mass outpouring of emotion far outnumbered even the turnouts for Sheikh Yassin and Dr Abdel Aziz Rantissi a decade later.

Some Qassam cells acted exclusively against suspected collaborators. Hamas has long deemed collaboration to be a heretical act at a time when the Palestinians were resisting the Israeli occupation. This, of course, is a highly controversial issue, but one that Hamas leaders parry by comparing their own position to that of the French Resistance against Nazi collaborators during the Second World War. Hamas's campaign against the collaborators was taken very seriously. 'Since our enemies are trying with all their might to obliterate our nation', stated one Qassam Brigades leader, '[so] cooperation with them is clearly a terrible crime.'[22]

In 1992 the targeting of collaborators rose steeply, with more than 150 killed by Hamas. Leaflets and sermons declared the offences for which supposed offenders would be brought to justice, among them 'supporting peace with the enemy', 'doing business with the enemy', and seeking to 'poison our society with their filth and vices and drug and alcohol taking, lust parties and outings'.[23] Hamas activists alleged that Israeli agents used hairdressing salons to supply young Palestinian women with alcohol and then filmed them in compromising positions to blackmail them into cooperating with Israel. Israeli agents were said to be luring hundreds of young Palestinian men into drug-taking and trafficking, with the same intention. Hamas leaders identified five categories of collaborator: ideological, political, economic, moral and security agents recruited by Israel to gather intelligence and assist in operations against Hamas.

Some Palestinians remember the fear of the Hamas 'vice squads'. 'I remember during the First Intifada when Hamas used to kill people and throw their bodies on the rubbish dump. They would say "this is a drug trafficker or collaborator" or something', said Dr Eyad Sarraj.

> Of course they were killing all these people under torture. To my knowledge Hamas killed more people than the Israelis during the First Intifada, at least in Gaza. To the extent that I was sitting once with Haider Abdel Shafi in his house and there was a knock on the door and it was a masked Palestinian militia. I was hoping it would be an Israeli soldier because you can deal with an Israeli soldier. And that was the wish of so many Palestinians at that time. We were too scared to open the door at night just in case it would be Palestinian militia, who would not have the time for discussion or argument, they would just shoot you and kill you. That state of fear and anxiety made the people immediately accept the Oslo agreement and the fact that Arafat and the PLO were coming, saying 'This is our rescue'.[24]

Hamas rejected calls from Palestinian nationalist leaders in the summer of 1992 to halt the collaborator killings and continued to defend their actions, even though there were many innocent casualties. As Sheikh Yassin declared from jail the following year:

> Collaboration can be defined as a contagious disease, like cancer or gangrene. We excise the affected member in order to prevent the disease from spreading to the body's healthy members. The collaborator declares a state of war between himself and his society, and passes on to the society's enemies information about his people and the reality in which they live. He recruits other people to help him in negative and unacceptable ways, and it is absolutely and utterly forbidden to remain silent about this or to ignore it.[25]

But it was reports of Hamas attacks on elements that it considered to be anti-social that caused most internal Palestinian concern. Young men and women were dragged before self-proclaimed Hamas 'courts' with masked judges, where they were accused and summarily sentenced.

Spreading web of violence

Once the Hamas military wing became established in Gaza its members began travelling to the West Bank to activate cells, particularly among the ranks of Gaza students attending university there. The founder of the Qassam Brigades in the West Bank was Sheikh Saleh al-Arouri, from a tiny village near Ramallah. Captured by Israel in October 1992, Arouri was jailed for fifteen years, accused of being the head of the military wing in the West Bank.

Even after his release from prison in March 2007, Arouri was guarded about his exact role within the Brigades. However, other Qassam members today describe him as the 'founder' in the West Bank. Arouri is an intense, inscrutable man with an expressionless face whose every phrase nevertheless betrays the precise vocabulary and cadences of the committed Islamist ideologue. Serving fizzy orange drinks in his remote West Bank village a decade and a half after the events, he maintained that the Israeli authorities were unable to 'prove anything' when they originally held him in administrative detention, and that he was accused of being the military head only after other Hamas detainees identified him during interrogation. After that, he said, he was subjected to extreme interrogation for seven months, including beatings, sleep deprivation, starvation and being chained to a wall and left out in the snow. Asked if he ever found out which of his colleagues named him, he shrugged slightly, replying: 'Naturally, I know. They were my friends.' Arouri insisted that he did not 'scorn or revile them because I knew they were under heavy pressure during interrogation'. But he allowed the façade to slip for just a few seconds, betraying a hint of bitterness. 'The pressure upon others was the same as on me, but no more. And there were many who did not break.'[26]

The Qassam network in the West Bank expanded and became, according to Arouri, an important 'link in the chain' of the wider Hamas movement by providing the means by which supporters could graduate from protest to military activities. 'It is a natural progression for people under occupation to take up to a method of resisting as civil resistance, and then gradually move into operational resistance.'[27]

Arouri said that one of the first Qassam cells in the southern West Bank was set up in 1990 by Sheikh Mohammed Abu Teir, the Jerusalemite Hamas veteran whose henna-dyed orange beard makes him one of the most distinctive public faces of the movement, both to Palestinians and to Israelis. Arouri said that Abu Teir's cell recruited people from Hebron, Ramallah and Jerusalem, but conceded that 'most of them were arrested' during one of the many Israeli crackdowns that inflicted setbacks on the Islamists' early military apparatus in the West Bank. Even when imprisoned, Arouri confirmed, Qassam activists remain closely involved with the movement outside – although he was careful only to admit to their 'moral and political influence'. Such contacts, he said, were maintained through smuggled mobile phones and regular visits with family and lawyers. 'The prisoners, whoever they belong to, are respected and highly regarded, even idolized by their own communities because of the respect that they have gained.'[28]

Such is the respect accorded to former prisoners that Abu Teir, who has spent more than twenty-five years behind Israeli bars, was placed second in Hamas's electoral list during the 2006 parliamentary elections, behind only Ismail Haniyeh. That Abu Teir has spent half a lifetime in jail is immediately apparent from his home, which lies down the narrowest of hillside roads in the East Jerusalem suburb of Umm Tuba. It is bedecked with prison art, including prisoners' models of the Dome of the Rock in bright pink, yellow and turquoise beads, and a bright green sailing ship adorned with Islamist slogans and the name Hamas.

Like so many Islamists, Abu Teir began his adult life in Fatah, working for Yasser Arafat in the movement's central security department in Jordan, Syria and Lebanon. He even served his first spell in an Israeli jail as a Fatah activist, after being arrested in 1974 for membership of the then banned organization. He gradually grew more disaffected and turned to religion, acquiring a degree in Islamic law and leaving Fatah in 1976, then going on to denounce his former colleagues for corruption and failing to serve the Palestinian people. He first established a cell of *Jamaa Islamiyya*, with which he remained until in 1985 he met Sheikh Yassin in Ashkelon jail, where he was recruited and states that 'I pledged my allegiance to his group.'[29] Abu Teir was in and out of Israeli jails in the 1980s and 1990s and was rearrested in 1998 for Hamas military activities after an intelligence operation which the Israeli media claimed had 'broken the Hamas military infrastructure in the West Bank'.[30]

The most senior Hamas figure assassinated in that high-profile operation was Adel Awadallah, who was killed with his brother Imad on 10 September 1998 at a house near Hebron. During the operation the Israelis recovered material which, according to Israeli newspaper reports, indicated that Awadallah was the commander of the military wing in the West Bank at the time. He was, according to the Israelis, the prime mover behind a wave of car bomb attacks between 1994 and 1998, having assembled bomb laboratories across the West Bank and liaised with the Hamas leadership in Jordan and inside Israeli jails. He had also, according to the Israeli reports, drawn up plans to kidnap prominent Israeli politicians – including the then mayor of Jerusalem and future prime minister,

Ehud Olmert – and to assassinate senior Israeli military officers. Evidence found in the raid led the Israelis to arrest Abu Teir for – among other things – trying to acquire rocket-propelled grenade launchers for Hamas, and being involved with a military cell of East Jerusalemites who had carried out car bombings in Tel Aviv and Jerusalem and tried to recover mines from an old minefield near Bethlehem to use the explosives for bombs.

The Israeli media claimed that during interrogation Abu Teir confessed his involvement in the kidnap plot, telling them 'I am a commander in the military [wing of] Hamas.'[31] However, during one of his brief spells at liberty Abu Teir, while confirming that his 1998 arrest resulted from the operation against Awadallah, insisted that the accusations against him were baseless. 'This was the excuse', he said. 'I say it very honestly that the last one didn't even deserve a year in prison because I had no military activities of the sort.' Abu Teir's lengthy spells of incarceration certainly appear not to have dented his commitment to the cause. 'I have experienced twenty-five years in jail because of my steadfastness to my beliefs and principles', he said. 'As I told Israeli Intelligence, I believe in fighting them until the Day of Judgment.'[32] In the 2006 elections Abu Teir won his seat in the Palestinian parliament. But months later the Israeli authorities arrested him and put him in jail again.

As the Qassam grew in size and sophistication in the early 1990s, it acquired cult-like status among Hamas supporters. From mosque pulpits and classrooms and at public rallies Hamas activists glorified the Qassam as defenders of the Palestinian people against Israeli repression, using every tool of public rhetoric and every media outlet to create a public base to rival the mainstream PLO. During the early 1990s, as peace negotiations gathered momentum from Madrid to Oslo, the Qassam accelerated its activities to undermine the peace process, carrying out attacks on Jewish settlements and shooting soldiers, settlers and civilians.

Suicide bombs

Although in 1993 a Qassam operative drove a truck at an Israeli target and died in the process,[33] Qassam veterans say suicide attacks at that point were 'not yet the policy of the movement'. According to Abu Khalil, they acknowledged that

> there were a few attempts in Gaza, but none of the attacks was successful, through lack of experience, failure to get close enough and not knowing how to make explosives. These failed attempts planted the seed of the idea, and from 1994 there was an official attempt to institute this policy. It was a decision made by the external leadership – then in Jordan – and was declared publicly.[34]

The real 'turning point' came the next year, in 1994, with Baruch Goldstein's attack on the Ibrahimi mosque in Hebron. The Qassam Brigades' response was the first suicide bomb attack, in the Israeli town of Afula, carried out by nineteen-year-old Raed Zakarneh, who killed eight Israelis and wounded thirty-four. In the weeks, months and years that followed – and until the order from Hamas's political leadership to shift away from the tactic of suicide bombing – this became the Qassam Brigades' modus operandi. They had discovered that with the suicide bomber they could strike at Israel 'throughout the length and breadth of Occupied Palestine'.[35] Israel's point of vulnerability had been discovered. In October 1994 Hamas carried out by far the largest suicide bombing yet, killing twenty-two people in an explosion on the no. 5 bus on Tel Aviv's Dizengoff Street.

The impact on Israel was seismic. Hamas bombers now had the potential to be in every street, café, shopping mall and bus. From Hamas's perspective its new tactic had succeeded, creating what Mushir al-Masri, a Hamas leader in Gaza, later called a 'strategic balance of terror'.[36] Other Hamas activists are less grandiose. 'Not a balance of terror', demurred one veteran Qassam fighter. 'We are trying to achieve some kind of balance, but they can destroy all of Gaza. We can only harm them. We are just sending a message to tell them: we can act against you. We can harm your children as you are doing ours. When our children can't go to school, your children will not go to school.'[37]

The suicide bombers compelled Israel to rethink its strategy – political, military, intelligence, economic, strategic – towards the Palestinians, and Hamas in particular. Hamas's actions also provoked controversy among senior Islamic scholars, with some objecting to the bomb attacks as counter to Islam and others, including Palestinian clerics, sanctioning them as permissible in defence of a land considered sacred to Islam and under foreign occupation. Sheikh Hamid Beitawi, a senior Muslim cleric from the West Bank city of Nablus – a major influence on Hamas – outlined his thinking on such operations as he entertained visitors in the salon of his home while robed in a dressing gown and prayer cap. He pontificated on the iniquities of Israel's long-standing occupation of Palestinian lands and then claimed that Hamas's attacks were legitimate, offering the argument that 'an occupied Muslim land must be legitimately defended by Muslims who adhere to the obligation of jihad'.[38]

The recruits

One of the reasons Palestinian militants have long flourished in Gaza is the unique characteristics of the 140 square mile coastal strip which is home to more than 1.5 million people. Gaza has always been the stronghold for Hamas because of its geography and religious and social

Photos 7.2   Hamas gunman at a rally in Gaza City, December 2006

conservativism. It is also one of the most densely populated areas on the globe. When Gaza's children stream for their schools at the end of a day of learning, it is as if buffalo are stampeding through the dust-filled streets. Beneath the miasma of dust and the cacophony of infant chatter are the hundreds of thousands of children who form the core of a Hamas generation. Indeed the average age of a Gazan inhabitant is seventeen, and nearly 50 per cent of the population is under the age of fourteen. Hamas has made a speciality of making these young people feel empowered. Unemployment rates for the male-dominated working population have risen steadily since the First Intifada. Today few opportunities exist for unskilled or semi-skilled men, who have subsequently joined the ever increasingly network of Hamas's armed ranks. The population density of Gaza prompted one senior Israeli intelligence officer after the 2006 Israel–Lebanon conflict to contrast the Islamist threat that it faces on its northern and southern frontiers. 'There is a difference between Hezbollah and Hamas. Hezbollah used the geography of south Lebanon very professionally, but in Gaza it is not topography, it is demography.'[39]

But since Israel withdrew its forces from Gaza in 2005, the coastal strip has also presented a far easier operating environment for Hamas's armed fighters, who do not have to face the scores of Israeli military bases and settlements which curtail their movements in the West Bank. 'Gaza's situation is different from ours', said the Jerusalemite Mohammed Abu Teir. 'Gaza is open to the sea to Egypt. Even when under occupation the armaments flowing into Gaza through tunnels and the sea were massive. Here it is very different. We don't have the same facilities.'[40] The result is that, in Gaza City, Khan Younis, Rafah or Jabalia refugee camp, fighters could hide within crowds or slip through narrow alleyways to hide from Israeli helicopters and spy drones overhead. They are not always successful, and Israel has assassinated many senior Hamas operatives. The most notorious of these killings came on the night of 22 July 2002, when an Israeli jet dropped a 1 tonne bomb on a house in a crowded area of Gaza City, killing Salah Shehadeh, the founder of the Izz ad-Din al-Qassam Brigades.

Beneath the rubble lay more than a dozen other dead Palestinians, including women and children. Among the first on the scene was Knel Deeb, twenty-seven, a Dubliner who was visiting his Palestinian cousins in a nearby building. He ran to the scene, where he saw

> pieces of flesh everywhere, one man running away holding a lump of flesh on a metal tray and another pulling out a baby boy with half his face blown away, obviously dead. Everyone was screaming, shouting, crying and shouting 'Revenge to the Israel child-killers'. The situation was extraordinary. I have never seen anything like it. I just kept thinking: if the British army wanted to take out Gerry Adams, would they use a bomb that size in a residential area like this?[41]

As thousands marched to the mosque for the funeral the next day, one Hamas official shouted through a loudspeaker: 'Who is your army?' 'Qassam', came the reply, followed by 'Revenge, revenge'. Nevertheless, the attack was a serious blow to the military wing of Hamas.

Initially Ariel Sharon, the Israeli prime minister, launched a robust defence of the attack, calling it 'one of our major successes'. But the line quickly changed as ministers registered the scale of international outrage at the pictures emerging from Gaza of the flag-draped bodies of the children killed and the injuries to 145 bystanders. Shimon Peres, the foreign minister, conceded that mistakes had been made. 'What happened is regrettable. It wasn't done intentionally. I think all of us feel sorry for the loss of life of innocent people, particularly children.'[42] Ultimately, Israel's courts ruled that such attacks were legitimate. However, in January 2009 a Spanish investigating magistrate, Judge Fernando Andreu, opened preliminary investigations into whether Israel's then defence minister and senior military officials could be prosecuted for crimes against humanity in a case brought to the court by the Gaza-based Palestinian Centre for Human Rights.[43]

Shehadeh was a well-known hawk opposed to any deals with Israel and blamed by Israeli security officials for dozens of suicide bombings. Yet the timing of the Israeli strike dismayed Palestinian leaders and European intelligence officials, who believed they were on the verge of getting Hamas to halt the violence. Just a few hours before the bomb, Mohammed Dahlan, Arafat's former security chief, was in Gaza holding discussions with Hamas, and indicated that he had secured their acceptance of the principles of a ceasefire announcement. Some suspected Israel of trying to spike any rapprochement with Hamas. However, Gideon Meir, an Israeli Foreign Ministry spokesman, insisted the strike was dictated by intelligence reports on Shehadeh's whereabouts at that precise time. 'The timing is nothing to do with politics. The decision to target this man was taken six months ago.' He also dismissed talk of Hamas signing a deal. 'Hamas is dedicated to the elimination of the state of Israel. There is no ceasefire, there was no ceasefire.'[44]

The man who took over from Shehadeh as head of the Qassam Brigades was Mohammed Deif, who spent thirteen years in jail, from 1982 to 1995, and has been Israel's most wanted man for more than a decade. Deif, wary of the more public profile of his assassinated predecessors, is a secretive figure who is rarely seen or interviewed by the media. His face is usually obscured behind a red *keffiyeh*. Deif has narrowly escaped various Israeli assassination attempts, but the injuries sustained in them have not put paid to his active role in leadership.

Ahmed Jaabari, who ran the Qassam Brigades on a day-to-day basis after Deif was badly injured in an Israeli missile strike and escaped to Egypt for medical attention, told an Al Jazeera television that his movement's aim was 'liberating the whole of Palestine'. Jaabari portrayed his quest as one of jihad. Israel holds him responsible for the Hamas 'build-up' policy from 2006 onwards, and he is believed to hold more radical and extremist views than the political leadership. Indeed, when interviewed on this subject by the television crew, he appeared dismissive of those within the movement who sought political office. 'I am a fighter for God. You will find me anywhere, anyplace, fighting the enemies of Islam. I will be honoured to represent Mohammed Deif on the battlefield. We don't seek positions in the government or leadership; our aim is to fight the enemies of Islam.'[45] By December 2008 it was estimated that Jaabari commanded some 20,000 fighters in the Qassam Brigades in Gaza and presided over a Hamas 'war cabinet' alongside other military hardliners such as the former interior minister Said Siam, Imad Akel and Ali Jundiyeh. An Israeli government analyst assessed both Deif and Jaabari as 'very important' within the movement, saying: 'They play a significant role in terror attacks and improving the military abilities of Hamas.'[46]

But rumours of serious internal rivalries between the political and military leadership – and within the military leadership itself – have also surfaced, centring on personality clashes as well as tensions over the best means by which to translate ideology into action. The principal tension is between those wedded to the armed struggle – what American counter-insurgency theorists in Iraq call the 'irreconcilables' – and those advocating a Sinn Fein-style transition to democratic means.

Intermittent talk of a ceasefire was linked to discussions about security, Israel, relations between Hamas and the PLO, reform of the PLO, elections and the future of the peace process. By the spring of 2003 Ismail Abu Shanab, one of the less hawkish of Hamas's political leaders, had come up with the conditions for a ceasefire that would see the Qassam bring an unprecedented halt to its operations and suicide bomb attacks against Israel. The Hamas leadership, including Sheikh Yassin, indicated that they would consider halting their attacks if Israel fulfilled three conditions: halt its operations against the Palestinians, free Palestinian prisoners and withdraw its troops from the Gaza Strip and West Bank.

Some in Hamas believed that Israel would reciprocate. Hardliners, however, believed that by compromising its principles Hamas would lose ground to Fatah and others who supported a two-state solution. Among these was Rantissi, who refused to countenance a ceasefire and insisted that the relationship with Israel had to be seen through the prism of conflict. 'Israel is the occupying force, and it is our right to wage a resistance against them. This is an inalienable right that others have enjoyed without complaint. Israel wages war on us, they want us gone [from this land], and we will fight them till the end.'[47]

Sayed Salem Abu Musameh, a white-bearded Hamas veteran from the southern Gaza Strip, says there are 'two main schools in the Islamic movement – hardliners and pragmatists'. Abu Musameh, who was one of the first four founding members of the Muslim Brotherhood in Rafah and

Photo 7.4   Hamas military wing members in Gaza, July 2005

Khan Younis, briefly led Hamas in Gaza when Sheikh Yassin was jailed in 1989. Now an elder figure, he later studied the strategy and thought of Islamic movements, and concedes that there are internal tensions inside Hamas. 'Haniyeh is from the pragmatic school, but there is great pressure on him from the hardliners',[48] he said in 2006, during one tussle between the two wings of the movement. The hardliners were widely believed to include Dr Mahmoud Zahar, Mohammed Deif and Meshaal and, before they died, Salah Shehadeh, Said Siam and Dr Abdel Aziz Rantissi.

However, the divisions within the military wing itself were to intensify after Hamas's military takeover of Gaza in June 2007. A few months later, in November of that year, when Mohammed Deif, the military leader, was smuggled back into Gaza through tunnels from Egypt, he encountered a challenge from Jaabari and his political patrons in the radical wing of Hamas, including Sheikh Nizar Rayan and Ali Jundiyeh. Rayan by this point was considered to be the strategic head of the Qassam Brigades, and the inspiration behind the takeover in June. He had a reputation as one of the most radical leaders, and his views, as shared from the pulpit in meetings and speeches to Hamas cadres, emphasized how dangerous any form of recognition of Israel would be to the movement's Islamist credentials. He often described the secular-nationalist government of the Palestinian Authority in Ramallah as *kufr* (infidel) and thus itself to be regarded as a legitimate target. Rayan, like Sheikh Izz ad-Din al-Qassam seventy years earlier, not only preached jihad from the pulpit but played an active role in planning armed activities. He was allegedly responsible for weapons production and procurement in Gaza.

Rayan and Jaabari represented a more radical, *salafi* or fundamentalist wing in the Brigades compared with the more 'pragmatic' Deif. To outsiders such distinctions might be academic, but it had wider significance in terms of the developing direction of the military wing of Hamas, its relationship to the political leadership, and the strategic direction of the conflict with Israel and Hamas's wider position as a Sunni Islamist organization in the Middle East.

In recent times some Hamas leaders have made a virtue out of their differences with other radical Islamist groups such as al-Qaeda, warning the West that to marginalize Hamas could provoke a radicalization in the Palestinian ranks and produce organizations far more dangerous than Hamas. Jamal Abu Hashem, a veteran Hamas 'pragmatist' and minister in the government of 2006–7, outlined such a prospect when referring to the West's continuing refusal to recognise Hamas in an elected unity government. 'Even if we were the majority in such a government', he warned, 'when compared to other religious elements such as al-Qaeda and the *salafis* we are a moderate movement.'[49]

By 2008, after Deif's return to Gaza, it became apparent that most of the senior leadership of the Qassam Brigades had embarked on a much more radical and *salafi* Islamic fundamentalist orientation than either he or many in the senior ranks of the political leadership desired. In private he reportedly bemoaned the radicalization, and warned that such tendencies could lead to developing links to al-Qaeda.

Internal tensions grew later that year, when the political leadership announced a *tahdiyah* (temporary truce) with Israel and ordered the military leadership to stand their men down. The *salafi* elements were furious, and in an attempt to undermine confidence in the ceasefire used their website to publish a list of attacks against Israel for which they had never previously taken responsibility. The power struggle came to the forefront. Deif complained to friends that he no longer wielded any real influence in the Qassam Brigades, and that 'the *salafis* had taken over'. In 2006 it was estimated that there had been only a small hard-core group of 200 *salafis* in the Qassam Brigades. This group had also made the first contacts with Moqdad Omar, an al-Qaeda leader. By 2009 the *salafi* group seemed to predominate. There were reports of internal incidents within the Qassam Brigades, and Fatah operatives also sought to envenom relations by waging attacks on the *salafis* in the hope that the traditionalists would be blamed.

The shift of power in Hamas towards the military wing and away from the political leadership allowed the *salafi* elements to challenge the political leaders directly on a number of occasions. The political leadership consequently had to harden its stance with the Brigades. The press reported on the strains within the Brigades, but Hamas leaders furiously denied the charges.

Bombs to rockets

The military wing was at the forefront of the Islamists' drive in Gaza towards the era of Hamas control. Although the world's attention was seized only when Hamas won the elections in January 2006, the foundations were laid the previous summer in the build-up to August 2005, when Ariel Sharon abruptly pulled Israel's troops and 8,000-plus Jewish settlers from the Gaza Strip.

Gaza overnight became a different world. Before 2005, movement around the Strip was controlled by Israeli checkpoints and watchtowers, but now Hamas, Islamic Jihad, Fatah, the Popular Front for the Liberation of Palestine and the Popular Resistance Committees suddenly had much more freedom. They could travel at will from one end of Gaza to the other in minutes instead of days.

Hamas lost no time in presenting the Israeli pullout as a victory for its armed campaign. The full Hamas propaganda machine went into overdrive. Huge rallies were organized where Hamas speakers claimed credit for leading the 'resistance' effort. Giant green banners appeared overnight in Gaza City proclaiming – in English for the benefit of the foreign media – 'Jerusalem and West Bank after Gaza – Hamas' and 'We Will Continue after Gaza – Hamas'. The media campaign was spearheaded by the Qassam Brigades' own dedicated media office. Faxes and emails bore the official crest 'Information Office – Izz ad-Din al-Qassam Brigades, Military Wing of Hamas Movement'. At press conferences on street corners or in orchards – to hide from Israeli aircraft – masked Qassam press officers spun the Hamas line in idiomatic English while wearing khaki jackets bearing the Qassam crest and words 'Information Office'.

As would-be suicide bombers and gunmen found it increasingly hard to reach Israeli towns from the West Bank because of Israel's separation barrier, Hamas and other factions increasingly turned to other means to attack Israelis. While its military wing continued to mount surprise 'spectacular' attacks, such as the kidnapping of the Israeli soldier Gilad Schalit during a tunnel raid on an Israeli border post on 25 June 2006, its principal weapon increasingly became the crude but potentially deadly Qassam rocket, which it and other factions manufactured in secret workshops across the Gaza Strip.

All Palestinian militant factions had used rockets before Israel's withdrawal from Gaza. Indeed, the settlements in Gaza were regular targets for mortar and rocket attacks, some of which proved fatal. But it became far easier for the militants to launch rockets after the Israelis withdrew because Israeli tanks and border guards were no longer in control of the narrow Philadelphi corridor which separated Gaza and Egypt. This made it simpler for Palestinian factions to smuggle in weapons from Egypt, using tunnels bored through the loose sandy soil underneath the border by criminal clans with decades of experience transporting weapons, drugs, cigarettes, alcohol and people. By 2010 Hamas enjoyed control over hundreds of these tunnels, using them to bypass Israel's policy of sealing off Gaza.

Though their attacks were rarely fatal, the sheer numbers of Qassams turned survival into a lottery in Israeli border towns such as Sderot, where the falling shrapnel killed, wounded and caused damage to buildings, vehicles and property. They were also unpredictable, setting off early warning sirens at all hours of the day and night and terrifying Israeli residents. Following its takeover of Gaza in 2006, Hamas was held responsible by Israel for all the rockets fired from an area under its control. By December 2008 Israel claimed that 10,000 rockets had been fired and responded with attacks on missile sites. But the rocket teams were usually long gone before the Israeli artillery could respond, and the property destruction and civilian deaths inflicted by the thousands of Israeli artillery shells fired into the crowded Gaza Strip drew condemnation from the international community about disproportionate use of force. Human rights groups also criticized Hamas for using weapons that indiscriminately targeted civilians. Indeed in 2009 the UN-ordered Goldstone Report into Israeli's military assault on Gaza also concluded that, in fact, the Hamas missiles launched indiscriminately at Israel constituted a war crime.

By 2008 the threat became graver as the Qassam Brigades had smuggled into Gaza longer-range Grad missiles capable of reaching Ashkelon and Beersheba. 'Yes, the Grads were a leap up. We don't have a military arsenal. Ours is tiny compared to them. But what we possess, these simple weapons, are effective against the Israelis',[50] boasted one Hamas rocketeer in northern Gaza, who gave the nom de guerre Abu Khaled. This prompted Israel to mount a large-scale attack on Jabalia refugee camp in northern Gaza in March 2008, in which sixty-one Palestinians were killed in one day – the bloodiest day since the 1980s. Explaining the scale of Israel's reaction, Tzipi Livni, Israel's foreign minister, said Hamas had begun to be more similar to a small army, and less a terrorist organization. 'Everybody needs to understand that Israeli citizens are being terrorized by rockets coming from Gaza Strip', she added, 'This is something that we cannot live with.'[51]

Assistance from abroad

In a rare admission – for a movement addicted to claiming credit for everything – Hamas officials confirm that the 2006 Hezbollah–Israeli war provided them with an insight into Israel's weakness against rocket attacks. For all the Jewish state's overpowering aerial superiority, its failure to halt Hezbollah's Katyusha missiles was noted. 'Many of the Arab regimes and international leaders were living under the illusion that the Israeli army was unbeatable', said Abu Bakr Nofal, a senior Hamas official in Gaza. 'This war has had a huge negative effect on the Israeli street, and it has sent a message that the occupation can never stand against the resistance if you have a really good resistance.'[52]

Israel claimed to have 'clear intelligence' about how many weapons Hamas had begun smuggling into the Gaza Strip through the Egyptian Sinai. However, in the aftermath of Hamas's election victory one senior Israeli intelligence official professed himself to be concerned more about the expertise Hamas was gleaning abroad than about the hardware it has smuggled. 'One of the bad fruits of the isolation of Hamas is the influence of Iran and its money', said Yuval Diskin, the director of Shin Bet:

> What we see that is more dangerous than any weapons is the training that Iran has promised Hamas. We know that Hamas has started to despatch people to Iran, tens with the promise of hundreds, for months and maybe years of training. I see this as the strategic challenge more than any smuggled weapons. You need expertise to use weapons, and in the long run the Iranian training is what is dangerous.[53]

While the Hamas leadership is reticent about its exact ties, on the ground in Gaza its fighters make no effort to deny that it receives help from Iran, pointing out that the ayatollahs are also – as Ariel Sharon noted several years earlier – sponsors of Hezbollah. 'As Hezbollah in Lebanon, as Hamas in Gaza', shrugged Abu Khaled, the Hamas rocket launcher in northern Gaza. 'To achieve our goal we are allowed to ask for help to obtain power from wherever we can, from whoever provides it . . . The only one that provides them is Tehran. If you go back to the First Intifada, some sons of Qassam used to buy the weapons from Israelis.'[54] Another Qassam Brigades leader admitted that he commanded men who had been trained in 'Iran . . . and Afghanistan, and Syria, Jordan and Egypt. We even have men who were trained by the FBI and then joined our ranks. It's not a question of special assistance from Iran. We'll use the experience of our men and training wherever they get it.'[55]

Nevertheless, Hamas is sensitive to the criticism that, by taking money and weapons from Iran, it is becoming a lackey of the clerical-led Shi'a regime in Tehran. Although Hamas officials are irritated by the accusation, they shrug with feigned unconcern, saying that, in the face of an Israeli and American-led boycott of Hamas-led Gaza, they will take help from anywhere so long as it comes without conditions that would compromise their principles.

Hamas's use of violence as a tool is deplored by Israelis and Palestinian moderates alike. Both argue – sometimes for very different reasons – that to try and scare Israel into giving the Palestinians a state is a fundamental misreading of Israeli society. 'The result was exactly the opposite. Their response was to surround Gaza and the West Bank with a wall', said Dr Eyad Sarraj, a Gaza psychiatrist and human rights activist. 'You made the Israelis, yes, frightened, but more determined to separate themselves, to live their own lives and make your life much more miserable, and kill you even before you think.'[56]

Avi Dichter, Israel's minister of public security and a former intelligence chief who claims, only half in jest, to have spent more years of his life in Gaza than Tel Aviv, argues that Palestinian advocates of violence utterly fail to comprehend the depth of Israelis' resilience. 'My parents lost their whole family during the Holocaust and they came to Israel. I don't have any intention to go anywhere, and believe me it's not going to happen. It is a question of time. What will happen first? Are we going to get tired or are they going to get tired? I can assure you, we are not going to get tired.'[57]

8

The Martyr Syndrome

There is no path except that of martyrdom – armed resistance and martyrdom operations. This is what will support Gaza. This is what will lift the oppression from you. We do not take up arms except in the face of the Zionist enemy. I call upon you to rise up. This is the time for the third Intifada.

Khaled Meshaal, Hamas leader[1]

It was 11 September 2001, and Jenin had only one hour left to revel in its status as the suicide attack capital of the globe. Nineteen hijackers who were at that very moment aboard airliners heading towards New York and Washington were about to change everything. But until then a small cluster of Hamas, Fatah and Islamic Jihad militants looking up nervously at the sky in a besieged Palestinian refugee camp were the most wanted suicide bombers in the world.

Since dawn Jenin refugee camp – a miserable, permanently half-finished concoction of dust, potholes and breezeblock homes and corner shops – had found itself surrounded by Israeli tanks and helicopter gunships. Israel had a list of the men that it suspected of masterminding suicide bombing – these men – and it wanted the Palestinian Authority to hand them over. The northernmost Palestinian town in the West Bank, just 6 miles from where Izz ad-Din al-Qassam was killed in a shoot-out with British forces sixty years earlier, Jenin had become a place of unknown terrors for Israel. It lay just on the other side of the Green Line which divided Israel proper from the West Bank.

Nearly a year into the Second Intifada that Green Line, although invisible on the ground, had at least served as a reassuring psychological construct for Israelis because it separated 'us' and 'them'. The West Bank was a place that could be sealed, checkpointed and – eventually – ringfenced off behind razor wire and concrete. But just two days before 9/11 Israelis had suffered an unexpected development: a suicide bomber not from 'over there', but from within their midst.

On 9 September 2001 an Israeli man blew himself up near the train station in the northern Israeli town of Nahariya, killing three of his fellow Israelis. The bomber belonged to Hamas, which was not unusual. But he was also an Israeli citizen, which was. Muhammad Shaker Ihbeishi, forty-eight, was the first suicide bomber to come not from the West Bank or Gaza, but from Israel's own Arab minority. Although Israel is often described as a Jewish state, it is more accurately a Jewish-majority one. One-fifth of its 7.4 million population – around 1.5 million people – are Palestinian Arabs. Ihbeishi was born in Israel, raised in Israel and lived in Israel. His Israeli Arab village of Abu Snaan was only 20 miles from Nazareth, the largest Arab city in Israel. In other words, he was both Israeli and Palestinian.

It was a frightening prospect for Israelis, who had long feared that the Palestinians living among them would become a fifth column during Israel's war with their cousins in the West Bank and Gaza. In fact Ihbeishi proved to be a one-off. But his attack had served its purpose for Hamas – to make Israelis worry about where the next bomb would come from. Hamas military planners said this was precisely their game plan, to create uncertainty among ordinary Israelis and avoid setting any pattern. 'To turn Arabs into a point of fear for Israelis, the most important thing was the variety of people who committed these suicide attacks', explained Mohammed, a bearded Izz ad-Din al-Qassam Brigades veteran in Gaza City in 2007.

> There were no veterans. First we started with university graduates. The Israelis used to say suicide bombers were a bunch of poor people, despairing of life, so at the beginning we used educated young university students. Sometimes it was an old man who had a family or a stable life. Sometimes it was women, although that wasn't the policy of Hamas at that time to use women. They came later. This had a very negative impact on the Israelis. They couldn't draw a profile of suicide bombers. It was anybody, in every category. It was absolutely deliberate that there should be no pattern. It was just honest, decent people who had a huge will to sacrifice for their own people. That was the only thing they had in common.[2]

In Jenin the besieged bomb-makers were delighted to see the Israeli consternation over the Nahariya bombing. But one Hamas fighter had a different perspective from his Gaza colleague. For him suicide bombings were a tactic born of desperate necessity, not a tool of psychological warfare. 'You have to understand nobody wants to die, there is no other way to achieve our goal. Suicide bombs are our Apache helicopters. They are all we have', he said.[3] One of his fellow wanted men, huddling close to a wall to avoid being spotted by Israeli spy drones, questioned what the Israelis had achieved by using F16s and Apaches. 'Now Israel cannot live in peace. There used to be immigration into Israel and now it is going the other way. Israeli factories are closing, they are suffering . . . We can bear these kind of conditions until 2005. Can they?'[4] It was a classic piece of bravado fusing two elements central to the Palestinian underdog narrative: redefining military weakness as moral superiority and survival as victory. These fighters gloried in their self-proclaimed capacity not only to inflict suffering on the enemy, but to be better at enduring it.

And about the ultimate goal, there was unanimity on the desired outcome. No matter what faction they belonged to, all said they now wanted the Hamas outcome for Palestine: control not just over the Palestinian territories occupied by Israel in 1967 but over Tel Aviv, Haifa, Nazareth and the rest of the land between the Mediterranean and the Jordan River – in other words, the end of the state of Israel. 'The time of making do with the West Bank and Gaza is over. Oslo is over. It is a page that has turned', said one of the fighters, his Le Coq Sportif tee-shirt stretched tight over his belly. 'There is no difference between Hamas and Fatah and PFLP. We are united.'[5]

Zealots

Hamas prizes martyrdom (*shahaada*) for Islam against what it denounces as the 'infidel' occupation of Palestinian land. For years it has generated a cult of sacrifice around the concept of martyrdom, Article 8 of its founding constitution proclaiming: 'Allah is its target, the Prophet is its model, the Koran its constitution: Jihad is its path and death for the sake of Allah is the loftiest of its wishes.'[6]

In June 2003, after Israel declared open season on the Hamas leadership, Hamas's founder Sheikh Ahmed Yassin scorned the threat of assassination, saying: 'If I saw the rocket coming I would jump and hug it'[7] – a vow given added force because he was a wheelchair-bound quadriplegic. He continued: 'If they kill Ahmed Yassin another 100 Ahmed Yassins will grow up . . . Our desire is martyrdom: the day we become martyrs is a wedding day for us. We are not afraid of their threats, and when we get killed it is the happiest day of our lives.'[8]

So unfathomable is the rationale of suicide bombing to most onlookers that the bombers – who are by definition unavailable to provide further explanation – become a blank canvas upon which all parties tend to project their own rationalizations. For Hamas or Fatah they are useful vehicles for videotaped propaganda messages; for Israelis they are the duped tools of evil despatchers who fill them with hatred for democracy, freedom and Zionism before sending them to their deaths. In family mourning tents after explosions, relatives and friends of the 'martyr' usually serve up, with dried dates and a thimbleful of coffee, explanations attributing their son or daughter's final gesture to despair, revenge or an attempt to burst out of a lifetime of powerlessness. For Israeli victims of the bomb attacks there is despair and even greater enmity. All see through their own prism an act which none can truly comprehend.

Although the concept of martyrdom is by no means exclusive to Islamist movements, the fusion of religion and armed struggle within the ideology identifies them most closely with the phenomenon of suicide bombings. Dr Eyad Sarraj, a Gaza psychiatrist and director of the Gaza Community Mental Health Programme, cites the prolonged effect of many decades of Israeli occupation on Palestinian society and the sway of religious movements such as Hamas. He argues that, for would-be bombers convinced that God is 'waiting for them on the other side', attacking Israel becomes a form of 'divine duty, the ultimate expression of faith . . . the ultimate expression of heroism'.[9] He maintains that, after the humiliation of the Arab states in the wars of 1948, 1967 and 1973 against Israel, the religious certainties imparted by groups such as Hamas – and Hezbollah in Lebanon – are welcomed by many Palestinians. Islamism, he says, gives them 'a new identity of victory and belonging to God compared to the identity of your father who was powerless and dying in defeat. This kind of new identity gives so much power.'[10]

Dr Sarraj and his staff even found themselves treating a rejected suicide bomber for feelings of inadequacy. 'He was at the top of the queue, but he was away from the phone when they called. He heard that somebody else had already done something in Israel, so he went to them and asked "Why wasn't it me?" They told him: "Well we looked for you but you were not there, so we chose the second in line." He was very depressed because he missed his chance, and came for treatment.'[11]

Others said that what was true of suicide bombers also holds for Hamas and Islamic Jihad fighters, who have less fear of death than their secular counterparts. 'They are fighting in the name of Allah', said one PLO militant. 'Their loyalty goes beyond our own.'[12] For Mohammed, a Hamas military wing veteran sitting in a Gaza refugee camp, the very impenetrability of such a philosophy to outsiders is a victory – because it instils in them fear of people with motivations they cannot fathom. 'It is natural that the Israelis cannot understand this language. It isn't part of the culture of the Israelis, the Jews. They love life and they can't under-stand or expect that someone will throw his life away like this. For us it is the ultimate sacrifice, for your children and for anyone, to give your life.'[13]

Cultivating martyrs

It is such religious-inspired zealotry – the name Hamas was chosen because it means 'zeal' in Arabic – that embodies the core concepts enshrined in the group's full name – the Islamic Resistance Movement.

Across the Middle East the concepts of martyrdom (*shahaada*), resistance (*muqawama*) and occupation (*ehtilaal*) are now ingrained in the identity of peoples who have for centuries lived under a succession of foreign invaders, from the Romans to the Mongols (Tatars), Ottomans and British. That historic desire to throw off the yoke of alien oppressors is shrewdly invoked by the Hamas Covenant, which places its struggle with Israel within this tradition:

> The Islamic Resistance Movement views seriously the defeat of the Crusaders at the hands of Salah ed-Din al-Ayyubi and the rescuing of Palestine from their hands, as well as the defeat of the Tatars at Ein Galot, breaking their power at the hands of Qataz and Al-Dhaher Bivers and saving the Arab world from the Tatar onslaught which aimed at the destruction of every meaning of human civilization. The Movement draws lessons and examples from all this. The present Zionist onslaught has also been preceded by Crusading raids from the West and other Tatar raids from the East. Just as the Moslems faced those raids and planned fighting and defeating them, they should be able to confront the Zionist invasion and defeat it.[14]

Of course Hamas has no monopoly on martyrdom, although it strives hard to make it appear so. But it has played on the powerful rhetoric and historical myths of the ancient Crusades made manifest in modern form in Israel and its American backers. As one scholar and Hamas supporter, Dr Atef Adwan, has argued, 'We understand the echo of history on our own land and that the banner of Islam can only be raised again in the face of Crusader occupation through resistance.'[15]

But in the 1960s and 1970s, long before Hamas existed, Yasser Arafat's PLO guerrillas were lionized by Palestinians as *fedayeen* – 'those who sacrifice' – and the word *shaheed* (martyr) is used across the Arab and Muslim world to invest the death of those killed in conflict with religious symbolism and significance. By no means all Palestinians support suicide attacks as a valid tactic, either morally or militarily. But for the vast majority of Palestinians, as for Arabs across the Middle East, they are called *a'maliyya istishhadiyya* (martyrdom operations) rather than *a'maliyya intihariiyye* (suicide operations). Hamas people are prone to admonish anyone who calls them suicide attacks in their presence. For many Palestinians, every victim of Israel's violence is a martyr, whose death is commemorated as a symbol of national sacrifice towards freedom and an end to Israeli occupation. They are celebrated as martyrs, be they masked PLO guerrillas shooting at Israelis in the 1960s, West Bank protesters killed by Israeli troops in the First Intifada, Israeli Arab demonstrators shot dead by Israeli police using rubber-coated steel bullets in 2000, Hamas suicide bombers in 2003, or children killed while sheltering from Israel's bombardment in a United Nations refuge during Israel's 2008–9 Operation Cast Lead assault on Gaza.

Within Palestinian and Arab societies death in conflict is increasingly glorified by political organizations and the media and transformed into a journey into paradise and the promise of heavenly pleasures. Indeed, jihadist mythology surrounding the promise to martyrs of seventy-two dark-eyed *houriyaat* (maidens of paradise) has entered the consciousness of the West as a stereotype of Islamic fundamentalism – a stereotype, but one grounded in the perception of some putative martyrs. 'If I don't get married now, that is all right, I have seventy-two maidens waiting for me in heaven', one hopeful young Al Aqsa Martyrs' Brigades fighter consoled himself during a break in fighting in Nablus in 2007.[16]

'Resistance' and 'occupation' are concepts so imbued with historical and emotional significance across the Muslim world – one positive, one overwhelmingly negative – that they are invoked by Islamist leaders from the Gaza Strip to Afghanistan seeking to make audiences empathize with their cause, just as Western politicians frequently invoke similarly powerful buzz words such as 'freedom' or 'democracy'. For most Westerners such concepts, so resonant among Arabs and Muslims, are merely euphemisms and obscure ideological rationalizations for the one phenomenon which strikes much closer to home: terrorism.

There is also the lingering sense after prolonged exposure to Palestinian militant groups that there is a huge flaw in their psychological readiness for war – raising the question whether victory or death is ultimately more important. Certainly in 2006, during Israel's summer war against the Lebanese Hezbollah, returning Israeli troops talked of encountering battle-hardened Hezbollah fighters constantly popping up from unknown hiding places, firing, and then vanishing again. A common theme of the Israeli accounts was that the Hezbollah fighters were not careless of their lives in the manner of Palestinian militants whom they had previously encountered, often apparently intent on glory through death.

Hamas has been accused of promoting a culture of martyrdom that has damaged Palestinian society. The cult of sacrifice was encouraged: theatre performances, student groups, pop chants and rap songs, films, poems, art, and impromptu memorials, websites, and posters, flags, postcards, necklaces – even slush puppies dubbed 'suicide reds'. Some websites allow their users to access hundreds of Hamas martyr or *shaheed* video clips, which follow a popular format of a succession of images of bearded gun-toting males interspersed with romanticized images of Arab steeds, red roses and Israeli soldiers being defeated on the battlefield. Each video is accompanied by a song, the lyrics of which talk about the nation, Islam and martyrdom.

By 2003–4 the fruits of the motivational efforts were ubiquitous. In Gaza City, Beit Hanoun, Jenin, Rafah and Hebron, martyrs' portraits hung from homes, shops, public buildings and traffic intersections, alongside advertisements for Nokia mobile phones and Samsung electronics. Martyrdom was everywhere.

Recruiters

Like Hezbollah in Lebanon and the Mahdi Army in Iraq, Hamas has a grass-roots network of mosques and social organizations which also serves as a recruiting tool for their armed wings. Preachers, instructors and youth activity leaders used to monitor promising young recruits carefully over months and even years to study their suitability, temperament and religious convictions before they are selected for an active role in the Izz ad-Din al-Qassam Brigades. Secrecy is paramount, it being a familiar refrain among family members that the first they learned of their son or daughter's involvement in the military wing or suicide cell is the posthumous video proclaiming their child as a martyr. Some Israelis assert that impressionable young Palestinians are exploited by Hamas to further its own ends and sometimes by families with a baser motive than jihad or glory: money.

In October 2002 the Israeli government accused Saudi Arabia and Iraq of channelling millions of dollars to families of suicide bombers during the Second Intifada, as a reward for attacking the Zionist enemy. A senior Israeli military official said that, while the Saudis donated 'much more' to individuals and organizations in total – $100 million as against $15 to $20 million from the Iraqis – Saddam Hussein's regime gained far more publicity by concentrating on suicide attackers. By prioritizing such missions – $25,000 per bomber compared with $5,000 from the Saudis – Iraq 'invested less money than the Saudis but they did it in a smart way'.

The Israelis' information came from documents and information said to have been gleaned from a captured middleman. After being arrested on 2 October 2002, this man allegedly told his Israeli interrogators that he had met regularly with Hamas and other organizations to speak with them 'about initiating terrorist activities against Israel', and that the Iraqi money was allegedly channelled from Baghdad through banks in Jordan and Ramallah. The Israelis said Iraqi donations came in three phases: up to August 2001, when Baghdad assigned $10,000 per attacker irrespective of type of attack; from August 2001 to March 2002, when Saddam began prioritizing suicide bombers by raising the reward to $15,000; and from March 2002 on, when suicide bombers' families received $25,000 and others only $10,000. According to an Israeli official: 'The mechanism is based on the knowledge of the suicide bombers and suicide bombers' families that after their son is martyred they are going to get a lot of money from the Iraqis. They know that they would get most of the money if their son is a martyr, but if he is an ordinary terrorist who was killed they would get only $10,000. If crippled, less.' He said that the Israeli authorities found documents from one family asking the middleman 'Why did we get only $10,000? Our son was a suicide bomber. Please give us the suicide bombers money. Please give us $25,000.'

He maintained that, although would-be bombers did not get the money in advance, they knew that their families would be taken care of. 'When they are trying to recruit them, part of the argument is that 'first you will contribute to the Palestinian cause, but you know that the future of your family is much better', he said. 'We know from the interrogation of suicide bombers who failed to kill themselves that the money was a consideration.'[17]

Hamas is contemptuous of Israeli assertions that its operations are motivated by financial reward. 'We struggle for freedom, not for money. Money won't buy a place in paradise for the martyr or his family', said Abu Ashraf, a Hamas military leader. 'Do you see the families of the martyrs living in luxury in the wake of their son's death? Or do you see them sitting in the shattered ruins of their homes as Israel's punishment?'[18] Sheikh Yassin, in an interview in 2003, remarked on the Hamas motive: 'This is a society raised on war and it wears the clothes of occupation. We have the right to retaliate if they kill our civilians and target them. And they have killed many more of our women and children than we have done.' He ended by declaring: 'A sacrifice in this way is for the nation and brings our people one step closer to liberation.'[19]

Waves

Palestinian suicide bombings against Israel came in two main waves – during the mid-1990s, when Hamas and Islamic Jihad were trying to wreck the Oslo peace process, and during the Second Intifada, when that process seemed to have broken down irretrievably. Between September 2000 and December 2005, according to the Israeli Intelligence and Terrorism Information Centre, Palestinians carried out 147 suicide bombings. The Israelis also claim that, although these were only a small fraction of the attacks during that period – the others were mainly shootings, stabbings and bombings – they were by far the deadliest single events, accounting for 525 of the 1,084 Israeli fatalities.[20]

While Israeli troops had encountered suicide bombings before in Lebanon, it was Hamas which carried out both the first Palestinian suicide bomb attack in Israel, in April 1994, and the worst, the March 2002 Passover bombing in Netanya which killed thirty people. Indeed March 2002 was by far the deadliest month for Israelis in the modern era of the Israeli–Palestinian conflict, with more than 130 Israelis and foreigners killed in Palestinian attacks.[21] Shocked though they may have been, there was little sympathy from Palestinians, who were dying in far greater numbers at the hands of the Israeli military. In the same month, March 2002, the Palestine Red Crescent Society recorded 234 Palestinians killed, at an average of sixty-one per month up to that point, nearly four times the Israeli rate.[22]

Both sides protest that numbers are misleading. Palestinians complain that the steady daily attrition suffered by them at the hands of Israeli attack helicopters, tanks, snipers and killer aerial drones is consistently underrepresented in international media reports, which tend to highlight high-profile 'spectaculars' such as suicide bombings. The Israelis protest that the higher Palestinian figures disguise a large number of combatants among the dead. It also maintains that – unlike Palestinian suicide bombers and rocket teams – Israeli soldiers and pilots do not intentionally target civilians. Unsurprisingly, both sides are deaf to the other's arguments.

While Hamas took grim satisfaction from the efficacy of the suicide bombings at the nadir of the Second Intifada, its rival Fatah, which had signed up to the peace process, was torn. Elements in Fatah argued that, because Hamas was capturing the imagination of the radicalized Palestinian street, with its cult of 'martyrdom operations', Fatah had no short-term choice but to follow or lose its decades-old primacy. They reflected a deep-seated Palestinian conviction, mirrored in countless opinion polls over the years, that the combination of force and negotiations against Israel is more effective than negotiations alone. Others argued that suicide bombings were a short-sighted policy that played into Hamas's hands, because it would push Fatah out into the political wilderness.

For Hamas leaders there was no such internal tension. It knew that such attacks were supported by its 'base' – the hundreds of thousands of Palestinian refugees who see Israelis living in the homes their grandfathers owned before 1948 and still dream – however unrealistically – of one day getting them back, by any means necessary. Explaining the extraordinary growth of the suicide bombing phenomenon, Ghassan Khatib, a political analyst and former Palestinian cabinet minister, said it was an emotional, not an intellectual, response:

> You are trying to treat the Palestinian activities as politicized in a rational way. They are not rational. They are instinctive reactions. It is just people wanting to take revenge and fight back. All the criticism is correct, but it will continue. It is like somebody is trying to stab you, and instinctively you find a nail and stab him back. It's not rational, it is how human nature works.[23]

The definition of a Hamas hardliner, the organization's deputy leader, Dr Abdel Aziz Rantissi, occupied a special position in Hamas mythology and Israeli demonology. An Egyptian-educated paediatrician, Rantissi was from the Arab village of Yibne, now the Israeli town of Yavne, which lies just over 20 miles from Gaza. A refugee, he would often talk about how his family's old home was still there, although now occupied by Israelis, and his dedication to the cause was driven by an intensely personal quest for his own right to return. Rantissi's anger never seemed to wane, whether at the Israelis or at Yasser Arafat's Palestinian Authority, which imprisoned and tortured him when Hamas sought to bomb into oblivion the Oslo peace process. Age certainly did not mellow him.

Photo 8.1   Hamas's deputy leader, Dr Abdel Aziz Rantissi, in one of the last photographs before his assassination in 2004

To younger Hamas members, fighters and supporters, Rantissi was a hero, having spent years in jail and exile. He survived several Israeli assassination attempts before the missiles which finally killed him in April 2004, only a month after he succeeded Sheikh Yassin as leader in

Gaza. Rantissi's medical qualifications made him an object of particular animosity in Israel, where he was reviled as the child doctor with no compunction about killing children. He never betrayed the slightest trace of embarrassment at the killings of Israeli civilians by suicide bombers, or any other means. Unlike some Palestinian militant leaders, who would try to deflect criticism with tortuous rationalizations or faux outrage, Rantissi never blinked, even when being challenged about killing Israeli children in pizza restaurants and outside discotheques. 'If they stop killing our civilians, we will stop killing theirs', came his unvarying justification. 'For us here every day we have a massacre, so we can't compare the two.'[24] For Rantissi, suicide bombs were a tool to be deployed according to the needs of the moment, as precisely and emotionlessly as the paediatric instruments he utilized in the examination room. 'The only reason we use it is because we don't have anything else to use. If we found something which could stop the enemy from killing us without killing ourselves, it would be much, much better', he said unemotionally.[25]

In one of his last interviews before he was assassinated, Rantissi sat in his familiar stance, legs wide apart, twirling his prayer beads with metronomic regularity, as his phalanx of bodyguards glanced nervously up at the sky and listened for the sound of helicopters, which were not to arrive for another month and five days. 'Does anyone at all know you are here?', asked one of the authors interviewing him at a secret, pre-arranged location. 'Only the Israelis', came the mordant, and prophetic, reply from one of his guards.[26]

Life in Rantissi's comfortable but far from luxurious Gaza City home could be a claustrophobic and paranoia-inducing experience. Fully aware that he was on Israel's target list, he never discussed his movements in advance over the mobile phone – one inadvertent mention of his intended destination had led to an earlier assassination attempt which narrowly failed to kill him. His wife, Umm Mohammed, also believed in the jihad being waged by Hamas. Speaking after her husband's death, she stated, 'For me this was a very direct work and contribution to the movement, backing my husband up. This was part of my jihad – within the home, backing him up while he engaged in the bigger jihad.'[27]

Moving in and out of hiding, Rantissi operated under the 100 per cent certainty that each of the three mobile phones lying on his living room table was monitored by Israel. Usually the game of cat and mouse pursuit was deadly serious, with Rantissi forced to receive important messages in code or by personal courier. He understood the price of his 'greater jihad'. At other times it bordered on farce, with the bizarre sight of Hamas's widely feared deputy leader shouting through his fax machine to Israel's data interceptors, asking them to clear the line quickly because he needed to send an urgent message. 'They have slow machinery. I can hear it delivering a copy to them after I have received a fax', he sighed, with a rare smile and a touch of theatricality. One of the few occasions on which

Rantissi would become aroused was when confronted with the accusation that after 9/11 Hamas made a grievous error by returning to suicide bombings, failing to realize the international opprobrium it would bring upon its head.

To accuse Rantissi of killing children and women drew not a blink. But to suggest that Hamas could err seemed to strike far deeper inside the man. 'What are we losing?', he interrupted. 'The international community did nothing against Israel despite their bulldozing and demolition of our homes, leaving women and children crying. We don't have the support to lose, anyway. Just give me one incident before the suicide attacks started where the Americans supported us against the Israelis for 200 years until now . . .'[28] Rantissi's words echoed the founder's sentiments. Sheikh Yassin himself has asked, 'When will the West tell the occupiers to leave our land? If we do not defend ourselves then who will?'[29]

Such outbursts gave an insight into the Hamas hardliner's view of the world – as a malevolent place at best uninterested and at worst inimical to Palestinian interests, and with an infinite capacity to tolerate Arab suffering, but none for that of the Israelis. For the many Palestinians who share this jaundiced perception, the West's tolerance differential is an unpleasant fact of life to be deplored. For Hamas's military wing it is an Achilles heel to be exploited with ruthless efficiency. If the world pays attention to Palestinians only when Israelis start dying, then the course of action was obvious to men such as Rantissi: kill Israelis. As he said, impassively:

> We were resisting occupation for twenty years, from 1967 to 1987. The whole world did not start reacting or calling for peace until after the First Intifada, when we began military attacks on Israel and Israelis started being killed. That is when the world started moving. For twenty years before that, nobody really cared. When the Palestinian Authority came, the military attacks decreased. When they decreased the Zionists, under the umbrella of negotiations, built more and more settlements and carried out the Judaization of Jerusalem, and so on. Over time, using negotiations, they created facts on the ground which stops the creation of a Palestinian state.[30]

To grab the world's attention by shocking it was not a strategy unique to Hamas. Indeed, Rantissi's tone was remarkably similar to that of the now ageing PLO plane hijackers of 1970, who to this day insist that it was their actions that brought the Palestinian cause to international attention – terror, or the threat of it, as attention-grabbing spectacle. One of Rantissi's favourite observations, a line he repeated more than once, was that Palestinians had the advantage over Israelis because they were more prepared to die for their cause. 'You have to understand that they value their life more than Muslims or Christians. They don't like to die. Their best wish to each other is to live 120 years.'[31] From the earliest years, the message of martyrdom, disseminated by Hamas preachers, youth camp trainers and television programmes, and on countless propaganda websites, videos, CDs and DVDs, was carried on by Rantissi's successors. Although the suicide missions later went into abeyance, the willingness to sacrifice for Hamas continued to be perpetuated among the ever growing youth ranks of the Hamas movement.

Opponents

Israel's military and psychological experts study the suicide and martyrdom phenomenon, looking for a profile upon which to draw up a defensive strategy. Some believe that the bombers reflect the very fabric of Palestinian society. 'There was no psychopathology to speak of. These were normal guys, just a cross-section of society', said Israeli expert Ariel Merari. 'I came to think that suicide terrorism is not a personal phenomenon – it is an organizational phenomenon, an organizational system.'[32]

Not all Palestinians, however, supported the notion of sacrificing themselves or their children, for any cause. At the height of the suicide bombings in the Second Intifada there was growing concern and disquiet among sections of the Palestinian leadership that extremist factions were inculcating a death wish in their children. There were periodic calls for an end to the bombings from those arguing that by glorifying martyrdom they risked losing an entire generation to fanaticism. In June 2002, fifty-five prominent Palestinian officials, academics and community leaders, including Hanan Ashrawi and Sari Nusseibeh, took out a full-page advertisement in the most influential Palestinian daily newspaper urging a halt to such attacks. 'We appeal to those who stand behind the military operations to rethink and reconsider these actions, and to stop sending young men to carry out such attacks targeting civilians in Israel', said the document. It called the attacks a counterproductive 'gift' to Israel's then prime minister, Ariel Sharon, by encouraging Israelis 'to continue their aggression and attacks against the Palestinian people'.[33]

However, the signatories came in for criticism among fellow Palestinians for voicing public dissent, even on such pragmatic, rather than moral, grounds. That same month an opinion poll showed 68 per cent of Palestinians supported suicide bombings, only slightly down from 74 per cent six months earlier. Determined to stamp out the threat from suicide bombers, Israel ordered tight closures on the West Bank.

In October 2002, outside the sealed-off city of Nablus, the Israeli commander of the area – who would identify himself only as Colonel Noam – said that Israel's policy of closures and checkpoints would stay in place to stop the suicide attacks. 'My job is to stop bombers getting to Tel Aviv, and I am determined to do it', he said. 'They will suffer until they understand. This is the price of terror.'[34] Inside the cordon around Nablus the Palestinian mayor of the city, Ghassan Shakah, cautioned that such measures would only provoke more violence among Nablus's 200,000 inhabitants. 'When you put pressure on a seventeen-year-old, he will react with bitterness and anger. The reaction will be to make bombs and commit suicide, because young people are losing hope', he warned.[35] It was a cause-and-effect argument. Israel said it needed more checkpoints, raids and assassinations to stop the bombing. Palestinians argued that the checkpoints, raids and assassinations were what had caused the bomb-ings in the first place.

Husam Khader, a Fatah member of the Palestinian parliament and resident of Nablus, lamented that support for radical Islamist groups such as Hamas and Hezbollah had soared in a city where youths already wore portraits of dead 'martyrs' around their necks. His eleven-year-old daughter Amani had already become dangerously infatuated with the idea of suicide:

> She says 'I recognize Fatah because of Yasser Arafat, but I am Hamas because they fight against Israel, because they are honest, they help the poor and they pray to God' . . . She said she wrote to her friend saying they wanted to make a military operation [suicide bombing]. I spent two or three hours a day saying, 'You should become a doctor, it will be better for your people, you are a child.'[36]

Most relatives of suicide bombers, at least in public, proclaim full support for their dead 'martyr', and accede to the intense pressure from family, neighbours and factions to bedeck their homes in the regalia of martyrdom and proclaim loyalty to the Palestinian cause. However, not all succumb to such peer pressure. In January 2004 the family of a seventeen-year-old Islamic Jihad bomber, Iyad al-Masri, accused the Islamist faction of exploiting his feelings of grief and rage at a vulnerable time, just after the Israeli army had killed his brother and cousin. Iyad's father, Bilal, said he blamed both the Israelis and Islamic Jihad for his son's death. The teen-ager had left his home in Nablus, heading for Jerusalem, but blew himself up when he was tracked down by Israeli troops, injuring no one.

> This family is very angry. The Israelis recruited my son as a martyr because they killed his brother in front of him. Then they killed his cousin in front of him too. Mohammed's brains were thrown all over Iyad. If he hadn't seen his brother and cousin die he would never have become a martyr. But those who sent him [as a suicide bomber] exploited his grief.[37]

Israel applied a range of military strategies to counter the suicide attacks. One approach was the reoccupation of parts of the Palestinian Territories and the blockade of Palestinian cities such as Nablus and

Ramallah. Other tactics included the targeted assassinations of Hamas leaders. Israel would also demolish the home of suicide bombers and impose curfews and other forms of collective punishment which were criticized by human rights groups. The Israel Defence Forces would also employ preventive measures such as mass arrest campaigns, roadblocks, travel restrictions, and raids on suspects. By 2003 Israel had embarked on its most radical counter-measure: physical separation by means of walls and fences. Once construction of the 500-mile barrier around the West Bank had begun (often sited on Palestinian territory occupied in 1967), Palestinians feared that the move was a prelude to annexation.

Martyrdom as power

So deeply ingrained were the Palestinian factions' conviction of the virtue of their cause that many failed to comprehend how their actions were seen in the wider world. On 11 September 2001, when the Palestinian Authority was quick to condemn al-Qaeda's attacks on the US, all the Palestinian factions appeared to realize the inadvisability of persisting with bombings in the immediate aftermath. Although they continued to kill Israelis with the gun, there was only one suicide attack in the next ten weeks.

Khalil Shikaki, a Palestinian opinion pollster and political analyst, said: 'Hamas and Islamic Jihad have concluded separately that it would be suicide for them to continue suicide attacks. They don't want to be the focus of American attention, and they don't want to be on the wrong side of the war. They would like to keep their war against Israel in a completely different realm.'[38] It did not last long. By early December, Fatah, Islamic Jihad and Hamas had all resumed their suicide campaigns, echoing Rantissi's attempts to justify them by blaming Israeli provocations. But, from their rhetoric and actions, they appeared so wedded to a tactic that inflicted damage on their enemy that they were blinded to how they were becoming international pariahs to those who saw no distinction between burning buses in Jerusalem and burning aeroplanes in New York. For Hamas there was genuine, or at least professed, astonishment that the world could not distinguish between 'our' and 'their' suicide bombings. 'We condemned 9/11', said Usama Hamdan, a senior Hamas leader in Beirut. 'We have condemned these acts in Iraq. But I will answer in one way: we don't have jets, we don't have tanks. So we made the decision. It is one of the ways we resist . . . there is nothing wrong with our way, because we are under occupation.'[39]

The unavoidable sense gained from scores of interviews with Hamas fighters and leaders, and with many ordinary Palestinians, is that many embrace suicide bombings because they inspire such a feeling of strength and empowerment by inflicting hurt on an otherwise near invincible enemy. One veteran member of Hamas's military wing said it returned to suicide bombings after 9/11 because Israel had taken advantage of events in Afghanistan and Iraq to hit the Palestinians hard while the world was distracted, and Hamas wanted to reassert its power. 'The moment Hamas went back to the suicide attacks they did stronger attacks, and they sent a message to everybody that whenever we want to stop we will stop, and when we want to initiate we can initiate', he boasted. 'That way you send a message to the whole world: you should respect Hamas.'[40]

But with a domestic backlash and Israel's construction of its West Bank barrier, suicide bombings became less easy. Increasingly rockets became the main Hamas tactic, a fulfilment of Rantissi's observation that Hamas would be delighted if it could find an effective way of striking 'without killing ourselves'.[41]

Hamas never publicly abandoned suicide bombing, but it did acknowledge that the tactic had outlived its usefulness and that the fight against Israel would be better served by developing its missile, rocket and mortar capacity. Israeli officials insisted that militant groups were still trying to carry out bombings, but that they were getting caught. But by 2005 there was a growing consensus that they were no longer the key to Hamas's strategy. 'There was a dilemma with the suicide bombs', said Mushir al-Masri, a Hamas MP. 'They stole the moral high ground that we enjoyed in terms of the international community. Palestinians have become a people that no longer enjoy the legitimate right to resist the occupation. The moral equivalency issue doesn't work in our favour. It's wrong to throw a bomb on a bus of women and children.'[42]

However, the favoured new weapon also presented difficulties. There was considerable opposition to the rocket-firing from farmers and civilians in northern Gaza because Israel's retaliatory artillery and missile fire often ruined their crops. In at least one case Islamic Jihad shot one protesting farmer in the foot as punishment for his dissent.[43] The inevitable civilian casualties inflicted by Israel's reprisals stoked Palestinian anger, and in June 2006 the Qassam Brigades resumed their rocket fire after Palestinians were outraged by video footage of a distraught eleven-year-old Palestinian girl, Huda Ghalia, crying for her dead father after her family were killed by an explosion while they were picnicking on a Gaza beach. The family said they came under Israeli artillery fire, and the video of the bereft crying young girl – broadcast repeatedly across the Arab world – infuriated Palestinians. Israel suspended all artillery fire into Gaza pending an internal investigation, but later denied that its shelling had killed the family.

After time, however, residents near the firing zones began to complain and put pressure on the factions, particularly after Hamas took control of the Gaza Strip in June 2007. 'Some people did try and stop them [the rocketeers], but they opened fire on them', said one resident of a favourite launching area. Abu Ali, a farmer, said his livelihood had been nearly

ruined. 'My crops were destroyed by Israel in retaliation for the rockets
– most of which never even fall outside of Gaza – and for the past year I
have received no help from Hamas to replace my trees, repair my irriga-
tion system, pumps and wells. Hamas have been exposed now – this is
their true face.'[44]

But grief trumps politics. On 8 November 2006 an Israeli artillery shell
struck a Palestinian home in Beit Hanoun in northern Gaza, killing nineteen Palestinians as they slept. Israel apologized immediately, blaming
a faulty targeting device on an artillery battery which was aiming at
a nearby area where rockets had been fired into Ashkelon the night
before.[45] The deaths caused fury. Ghazi Hamad, a Hamas spokesman in
Gaza, denounced Israel as 'a state that believes in killing, and therefore
this state should cease to exist'.[46]

At the graveside of the nineteen victims, laid out in a long row in
the ground, there was heated debate about whether the rocket attacks
should continue. But it quickly became apparent that the main concern
was that rockets caused too little – not too much – destruction. 'It is time
for the resistance to think clearly, to be responsible', vouchsafed Gazan
Mohammed Yasji. 'The resistance should have a strategy, a more studied
approach. It makes no sense to fire rockets from within a civilian population when you know how Israel will react. We are steadfast, but there is
no need to inflict this suffering upon us.'[47] Yasji was shouted down by
others in the crowd, who saw the rockets as at least a token expression
of resistance to Israeli force. 'We are with firing the rockets. Israel are the
occupiers. It's us or them', said Abu Sharif Basyouni, a 24-year-old PA
security official. 'When they are firing their artillery at Jabalia, do you
think they care about hitting civilians? They want to erase a generation of
Palestinians. They want to break our will.'[48]

But it quickly transpired that Mr Yasji's scruples were based on a
ruthless assessment of their impact, not upon principle. For him – and
everyone in the gathered crowd – suicide bombings were a better tactic,
because they killed more of the Israelis who were killing them. 'I support
martyrdom operations inside Israel', he said. 'Let them know how it feels
to see civilians die. Suicide bombs make me feel strong because I penetrate their security.'

Human shields

One of the principal accusations levelled by Israel against Hamas and
other Palestinian factions is that, by making use of their own civilian
population as human shields, their fighters are frequently too ready
to sacrifice others. The allegations became particularly heated during
the battle for Jenin refugee camp in April 2002, in which twenty-three
Israeli soldiers and more than fifty Palestinians were killed, most of them

militants. Israel accused Palestinian gunmen of waging war from behind their own civilian populace. 'Terrorists used groups of civilians, women and children to get close to our troops', said Major Rafi Laderman, an Israeli reservist who fought in the battle.

> In one case a man with an explosive belt on him was inside a group. He was separated from the group and refused to undress himself and was shot dead . . . In another case when a group of civilians, women and children surrendered themselves and came out into an alley two terrorists emerged from this group and shot at a group of soldiers, injuring them, one critically.[49]

Israel's Shin Bet reiterated the allegations later, in a January 2003 report, saying that 'Salim Haja, a senior Hamas operative arrested during Operation Defensive Shield, admitted during questioning that he placed a bomb laboratory close to a school, and that the operatives in the laboratory were disguised as pupils carrying schoolbags and books.'[50]

But the issue was highlighted as never before when Israeli tanks and fighter-bombers pounded Gaza during the hugely controversial three-week Israeli assault on Gaza in 2008–9, designed to curb Hamas's rocket fire into neighbouring Israeli towns. Israelis consistently sought to use the human shield criticism to explain the unprecedentedly high rate of civilian casualties among the more than 1,300 Palestinian dead. 'Once we go into Gaza, we're of course faced with a terrorist organization which operates from within civilian surroundings. For example, they fire rockets from the homes of people. And actually, the families are accomplices', stated Isaac Herzog, Israel's minister of welfare and social services.[51] İlan Tal, an Israeli military spokesman, argued that Hamas, not Israel, was responsible for the high number of civilian losses. 'We are under attack from Hamas. We are retaliating and our target is Hamas, not civilians. Civilians have been killed. This is the consequence of Hamas using civilians as human shields. Hamas does not value the human life of Israelis or Palestinians.'[52]

International organizations censured Hamas during the operation. In January 2009 the human rights campaign group Amnesty International warned Hamas that if it was using Palestinian civilians as human shields it would be in contravention of the Geneva Convention: 'Hamas fighters also put civilians in danger by firing from homes', it claimed. 'The use of these tactics at a time when armed confrontations are taking place in streets in the middle of densely populated residential areas underlines the failure of both sides to respect the protected status of civilians in armed conflict.'[53] Hamas responds to the human shield accusations by saying that, with Gaza sealed off from the outside world – by Israel – it has little choice but to wage war in the deeply densely populated city centres and refugee camps where it lives.

On the ground there is often considerable grey area about how much the so-called human shields are willing participants. In 2006, after Israel began using F16 strikes to destroy suspected militants' homes, Gazan civilians in Beit Hanoun began standing on rooftops to make the Israelis abort the raids. They often responded voluntarily to appeals broadcast over mosque loudspeakers and radios, rushing to the threatened build-ing within minutes to stand on the roof, giving the Israeli pilots no option but to cancel the bombing mission or kill scores of civilians. But during the 2008–9 offensive many Gazan civilians complained that Israeli troops were attacking them under the guise of targeting the armed fighters. 'The streets are totally empty', said one resident. 'Those that dared to leave only went to buy food for their families . . . but we were targeted by Israel in our homes, on the street, in our schools, in ambulances and refuges run by the UN that were supposed to protect us', said Umm Subhi from Gaza City. 'We spent all night reading the Koran and praying to God that the attacks would stop, and still they targeted us.'[54]

In September 2009 the UN Human Rights Council's fact-finding mission into the operation criticized Israel, accusing its military of using disproportionate force against the civilian population of Gaza, of carry-ing out a deliberate and systematic policy to target Palestinian industrial sites, water installations and homes, and of using Palestinian civilians as human shields during the conflict. Israel's prime minister, Binyamin Netanyahu, reacted angrily, accusing the Human Rights Council of having 'made more decisions against Israel than against all other 180 countries in the world' in recent years, and warning that, by criticizing Israel, the 'victim', it risked legitimizing 'terrorists who fire upon civilians and who hide behind civilians'.[55]

Sacrifice worth making

By far the deadliest suicide bombing in Israel was the 27 March 2002 attack on the Park Hotel in Netanya, in which thirty Passover celebrants were killed by Abdel Basset Odeh, a 25-year-old member of Hamas's mili-tary wing. At Odeh's family home in the Palestinian town of Tulkarem, less than 10 miles from Netanya, his family still have his portraits on the wall, brandishing a semi-automatic rifle, in his Hamas bandana, with the Hamas military logo prominently displayed. They insist they knew nothing of his intentions in advance, but attribute it to the 'accumulated' pressures of being a Palestinian, talking of how he was detained during the First Intifada as a child and suffered the impotence and frustration of a young man forced to submit to Israeli soldiers at checkpoints. 'There are many who say that they are fed up with this life, are frustrated and they don't want to live any more', said his father, Mohammed, five years after the attack. 'People get so frustrated and so oppressed. Not only Abdel Basset but every Palestinian feels that he has suffered and he has lived a bitter life.' Certainly Odeh's life did become harder in his final months, a time during which his appearance changed dramatically from a clean-shaven and bespectacled youth to a heavily bearded, turban-wearing Islamist straight out of Hollywood central casting.

Although he was engaged to a Palestinian from Iraq and had made all the arrangements, including obtaining a furnished apartment, his family say he found it increasingly difficult to travel to neighbouring Jordan to meet his fiancée's relatives. Finally, in the summer of 2001 – nine months before the bombing – the Israelis refused him passage through the border, denying him a chance to make a future and a family for himself. Soon afterwards Odeh disappeared, they said, just as the Israelis were beginning to ask awkward questions about him. Odeh's father professes his son's actions a 'good operation' which 'made people very happy. They hit the street in joy the minute they heard of the attack.'[56]

In its essentials, Odeh's tale is little different from hundreds of others in which anger, desperation or frustration did not escalate into suicidal slaughter. Furthermore, suicide bombing is by no means the only form of martyrdom to which impressionable youngsters can succumb. As Israeli battle tanks fought Palestinian militants in Gaza's Jabalia district in 2006, Muhammad Zakout ordered his children to stay indoors. The 44-year-old labourer left his house briefly to check on his elderly mother, and when he arrived back home he found that his fourteen-year-old son Ala'a had sneaked out of the house to throw stones at Israeli soldiers, and had been shot in the shoulder. 'He doesn't listen to me', lamented Mr Zakout at his son's hospital bedside in Gaza City. 'It's very hard to keep him away. If he's older and he chooses to join the resistance I could understand. But not why they throw stones. It is because they don't have a real life. They are looking for excitement.'

Inside the hospital, Ala'a's grandmother and mother asked why he wanted to die: 'Is it to meet the martyrs? To see the next life? Has the cat got your tongue?' As they did so, Mr Zakout continued to expostulate. 'It is not easy to raise a child in this society', he said, leaning against a door bearing a picture of Sheikh Hassan Nasrallah, the leader of Lebanese Hezbollah.

> He becomes a young man and all of a sudden you lose him. He promises me he won't go to these things, and the next day he goes. I blame both the Israelis and the big Palestinian politicians. I have nothing against fighting the occupation. They are the terrorists and the ones with the upper hand. If you don't stop them at a certain point they will carry on and on. If you are occupied, it is your right to resist. But older people can make the choice. It is the duty of the mosques and the teachers to tell children that is not their role.

Eventually the wounded Ala'a, wincing from an injured shoulder, provided an answer to his family's questions about his apparent death wish. 'I'll tell you why', he finally mumbled. 'We are just bored of this life and we want to die.'[57] Asked what they want to do when they grow up, the injured boy's teenage friends looked blank, seeing no possibilities in a Gaza Strip steadily being degraded by year after year of Israeli attacks and Palestinian civil war. Twenty years previously, Palestinian refugees dreamed of professions in medicine, engineering and education. Now the young, who form the majority of Gaza's population, look around them and see no hope, no peace, no prosperity, and no economic future. 'We have already grown up', shrugged his friend Muhammad Abu al-Jidyan.

> We have no chance to do anything else. Probably when we grow up a little more we will just carry Kalashnikovs and fight. What else do we have to do? The resistance don't ask us to throw stones, they kick our asses for it. But we do it anyway. At least it means the soldiers will not be able to put their heads out of the tank to shoot people, or to move into buildings. We want to become martyrs and we want to help the resistance, whether they like it or not.[58]

That proclamation of the willingness to sacrifice life continued to define Hamas nearly a quarter century after its creation.

On 30 December 2008, at the height of Operation Cast Lead, Hamas's TV channel broadcast messages from Hamas women who declared themselves ready for martyrdom. One masked woman declaimed:

> I, Umm Suheib, have dedicated myself for the sake of Allah, and for the sake of redeeming my family, from which I have lost eight martyrs so far. I swear by Allah that I will turn my body parts into a fire that will burn the occupation soldiers, if they move towards my house. My beloved people, if Allah supports you, no one will be able to overcome you. We are confident of the support of Allah. There are thousands of martyrdom-seeking women like me, waiting for the occupier . . . I pledge to my people that I will continue on the path of my family, and avenge the widows and the orphans.[59]

It did not happen. In fact Israel lost only nine soldiers in the three-week operation, four of them killed by one of their own artillery shells that 'misfired'.[60]

During the battle Hamas did lose two senior leaders, Said Siam and Nizar Rayan, a religious and ideological hardliner who sent one of his own sons on a suicide mission in 2001 that killed two Israelis. Rayan, forty-nine, died alongside his four wives and nine of his children because he refused to leave his home in Jabalia refugee camp, and was inside it on 1 January when Israel dropped a 2,000 lb bomb during an air strike. In his last interview, with Hamas TV the day before he died, Rayan proclaimed the same sentiments about martyrdom that led to the deaths of seventy members of his mosque. 'Oh fighters, know that you will be victorious', he said. 'God promises us either victory or martyrdom. God is greater than they are, God is greater than their planes, God is greater than their rockets.'[61]

But although there were numerous accounts of Hamas laying booby-traps and losing hundreds of fighters, the movement appeared to withhold most of its fighting forces, declining to throw them in suicide missions towards the thousands of Israeli troops. It claimed to have lost just under fifty fighters, and its veiled threats of new weapons and 'surprises' – a direct steal from Hezbollah in Lebanon two years earlier – also failed to materialize, along with the promised Israeli casualties. The outcome of Gaza 2009 was that the rhetoric of martyrdom was fulfilled, but often by civilians – the innocent men, women and children who died in their homes, United Nations schools and other places of refuge from the battle between Israel and the Hamas fighters in their midst.

Amid the rubble and freshly dug graves, anger was directed at Israel. Ahmed Mohammed Dardona, a 23-year-old policeman who lost his leg, was hobbling around the destruction of his east Jabalia neighbourhood on crutches. 'The solution is we want peace. We don't want the Israelis to come here and destroy our houses. We must restore a national unity government to stop the firing of rockets towards the Israelis. We are fed up, our houses are destroyed and we are suffering in very bad conditions', he said.[62] There were near universal nods of agreement from a dozen young men in their twenties all around him, only one dissenting. Issaber Aziz compared the destruction to that of 1948 and 1967, after three years of siege. 'Israel didn't fight Hamas, but fought the Palestinian people themselves. They destroyed four houses belonging to me and my brothers. We didn't do anything. We are not in Hamas, we are pro-Fatah. Now we are homeless, without shelters. We are sleeping in the homes of our relatives.'[63]

The angriest people were in some of the most devastated areas, such as the Izbit Abed Rabbo neighbourhood of east Jabalia, where people said they heard no fighting between Hamas and Israelis. Shahab ad-Din Abul el-Aish said: 'There were no clashes here. They were shelling towards civilians. We didn't see any [Israeli] shooting or fighting.' Four of his daughters were killed on 16 January when a shell hit their home. 'We the people paid the price. We fought, but not the leaders of both sides, neither Fatah nor Hamas. They didn't lose anything, either side. We, the people, paid the price.'[64] Only the months and years ahead would tell whether Hamas would pay a price for asking so much while sacrificing – and delivering – relatively little on the battlefield in the winter of 2008–9.

This was certainly what Israel hoped for, in defiance of international outrage and accusations of disproportionate force because of the 100 to 1 ratio of Palestinian to Israeli deaths. 'If our civilians are attacked by you, we are not going to respond in proportion but will use all means we have to cause you such damage that you will think twice in the future', said Giora Eiland, a former Israeli national security adviser, answering the criticism. 'The [Hamas] regime will be under pressure to stop the violence and will be careful not to repeat this experience again . . . Due to the terrible devastation on the ground, there will be a lot of political pressure.'[65] In essence, Israel's strategy of deterrence in 2009 was the same as Colonel Noam's in Nablus seven years earlier: 'They will suffer until they understand.'

But its effectiveness is unclear, judging from the reactions of Palestinians inured to hardship after years of Israeli arrests and reprisals. As he watched the scale of the vengeance brought down on Gazans by the Hamas rockets, one Palestinian film-maker in the West Bank capital of Ramallah said he nevertheless supported Hamas's rocket-firing because it was a gesture that Palestinians would not lie down and accept Israel's forty-year military rule over them, even if it cost their lives. 'Just to say no', he said. 'I don't have a job. I don't have a life. I can't study. We are a nation of farmers without our lands, and fishermen without a sea. That will make for frustration, and there will be a reaction.'[66]

9

Harvesting

We build for you, and we also resist for you.

Mushir al-Masri, Hamas rally, 2006[1]

The football soars high above the schoolyard towards the makeshift goalmouth, positioned beneath green and white Hamas banners. It is a goal, and victory to the boy's team, named after a 'martyred' Hamas hero – except all the teams here are named after dead Hamas heroes. As the young players take a breather on the sidelines, Hamas volunteers provide them with green bottles of Mecca Cola. Even the refreshment is political: the bottles are stamped 'The Taste of Freedom' and 'Made in Palestine'. When they see the authors, a group of young boys rush forward, shouting: 'We are Hamas. Are you Hamas or Fatah?' At the mention of Fatah and its West Bank stronghold Ramallah, the youngsters draw fingers across their throats, in a slitting motion.

This is summer camp, Hamas-style, for thirteen- to fifteen-year-old schoolboys in what used to be known as the 'Hill of Winds' district of Gaza City but increasingly reverted to the 'Hill of Islam' – one of its old names – after Hamas's 2007 takeover of the Gaza Strip. The camp is just one of the hundreds of community, education and social projects in Gaza and the West Bank which provide the grass-roots foundation for Hamas's political and military activities. The movement is by no means alone in running such camps. Each summer along Gaza's Mediterranean coastline boys could be seen doing press-ups and shuttle sprints between lessons in makeshift beachside classrooms during similar activities run by Fatah and other factions such as Islamic Jihad. The UN refugee agency UNRWA also runs summer camps, where boys and girls attend together. But Hamas runs the most. By 2009 the movement said that it hoped 100,000 children would attend its summer camps over a two-month period, and it also introduced specialized Koranic recitation camps for up to 10,000 schoolchildren.

Hamas's programme to Islamize Palestinian society has always had

a particularly strong social and welfare dimension. In keeping with
the principles of the Egyptian Muslim Brotherhood, of which he was
a disciple, Sheikh Ahmed Yassin, believed that personal example and
preaching, or *da'wa* – literally, 'the call' – were the best means to disseminate the Islamist message. No one is so receptive as the malleable
young and the desperate poor. For this reason much of Hamas's annual
budget – which runs to tens of millions of dollars a year – is devoted to
an extensive social services network of health, education, social welfare,
women's training and other projects, much funded by overseas donors
and sympathizers. Every dollar spent on building schools, hospitals and
religious institutions had double value. It was both a plus in the Hamas
column and a minus in that of the Fatah-dominated Palestinian Authority
(PA), which was widely scorned as being too mired in corruption and
incompetence to deliver such services efficiently.

During its decade or so of Fatah control, from 1994 to 2006, PA officials
would protest loudly, with some justification, that they got no credit for
delivering hundreds of millions in aid, whereas Hamas was lionized for
providing a fraction of those sums. But the PA was a government which
was resented for every dollar – and there were millions – that went missing
through corruption or mismanagement, whereas Hamas's programmes
were run through Islamic societies and charitable institutions, which
earned gratitude for every penny donated. Hamas's decades of investment
in such social projects were a crucial factor in its January 2006 parliamentary election victory. If Hamas were only a network of armed cells it would
be nothing more than a violent rejectionist splinter group existing on the
fringe of Palestinian society, with little to distinguish it from its older, but
far smaller, rival Islamic Jihad. 'Hamas gives a lot more attention to charitable work and popular activism, which ensures a mass public base', said
Ghassan Khatib, a former Palestinian cabinet minister. 'Islamic Jihad sticks
to military means, [and] it is more extreme and rigid.'[2]

In the West this aspect of Hamas is often underestimated. To television audiences and newspaper readerships, through images of shrouded
Israeli corpses and the gutted shells of passenger buses burned down to
their tyre rims, Hamas is understandably defined by its violence. This
is the face of the movement which is seen and reviled. Palestinians,
however, see other faces. To them Hamas is also the incorruptible social
reforming organization, providing an Islamically inspired network of
schools and charity organizations caring for orphans and delivering food
to widows. These carefully laid foundations are precisely why Hamas's
full name is the wider 'Islamic Resistance Movement' – not the narrower
'Islamic Resistance Party' or 'Islamic Resistance Army'. The political
section and military wing are integral parts of the movement, but they are
not the whole. 'The election victory was a harvest of all the well-organized
benevolent work done by Hamas and the Mujamma over the years since
the 1970s under Sheikh Yassin: the schools, the charities, the clinics, the

orphanages and the mobilization of the people', concluded Amjad Shawa, an experienced Palestinian humanitarian coordinator in Gaza City, who has watched Hamas grow from Islamist seedling to election victor.[3]

Israel is also clear-eyed about Hamas's social role, while insisting that it is inseparable from the movement's military activities. In March 2007, a year after Hamas won the election, the head of Israel's Shin Bet domestic security agency, Yuval Diskin, said that Hamas's leaders regarded the Palestinian Authority's social, or *da'wa*, ministries such as education and social welfare as important prizes. 'The *da'wa* is there to recruit people to the Hamas movement', he said. 'For Hamas, the government is only a tool to serve the movement. They still think like a movement, not like a government.'[4]

Hill of Islam

Back at the 'Hill of Islam' summer camp, the boys' next activity is marching drills. They practise flag-bearing and parade ground formations, wearing Hamas caps and motivational Hamas tee-shirts bearing a logo of Gaza wrapped in barbed wire and the slogan: 'Despite the Siege, We Are Steadfast'. In the building behind them, more boys are packed into a classroom for a religious knowledge quiz in which bearded instructors instil knowledge of the Koran and Islamic history using the top-of-the-form quiz format. In rapid succession they fire off questions to the competing teams from Fallah, Amin and Hidayah mosques: 'What was the name of the cave where the Prophet Mohammed received the message from God? . . . What was the surname of his wife Aisha? . . .'

Asked how they select recruits for the camps – a popular summer activity in the fun- and money-starved Gaza Strip – one of the organizers said it was open to all. 'The goals of the movement's summer camps are to continue the education of the children and to teach them about the movement, and religion, and how to be a good Muslim. It also goes with the general goals of Hamas to create a new generation which is able to face the problems and hard life we face.'[5]

The movement does not restrict its camps only to boys who are already religious or committed to the struggle against occupation, for that would be preaching to the converted. It makes a point also of drawing in the secular and the apathetic, to begin remaking them in Hamas's image. 'We target boys who go to mosque, and those who don't go to mosque', said one of the camp's bearded organizers. 'Even those whose fathers are in Fatah can come, even those who don't believe in any faction.'[6] Crucially, in a strife-torn region where parents want to know that their boys are being kept out of danger, Hamas promises security alongside religion. 'People come to participate in our camps because they trust that their children are in safe hands', he added.

Photo 9.1　A Hamas summer camp for boys in Gaza

Girls, of course, are nowhere to be seen. They are half a mile away in another school entirely, learning to be dutiful daughters and future mothers under the watchful eye of Hamas women teachers, and trusted, bearded minders.

Across the high razor wire fence and closed borders that separate Gaza from the Jewish state, Israeli officials excoriate Hamas and other militant groups for mixing indoctrination with youth activities. 'In addition to the encouragement of children through the media, the Palestinian educational institutions and summer camps are also involved in inciting, brainwashing and indoctrinating Palestinian children and youth. Children are indoctrinated with extreme Islamic ideas, calling for support and encouragement of the Jihad against Israel', declares an Israeli Foreign Ministry report. 'At the camps, the children are taught about the history of Islam, and pictures of martyrs are hung in every place. In this way, the seeds of hatred towards Israel are planted in the children.'[7] The Islamists do not deny that the promotion of Islam is the prime purpose of such activities. Indeed they proclaim it. 'The most important thing in our camp is to teach them the rules of our religion', says Riham al-Wakil, one of the girls' instructors. 'We teach them all the ideas from the Koran, how to be mothers, how to treat their relatives and fathers, and how to respect them.'[8]

As for the anti-Israel ethos, Hamas makes no attempt to hide it. As he drank the green-bottled Mecca Cola, a camp instructor sought to dispel notions that it is a crudely anti-Jewish organization by drawing a distinction between Jews living outside Israel – with whom Hamas had no argument – and those inside it helping to implement the Zionist project, and therefore denying the Palestinians their land. 'The Jews raise their children to hate Palestinians, and especially Muslims', he said, as if stating a self-evident proposition.

> The Jews are always trying to educate their younger generations to be isolated and distinct, to be proud that they are better than others and to live within a ghetto away from other communities. Even the separation wall of the West Bank is a mode of Jewish thoughts towards the others. We teach the children how to respect others, to be open to other civilizations and cultures, and to respect others' points of view. We teach them that the Christians and Jews pray to the same God. We must respect them and we must not attack them unless they attack, occupy or fight us. In that case we will fight them. For the Israelis, the Zionist country, there is special treatment. We teach the children here that Israel must be fought and must be removed because it is illegitimate, and the Jews came from different places around the world to occupy a land which did not belong to them . . . We respect the Jews who live in England and the USA. We respect their thoughts if they don't occupy our land, and don't help the Israelis.[9]

Principle

The principle behind many of Hamas's youth, kindergarten and educational projects is an Islamist adaptation of one long familiar in the West: 'Give me a child until the age of seven, and I will show you the man.' Indeed the principle of inculcating Islamic values early is enshrined in Hamas's founding covenant, under the section: 'Strategies and Methods'. Article 16 reads:

> It is necessary to follow Islamic orientation in educating the Islamic genera-
> tions in our region by teaching the religious duties, comprehensive study of
> the Koran, the study of the Prophet's Sunna [his sayings and doings], and
> learning about Islamic history and heritage from their authentic sources.
> This should be done by specialized and learned people, using a curriculum
> that would healthily form the thoughts and faith of the Muslim student.[10]

Likewise section 21, the section 'Social Mutual Responsibility', spells out clearly the long-term benefits to the movement and the religion of tending to the needs of the underprivileged:

> Mutual social responsibility means extending assistance, financial or moral,
> to all those who are in need and joining in the execution of some of the work.
> Members of the Islamic Resistance Movement should consider the interests
> of the masses as their own personal interests. They must spare no effort in
> achieving and preserving them. They must prevent any foul play with the
> future of the upcoming generations and anything that could cause loss to
> society. The masses are part of them and they are part of the masses. Their
> strength is theirs, and their future is theirs.

Making explicit the recruitment agenda behind such attempts to promote social solidarity, it concludes: 'The ranks will be solidified to confront the enemies.'[11]

Such principles of social activism have been a cornerstone of movements such as the Muslim Brotherhood. In this way Hamas's value system is transmitted through its social and welfare programme. Hamas, then, hopes to shape the social values of Palestinian society according to its own understandings of Islamism. The impacts are apparent in realms that pertain to law, religious law, marriage, segregation of the sexes, moral and family matters, dress codes, young people, women, sexuality, education, and attitudes towards alcohol, drugs and social recreation activities.

Money

Social programmes are by their nature long-term and expensive. Hamas's predecessor, the Mujamma, had always made a point of tying charity funding to its burgeoning welfare and social programmes. This is known as *zakat*, a voluntary 7 per cent tax on income for alms which is a fundamental tenet of Islam. Each project needed money, whether it was a library, clinics, a kindergarten, a sporting club or mosque refurbishment. In Gaza, the Mujamma, and later Hamas, encouraged their supporters to contribute. Through the *zakat* committees and other funding mechanisms in the Gaza Strip Hamas has been able to control funding for projects to the poor. In the West Bank both Israel and the PA have targeted *zakat* committees and other Muslim charitable projects, claiming they are a front for Hamas terror.

By 2009 Palestinian officials in the West Bank were determined to close down Hamas's access to such important networks of influence and patronage. A senior PA official leading the campaign against Hamas-affiliated civil society organizations was frank in his assessment that such activities were an important part of the 'anti-terror' effort of the Palestinian security forces against Hamas. He acknowledged that he had 'forced personnel changes on the administrative boards of many local charities, ousting Hamas and ushering in "independents"'. He also said that he had 'arranged for such independents to win internal elections, stuffing [ballot] boxes to get results before the votes'. There were, however, problems. The official admitted that ousting Hamas and not replacing its funding and community-based support system was leaving a vacuum:

> What we are doing is like sending soldiers into battle without weapons. It doesn't solve the problem to appoint a new leadership and then let it fail. Even the guys we appointed are thinking of quitting. I have changed 95 per cent of the societies and they are destroying themselves from within. I've changed personalities but I have not given them the tools to succeed. Fatah is not benefiting from this effort.[12]

Much of Hamas's funding has always come from Palestinian expatriates and Muslim donors abroad. Particularly since 9/11 the American government has taken the lead in seeking to cut off the flow by freezing the assets of organizations, charities, banks and front companies which it suspects of channelling money to Hamas, Hezbollah, al-Qaeda and other groups that it deems to be terrorist organizations. In 2002 a senior Israeli official reporting to Ariel Sharon's government said that this American action post-9/11 radically changed Hamas's sources of funding. Before 2001, he said, 'Hamas used to be an independent terror organization – it used to count on income and money from Saudi, England, Germany, other countries but especially from Saudi.' After September 11, American pressure on its donors in the United States, and on the Saudis, cut off these sources of funds. 'We have seen that Hamas is getting more and more close to Iran . . . Iran became during the last year the number one carrying out terror activity.'[13]

A year later Israeli intelligence calculated that Hamas had an 'extensive network of financial sources operating within the framework of *da'wa* activity' which gave it income to a 'total value of tens of millions of dollars a year'. An Israeli report said that a 'considerable proportion' of this came from Gulf Arab states – with an estimated $12 million a year from Saudi Arabian sources and $3 million from Iran. The report also identified charity associations and foundations in countries such as Great Britain, the USA, Germany, Denmark, Belgium, the Netherlands and France, with 'limited' Hamas activity in Asia and Africa.[14]

By this time – somewhat tardily after years during the 1980s of turning a blind eye because they wanted to encourage a rival to Arafat – the Israelis were cautioning that the generous funds available to Hamas were contributing 'to the enhancement of its standing on the Palestinian street' and could 'eventually pose a threat' to the legitimacy of Arafat's PA. The fund-raising, Israel claims, is an important function of Hamas's outside political leadership, which lives in exile, particularly after the Israeli and Egyptian decision to close Gaza's land crossings following Hamas's 2006 election victory. The Israelis say that money is channelled into Hamas's coffers through 'bank transfers, moneychangers, private money services, unofficial networks for the transfer of funds' and other 'unsuspecting' agents, and is then distributed for different purposes:

> All the monies flow into a common fund, and are then channelled to the relevant activities, in accordance with needs and in coordination with the functions of the organization in the territories and abroad. . . . Thus, in view of the great difficulty in tracing the source of the money, its address and the motives behind the transfer of funds, it is essential that a strict and vigilant approach be adopted towards the entire fundraising network, operating within the framework of *Da'wa* activity.[15]

The Americans were similarly robust in monitoring and seeking to curtail Hamas's money-raising activities long before 9/11 or Hamas's election victory in 2006. This dates back to when Hamas was a perceived threat to the Oslo peace process in the 1990s. In 1995 the White House designated it as a terrorist organization, along with eleven other organizations, and issued an executive order 'prohibiting transactions with terrorists who threaten to disrupt the Middle East peace process'. The list included Hezbollah, the Popular Front for the Liberation of Palestine, the PFLP–General Command and two Jewish extremist organizations, Kach and Kahane Chai.[16]

Hamas was further listed two years later, in 1997, as a foreign terrorist organization and on 23 September 2001 as 'a Specially Designated Global Terrorist' (SDGT) organization under President Bush's post-9/11 executive order 13224, designed as a tool to 'impede terrorist funding' by authorizing the US government to block assets of individuals and entities, and their 'subsidiaries, front organizations, agents and associates'.[17] On 22 August 2003, four months after Hamas rejected President Bush's Roadmap for Middle East peace, the Bush administration announced that the US Treasury was naming six Hamas leaders and five Hamas-related charities as Specially Designated Global Terrorists. The designation came three days after Hamas claimed responsibility for a suicide bomb which killed twenty-three people on a bus in Jerusalem. Israel retaliated the following day by assassinating Hamas leader Ismail Abu Shanab. The violence effectively ended the Hamas ceasefire of 29 June.

The six leaders named by the US Treasury were:

1 Sheikh Ahmed Yassin, identified as 'the leader of Hamas in Gaza'. Yassin, an accompanying Treasury document said, 'maintains a direct line of communication with other Hamas leaders on coordination of Hamas's military activities . . . Yassin also conveys messages about operational planning to other Palestinian terrorist organizations.'
2 Imad Khalil al-Alami, identified as a 'member of Hamas's Political Bureau' in Damascus and a 'military operations leader' who 'has had oversight responsibility for the military wing of Hamas within the Palestinian territories. As a Hamas military leader, al-Alami directs sending personnel and funding to the West Bank and Gaza.'
3 Usama Hamdan, a 'senior Hamas official based in Lebanon' who, according to the Treasury, 'maintains contact with representatives with other terrorist organizations' and 'has worked with other Hamas and Hezbollah leaders on initiatives to develop and activate the military network inside the Palestinian territories in support of the current intifada, including the movement of weapons, explosives and personnel to the West Bank and Gaza for Hamas fighters.' It also alleged that 'funds transferred from charitable donations to Hamas for distribution to the families of Palestinian "martyrs" have been transferred to the bank account of Hamdan and used to support Hamas military operations in Israel.'
4 Khaled Meshaal, described as 'chief of Hamas's Political Bureau' in Damascus and head of its Executive Committee and Special Office. He was said personally to control 'cells in the military wing based in the West Bank' and to have been 'responsible for supervising assassination operations, bombings and the killing of Israeli settlers' through a 'direct link' to Abdel Aziz Rantissi. He too was alleged to have received charitable funds into his bank account, which were later 'used to support Hamas military operations in Israel'.
5 Musa Abu Marzouq, described as 'Deputy Chief of the Political Bureau' in Damascus, who was accused of 'directing and coordinating terrorist acts' and of providing 'start-up funding and instructions' to one of the designated charities.
6 Abdel Aziz Rantissi, 'a Hamas leader in Gaza reporting to Sheikh Yassin', who was said to be 'operating directly under Hamas leader

Sheikh Yassin' and to be coordinating military activities with Yassin and Meshaal.

The charities were based in France, Switzerland, Britain, Austria and Lebanon. Like the six leaders, all their assets in the US were frozen, and US nationals were prohibited from having transactions with them.[18]

The US Treasury's anti-money laundering and counter-terrorist financing branches allege that Hamas raises 'tens of millions of dollars per year' throughout the world by using charitable fund-raising as cover:

> While Hamas may provide money for legitimate charitable work, this work is a primary recruiting tool for the organization's militant causes . . . Hamas uses a web of charities to facilitate funding and to funnel money. Charitable donations to non-governmental organizations are commingled, moved between charities in ways that hide the money trail, and are then often diverted or siphoned to support terrorism.[19]

In Lebanon, Usama Hamdan, one of the Hamas leaders named in the order, concedes that one of the functions of the Hamas leadership outside Palestine is to raise money: 'This is one of the important roles towards the government.' But he insists that charitable funds do not go towards weapons. 'We don't use the money of the charities to finance Hamas', he said. 'Those monies were sent to the people inside Palestine, and they helped the people inside Palestine.'[20] Hamdan believed that one intended effect of the American and Israeli allegations that charity money goes towards weapons is

> putting pressure on the Palestinian people, turning them against Hamas. Everyone knows that, according to our beliefs or religion, we are not supposed to use the charities or their money to finance Hamas as a group, either a militant or a political group . . . They want to turn the people against Hamas. They know well that Hamas is not taking any part of this money.

Questioned about whether Arabs living in the West channel money to Hamas, he responded that US legislation prevents them from sending direct support to Hamas-related organizations. 'But that doesn't mean they can't do anything for Palestine. They can work for the Palestinian people and they can work directly; they don't have to work through an organization.'[21]

The British government, like the European Union, has a list of targets for financial sanctions which includes Hamas. Since 2001 Hamas's Izz ad-Din al-Qassam armed wing – and since 2003 Hamas as a whole – have been on the UK Treasury's 'consolidated list of financial sanctions targets,'[22] meaning that their assets are frozen and they cannot receive financial support from anyone. Meshaal, Hamdan, Marzouq and Alami were added in 2004. Any organization or individual breaching the sanctions can be jailed for seven years under British legislation and for two years in European Community regimes. The European Union has a similar list of 'persons, groups and entities involved in terrorist acts' whose assets are frozen, including Hamas.[23]

After Hamas's victory in the 2006 election the international community set out to isolate the organization even further, until it renounced violence, recognized Israel and consented to abide by previous agreements signed by previous Palestinian leaders. 'The military wing of Hamas is proscribed in the UK as a terrorist organization: they fire rockets at innocent civilians and put ordinary Palestinians in harm's way', a Foreign and Commonwealth Office spokesperson said in mid-2009. 'We believe that to talk to Hamas directly at this time would simply undermine those Palestinians who are committed to peace.'[24] However, the British government acknowledges that others are in contact with Hamas, and that it receives briefings on those contacts. According to the FCO spokesperson,

> The Arab League has mandated Egypt to communicate with Hamas. We are in regular contact with both the Arab League and Egypt. Turkey, Syria, Qatar and others are also speaking to Hamas. The UK strongly supports intra-Palestinian reconciliation behind President Abbas, which is the key for peace, stability and development. If distributing aid requires contact and cooperation with Hamas, then we would not wish agencies to let that stand in their way. But, given Hamas's commitment to violence and their rejection of the legitimate Palestinian Authority, we urge aid agencies to ensure that they maintain the greatest possible distance from Hamas.[25]

Some made no secret that the intent was to crush the organization and its 'hearts and minds' activities. At a meeting of the United States House of Representatives Committee on International Relations on 2 March 2006 to discuss US policy towards the Palestinians in the aftermath of Hamas's parliamentary victory, Democrat Representative Tom Lantos said the US had to do everything in its power to make sure that Hamas could not reap political benefits from American money entering the PA. 'Simply ending direct assistance to the PA does not cut it. There must be an end to all non-humanitarian assistance that could benefit Hamas', he said. 'The last thing in the world we in Congress want to do is to let a Hamas government reap the credit for development projects that are funded by the American taxpayer.'[26] Others urged caution. Robert Malley, a director of the International Crisis Group and a former Middle East negotiator under US President Bill Clinton, said he understood the 'temptation' to try and bring about Hamas's failure by cutting funding to the Palestinians, but warned:

If the US and Israel and others are perceived as trying to engineer Hamas's downfall and quick disruption of the government, the Palestinian people are not going to take from that the lesson that Hamas failed them, but that others failed them. And in that sense, Hamas's failure may not necessarily be America's success. It depends very much how it fails. If we see more despair, more poverty on the Palestinian side, who in this room thinks that that's going to help the moderates on the Palestinian side? History doesn't suggest that.

A prescient Malley then warned about one possible and potentially threatening outcome: 'If the Palestinians are starved of funding and they turn to Iran, is that going to serve our interests?'[27]

Hamas refused to meet the conditions laid down by the international community, which imposed a direct aid embargo with donors refusing to provide money to the Hamas-controlled Palestinian Authority. This was eased in June 2007 after the Hamas takeover in Gaza, after which President Abbas effectively split the PA in two by appointing Salam Fayyad as prime minister in the West Bank. Governments and international organizations were prepared to deal with the highly respected former World Bank and IMF official, a non-Fatah member of the tiny Third Way party, who earned a reputation for transparency and reforming zeal during his spell as finance minister from 2002 to 2005 when he was imposed by the international community on an unwilling but increasingly powerless Yasser Arafat.

With the Abbas and Fayyad-led PA attempting to get back to business as usual in the West Bank, Hamas – insisting that it was still the legitimate and democratically elected government – remained frozen out in Gaza. But funds continued to reach it, as the movement went to parties that were willing to fund them both as a movement and as a government. When asked if the newly empowered Hamas was siphoning off funds from the branches of the PA which had recently come under its control, Yuval Diskin, the head of Shin Bet, said: 'Hamas doesn't need the PA's money, they smuggle money in. They have plenty of their own money.' He then admitted that 'one of the bad fruits of the international siege on Hamas is that, once all the doors were closed, the only window open was to Iran.'[28]

Such views were affirmed by the leader of Gaza's civil police force. A year after Hamas's 2007 military takeover, Tawfiq Jabr sat in the newly refurbished offices and premises of the blue-uniformed civil police – which had been integrated with Hamas's *Tanfithiya* force. Sitting at a huge executive desk with a 52-inch plasma TV behind him, the police chief said he wanted for nothing when asked if he needed money to rebuild the force. On the adjacent drill ground hundreds of policemen were parading in new uniforms and police cars, with the force's new insignia, were parked on full display. 'For the first time in the history of Gaza there has been a 95 per cent decline in criminality', declared Jabr. 'The people feel safe, we meet our social responsibility and there is order.'[29] The money was coming despite the siege, and was being spent by Hamas on social control. Six months later, after the first aerial wave of Israel's December 2008 Gaza bombing offensive, Jabr was lying dead on the very same parade ground, among dozens of police bodies and the rubble of the refurbished headquarters.

In a revealing document the same year the US Treasury disclosed that, as of 2007, it had blocked $8,658,832 of Hamas's assets in the United States relating to anti-terrorist funding programmes. The Hamas total compared with around half that – $437,281 – for Hezbollah, and a paltry $63,508 for Islamic Jihad. In the list of nine organizations, only al-Qaeda had more blocked funds, with $11,324,361.[30]

Hamas, meanwhile, tried to shrug off the intense scrutiny on its reliance on foreign money, pointing out that under Fatah control in previous years the PA had been almost entirely dependent on external assistance, with little by way of proper mechanisms of accountability. 'The West funded the PA and the PLO squandered it living the playboy lifestyle', declared Ismail Haniyeh. 'We are accountable to the people and God above for every cent that is spent providing services to the people. We do not squander it but invest it in the welfare and safety of our steadfast nation.'[31] Hamas made no attempt to hide the fact that it was receiving foreign donations; indeed, in the first few months after its election Hamas leaders held press conferences in Gaza gleefully trumpeting promises of aid from Arab and Muslim countries. The aim appeared to be an attempt to switch from reliance on European and Western sources of direct funding to a 'Look East' policy championed by the newly appointed foreign minister, Mahmoud Zahar. The culmination of these defiant money-raising efforts came in the autumn of 2006, when Hamas ministers brought suitcases full of foreign cash across the border from Egypt to Gaza, declaring to the European Union Border Assistance Mission stationed at the Rafah crossing that they were funds for depleted PA coffers. One Hamas official confirmed that $2 million had been brought in to pay public servants such as police officers, doctors and teachers who hadn't received their salary in months.[32]

In the days that followed, Palestinian civil servants received their first payouts. Hamas declared the money to be Ramadan 'Eid' payments, pledging that, despite the hardships that thousands had endured because of the boycott, there would be money for food as Palestinians celebrated the most important religious event in the Muslim calendar. Hundreds of workers streamed to PA pay-offices and banks to receive their meagre cheques of $50 each. When Israel progressively sealed this easy land route following Hamas's election victory and military takeover of Gaza the following year, Hamas used tunnels from Egypt to bring funds into the increasingly impoverished Strip. But, for all its claims of honesty and integrity, Hamas could not replace the vast sums of foreign aid that had kept the Palestinian Authority, and the entire Palestinian economy, afloat. Repeated Friday sermons by the charismatic new prime minister, Ismail Haniyeh, preaching the virtues of thrift, honesty and steadfastness did little to fill Palestinians' pockets, or tables. 'We'll eat *za'atar* leaves, weeds and salt, but we won't be traitors and we won't be humiliated!' declared Haniyeh before a crowd in the Gaza Strip on 14 April 2006.[33] Poverty drove more and more into dependency on humanitarian food parcels and handouts from UN agencies and other charities as the funding cuts hit Gaza's already fragile economy and social and welfare sector.

On the ground in the West Bank, meanwhile, Hamas found it far harder to operate its charitable network. The Israeli army and intelligence services launched frequent raids against organizations suspected of involvement with Hamas. One such came in February 2008, when the Israeli military issued orders to close down half a dozen departments of the Islamic Charitable Society in Hebron, accusing it of being a Hamas front. The charity was founded in 1962 to help orphans, including, its organizers claimed, the children of Palestinian collaborators who were killed for cooperating with Israel. The society also ran eight local schools, bakeries, housing projects and garment factories employing up to 550 people.[34] The Israeli raids shut down the bakeries and a clothing factory which earned money for the orphans, said the charity organizers. Israel alleged that the society was 'a Hamas terror organization fund operating under the guise of charity' and that the equipment and possessions seized by the army and Shin Bet were 'important Hamas sources of profit used to fund terrorist activity in Hebron'. It said the institution was part of Hamas's attempt to increase its standing among the civilian population in the West Bank. It accused the Hebron organization of having delivered money to terror operatives and members of their families, training youths in the spirit of jihad, providing financial incentives to families of suicide bombers and prisoners, and spreading Hamas principles among the Palestinian population. 'With such actions Hamas exploits Palestinian society, particularly its lowest socio-economic strata, in order to gather a terror following.'[35]

The Islamic Charitable Society said it had an income of $3 to $5 million a year but had nothing to do with Hamas, pointing out that it was not among the scores of Hamas-affiliated organizations which had been shut down by the Fatah-dominated PA in the West Bank during an earlier wave of closures. 'There is no connection whatever with the Hamas movement. If there was the smallest proof, Israel would have found out about it and the PA would have taken all steps to close the place down', said Ghassan Mohammed, the society's supervisor. Touring the wreckage of the Israeli raid at the orphanage, charity bakery and school, he said the Israelis

> confiscated buses used for transferring orphans to school, bakeries that we
> used to give the orphans food and workshops where they make clothes. If

they had found any rockets or tools for fighting they would have closed the whole place and the whole world would have found out about it. They merely have a general plan to fight terror, but they don't have any proof that this institution is part of that.[36]

The agenda

One persistent criticism of Hamas is that its social programmes come with an expensive price label: social order, the Hamas way. Aside from the repeated and well-documented reports of Islamist enforcers bullying women into conforming to Islamic behaviour codes, Hamas and other Islamist organizations have curbed other social activities of which they disapprove.

In 2005, soon after winning control of the West Bank town of Qalqilya in municipal elections, Hamas banned a decade-old dance and music festival – initially on the pretext that it wanted to protect the grass in the town's football stadium. The same year, Islamist gunmen also stopped a rap band performing on the site of an evacuated Jewish settlement during celebrations of Israel's withdrawal from Gaza. Adding fuel to the critics, after Hamas won the election its Education Ministry ordered a 400-page anthology of forty-five Palestinian folk tales, including a tale called 'The little bird', about sexual awakening, to be pulled off school library shelves. The then education minister, Dr Nasser Eddin al-Shaer, confirmed that the title had been removed, saying that the book was 'full of clear sexual expressions'.[37] The move was quickly condemned internationally and domestically, including by Hani al-Masri, the director of the Palestine Media, Research and Studies Centre in the West Bank city of Ramallah. 'I think it is a dangerous decision that shows us the hidden face of Hamas', he said. 'Hamas have always wanted Palestinian society to be more Islamic, and the ban shows this.'[38] The public outcry forced Hamas to backtrack, and the book was quickly reinstated. Mr Shaer backed down, calling the row a 'storm in a teacup'.[39]

In a conflict within which ideologues often argue that any activity which distracts from the central goal of liberation through armed struggle is an unworthy distraction, such acts are by no means confined to Hamas. In the same month as Hamas's dance ban in Qalqilya, gunmen belonging to Fatah shot in the air and ended a concert by the Palestinian singer Ammar Hassan in Nablus, objecting to his 'immoral' songs.[40] But such disapproval is actually enshrined in Hamas's constitution, one section of its founding covenant being dedicated to 'The role of Islamic art in the battle of liberation':

Man is a unique and wonderful creature, made out of a handful of clay and a breath from Allah. Islamic art addresses man on this basis, while pre-Islamic art addresses the body giving preference to the clay component in it. The road is long and suffering is plenty. The soul will be bored, but Islamic art renews the energies, resurrects the movement, arousing in them lofty meanings and proper conduct.[41]

The anti-dancing edict was defended by Dr Mahmoud Zahar, Hamas's elder statesman. 'A man holds a woman by the hand and dances with her in front of everyone. Does that serve the national interest?' Zahar asked the Arabic website Elaph. 'If so, why have the phenomena of corruption and prostitution become pervasive in recent years?' Zahar also condemned homosexual marriage, saying: 'Are these the laws for which the Palestinian street is waiting? For us to give rights to homosexuals and to lesbians, a minority of perverts and the mentally and morally sick?'[42] Such intolerance instils genuine fear among social liberals in the Palestinian Territories. 'Hamas doesn't only impose its social agenda, it imposes a political, legal and social agenda', said Naima al-Sheikh Ali, a Fatah activist in Gaza. 'Their attempt to impose their presence by force of weapons proves how strongly they are trying to impose their political and social agenda.'[43]

Certainly in the Hamas summer camps for girls the emphasis was on the role predestined for them, according to the movement's interpretation of Islam. 'Fatah used to run the camps only to indoctrinate for Fatah, but we are the opposite', explained Riham al-Wakil, one of the camp instructors who had volunteered from the Hamas women's student association. 'Yes, we are Hamas', she continued, 'but we teach the girls about the rules of our religion first. We show them how to be mothers and to respect the wishes of their father.'[44] The thirteen- to fifteen-year-old girls attending the camp were instructed in how to perform prayers, about relationships within the family and about the *hadith* and *tafsir* (commentary) on the Koran. They also put on exhibitions, one about the Prophet Mohammed and another on the Hamas-supported boycott of Danish goods in the aftermath of the controversy about Danish cartoons of the Prophet. The girls sang songs about being a good daughter and then, amid paper flowers and crafts made from glitter and sequins, one young star was singled out to perform back flips, cartwheels and acrobatics for the women-only viewers.

Other victims of the new Islamization were Gaza's Nawar (domari gypsies). In 2006 they complained that, since the outbreak of the Second Intifada in 2000, the Islamists had steadily put an end to their ancient traditions of song and dance at weddings and celebrations. 'We went from city to city, to Rafah, Khan Younis, Jabalia. We would set up tents and would play the *oud* and the drums. Some of us wandered as far as Egypt, Syria and Jordan', said Fatima, forty-nine, a Nawar singer. She and her fellow dancers and entertainers were able to thrive in licensed clubs and dance halls set up along the seafront after the creation of Yasser Arafat's

PA in 1994. But it lasted only a few years, said Sheikh Abu Mohammed, the Nawar patriarch. After the outbreak of the Second Intifada, Islamists began to enforce their writ, accusing the Nawar of being prostitutes, depriving them of their living and forcing them into begging in the streets and markets. 'The extremists burned and closed all the clubs. They said it was *"haraam"* (forbidden) that girls dance and sing. Our ancient life has vanished into thin air and it will not come back.'[45]

The good times were also over for bar and nightclub owners. Although restaurants serving alcohol are a feature of liberal West Bank towns such as Ramallah – indeed, there is a brewery in the 100 per cent Christian village of Taibeh – there is no such freedom in Gaza. An empty, burned-out cinema has stood in the centre of Gaza City for years, a daily reminder to everyone of what happens when social and entertainment institutions fall foul of the Islamists. By December 2005 there was only one bar left selling alcohol in Gaza, and that was inside a United Nations beachside compound. Even this was bombed over the New Year's holiday, never to reopen.

Other Palestinian-run bars had long gone. One former club proprietor, Nabil Kafarneh, lamented that he lost $250,000 when his Gaza beachside clubs, the Sheherazade and the Appointment, were burned down in 2000, even though they had PA licences to operate legally. He said his night-clubs were torched after a Hamas rally in which the crowd was exhorted to 'burn casinos'. 'I had thirty dancers', said a miserable Mr Kafarneh, as he sat in the gloomy, cold and damp lounge of his home, replaying on a large television monitor the only memory he has of the liberal 'old days' – a grainy video of Arab women dancers gyrating round a series of tables occupied by men eating meat and fruit and smoking *nargilas*. 'The dances we were offering were for art. I had a licence for alcohol and hundreds of people used to come and enjoy themselves here, and hundreds more were beneficiaries in terms of employment.' He complained that he could find no one brave enough to help him reopen the clubs under a Hamas regime. 'There were no previous warnings, it was a random attack', he said.[46]

During the same period, as Hamas was consolidating its rule, a hitherto unknown Islamist organization calling itself the Swords of Islamic Righteousness began bombing internet cafes and chemists, accusing them of peddling pornography and illicit drugs. With Gaza's ineffective security agencies distracted by the civil war then raging between Hamas and Fatah gunmen, the group distributed communiqués in which they threatened to 'execute the laws of God' at cybercafés 'which are trying to make a whole generation preoccupied with matters other than jihad and worship'. The group also claimed attacks on unveiled women, threatened 'university girls putting on makeup and dressing in a satanic way', music shops and motorists playing loud music.[47]

Fawzi Barhoum, a Hamas spokesman, denied that Hamas had anything to do with the attacks, protesting that it was 'among those most damaged by the lack of security'. He maintained that

> Our programme of change and reform regarding corruption and vice is not based on any sort of violence or fighting, but in an educated, civilized way that represents the culture of the Palestinian people and their faith. We adopt an Islamic approach to reach our targets. All sorts of violence, starting with kidnapping, assassinations, internal fighting, destroying and burning headquarters and civil society buildings, kidnapping journalists and assaulting the public places, only serves the occupation and has a very negative effect on the Palestinian people.[48]

Yet once Hamas had assumed total control of the Gaza Strip in June 2007 it instituted measures that would restrict people's freedoms according to its strict social agenda. It issued an edict imposing an internet filter which disrupted business and slowed down traffic so much, café owners complained, that it succeeded in closing down stores which had survived the earlier Islamist purges. 'I think it's because the government is trying to stop people from accessing porn', said one internet café owner, who only agreed to speak on condition of anonymity, fearing reprisals. 'It is a useless decision because people always find a way around the controls. It is a form of trespass on individual rights, and I have lost customers because the filters slow considerably all the internet traffic in Gaza.'[49] Another internet café owner spoke of persistent harassment since Hamas had taken over. 'Their police have raided my premises many times looking for Fatah flags and pornography. They've arrested me more than once, and now people are afraid to spend time in the internet café.'[50]

Hamas was accused of imposing other social edicts, including the announcement by a senior judge of a dress code under which female lawyers would have to wear conservative robes and headscarves in court, and a ban on women riding motorbikes. Rumours also spread that it had banned the sale of sexual performance-enhancing drugs such as Viagra. Hamas – according to the rumour – did not want the indolent and the unemployed engaged in prolonged carnal pleasures. Arson attacks and other violence continued against individuals, social clubs and cafés. Human rights groups in Gaza and elsewhere say that, even if attacks are not being carried out by Hamas under the cover of anonymity – as many suspect – at the very least Hamas and its preachers, youth teachers, summer camps and public rallies are responsible for creating the atmosphere of intolerance and social oppression within which such attacks take place. Indeed, Hamas has produced a large cadre of social enforcers, and this network is a direct outcome of the decades invested by Hamas in running youth, social and charity programmes in the Gaza Strip in particular – creating a receptive audience for its message to ensure that today's audience are tomorrow's enforcers.

Islamic society – a cameo

It was June 2002, the height of the Second Intifada, and Hamas bombers were blowing up buses and cafés in Jerusalem and Tel Aviv. The latter is just 40 miles north of Jabalia refugee camp in the northern Gaza Strip, but the two could be in different worlds. Tel Aviv is a cosmopolitan Israeli city of Bauhaus architecture, embassies, art boutiques and seafront bars. Jabalia is a claustrophobic zigzag of identical grey streets and permanently unfinished breezeblock homes packed together closer than houses in Tudor London. More than 195,000 people live in the camp area of just 1.4 sq. km. Here in a back street was the *Jamia Islamiyya*, or Islamic Society. Founded in 1976 in Gaza, it is a benevolent society which pre-dates Hamas by more than a decade, but it was established by the same Islamist network and forms part of the Hamas movement's wider social services network. Its main aim, according to the manager Mohammed Shahab, is 'to bring people to the Islamic religion and to build a full Palestinian life, bringing them mosques, faith and education by introducing them to science, physically by offering them sports, socially by lifting their spirits and morally by bringing them employment'.[51]

As he organized volunteers, Mr Shahab explained how the society's social committee looked after the needy children of Palestinians killed during the conflict – distributing meat, clothing and school bags, and running a blood bank. Shahab insisted that his society did not take money from the Palestinian Authority, which was then still run by Fatah, but instead received funding from organizations in Britain, Europe, the Muslim world and, closer to home, from the overwhelmingly Arab city of Nazareth in northern Israel. The poorest unemployed people in the area were selected by volunteers familiar with each district in Jabalia, and were given food: 5 kg of sugar, 2 kg of tea, 2 kg of lentils, 3 kg of beans, 2 kg of hummous, 6 kg of rice, 4 litres of cooking oil, two cans of meat, tomato sauce and 25 kg of flour. Among the recipients was Mohammed Azaliya, thirty-eight, a father of six children who once earned 220 shekels (£25) a day as a construction worker in Tel Aviv, but who lost his job when the escalation in violence prompted Israel to slow down and finally stop the flow of Palestinian day labourers who used to pass through the Israeli-controlled crossing between the Gaza Strip and Israel.

The society had a kindergarten, mostly for the children of unemployed former workers in Israel such as Mr Azaliya. The charges were 30 shekels (£4) a month per child and the same amount for the bus. Some workers owed the Islamic Society as much as 30,000 shekels for two years' education, which they had to pay back only if they found work. Orphans and hardship cases received education for free. 'Where else can I go? To the mafia?' asked Mr Azaliya, using the pejorative local slang term for the PA. 'They [the PA] give each of us 500 shekels [£70] a year. All of them have many millions of dollars and have smuggled it abroad. We thank

God for the Islamic Society, otherwise a lot of people would be starving now.'

Standing in the dingy office, the recipients poured scorn on the PA, accusing its officials of stealing food coupons. 'I was meant to get twelve or thirteen but I only got two, which means ten disappeared', says Mr Azaliya. 'Hamas are not thieves like the others. They don't make concessions about our homeland. The others are traitors and mafia.'[52] Mohammed, the organizer, beamed as his clients insulted the Fatah-dominated PA, but emphasized his society did not insist, or need to insist, on a religious quid pro quo for the aid it handed out. 'We don't impose any conditions', he said. 'We are the Islamic Society but we don't make them follow what we do. It's not political, it is our religion. Some of these people will eventually come to God. We want them to become more religious, more clear, more pure.'

Islamic Society headquarters in Gaza were among the institutions targeted and destroyed by Israel's intensive bombing strikes as part of Operation Cast Lead, from December 2008 to January 2009.

But the work of the Islamic Society and the rest of Hamas's network in the decades up to, during and after the Second Intifada, when families needed it most, represented not so much a donation as an investment by Hamas, one that reaped a lucrative political dividend in the 2006 election.

Link in the chain

There is, of course, no direct one-to-one correlation between every charitable act and every Hamas member and voter recruited, but few question that Hamas's military wing operates as a 'link in the chain' of the wider movement. It is for this reason that Israel refuses to recognize any distinction between Hamas's social organization and its military wing. Indeed it has targeted the social institutions for attack – destroying schools, offices and storage warehouses. All are seen as part of the infrastructure of terror.

In November 2006, citing a wave of rocket attacks from Gaza into Israeli border towns, the Israeli political-security cabinet authorized strikes not only against 'missile-launching areas' but 'against Hamas institutions in the Gaza Strip'.[53] The Israeli attacks were met with a fatalistic shrug by Sakkar Abu Hein, the head of the Mujamma. 'They hit us last week, they hit our branch in Shejaiyah', he confirmed in his office in Gaza shortly after the attack. 'The building we had is three storeys: the first is a mosque, the second is a library and the third is a workshop for women to teach them how to sew and knit. The fourth', he added, in a rare flash of Islamist humour, 'is a nuclear bomb factory.' Asked if the building had Hamas military personnel defending it he said no, again resorting to sardonic wit.

'We have Patriot missiles upstairs to intercept their weapons. What can we do? We have nothing. We have nothing except the power of Allah.'

Mr Abu Hein confirmed that his organization was created in 1973 by Sheikh Yassin. But he maintained that, as the head of the Mujamma bloc, he and his 250 employees, plus another 100 teachers, are entirely separate from Hamas's armed activities. 'We can work in everything except politics and the military. We provide social, medical, educational and charities for poor people, orphans and others. All kinds of charitable services', he said. Those services have expanded significantly over the decades. It began with one kindergarten serving 200 children in Gaza City. By 2006 it had twenty kindergartens looking after 4,000 children. In 1990 it looked after 500 orphans; by 2006 around 5,000 were receiving a monthly payment. 'Our message is defending humanity, fighting poverty, fighting sickness, developing women and protecting children. All the benevolent societies have a board of trustees, totally separate from the political and military work of Hamas', he said. 'I am head of the Mujamma bloc. I only work with social work. I have nothing to do with politics, military or any other kind of organization within Hamas. My job is to run the Mujamma.'

Mr Abu Hein said his organization's budget was $2.5 to $3 million a year but that, because of the international sanctions and crackdown on funding to Hamas, 50 per cent of it had not arrived. 'The Americans, British and Europeans in particular have stopped money coming from organizations which help us.' The largest amount was from Europe, he said, principally from non-governmental organizations in France, Britain, the Netherlands and Belgium. He claimed that both Muslim and non-Muslim NGOs contributed to their activities and that he received funds from Yemen, Sudan and Egypt. Challenged about allegations that money donated to the Hamas-led government – or to its pre-existing network of associated charities – can easily be diverted to its armed wing, he insisted that money to the government goes to the Ministry of Finance and that that money donated through the network of Islamic charities goes straight from the banks into the accounts of the benevolent societies to which it is donated, into separate accounts for different projects. 'Firstly, you can visit all our institutions and check if we have any weapons', he said.

> Secondly, the donors sponsor individual projects and make sure each project is completed as described. We take 10 per cent out of this money to pay for our services, to run the project. We are an open book. Anyone can follow the money from the minute it comes to the project until it is spent. Anyone can monitor us, all of our accounts are open.[54]

The same month as Mr Abu Hein was speaking, November 2006, the United Nations Office for the Coordination of Humanitarian Affairs in Israeli-occupied East Jerusalem reported that Israeli army raids had 'closed down four Islamic charities in recent months and raided many more in a string of targeted raids across the West Bank which have left more than 4,450 orphans, 157 widows and 3,000 destitute families without a local humanitarian safety net.'[55]

Welfare weddings

One factor that should not be overlooked is that Hamas as a movement knows full well, in an environment of penury and hardship, the value of spectacle. It has an ability – appetite even – for showmanship. It will sometimes enliven a public rally in Gaza with a recorded message from its supreme leader, Khaled Meshaal, in Damascus, because as a wanted man he can never visit Gaza. Other attractions may include a Hamas DJ and sound system to whip up the crowd, or the sudden appearance of masked fighters rappelling down nearby buildings on ropes, to the delight of watching children bored by the political rhetoric.

Every so often Hamas will also use its cash to hold mass weddings in Gaza, putting on a huge show for would-be bridegrooms who could not otherwise afford any ceremony. As a socially conservative religious movement, Hamas not only abhors the concept of sex outside marriage but has also promoted marriage as a form of resistance – a union of man and woman producing future generations to wage jihad against Israel. During the First Intifada, Hamas in Gaza endorsed the marriage of girls and women as young as thirteen to Palestinian men as progenitors of jihad in a demographic war against Israel. In later years it organized such weddings to secure husbands for the widows of their fighters killed in earlier battles and encounters with Israel.

In September 2006, nine months after the election victory, the Islamic Society held one such mass wedding ceremony at the football stadium in the southern Gaza border town of Rafah. There was a heavy presence of bearded and armed Palestinian police loyal to Hamas as a band played and men on horses and camels raced up and down before the flower-bedecked stage, waving Hamas flags. The brides were not there – they had had a separate ceremony two days earlier and were banned from this particular part of their own wedding. But relatives of the grooms were there – men and women sitting on different sides of the football pitch, drinking orange juice and eating roasted nuts and sunflower seeds.

Among the eighty-four grooms present, Saher Jarbouah, a 24-year-old accountancy student, said that he was among the two-thirds who were not religious, but professed his gratitude to the Islamists for saving him the thousands of dollars he could not afford and for laying on a ceremony in front of 10,000 people to mark the beginning of his married life. 'Of course this is useful for us', he said. 'It would cost a lot of money if you have to organize a wedding celebration yourself, hiring the band, the chairs, the video and so on. Most people can afford only a small celebration, but this

Photo 9.2   Palestinian bridegrooms at a mass wedding in Rafah, Gaza, paid for by Hamas

way you have the chance to be part of a really big event.' Gazing around him, he declared, 'It saves people money, it brings joy and happiness and it brings people together. It unites the families of eighty-four people, so that rich and poor can celebrate, not just the wealthy.'[56]

Nasser Barhoum, the event organizer, said that Hamas had held similar events since 1996 – halting only for three years at the worst of the post-2000 violence because of the regular Israeli raids. The $10,000 cost of the wedding was 'money well spent' for the movement, he assessed. 'In a poor town like Rafah there is a huge percentage of bachelors who cannot afford their own ceremonies. We recognize the importance of the institution of marriage and we are doing our best to make good Palestinian families. The Islamic Society's main job is to take care of poor families and their welfare, and Rafah is the poorest place.'[57] And, of course, the Hamas message ran through the wedding ceremony like marzipan through the cake. Addressing the crowd, Ghazi Hamad, a Hamas official, proclaimed that such events were a statement that Palestinians could not be broken. 'It is a message to the whole world that our happiness overpasses our sadness. No matter how hard and bitter our life is, we will overcome it. We will not give up. We will not be divided. That is why we are going to be victorious',[58] he said, to cheers.

Hamas's leaders seemed to be fully aware of the benefits of occasionally giving Gaza residents – and future voters – a break from the miserable circumstances in which they lived. The event was held the same week that the United Nations trade and development agency, UNCTAD, said that the Western aid freeze and Israel's closures and confiscation of $65 million (£35 million) a month in Palestinian tax revenues after Hamas's victory had left the Palestinian economy 'on the verge of collapse', and that unemployment, then standing at 35 per cent, was likely to rise to half the Palestinian workforce.[59]

Countering the Palestinian complaints of hardship, Shlomo Dror, the spokesman for the Israeli government's coordinator of government activities in the West Bank and Gaza, insisted that Israel opened the Karni goods and Rafah passenger crossings into Gaza whenever it could. He blamed Hamas and other militant groups for continuing with their violent approach, leaving Israel with no choice but to defend itself by closing the borders and crossings, hence stopping the movement of goods and access in and out of Gaza. 'I agree that the situation in Gaza is very bad. Nobody will tell you that it is good', he said. 'The issue is that the Palestinians have to take responsibility for the situation. They put snipers on the roof to target our civilian staff at Karni crossing and dig tunnels to attack them. When we offer to use other crossings, they refuse.' Mr Dror added: 'I think Hamas wants the situation to be very bad because this is the way that they can get money from Europe and America.'[60]

Whatever the criticisms, Hamas officials say they have learned one lesson from watching Fatah dominate the PLO for decades and the PA from 1994 to 2006. They say that Hamas will remain careful to maintain the distinction between a government – which can quickly be voted out of power – and a movement, which continues whether its MPs are in the cabinet or in opposition. Hamas early came to the conclusion that Yasser Arafat made a grave error by allowing Fatah the movement to integrate so closely with Fatah the government, to the point that, when Fatah the government fell from power, Fatah the movement had atrophied politically and organizationally. 'In the PLO's and Fatah's time the mix between government and the organization created many problems', said Riham al-Wakil, the Hamas summer camp organizer. 'The mistake of Fatah was to mix the movement, the youth wing, the PA, everything. It was all mixed together. That led to corruption and led to individual power bases, struggles between those bases and the creation of special interests. We are aware of those issues. There is total separation between the movement and government.'[61]

For an organization long dedicated to destruction, Hamas had learned from its larger and better-equipped fellow Islamist organizations – such as Hezbollah – that construction can be just as potent a tool. 'We build for you, and we also resist for you', Mushir al-Masri, a former Hamas spokesman and newly elected MP, shouted to a crowd of delighted supporters at one post-election rally in Gaza City.[62]

Indeed, this is likely to prove essential to Hamas's very survival. After Israel's winter offensive of December 2008 to January 2009 destroyed scores of buildings, it became clear that, in trying to destroy one battle-field, Israel's onslaught had created another: Hamas's head-on struggle with Fatah to own the reconstruction of Gaza.

A few days after the offensive ended, Ismail al-Ashqar, a Hamas MP and strategist, made no effort to conceal his anger, not just at Israel, but at Fatah's president, Mahmoud Abbas, for – as he saw it – doing too little to stop the bloodshed. Normally urbane, Ashqar had just lost a brother, a nephew and four cousins in the month-long Israeli operation, and was in an unusually venomous mood as he said that Hamas had no inten-tion of allowing Fatah, once the guns fell silent, to sweep in to Gaza with millions of dollars in European funds to begin rebuilding and taking the credit for it. Standing in the rubble of the parliament building, he pointed out – accurately – that the reality on the ground was that Hamas had near total military control over Gaza since its 2007 takeover, and that no Fatah reconstruction effort could operate there without Hamas's consent. Especially if, he said darkly, international players wanted to boost President Abbas and the Abbas-appointed West Bank prime minister, Salam Fayyad, by pumping millions of dollars into the rebuilding effort through Fatah rather than through Hamas.

'Europe and the US are part of the conspiracy, and this money is politi-cal money, it is dirty money', Mr Ashqar said. 'We think that they want to give this money to the Palestinian people through people who don't really represent us, like Fayyad.' Hamas, he insisted, would allow money into Gaza only through respectable international humanitarian organizations, the United Nations and overseas banks, or through their own govern-ment in Gaza, supervised by the donors. 'If they want to use it for their own ends, we tell them that that money will never get here', he stated. 'We do not allow the Fayyad government to work in Gaza. It is an illegal government.'[63]

10

Women

She is the maker of men. Her role in guiding and educating the new generations is great.

Hamas's Covenant[1]

Ultimately it comes back to the name: the Muslim Brotherhood. Hamas's well-drilled and energetic women's movement has drawn a huge amount of domestic and international media attention since the election victory in 2006, but even its senior members concede that such high-profile activities have not changed how the movement is run. It is men who monopolize control. The Brotherhood continues to take the decisions while the Sisterhood has, at best, a supporting role. Hamas remains patriarchal and conservative and defines the role for women in the movement.

In the wake of the election victory, Jamila al-Shanti, the Gaza-based Islamist who headed Hamas's list of women candidates, was asked if there had ever been any women on the organization's main *shura* council, its supreme decision-making body. 'No, not until now', she conceded. 'We are not part of this *shura* council.' Shanti played down the omission, saying she and her fellow women Islamists were content to have 'our own organizations within Hamas'. She even, less than convincingly, sought to portray their exclusion as an advantage, arguing: 'We have our own needs. Why should we be only a minority within a *shura* council in which the majority are men and their decisions have influence on us? No, we have two separate movements, the men and the women, and we work according to our needs. We have our own *shura*, our own movement.'[2] Hamas did appoint Mariam Saleh as the minister for women's affairs in its government of 2006. This was only natural given the strict segregationist tendencies of the movement.

Despite Hamas's claim to involve women at all levels, its critics maintain that it is a rigidly conservative organization whose own founding manifesto defines women principally through a biological function as 'makers of men'. In the areas where it is strongest – most notably the

Gaza Strip – Hamas has mounted a sustained campaign of Islamization, using preachers, social pressure and even intimidation to compel women to act and dress according to its own interpretation of Islam. This has drawn vociferous domestic and international criticism that, in so doing, it has restricted women's freedoms and tolerated violence against them. Indeed, its attitude to a woman's place in society and politics has become a key batttlefield between Hamas and its secular opponents.

But as the huge women's turnout for Hamas in the 2006 elections testifies – and as even Fatah women activists reluctantly concede – Hamas has in recent years comprehensively outmanoeuvred its secular opponents in the battle for the hearts, souls and votes of Palestinian women. It has mobilized them to win power and wage resistance against Israel. Why did Hamas single out women as a constituency likely to prove such willing recipients – and carriers – of its message? And how did it win them over in the face of competition from much larger and longer-established Palestinian women's organizations?

Covenant

When the Hamas movement was created during the opening days of the First Palestinian Intifada in 1987, it considered itself to be the Palestinian wing of the Muslim Brotherhood, founded in Egypt in 1928. The 'Brothers', or Ikhwan as they were known, were the exclusively male founders who established its structures and made all decisions about the movement's agenda through the traditional Islamic method of consultation (*shura*). In its founding Covenant, printed on illegal presses, Hamas spelled out its vision, including its view of how women could contribute to the cause. Its leaders believed that a crisis of faith was afflicting Palestinian society, leaving it weakened and ill-prepared to confront Israel's occupation forces. They maintained that individuals had to return to their faith and control themselves through the fundamental pillars of Islam. And part of this was for men to exert their rightful control over women, as ordained in the faith. From the very outset Hamas also laid claim to the powerful motif of women as the mothers of martyrs. The Covenant depicts women as passive bearers of future generations of jihadists, and the Hamas ideal of Palestinian womanhood is evident from sections dedicated to their role in the home, and society:

> The Muslim woman has a role no less important than that of the Muslim man in the battle of liberation. She is the maker of men. Her role in guiding and educating the new generations is great.
>
> Woman in the home of the fighting family, whether she is a mother or a sister, plays the most important role in looking after the family, rearing the children and imbuing them with moral values and thoughts derived from

Islam. She has to teach them to perform the religious duties in preparation for the role of fighting awaiting them. That is why it is necessary to pay great attention to schools and the curriculum followed in educating Muslim girls, so that they would grow up to be good mothers, aware of their role in the battle of liberation.

   She has to be of sufficient knowledge and understanding where the performance of housekeeping matters are concerned, because economy and avoidance of waste of the family budget is one of the requirements for the ability to continue moving forward in the difficult conditions surrounding us. She should put before her eyes the fact that the money available to her is just like blood which should never flow except through the veins so that both children and grown-ups could continue to live.[3]

The Covenant defines the limits of any role which a Palestinian might wish to play within the ideological bounds of a conservative Islamist movement. In Hamas's battle with Israel, women are confined to a support function on the home front, using their bodies and reproductive capacity to produce fighters. Hamas, like other actors in this conflict, understands the politics of demographics.

Historical role

Palestinian movements have long sought to depict women as being integral to their society's resistance against Israeli occupation. Hamas is no exception. Even as Izz ad-Din al-Qassam organized his peasant rebel bands during the British Mandate in the early twentieth century, Palestinian women protested, demonstrated, and wrote petitions to British officials to oppose the changes transforming their society during the period of mass Jewish immigration to their country. Al-Qassam, conservative Islamist that he was, believed that women should be neither seen nor heard. In the 1930s he had issued a ruling against the attendance, and wailing, of women at funeral services. He also opposed the 'blatant mingling of men and women'.[4]

   In 1936, Palestinian women founded their own Congress and Executive, and were militant in their rejection of British rule and demands for Palestinian independence. The British authorities were not above calling on Palestinian male leaders to 'restrain their women'. But it was not enough to deter both Muslim and Christian women from banding together and engaging in forms of resistance. These women were motivated far less by feminist ideas of women's emancipation and equality than by the political impulses of nationalism and independence.

   In the late 1940s, after the UN approval of the partition of Palestine and expulsion of Palestinians from their homes and villages, many thousands of women fled into exile in refugee camps in Lebanon, Syria, Jordan, the

West Bank and Gaza Strip, where they passed on accounts of brutality, massacre and martyrdom to younger generations. Inspired, the daughters of these women became politically active in the 1960s and 1970s, signing up to join Palestinian nationalist *fedayeen* – guerrilla groups. In training camps across the Arab world, many participated in PLO activities, taking heed of the role that women were playing in other liberation struggles, such as in Algeria. These women faced tough choices in their dual struggle for Palestine and for the women's movement. But they were part of a nationalist struggle against Israel, not fighting a jihad in the name of Islam. This distinction between such early activists and the Hamas model emerges from discussions with veteran women's campaigners who were involved in the struggles of the 1960s and 1970s, and who now see the changes wrought on their lives and their society by the rise of the Islamists.

Bareheaded, and chain-smoking Viceroy cigarettes, Dr Mariam Abu Dagga now sits in her Popular Front for the Liberation of Palestine office in Gaza City, recalling how in the late 1960s she was a military activist in the leftist faction's 'Martyr Guevara' group, named after Che Guevara. Jailed and deported by Israel in the early 1970s, she returned more than two decades later in 1994 to a post-Intifada Gaza she did not recognize, where being without a headscarf (*hijab*) made her the exception rather than the norm. At her 'welcome home' party, she remembers, an uncle sidled up to her and said it would be 'better' if she wore a *hijab*. 'I told him: "I like you as a brother, not because of the way you dress. If you come to me would I force you to wear shorts?" He didn't say anything more.' When she tried to take part in political and business meetings she found herself isolated, and was made to feel unwelcome, even un-Palestinian. 'I was the only woman at meetings', she recalls. 'When I arrived they said "The bride has come". I asked, "Why are you saying this?" and they said, "Because we don't see women here except when she is a bride at her wedding". Other times they would say to me: "Hello, how are you? Are you Jewish? Are you a foreigner?"'[5]

Certainly, the dual struggles of feminism and national liberation have not always coexisted in harmony. Islamist groups, including Hamas, have excoriated secular Palestinian women's movements, denigrating them as anti-national and pro-Western.

The women's Intifada

Palestinian women have always been active politically, especially compared with their sisters in other parts of the Arab world. The Gaza which Dr Mariam Abu Dagga left in the 1960s was more socially liberal than the one she returned to in 1994 because, under the popular Egyptian nationalist leader Gamal Abdel Nasser, Egyptians and Gazans enjoyed the same social freedoms as other relatively 'progressive' Arab countries of that era. Pan-Arabism and socialism were the dominant ideologies and the Islamists, chiefly of the Muslim Brotherhood variety, barely existed in Gaza. They were certainly marginal in debates about politics and society. Women such as Mariam were politicized and played their part in the liberation struggle.

Later, during the first two decades of Israel's occupation of the West Bank, East Jerusalem and Gaza, from 1967 to 1987, Palestinian women participated in demonstrations, organized petitions and carried out other activities in support of the national struggle. Some were legends, lionized by the propaganda organs of the PLO. Among them was Laila Khaled, a member of the radical leftist PFLP, who in 1969 took part in the hijacking of a Trans World Airlines passenger jet, and was arrested and jailed the following year after a failed attempt to hijack an El Al plane. Wearing a *keffiyeh*, carrying a gun, and sporting a home-made ring fashioned from the pin of a grenade and a bullet, she became an icon of the Palestinian movement, representing to her admirers a fusion of feminism, national struggle and guerrilla warfare. She was jailed for her part in the second hijack attempt, but was released within weeks in a prisoner exchange deal and was later elevated to the central committee of the PFLP.

Other female icons were the writer and women's emancipation activist Sahar Khalifa and the poet Fadwa Touqan, both from Nablus, and even Raymonda Tawil, a Christian Palestinian nationalist writer, whose daughter Suha married Yasser Arafat. In their different ways these women came to symbolize the Palestinian national struggle, but there was barely a headscarf between them. Even in the socially conservative Gaza Strip women went bareheaded and wore short skirts on university campuses.

In the early 1980s things began to change. Hamas's Islamist forerunners in the Muslim Brotherhood and Mujamma frowned upon the socially liberal outlook of the PLO towards the attire, behaviour and public role of women. They began harassing them and coercing them to wear clothes which conformed to their own strict interpretation of Islam. Men were urged to grow their beards long and to wear long, loose clothes and some form of head covering for prayer. Women were pressured to abandon their short skirts, bare heads and even the traditional embroidered *thobe* worn by many Palestinian women in favour of what became known as *shari'a* dress – the *hijabs* and *jilbabs* which became ubiquitous on the campus of educational institutions such as the Islamic University of Gaza (IUG) and Hebron Polytechnic in the West Bank.

At the IUG, gender segregation was enforced and poorer female students received free clothing coupons donated by rich Gulf patrons which could only be redeemed for strict Islamic forms of dress purchased from local dress stores and boutiques. As Randa, a well-known Palestinian women activist, remarked, 'They thought our hemlines were a threat to the national struggle and forgot that with our brains we could make all the difference to achieving our political goals as a nation. The problem was them, not us.'[6]

The outbreak of the First Intifada in December 1987 was to bring an escalation of the Islamization campaign, amid the huge social and political changes that the uprising wrought across every sector of Palestinian society. During the Intifada women were suddenly everywhere, experiencing a hitherto unprecedented level of visibility and public involvement in the political struggle. Thousands turned out for the funerals of Palestinians killed by Israel, as demonstrations erupted first in Gaza, then in Jerusalem and the West Bank.

In every city, town and village women threw aside their daily household chores to march, build barricades or join popular committees that were organizing everything from food distribution to medical supplies. As Umm (Mother of) Mohammed, from Bethlehem's Aida refugee camp, recalled: 'I knew that I had to do my duty and play my part . . . our time had come and I was going to be part of it.'[7] Traditional women, camp women, urban women, village women, the educated and the illiterate, religious and secular, bareheaded and *hijab*ed – all took the lead in boycott campaigns against Israeli goods, often producing home-made replacements for the boycotted products. Neighbourhood groups, factional committees and families organized an alternative food economy based on home-made products such as cheese, pickles, olives and bread. If the bakeries were closed because of a curfew, then old *taboun* bread ovens were fired up again and used by women to make as much bread as their flour supplies allowed. Almost anything that grew was pickled in pink vinegar and preserved by women, who harvested fields and scavenged the local countryside for edibles that Palestinians could consume while Israel laid siege to them in an attempt to break the uprising.

This new social-national empowerment of Palestinian women only increased when Israel began to arrest thousands of Palestinian men in an effort to break the Intifada. Women were left to support their families financially as well as emotionally. Many turned to the lowest-paid jobs in Israel as day migrants and became the head of their households when husbands, brothers and sons were in prison or incapacitated by Israeli bullets. Wearing a full-face veil, known as a *niqb*, and gloves, and clothed in green with a cream *hijab*, Dr Abdel Aziz Rantissi's wife, Umm Mohammed, remembers that this was the era in which she too became involved in the Islamic movement:

For certain periods of time my husband was imprisoned or deported, and I shouldered the burden. I was the wife of one of the most well-known leaders. I stood by him and supported him in the way that he chose. It was a simple role as a woman. I often had to carry the burden of the whole family because he wasn't there – I had to raise the children.[8]

It was women who led the campaign to set up underground schools and community education when Israel ordered the closure of Palestinian schools and universities. They taught under threat of discovery and arrest by Israeli soldiers. However, not everyone was happy about the new emancipation that was evolving out of necessity in the new social and political order.

Founded in the opening days of the intifada, Hamas was the newest player on the scene. Determined to establish its credentials in a popular uprising, it quickly seized upon the role of women. For Hamas, a woman's place was in the home and not out fighting the occupation in the street. This became apparent within just a few months, as it organized its supporters to mount a campaign centred on the most visible sign of women's status in society: whether they were bareheaded or wearing a *hijab*.

Even after years of creeping Islamization there were at that time some public spaces where in places such as Gaza women still enjoyed greater freedom. But social pressure increased until those spaces became squeezed and then almost non-existent. Today one can barely travel a few metres down any major shopping thoroughfare in the Gaza Strip before encountering a small store outside which are displayed a colourful and glittering array of *hijabs*. The garments, and the necessary accoutrements of pins, visors and under-scarves, are laid out on plastic-coated racks in a rainbow of colours.

The ubiquity of the *hijab* was achieved quickly, within a year of so of the creation of Hamas. Of course some Palestinian women had always worn the *hijab*, or other forms of head-covering indigenous to a conservative, tribal society. Gaza was never Cannes or St Tropez. If women went with their families on a Friday to picnic at the beaches, they were dressed for a society that was socially conservative. This meant that, despite the summer heat of the Mediterranean, they never wore bathing costumes or bikinis. Many village women and those from peasant backgrounds in refugee camps wore a white muslin head-cover when at work. Their mothers and grandmothers had worn such scarves and they retained the custom, unquestioningly.

But a large number of women, especially in the urban middle classes, like their Arab sisters in Cairo, Baghdad, Beirut and Damascus, had dispensed with the *hijab* altogether. It was against these women that Hamas directed its *hijab* campaign, sometimes even using violence and often intense social pressure to enforce its will, regardless of the fissures it created in Palestinian society at a time when there was otherwise great emphasis placed on the need for unity and solidarity within the community.

Acid and stones

'Daughter of Islam, abide by *shari'a* dress!' ordered the graffiti on the walls of many a Gazan street. Gangs of Hamas 'enforcers' stormed into classrooms demanding that bareheaded girls put on the *hijab*. 'Before 1987 everything was normal, it was a personal freedom not to wear the *hijab*', said Naima al-Sheikh Ali, the director of Fatah's women's section in Gaza. After that, she recalls, 'Hamas began imposing its agenda on the hijab in Gaza. Whenever they saw a woman without a veil they attacked her and sometimes threw acid in her face.'[9]

Before long, bareheaded women were being stoned and abused in the street; their moral and national commitment was openly ques-tioned. Gangs of young men or boys with Hamas affiliations would roam Gaza's streets looking for bareheaded women whom they would target. Violence against women was never far from the equation in such encounters. If males were accompanying bareheaded women, then they would be told to order 'their' women to cover up or share the shame of the bareheaded one. Such women were portrayed as symbols of cor-ruption and national betrayal, as Hamas communiqués, leaflets and articles warned that beauty salons, hairdressing salons and dress shops were dens of iniquity where Israeli intelligence operatives ensnared Palestinian women, then used their sexuality to lure Palestinian men into becoming collaborators. Hamas and other Islamists cultivated the image of the Palestinian collaborator as the bareheaded, loose and morally bankrupt woman tricked into submitting to Israel for the thrill of illicit sex, alcohol or drugs. This was explicitly spelled out in Article 17 of the covenant:

> The enemies have realized the importance of her role. They consider that if they are able to direct and bring her up the way they wish, far from Islam, they would have won the battle. That is why you find them giving these attempts constant attention through information campaigns, films, and the school curriculum, using for that purpose their lackeys who are infiltrated through Zionist organizations under various names and shapes, such as Freemasons, Rotary Clubs, espionage groups and others, which are all nothing more than cells of subversion and saboteurs.[10]

The propagation of the canard that women are weak and vulnerable to exploitation by Israel through seduction – *ighraa* in Arabic – provided Hamas with yet another rationalization to exert greater control. Its solu-tion to such Israeli subversion was, of course, religion: 'The day Islam is in control of guiding the affairs of life, these organizations, hostile to human-ity and Islam, will be obliterated.'[11]

As it grew stronger, Hamas began to denounce secular Palestinian women's organizations as being part of a liberal feminist plot to under-mine the Muslim family. 'She is a woman, she is a Christian and she smokes',[12] the Hamas hardliner Dr Mahmoud Zahar sneered of Dr Hanan Ashrawi, an erudite and articulate Palestinian adademic from Ramallah who rapidly ascended to international media stardom when she became

Photo 10.1 A woman wearing a hijab in front of a graffiti-covered wall in Gaza

the public face of the PLO and a negotiator during the peace talks of the early 1990s.

Mascara and martyrs

One factor aiding Hamas's campaign was the tardiness of the secular political establishment to realize the significance of the new drive to social conformity, the targeting and attacks on women, and its unwillingness to stand against it. By the time that the United National Leadership of the Uprising (UNLU) responded with a special annex to one of its regular communiqués decrying attacks against women on the basis of their dress during the Intifada, the damage had been done, at least in Gaza.

Hamas was by no means alone among the armed factions in regarding the Intifada as a time of sacrifice across society, one in which individuals should not indulge petty vanities or waste money on fripperies while the families of martyrs were living in poverty. At such a time of heightened nationalist feelings, even for secular organizations mascara and martyr- dom did not mix. When the UNLU statement finally emerged its force was blunted by a stipulation that its leadership, too, was against 'exces- sive vanity' and 'cosmetics'. As so often across the Islamic world, it was hard for devout but moderate Muslims to argue against those playing the religious card without fear of being branded 'bad Muslims' from the pulpit and within their own tight-knit communities.

Zeinab al-Ghunaimi, director of the Centre for Women's Legal Research and Consulting in Gaza City, said that, when she stood for election in Gaza, her own sister tried to get her to drop out of the election after Hamas started vilifying her in public for not wearing a *hijab*. One of the secrets of Hamas's success, she concluded, was that it 'successfully estab- lished a belief that their politics is about Islam and their Islam is about the right kind of politics. So whatever the initiative people cannot reject it, because it would the same as rejecting the religion itself.'[13]

Others, even within the secular mainstream, believe that their own PLO leadership was simply too slow to realize the threat from an Islamist movement with a coherent, well-planned social agenda that dovetailed perfectly with its political and religious platform. 'Of course the PLO's address to the women was weak', said Naima al-Sheikh Ali, the Fatah women's activist. 'We blame the PLO factions for this. We warned them . . . The PLO factions had no clear agenda on women's issues.' They failed, she believes, to see 'that the *hijab* is a symbol of an Islamic state that I have not chosen to live in . . . I'll choose my state when I have got independ- ence, and I'll do it through the ballot box, not the mosque.'[14] Within a few years Hamas's campaigns had succeeded in ensuring that many of the women who had led the Intifada were now back at home, and silent in any public space.

Enforcers

One who fell victim to the new 'morality' was Yusra al-Azzam, a twenty-year-old Gazan who was killed by Hamas's self-appointed religious police for the offence of picnicking on a beach with an unmarried man who was not her relative. In April 2005 Yusra was returning from a day out at the beach with her fiancé, her sister and his brother when a white Mitsubishi car filled with Hamas 'enforcers' ordered the car to pull over, and opened fire when the driver refused to stop. Yusra was hit by the gunfire and died. Hamas initially denied involvement, but then admitted that the gunmen were Hamas. As the death began to generate much negative publicity, the movement quickly distanced itself from the killers, saying that they had acted without authority. But the gunmen belonged to powerful Gaza clans and were soon released from jail. With few relying on official courts at a time of near complete lawlessness, the dispute went to arbitration in the traditional way. After judging the death to have been 'accidental', the mufti of Gaza ordered that Yusra's relatives be paid 25,000 Jordanian dinars (£19,000) in 'blood money'. He applied the standard yardstick of 4.25 kg (150 oz) of gold for a dead man, and half that for a woman.

Interviewed a year after the death in their dilapidated house in Beit Lahiya, Yusra's parents were bitter but still fearful. Her father repeatedly emphasized that he considered the dispute officially closed, sitting beneath a portrait of his dead daughter on the wall as he murmured, over and over again: 'It is the will of Allah.' Yet Yusra's mother, Suhair, after remaining quiet for more than half an hour, suddenly exploded with impotent anger: 'We want them to be punished more. But as long as the old men take responsibility for these situations, we can't do anything.'[15]

Although Yusra's death was unusual in its circumstances, honour killings – including those allegedly carried out or sanctioned by Hamas 'enforcers' – are by no means rare. In August 2008 the Palestinian Centre for Human Rights documented thirty such killings between 2006 and 2008 in the occupied Palestinian Territories, twenty-four of them in the Gaza Strip. With Hamas in charge of Gaza, the rate of such attacks and killings increased, and Hamas officials refused to answer why they were failing to issue government statements and communiqués taking an unequivocal stance against them. Silence, in this case, was understood as a nod of aquiesence in the face of hate crimes against defenceless women. 'It is the government's duty to protect all its citizens, not just the men', said Reem, a local university graduate. 'I know that if I am even suspected of stepping beyond the bounds that my very life could be endangered.'[16]

Home front

Hamas's agenda for women had other dimensions. During the First Intifada it was a powerful advocate of forcing women back into the homes (*beit al ta'a*) and marrying off girls as young as thirteen. The rationale for early marriage was twofold: to protect the women, and to acceler-ate the reproduction of the 'living legacy' – a new generation of fighters. Hamas also believed that, if schools and universities were closed, girls and women should remain in the home and away from the streets, public squares, markets and other places in order to 'preserve' their honour. One such young woman whose life was confined by the new order was Hanan, a fourteen-year-old who was among 70,000 refugees living in the Khan Younis camp in southern Gaza in 1989.

Hanan's family were supporters of the leftist PFLP faction. Her father, a schoolteacher with the refugee agency UNRWA, was fiercely critical of Hamas's Islamic social agenda, and his outspoken views brought reprisal attacks down upon him, such as beatings. Cowed into submission by Hamas 'enforcers', he underwent a customary public corrective meted out to dissenters – he was forced to spend hours in the nearby mosque ensuring that everyone could observe him being a 'good Muslim', while his daughter, who until the Intifada had enjoyed school life, found herself virtually confined to home because Israeli curfews closed her school, and her father was too scared to let her out into the street for fear that Hamas would cast doubt upon her virtue.

Hanan's strategy was to make the most of the situation. She would sit in a corner of the main room – where the family spent the day, ate and slept at night – with her old school books and relearn what she had already learned. Although she wanted to be a teacher – 'like my father' – circum-stances turned her into the essence of a Hamas woman.[17] With a teaching career all but impossible, she was married off to her first cousin at the age of sixteen and had her first child within a year. Hanan's story has been replicated a thousand times over as Hamas has sought to redefine the social environment in which women exist in Gaza.

Hamas supporters consistently protest that it does not restrict women's rights, and claim that the West unfairly views all Islamists through the distorting prism of perhaps the most notorious anti-women's move-ment of all: the Afghan Taliban. 'They know nothing about the Taliban', responded an irritated Dr Mahmoud Zahar when confronted with the comparison in January 2006, shortly after Hamas's election victory.

> I will give you a personal example. My wife was a teacher, until the Israelis attacked my house and broke her back. My first daughter is an engineer . . .. The [second] is an English teacher. The third has graduated from accounting high school. The younger three boys are candidates for university. So I think this is a good answer to your question.[18]

His message is that hammered home by those from the senior leadership to the grass roots: that as Hamas encourages women to be educated and to contribute to resistance against Israel, it cannot therefore be accused of holding them back. At the Islamic University of Gaza, where Dr Zahar once taught, Iman Abu Jazar, the leader of the Hamas women's student bloc, insists that Hamas 'is not what people think'. A veiled medical student, Iman is dressed in a full-length *jilbab* and blue cotton gloves and was chaperoned by Hamas minders throughout the interview in the offices of the university's segregated campus. 'In Hamas women occupy every role, as doctors and engineers. They are on the councils and they are the mothers of many martyrs', she says. Restrictions on women, she argues, arise from the traditional conservative nature of Palestinian tribal society, 'not from Islam. I think women from the West come here and see Palestinian women, [and] we hear people say even in Palestine that Islam does not give women any of her rights. But I think it is not true. Hamas gives woman her rights.'[19]

However, women's rights campaigners maintain that, by focusing on education, Hamas deflects attention from more serious underlying issues. Dr Hanan Ashrawi, a former Palestinian cabinet minister and PLO negotiator, said that, for all their claims, the Islamists' agenda remains anti-progressive. 'They say that women have the right to education and the right to work provided that these don't interfere with her responsibilities as a home-maker and blah blah blah, but they will never accept the fact that women are equal. The question of equality is out of their agenda', she said, at her office in the West Bank city of Ramallah. A Christian Palestinian who now sits in the Palestinian parliament as a member of the Third Way party, she accepts criticism of the secular mainstream Palestinian leadership over the years on women's issues, conceding that it was 'not gender sensitive and did not work for gender parity at all'. But she discounts glib theories that Hamas's women's movement succeeded because it was uniquely well organized. She argues that the secular women's movements were similarly active within their communities, but that they focused on achieving necessarily gradual improvements in women's issues and other civil society agendas within a conservative society. Hamas, by contrast, deployed its women's movement – and charitable arms – as highly politicized recruitment tools. 'Civil society, particularly the women's movements, were all depoliticized. What did the secular nationalist women do at the elections? All civil society organizations became observers', Dr Ashrawi said.

> All these years they had been working in a non-political way, training for awareness, public consciousness, capacity-building, but not giving the services that the Hamas organizations were giving. And they were not conditional – I will give you this service provided you bring another woman with you, or I will do this if you do that, expanding their constituencies . . .

Hamas's organizations were politicized: schools, charitable organizations, day care centres, whatever.[20]

Naima al-Sheikh Ali, director of the women's section of Fatah in Gaza, shares Dr Ashrawi's viewpoint that arguments about whether or not Hamas allows women to gain academic qualifications or finish school distract from the real issues of women's empowerment and equality. 'Being a doctor or engineer is not the issue; the issue is that she must enjoy independence and freedom of decision', she said in her crowded Gaza City office, which was packed with dozens of women and children seeking assistance. She is irritated that Hamas seeks to portray itself as having 'sole possession' of the women's issue as if before it, women's activism simply did not exist: 'They are trying to ignore all the history of women's movements in Palestine, just as they tried to ignore all the history of the PLO.' She argues that Hamas is interested only in imposing its own political and social agenda, by force of arms if necessary, and has consistently shown no interest in advancing the cause of Palestinian women by obtaining legal safeguards for them, such as securing access to children for divorcees, achieving equal employment rights for women in government jobs, introducing a family code to enshrine protection for women and children, and protecting young women by raising the minimum age at which they can be married off by their families. 'Does Hamas oppose you on all those issues?', she is asked. 'Of course', she says.

Although opposed to the imposition of the *hijab* by force, Ali and other women's campaigners are also visibly irritated at what they regard as a Western obsession with the subject, pointing out that, in an environment of economic hardship such as Gaza, the principal concern of most women is how to feed their families, not what they wear on their heads:

I can't dare to speak with women about the *hijab* while she can't find milk for her children, and I can't speak to women about freedom issues while they are unable to feed their children. It would be as if we are speaking about luxuries. When there is economic stability, then we can handle these issues. But today, under this economic situation, our women's movement has been paralysed.[21]

Women suicide bombers

One controversy surrounding women's participation in Hamas is that of military operations – chiefly, but not exclusively – suicide bombings. The vast majority of Palestinian suicide bombings have been carried out by men. Of the 147 attacks in the five years from September 2000 to December 2005 – some involving more than one person – 156 of the bombers were male and only eight female.[22] The first suicide bombing by a Palestinian woman was on 27 January 2002, by Fatah's Al Aqsa Martyrs' Brigades. Wafa Idris, a 28-year-old refugee from Ramallah's al-Amari refugee camp, killed an 81-year-old man and wounded more than 150 people when she blew herself up in Jerusalem's Jaffa Street.[23]

Usually determined to set the agenda on innovatory military tactics, Hamas found itself behind, and confronted with a dilemma. On the one hand women aroused less suspicion at checkpoints, were often searched less, and could conceal bombs beneath their robes. On the other hand Sheikh Yassin was, according to some Hamas figures close to him, personally reluctant to deploy women as bombers. Faced with a wave of applications from women wanting to die for the cause, he delivered an ambivalent ruling – that Hamas would not permit women bombers for now, but would leave the possibility open for later in the struggle. 'I'm saying that in this phase the participation of women is not needed in martyr operations, like men', Yassin told the London-based newspaper *Asharq al-Awsat*. 'We can't meet the growing demands of young men who wish to carry out martyr operations.' Yassin said that 'women form the second line of defence in the resistance to the occupation' but that once the sixteen-month-old Intifada entered the 'decisive phase, everyone will participate without exception'. But he stipulated that, if a Hamas woman wanted to carry out an attack, she had to abide by the usual Islamic constraints and be 'accompanied by a man', such as a relative, 'if the operation requires an absence of more than a day and a night'.[24]

Hamas's West Bank spokesman, Sheikh Hassan Yousef, clarified Yassin's remarks by adding that he believed there was no religious precept prohibiting a woman's involvement. 'It is Muslim women's right to fight against occupation, and no fatwa forbids them from joining the struggle', he said.[25] His assessment was supported by Ismail al-Ashqar, a Hamas MP in Gaza, who said the issue was not one of a blanket religious prohibition, but of the circumstances in which it was suitable. 'Is it allowed by religion or not?, is the first question', he said in his office in Gaza City. 'It is allowed. When to use it, this is the question.'[26]

Dareen

Within a month one zealous young woman Hamas activist tested Yassin's ban, and found a way to get around it. Dareen Abu Aisheh was a 22-year-old from the village of Beit Wazan, near Nablus, who was a fourth-year English literature undergraduate at the city's an-Najah University. Always the first to Hamas's Islamist party's rallies, she was a student of Shakespeare, gave Koranic lessons at al-Rahmari mosque in the village, and studied karate. Poverty was not a factor: she came from an affluent family whose comfortable single storey home on a hilltop outside the city sat among date palm trees, grape vines and almond trees.

But on 27 February 2002 two Fatah activists drove her from Jerusalem to Tel Aviv. When Israeli police asked her to show her documents at the Maccabim roadblock, she detonated the explosives strapped to her waist, injuring two Israeli policemen and killing herself. Fatah claimed responsibility, but in Beit Wazan the next day her family said she had first approached Hamas, only to be refused permission to blow herself up. They disclosed that her seventeen-year-old cousin Safwat had carried out a suicide bombing the month before in Tel Aviv, wounding twenty-three people near the old central bus station. 'She came to me and said: "Women should carry out such operations, but Hamas won't allow us". I think it was the death of her cousin last month that was zero hour for her', her uncle Omar said.

Although her family had no idea in advance what she was going to do, Dareen had shocked her mother, Wafika, shortly before her death, by dipping her handkerchief in the blood of a Palestinian policeman who was killed in her home town – a handkerchief she left with her family with a note reading 'so that nobody forgets'.[27] Holding the still-bloodstained handkerchief, her mother said that it was the recent deaths of Palestinians in Nablus which had driven her to it, and that Dareen had frequently talked about the example set by Wafa Idris. 'She kept talking about it and said women should be involved as well as men, but maybe later when the men have played their part', said Mrs Abu Aisheh. 'She also mentioned pregnant women dying at checkpoints and said "It's not like the Israelis are treating women differently from men; they are treating them as equals and killing them as equals".' As her mother was consoled by women relatives, women members of her family disagreed about Dareen's act. 'According to the Islamic religion women should only be pilgrims to Mecca', said her sister. 'Only in very special situations should a woman do this. She used to see very difficult scenes of people being killed, injured and bloody and women giving birth at checkpoints. There was a pregnant woman shot at a checkpoint three days ago, she was touched by this.' One of her cousins echoed Sheikh Yassin's pronouncement: 'In our religion it says a woman can share in jihad and fight the enemies, but in the present time it should not be allowed.'[28]

In nearby Ramallah a few days later Sheikh Hassan Yousef bridled when presented with Dareen's posthumously relayed criticism of Hamas's reluctance to use women. But, despite being repeatedly pressed, he confined himself to generalities, in an apparent effort either not to reveal Hamas's thinking or not to get ahead of the movement's Gaza and Damascus leadership. 'We believe in the right of women to resist the occupation, side by side with men. We have no reservations', he said.[29]

There had been one early indication of the glorification of martrydom by Dareen and her peers. Six months before her death, Dareen's student wing of Hamas at an-Najah University had erected a re-creation of the Sbarro pizzeria to 'celebrate' the Hamas suicide bombing which killed fifteen people in Jerusalem in August 2001. The grisly exhibit included bloodstained plastic body parts hanging from the ceiling, as if they were flying through the air from the force of the explosion. Israeli intelligence says the person who led the bomber to the Sbarro pizza restaurant was a woman named Ahlam Tamimi, a twenty-year-old student originally from Jordan, who lived in Ramallah and had been recruited by Hamas a few months before the bombing. According to Israel's Shin Bet, during interrogation Tamimi admitted that she tried to look like a tourist by carrying a camera and speaking in English, while the male bomber carried a guitar case with the explosives inside.[30]

Dareen was not the last woman to pressure Hamas to become a suicide 'martyr'. As the post-2002 construction of Israel's West Bank barrier made it harder and harder for men to slip into Israel, Hamas softened its opposition. On 14 January 2004, Reem al-Riyashi, a 22-year-old mother of two, became the first Hamas woman suicide bomber when she blew herself up at the Erez Crossing in the Gaza Strip, killing four Israeli soldiers and guards. The Israelis said that, when she reached the zone where Palestinian workers are inspected, Riyashi told the guards that she had a metal plate in her leg which could set off an alarm, and a woman soldier was sent to inspect her. While she was waiting Riyashi 'apparently succeeded in penetrating a meter or two into the inspection hall, and blew herself up'.[31] Mohammed, a veteran Hamas military wing member in Gaza, said that Riyashi was accepted because her attack came 'during a very tight security atmosphere which meant no man could get close to the Israelis at Erez'. He reported that it was Sheikh Yassin personally who took the decision to relax the ban. 'She put a lot of pressure on Sheikh Yassin, and she wasn't the only one . . . Many women were putting pressure on Yassin because they wanted to be operational.'[32]

Jamila al-Shanti confirmed the account, saying that many Palestinian women had 'grown accustomed over decades of conflict to living in houses where military equipment was stored, so many sought to be trained in weapons'. She stated that Riyashi decided to undertake the attack because 'she felt that the Israelis destroyed everything around her, killed everything. She took the decision that she was going to the resistance and she wanted to do something to express her anger.' Hamas's view, said Shanti, was that 'it is open for us to use any method to defend ourselves'.[33]

Riyashi's case was commemorated by Hamas. The movement subsequently made and screened a video on its own Al Aqsa television station which re-enacted the scene in her home the night before she blew herself up. It showed a four-year-old daughter watching her mother get dressed, and singing: 'Mummy, what are you carrying in your arms instead of me?' The next day she finds out it was a bomb. The two and a half minute video is dubbed with the haunting lament of the little girl. After the attack

Hamas also broadcast interviews with Riyashi's two kindergarten-age children, asking them about their mother and the attack she perpetrated. Duha, her daughter, is asked, 'Where is your Mama?' Her tiny voice piped up that her mother was in paradise as a martyr. Her young brother fidgets throughout the encounter as the bearded interviewer persists in asking the children questions, such as 'How many Jews did Mama kill?, Do you love Mama?, Do you miss her?'[34]

However, in 2007 an article in *Time* magazine alleged that Riyashi was blackmailed into carrying out the bombing after her husband discovered that she was having an affair with a senior Hamas commander, and she was offered the chance to blow herself up to restore her honour.[35] Indeed, the Israelis accuse Palestinian organizations of 'cynical exploitation of innocent and unstable young women', stating that many of those used to carry out attacks are chosen precisely because they have a large amount of 'personal baggage'.[36] They say that women bombers often try to look more Western by wearing short skirts, pregnancy clothing and modern hairstyles, but that many are actually 'from the margins of Palestinian society', the usual motive for their involvement being personal, including 'romantic links with the militants involved in recruiting them' or despair over their personal lives.[37]

At the other end of the spectrum from young, despairing women was Fatima Najjar, a seventy-year-old great-grandmother who blew herself up in northern Gaza during an Israeli raid in November 2006. Despite the fact that she injured two soldiers only slightly, she was awarded the posthumous nom de guerre Umm Fidayeeat – Mother of the Women Fighters. Hamas said that Najjar approached Hamas fighters who were unable to get near Israeli soldiers duiring the raid and told them, 'If you can't do something I can, because my house is close to the Israeli position.' Hamas's Jamila al-Shanti explained: 'Her land had been taken away from her. Who could prevent her? But it is not the policy of the movement. If someone volunteers, we will not stand against it, but it is not our policy to go and ask women.'[38]

Her family said that Najjar, who had nine children, forty-two grand-children and two dozen great-grandchildren, had become radicalized after Israeli troops blew up her home in 1990 during the First Intifada. In the weeks before her death she had smuggled food, water and ammunition to Hamas fighters, and earlier in November she had also taken part in a women's march to break a siege on Palestinian fighters who were trapped by Israeli troops near a mosque in Beit Hanoun. Hoping to be 'martyred', she was bitterly disappointed when other women were killed, but she survived. 'When she came back she was happy when she heard that everyone had got out of the mosque alive, but very sad when she heard some women had become martyrs and she hadn't, even though she was the first there', said one of her sons, Saber.[39] Other family members declared that, having raised such a large family, Najjar believed she had fulfilled her wifely and maternal duties and wanted to contribute in a more direct way to the 'resistance'. Majdi Hamouda said:

> You in the West find it hard to understand why a Palestinian woman would do such a thing. But she wanted to send a message to Israel, Europe and the West. Israel says that the Palestinian mothers send their sons and their grandchildren to death. But she wanted to say that the Palestinian mother dies for her sons and grandsons, for their dignity and their freedom.[40]

The women's march in which Najjar participated – and in which she had hoped to die – was unprecedented. On 3 November 2006 hundreds of women had walked and run through the streets of Beit Hanoun at first light, responding to all-night appeals over Hamas's Al Aqsa radio to come out onto the streets of the northern Gaza town after its fighters were trapped in a mosque there. Two women were killed and dozens injured when Israeli troops opened fire, Israeli commanders saying that they shot at militants who were escaping disguised as women. A spokeswoman for the Israeli military condemned militants for acting 'with no shame' by using human shields, 'knowing the IDF would not shoot at women and children'.[41]

By noon on the day of the deaths schoolchildren were handing out freshly printed leaflets bearing the Izz ad-Din al-Qassam Brigades logo and proclaiming: 'The women of north Gaza arose to help Beit Hanoun.' But as the day wore on Hamas appeared embarrassed by the deaths and the manner of their fighters' escape. Challenged by journalists about whether the gunmen had got the women killed by using them as cover, Abu Obaida, a masked Hamas military spokesman, would no longer confirm that smuggling the men out in dresses was part of the original plan, saying only that 'The women were coordinated to go in different directions so that the Israelis would be distracted.' When pressed, he mumbled testily about the movement's 'legitimate right to use popular resistance besides military resistance', before trying to turn the accusation back on Israel: 'They are destroying civilian infrastructure and have been using Palestinians as human shields for years, which is well documented by Israeli and international human rights groups.'[42]

Hamas still seems prepared to accept women into their military wing. In 2005, amid much publicity, it announced the formation of a women's own military wing with the declared aim of 'jihad and resistance'. The woman commander of the unit gave an interview, published in the Islamic press, which lauded the actions of suicide bombers. 'The martyr Reem Al-Riyashi is like a crown on our heads and a pioneer of the resistance. Nobody can fathom the magnitude of her sacrifice', she said. The interviewer then asked the most mundane question of all: 'How do you manage to combine membership in a military unit, educating [your] children, and taking care of [your] husbands and your households?' The answer came: 'That's something completely normal. We manage our time and know our duties, like every working woman.'[43]

A rose by any other name

The first indication that Hamas could achieve its stated, but widely discounted, goal of attaining power democratically came in the municipal elections of 2005, a harbinger of the general election which it was to win a year later.

In the northern Gaza town of Beit Lahiya, Aziza Abu Ghabin was one of Hamas's successful women candidates, running her campaign from a basement office in the women's Islamic centre. Meetings were all-women and children affairs, the only adult men in sight being armed Hamas militants acting as chaperones when foreigners came to call. During meetings the chants arising from the women gathered in the basement were an indication of the strength and fervour of a hitherto overlooked dimension of the movement, an oversight which its political rivals were soon to regret. But the chants, although by women, were all in support for Hamas's (male) leadership and (male) martyrs. And the activities undertaken by the women were circumscribed by the men who dominate the movement, leaving these 'Muslim sisters' to hold training courses in homemaking, beauty and computer skills. Other initiatives included preaching, youth education, women's literacy and charitable activities for the needy – orphans in particular.

The women's campaigns were segregated: election rallies, canvassing, public meetings, and other events were women-only affairs except for the obligatory musclemen chaperones. By Hamas edict, Aziza's face – like those of other women candidates – did not appear on election posters next to the photographs of the men. Instead the spaces by their names were blanked out and replaced with a picture of a rose. A rose by any other name in these circumstances meant a Hamas woman electoral candidate.

Aziza won 5,000 votes and a seat on Beit Lahiya municipal council, insisting that she was not going to confine herself to women's issues: 'I am a Muslim and I want to play an active role in the municipality in all its affairs.' Women, she insisted, would help set the council's priorities and be decision-makers. 'This is our right preserved for hundreds of years. I know my rights in Islam.'[44] However, these stated ambitions were dismissed by her secular rivals. 'They emphasize that the women's role is to stay in the house and bring up the children,' sniffed one PFLP rival. 'Even their women MPs were for show. Most of their doctors are doctors in *sharia* law.'[45] Certainly in Beit Hanoun, a few miles away from Aziza's office, the Hamas mayor, Dr Mohammed el-Kafarneh, appeared to give women's issues a low priority. First-time female visitors to his office were immediately and insistently reminded by his assistant that the mayor would not shake hands with women, and that a *hijab* was the preferred mode of dress.

The mayor outlined his plans for municipal reform and regeneration: buses for schools, free medicines for the needy, rubbish collection and neighbourhood committees to promote local democracy. When asked about female representation on the committees he was first evasive, then admitted that there were no women members. 'Wives can make their complaints to their husbands and they will bring it to the committee, and in this way we hear what they are saying', he finally explained. He then embarked on a lengthy discourse with other men in the room about how Muslim men put their love for their mothers above that of even their wives. 'I respect women so much. Every day before I come to work I stop by my mother's house and give her my respect, and every evening before I go to my own home I stop by my mother's house and give her my respect.' Pushed further on the issue of women's rights in his municipality, he said he had set up a 'women's affairs unit', staffed by the only two women elected to the council, to deal with 'lectures to women so that they might know their rights in this society . . . The role of women in Islam should be respected.'[46]

Some women chafe at what they complain is a huge gap between Hamas's rhetoric and the reality. Privately, one elected candidate from the leftist PFLP complained that, with the Islamists in control of the municipality, issues of women's rights had been bound 'hand and foot' to Hamas's 'conservative Muslim logic of subordination'.[47] But after its successes in the municipal elections, in which Hamas fielded female candidates for two quota seats per council, it put women up again for the January 2006 parliamentary general election, in which electoral legislation mandated a one-third quota of women.

Once it decided to drop its rejectionist stance to national elections, Hamas competed hard for women's votes. Thousands of women were repeatedly canvassed and huge amounts were spent organizing women-only Hamas rallies and festivals. Its women candidates were a mixture of seasoned politicians, technocrats and cult figures. The most prominent of the six Hamas women MPs elected were Jamila al-Shanti and Maryam Farahat. Shanti was a well-known academic and administrator, with years of experience working within Hamas. Farahat, known as Umm Nidal (Mother of the Struggle), was the complete opposite. She had no political experience but was a folk heroine to Hamas diehards after having given three of her sons as 'martyrs' to the cause. She was even filmed with her youngest son before the suicide mission in which he died, telling him not to come back to her unless he was a '*shaheed*' (martyr). Then she said to the camera: 'I gave my sons to the jihad for Allah . . . it is our religious obligation.'[48]

After weeks of huge election rallies, where women such as Umm Nidal were billed as the 'star attraction', and a carefully orchestrated television and newspaper campaign, Hamas sprung one more surprise on its opponents on election day. When voters emerged from their homes to head to the polling booths they were confronted with droves of Hamas women activists, all wearing green sashes and green and white headbands, chanting and carrying posters and leaflets. Their presence had an electrifying effect on voters and rival parties because it was so unexpected, and heightened the already existing sense that Fatah had yet again been taken by surprise at the end of a complacent, half-baked campaign rooted in the past. It was also a masterstroke of news management – capturing the news cycle on election day when the Palestinian and Western media were in full attendance. With television cameras and newspaper photographers giving the 'Sisterhood' saturation coverage, it helped transform the public image of Hamas.

Days later Umm Nidal was back in front of the news media proclaiming her success at the polls. 'People see in me a symbol of sacrifice and struggle', she declared, as she received plaudits from supporters at her house, and later from adoring women students during a victory rally at the Islamic University of Gaza. 'If I didn't give my sons to jihad, I would be a sinner.' But Umm Nidal provoked controversy after newspaper reports that she planned to introduce legislation forcing women to wear the *hijab*. She insisted that she was misquoted. 'I said I hoped all woman would cover their heads, but I never said it should be compulsory.'[49]

Dr Hanan Ashrawi, who also won a parliamentary seat in the 2006 election, said that she had begun to notice the emergence of Hamas's black-veiled, green-sashed women's brigade during the municipal polls the year before. 'I saw some of it, but the extent, the pervasiveness, came out in the [2006] election', she recalls.

> That meant that they had been working for some time, because all of a sudden you saw these women come out. At every polling station the Hamas women were there, dressed almost in uniform. All of them! And not shy or demure – out there lobbying, asking you to vote, vote for Hamas, and so on. And they went from house to house to bring out the votes.[50]

When Hamas emerged as victors there was immediate panic among moderate Palestinians that the new masters would issue instant edicts mandating Islamist dress codes and behaviour in the Gaza Strip, the area most firmly under the organization's control. These did not materialize. There was no sweeping crackdown, and Gaza's liberal middle classes were still able to slip away to a select few restaurants and beachside hotels where women could smoke cigarettes and waterpipes, and sit bareheaded talking to men, if they chose. But, as Hamas tightened its grip in the wake of its June 2007 takeover of the Gaza Strip, its ideological opponents began to live in fear of the slow, creeping Islamization that has over decades seen the decline and then disappearance of Gaza's public cinemas, nightclubs and bars serving alcohol. Indeed, by January 2009, two years after the election, not only was alcohol banned from public sale in the Gaza Strip but Hamas border agents were searching the bags of visitors to Gaza, looking for alcoholic contraband.

Victory for women does not equal liberation or equality

Women activists and others have complained that, since it came to power, the Hamas government has failed to address the rising incidence of women killed for alleged 'honour crimes', choosing neither to condemn such acts nor to distance itself from rumours that they are sanctioned by the movement's leadership. 'The people who are most afraid of Hamas taking power are the women's movement because in oriental society the woman is always the weakest sector', sighed Naima al-Sheikh Ali.[51] Indeed, upon acceding to power the Hamas government made no statement on equality, and on International Women's Day in March 2007 the Hamas head of the PLC refused to meet the annual delegation of women handing in their petition for equal rights.

In a Hamas publication the same week, a short story written by a Hamas PLC member and leader, Salah Bardaweel, effectively made a mockery of the Palestinian women's movement and their preoccupation with 'gender' issues at a time, its author clearly believed, when Palestinian women should be supporting and demonstrating on behalf of their jailed sons and dead husbands. In an exchange between the two principals of the story, Umm Karim (the mother of a jailed son) addresses a secular woman, who is described as a 'fat woman, whose flesh was bursting out of her tight clothes in all directions and her aggressive hair was poking the faces of other women like feathers of porcupine'. Bardaweel then sneers: 'Who is the Palestinian woman if she is not the mother of martyr, the mother of prisoner, the mother of wounded and the mother of the Mujahid?'[52]

Within a year of its takeover, Hamas's image for cleanliness and incorruptibility was still a decisive factor in its favour on the streets of Gaza, despite the economic hardships caused by the international isolation and Israeli border closures imposed on the Hamas-led Palestinian Authority because of its refusal to renounce violence or recognize Israel. This played well with some women constituents: 'It is enough for us that our leadership and our government are standing with people', said Umm Usama, a 45-year-old woman who attended a pro-Hamas rally in front of Gaza's parliament building in September 2006. 'Until now they haven't got their salaries either. They sold their women's gold to survive, like the rest of the population. That is good enough for us.'[53] Her fellow demonstrator Zainab, forty, said that her only means of support came from the Islamists' food coupons, United Nations handouts and the income of her husband's one brother – out of eight – who still had a job. Her bitterness was not directed at Hamas but at its internal and external enemies. 'No matter how much they starve us we will continue to support this government. We will never stop', she said. 'The world pushed for Hamas to participate in the elections, and when the outcome wasn't the one they wanted, they retreated on democracy.'[54]

But other women were left deeply uneasy at Hamas's quiet efforts to impose its social, political and religious agenda. Suha – she would identify herself only by her first name – was, in March 2007, the principal of an elementary school in the Gaza Strip where, she claims, three armed members of Hamas's paramilitary Executive Forces came into the school unannounced and demanded to see her. Angered that the rest of their paramilitary unit was standing in the school grounds, fully armed, she confronted them:

> I immediately said, 'What are you doing here? You know that it is forbidden to come to a school with weapons.' They told me that they had come to the school to 'suggest' a way to guide the girls of the school to go through the streets. They wanted us, as school principals and teachers, to say to the students that the girls should walk on, for example, the left side of the street to and from home, and the boys on the other side. I was astonished.

She continued nervously, asking once again for anonymity. 'I told them I rejected the idea, it was interfering in our personal freedoms. I told them, "I don't take orders from you". But they said, "It is the orders of our leadership".'[55] Hamas officials in Gaza City later said they had no knowledge of any such edict.

Women's organizations also complain of being raided, of having their computer disks seized, and of incitement in mosques against any who defy Islamist edicts on behaviour and dress.

Why women vote for Hamas

There were many theories offered for Hamas's election victory and for its success in appealing to women. Hamas supporters attributed this success to its grass-roots network of food distribution centres, medical clinics and nurseries and its reputation for honesty. They also cited both widespread disillusionment at the corruption and inefficiency of Fatah and its failure to secure peace or a viable Palestinian state after more than a decade of negotiations with Israel, and anger at the lawlessness and gang warfare between armed factions on the streets of the West Bank and, particularly, Gaza.

Giving a post-mortem on her own party's election defeat and the role played by women in that, the Fatah women's activist Naima al-Sheikh Ali believed Hamas's success lay in its skilful exploitation of women's fears – of poverty, of Israel, and of corrupt Palestinian Authority officials looking after their own at the expense of the deserving poor – and also in Hamas's promotion of religious certainty as the balm for that fear.

> We are a conservative, poor society, and always where there is poverty the belief in religion and belief in abstract and unknown things plays an effective role in society. So the debate involved frightening women by saying: 'Those people are secular infidels, communists' and the like. In addition to that, Hamas had the capability to provide money and food. Bear in mind that it is part of an international organization, the Muslim Brotherhood, not like the other organizations, which only extend locally in Palestinian society.[56]

However, Mona Shawa, of the Palestinian Centre for Human Rights in Gaza City, believed that Hamas's rise had less to do with its provision of food coupons and more to do with its success in persuading women that, amid increasing instability, there was only one public refuge where they could feel secure. 'The place that they feel safest to go, and their husbands, brothers and fathers allow them to go, is the mosque', she said.

> The mosque is where women can go with no objections, and I have seen them. At prayer time they offer seminars. The ladies take lectures on religion there. In this way the mosque becomes the only space outside the home for every Palestinian girl and woman in the Gaza Strip, irrespective of their social status, level of education, whether they are single, married or widowed, literate or illiterate, refugee or city dweller. Many women go to the mosque, and Hamas is related more to religion than other movements, so they become closer to Hamas than other factions. This is very new.[57]

For the women of Hamas, electoral victory brought them – or so they hoped – closer to their ultimate goal of ending Israel's occupation and establishing a true Muslim society and state in an independent Palestine. Huda Naim, a Hamas woman MP, offers a vision of women participating in the struggle, and even expanding their role, but always within the context of Islam. 'It is time to change. Palestinian women should have all their rights, including in marriage, where our religion allows for a free choice', she said. 'We must prepare for the jihad, and we women as mothers have a role in raising fighters ready for sacrifice for the homeland.'[58]

Other Hamas women activists insist that the West misrepresents its ethos. The student activist Iman Abu Jazar says that she works within a Hamas structure where the men have their decision-making councils and the women have theirs. 'When Hamas won the elections all the Western media said Hamas would force everyone to be Islamic in everything. No. We are working with people to help give them the right way. We are working with the people politically. Islam is our reference.' Her enthusiasm growing, and barely confined by the small office she occupies in the segregated campus of the Islamic University of Gaza, she declares: 'Hamas shelters women in every place . . . it gave women rights. Hamas is no Taliban. The women saw that Hamas is her ambition fulfilled.'[59] Others are less charitable. Dr Hanan Ashrawi believes Hamas's rhetoric about involving women conceals the reality:

> The fact that the Hamas women are saying that they have the right to work and the right to education gives the semblance that Hamas is out there helping women. I know there are some women and some in civil society who are justifying this and who are saying the Hamas women's story is a success story. But it is not a success story because it didn't really empower women. It only made their traditional moulds and confines a bit more comfortable in terms of work and education, but it didn't really change attitudes.[60]

In 2009, in the wake of Israel's Operation Cast Lead in the Gaza Strip, where women were counted among the dead, injured, homeless and bereaved, their sacrifice and struggle was counted on by the leadership. Throughout the war Hamas's women supporters had attempted to protect their families, pray to Allah to keep them safe, cook food when there was an opportunity, and fulfil the many other roles that they play. That support function is the truest manifestation of the limits to which women will always operate in the Hamas movement. 'No doubt our work is totally supportive', says the widow of Hamas leader Dr Abdel Aziz Rantissi, 'because we are part of that movement.'[61]

Whatever way Palestinian women play their politics for Hamas – whether out of support for the resistance against Israel and affection for Hamas leaders, or because there is no credible alternative, Hamas leaders understand how important they are. On the segregated campus of the Islamic University a young male student marvelled at the chants of female students attending an Islamist rally: 'In every family in Gaza you will now find these women', said Abed Hamdan. 'In that family – the one of her father or the one of her husband – she will carry the torch.'[62]

11

A House Divided

They put us in jail, tortured us, took our guns and cooperated with the Israelis to catch us . . . Our gun brought with our own money is for self-defence.

Dr Mahmoud Zahar[1]

The rivalry between Hamas and Fatah is long-standing and replete with blood. Rarely have the two organizations coexisted peacefully. Hamas sees Fatah and the PLO as the principal internal obstacles to its goal of Islamizing Palestinians. To this end, it has fought them for the heart and soul of the Palestinian people. It has also accused its nationalist rivals of being traitors and collaborators and of betraying the cause of liberation, regularly condemning PLO leaders as 'heretics', 'infidels' and 'apostates'. As one secular opponent remarks, 'The ideology they circulate among the people has encircled them so that everything becomes *haraam* [forbidden]!'[2] From the very moment the Palestinian Authority (PA) was established in the mid-1990s, Hamas accused its officials of stealing public funds and public lands and of nepotism, patronage and behaving like infidels. The land accusation was particularly potent, land being for many Palestinians the core of the conflict with Israel.

Hamas believes it can outsmart, outgun and outlive the PLO and Fatah. An incipient tension that was evident in the late 1970s when the two movements first began to clash for power has escalated over the years into a deep-seated enmity that has thus far surpassed attempts to overcome it through internal ceasefire, common cause against Israel, unity in the name of the Palestinian people, or power-sharing in the name of democracy and good governance. So deep is the enmity that some Israelis believe their best hope is for the Palestinians to destroy themselves with infighting.

Seeds of conflict

In the 1950s many nationalists who later led the Fatah movement had flirted with membership of the Muslim Brotherhood, studied in Egyptian universities alongside many founding members of the Mujamma and Hamas, and worked alongside the Islamists in Gaza. Figures such as Fathi Balawi, Salah Khalaf (Abu Iyad) and Khalil al-Wazir (Abu Jihad), who were involved in the Muslim Brotherhood, defected to the new Palestinian nationalist trend that grew in popularity during the late 1950s and early 1960s. Such figures were popular elements of the Brotherhood. 'Balawi was my teacher', says one former student member.

> He was a favourite and very well known. Sometimes he would lock the door of the class and talk about politics to us . . . He was always attacking the government and the students admired him. He talked about [Hassan] al-Banna and [Sayyed] Qutb, and we read their publications and passed them round in secret. He was arrested many times and then went into exile to the Gulf.[3]

By that point there was a working assumption that one trend would ultimately prevail over the other – and that the victor would be nationalism of the Palestinian variety in the form of Fatah, the secular nationalist faction founded by Yasser Arafat in the late 1950s, and the umbrella Palestine Liberation Organization (PLO) ,which Fatah later came to dominate.

As Fatah reached its zenith in the 1960s and 1970s its activists believed there was little to worry about from their old friends in the *Ikhwan*. By the early 1980s, when it became apparent that Sheikh Yassin and others were marshalling their energies into a new organization, the Fatah leadership, now in exile and very distant from internal turmoil and disputes in Gaza and the West Bank, decided on a strategy of supporting its own 'Islamist' elements. In the mid-1970s Fatah's Abu Jihad and Munir Shafiq helped support an Islamic Jihad faction, led by Sheikh As'ad Bayyud Tamimi. Islamic Jihad, in contrast with Sheikh Yassin's emphasis on social welfare and preaching, was concerned chiefly with the reconquest of Palestine. The rivalry was always apparent.

Dominance breeds arrogance and arrogance the danger of underestimating new forces which rise to challenge you. In the late 1960s and early 1970s the PLO's numerous factions launched attacks on Israel, and by the mid- to late 1970s its armed wings, the *fedayeen*, enjoyed unquestioned loyalty from Palestinians living under Israeli occupation and in the refugee camps outside Palestine. The PLO revelled in its popularity and continued to secure funds and run a support infrastructure that included welfare payments to the most needy, free education, medical services and a sense of national objective – continuing the struggle against Israel. In Jordan the PLO had effectively become a 'state within a state', posing a serious threat to King Hussein. In 1970 open conflict – effectively a civil war – broke out between the PLO and the Jordanian army, which ended with Arafat and his forces being routed and forced at gunpoint out of Jordan and into the Palestinian refugee camps of Lebanon.

Israel, for its part, had made it clear to the world that it would never negotiate with the PLO, which it regarded as the cradle of terrorism. Israel was prepared to use force to meet the threat posed by the Palestinians, and was intent on destroying the PLO by any means possible. In 1970 Ariel Sharon, head of the Israeli army's southern command, bulldozed dozens of shanty town homes in Gaza's Shatti refugee camp to crush the *fedayeen* on their home turf. Today Shatti's 'Wreckage Street' remains testament to Sharon's actions decades earlier. By the end of 1971 more than 16,000 Palestinians had been displaced from 2,000 shanties. Hundreds of young men and women were arrested and deported, and some 600 of their relatives were sent to detention camps in the Sinai desert. Palestinians saw this as a 'policy of liquidation' directed against the PLO and its supporters. Israel's campaign against the PLO would extend to Lebanon in 1978 and again in 1982. Its strategy of liquidating PLO terrorists was pursued relentlessly across the globe.

A foil to the PLO

Israel also understood that, by encouraging a local foil to the PLO, the movement would be further weakened. That foil, of course, was the Islamic movement. It is not hard to understand why Israel chose to take a benign attitude to the Islamists, or why the Islamists abhorred the leftist secular influences of the PLO on impressionable Palestinian youth more than they did the Israeli occupation. In the 1970s this coalesced into a mutual antipathy of the PLO. Gaza's nascent Islamists believed that redemption would be a staged process: first to return Muslims to the 'straight path' and then, once they had established a strong redoubt of Islam, to take on their opponents.

Assad Saftawi, a leading Islamist figure whose own sons were mujahidin for the Palestinian Islamic Jihad, explained that, during this period: 'The *Ikhwan al-Muslimeen* [Muslim Brotherhood] took the conscious decision not to engage . . . in the *fedayeen* struggle . . . Its biggest priority was to reconstitute and reorganize after years of repression under Nasser.'[4] He also contended that 'Israel turned a blind eye, and we [Islamists] employed a degree of wisdom in this decision not to alienate the authorities and invite a crackdown. We were trying to lessen the influence of the leftist movement, which was disproportionate at the time.' The Islamists were also able to exploit Israel's policy of non-intervention and benign attitude to the formation and licensing of the Islamic Society, Mujamma and other Muslim organizations.

Others perceived the Islamists with antipathy, and some contended that they had collaborationist tendencies towards Israel. Assad Saftawi defended the Islamists against charges of collaboration, saying they were 'working towards a goal of comprehensive national unity'. But then, as now, the means to that goal included attacks on secular institutions, violent clashes and the destruction of 'liquor stores and casinos' throughout the Gaza Strip.

By the mid-1980s Israel had invaded Lebanon and routed the PLO, so the Islamists felt emboldened to take on Fatah itself, not just the PLO's smaller factions. Saftawi, who by this point had left the Islamist camp and defected to the PLO, said that after 1982 Israel allowed the Islamists 'free rein' as part of its attempt to undermine the PLO in the Gaza Strip and weaken institutions such as the universities, which the PLO had controlled up to that point.[5]

Confrontations escalated between Fatah and the Mujamma. Yet even at this point the PLO was often complacent, both about the support it enjoyed in the West Bank and Gaza Strip and about its ability to see off the threat posed by what it contemptuously referred to as the Mujamma 'putschists'. Even two decades later, half way through the First Intifada, PLO leaders believed that the Islamists could never take over because neighbouring Arab states such as Egypt, Jordan and Syria would not allow an Islamist state in Palestine. They also managed to persuade themselves that Palestine was not as fertile a soil for Islamist movements as Iran – a common refrain to this day – and that the Islamist newcomers could not gain traction among the population because they had no track record of 'struggle' against Israel. 'They cannot make up for this lost time. The Palestinian people know who has been there', said one nationalist leader.[6]

In the West Bank the PLO rallied to oppose the new Islamists. Their strongest accusation was that the newcomers were collaborators with Israel. As Saftawi conceded: 'Their continuing hostile stand towards the PLO was not endearing them to the people.'[7] Leftist elements in Gaza were more forthright in their accusations. 'They [the Mujamma] had been encouraged by Israel', said Abu Mahmoud, a member of the Democratic Front for the Liberation of Palestine. 'The Israelis turned their heads away and in some cases even armed them with knives and guns. The Israelis were clever and they succeeded for a time with their goal: the Mujamma would do their dirty work, causing conflict and strife, attempting to eliminate us nationalists.'[8]

In the West Bank, PLO factions were able to organize against the Islamists' attempts to dominate public institutions such as universities, student councils and professional associations. This is not to say that there weren't some successes, but the secular nationalists were able to stave off the challenge longer than their counterparts in Gaza. On the university campus the Islamists tried to dominate the PLO in debates, rallies and student council elections. For a stateless nation living under Israeli occupation, such student elections were often the only opportunity for Palestinians to determine which way the political winds were blowing in their own society and to participate in the electoral process. 'Although we were called collaborators by the secularists at university, we decided to form the *Kutla Islamiyya* [Islamic Movement]', says Hamas PLC member Sheikh Mahmoud Musleh of his student experiences in the late 1970s and early 1980s. 'It polarized the students to either Islamist or the PLO.'[9]

However, Islamist leaders and activists were prepared to use blunt rhetoric and brute force. One Islamist student leader in the West Bank was fond of declaring, 'We tried the fiasco of liberalism in 1948 and we lost half of Palestine. We tried socialist communism in 1967 and we lost the rest of Palestine. We need to be more doctrinaire if Israel is to be overthrown. We need an Islamic state founded on the principles of the Koran.'[10] The brute force was evident in successive attacks organized by Islamist students against secular targets. The Israeli authorities were once again accused by the secular nationalists of giving the Islamists free rein – only this time in the West Bank. 'There was no interference whatsoever by the Israelis', said Dr Abu Dajani, in Nablus. 'The Israeli authority promoted and encouraged divisions to indirectly strengthen one current over another. They were trying to maintain a balance of power and prevent the nationalist movement from becoming too powerful.'[11] This accusation was the strongest weapon that the nationalists had against their Islamist foes. However, the Israeli–Islamist conspiracy theory was also evidence of the PLO's weakness at this point, and Islamists countered that it was exaggerated by nationalists to use as a propaganda tool against them. 'It's a well known policy of Arafat', contended Hamas leader Mahmoud Zahar in 1990, 'to seek to cause divisions among us all.'[12]

By the late 1980s it was already apparent that the PLO's dominance had been dented, partly by the Islamists and partly through its own infighting.

An intimate rivalry: the First Intifada

In 1987, as Palestinians in the West Bank, East Jerusalem and Gaza Strip entered their twentieth year of Israeli occupation, the internal rivalries seemed insignificant in comparison to the deeper political issue of the Palestinian struggle for self-determination and independence. Israel had by then built settlements throughout the West Bank, Gaza Strip and Arab East Jerusalem. Palestinians were hemmed in by a labyrinthine system of permits issued by the military and civil Israeli occupation authorities. Political organization, except through channels organized by the Mujamma, was expressly prohibited by the Israeli authorities, to the extent that even the colours of the Palestinian flag – red, green, black and white – if worn together by a Palestinian, could result in arrest and imprisonment. What neither the leadership of the Mujamma nor that of the PLO could predict, however, was that Palestinian resentment would blow up into a full-scale uprising against the occupation. The uprising would present opportunities for both movements in their struggle to be the true voice of the Palestinian people in the battle against Israel. But neither truly found common cause in adversity.

In the overcrowded refugee camp of Jabalia in the Gaza Strip, the cemetery is a reminder of the many Palestinians who were 'martyred' during the Intifada of 1987. 'I was really just a kid myself, but we remember the funerals as much as the battles that brought them to us . . . killed for throwing stones at the most well-armed army in the world . . . killed for just being a Palestinian in the street . . . this was our battle', remembers Ashraf al-Masri,[13] a Gaza taxi driver, as he passes the cemetery. Now, as then, the graves of the martyrs are bestrewn with photos of the dead, the dried fronds of palm leaves and a token of their faction.

It was at the cemeteries and during the funerals of the first martyrs of the Intifada that the new movement, Hamas, began to seep into the public consciousness. Amid prayers for the dead, the chants of '*Allahu akbar*' (God is great) rose from the mourners, along with promises to redeem the blood of their martyrs in revenge against Israel. In the mourning tents, sheikhs, preachers and their young activists would attend in their hundreds to support the bereaved. At this early stage, though, it was not the heirs of the Mujamma who captured the popular imagination but elements who had split from them in the early 1980s to form the more radical Palestinian Islamic Jihad (PIJ), led by Fathi Shiqaqi and Sheikh Abdel Aziz Auda. PIJ, a small but deeply potent and radical Islamist faction, had waged armed attacks on Israel since the mid-1980s. Its leaders were inspired by the Iranian revolution of 1979 and contended that armed jihad against Israel would be the only route to liberation.

Hamas, however, sought to create its own brand identity, distinct from PIJ and the PLO. Its propaganda claimed the uprising in their name. One early communiqué declared: 'At this time the Islamist uprising has been intensified . . . In all the villages, all the refugee camps our martyrs have fallen . . . But they have died in the name of God and their cries are those of victory . . . In the name of God, God is Great, the Hour of Khaybar has arrived, Death to occupation.'[14] Khaybar is a reference to the victory of the Prophet Mohammed and his supporters over the Jews of Khaybar in Arabia in the seventh century – a clear attempt by Hamas to make the Intifada its own, and to portray victories as Muslim in inspiration and execution.

Hamas also made no secret of its antipathy towards the PLO. First, it rejected the notion of Palestinian nationalism as alien and Western in inspiration: 'Secularism completely contradicts religious ideology', declared Dr Mahmoud Zahar. Nationalism, he argued, 'was an anathema produced by orientalists, missionaries and imperialists'.[15] Dr Abdel Aziz

Rantissi also claimed that only Hamas could deliver the Palestinians from Israel: 'If we want liberation, then we must rely on Islam and not the false charlatans of the PLO, who do nothing for peace except of Israel and America.'[16]

For Hamas, nationalism meant an expression of faith as 'a religious precept', and the good Muslim was a good nationalist. As Dr Zahar declared, The most honest *watani* [nationalist] in the world is a Muslim. He considers the land as holy land.'[17] And although he was often more nuanced in his approach to internal Palestinian relations, Sheikh Yassin also argued that the PLO's approach was fatally flawed because it was Islamic neither in its inspiration nor in its end goal. He maintained that 'The future of the PLO lies with Hamas as much as any other faction . . . It is time to lead all the Palestinians to a real chance of independence and statehood for those that were exiled to come home and for occupation to end.'[18] Hamas criticized the nationalists and the PLO for 'capitalizing on the successes of the Intifada' and instead warned that 'All Palestine is the right of the Muslim, past, present and future . . . No Palestinian has the right to give up the land soaked in the martyrs blood.'[19]

Israel was initially prepared to let Hamas chart its own course and consolidate itself as the internal challengers to the PLO. When Hamas activists enforced commercial and general strike actions on the Palestinian people, many reported that Israeli soldiers stood by. When the nationalists engaged in such acts the Israeli army used its full force to open shops, to break strikes, to arrest strikers and to punish them in other ways. Israeli political leaders also embarked on a dialogue with Hamas leaders. At a time when Israeli politicians refused to engage in dialogue with the PLO because it was considered a terrorist organization, they were more than happy to talk with the people they described as 'Islamic fundamentalists'.

The relationship between Israel and the Hamas leadership, bound by a common foe, peaked during the second year of the uprising. Hamas leaders were filmed attending high-level meetings with the Israelis, and Israel sought to communicate the message that Hamas rather than the PLO was the address of choice. It appeared that Israeli policy-makers were oblivious to the message of Hamas's jihad against the Israeli occupation. They tolerated much from Hamas while turning a blind eye to the large amounts of money flowing into its coffers from abroad, and both sides revelled in the shared antipathy towards the PLO.

As the Intifada progressed, and as the PLO moved into the peace camp, entered negotiations with Israel and began the lengthy process of political rehabilitation, Hamas emerged as the polar opposite. Indeed, the prospect of peace talks in the early 1990s led to the emergence of very public disputes between Hamas and the PLO. Hamas vehemently opposed negotiation with Israel (despite the earlier talks between their own leadership and the Israeli political elite) and condemned the PLO

when it participated in the historic Madrid peace talks of 1991. Clashes
were reported throughout Nablus between rival supporters of the two
factions. In June that year more than a thousand mostly masked Hamas
supporters had marched through the city. Hamas gunmen opened fire on
a Fatah activist and a general strike was organized. By September, further
clashes in Nablus and neighbouring Salfit had led to one man being shot
dead and four others wounded.

Fatwa and prison politics

Hamas leaders issued a *fatwa* (ruling) condemning the PLO for talks
with Israel. The *fatwa* was a specific weapon in the bearpit of Palestinian
politics that it could use against its secular nationalist opponents. Ever
since the *fatwa* death sentence issued by the Iranian revolutionary cleric
Ayatollah Khomeini against the author Salman Rushdie, Islamists have
gained notoriety for such declarations. Yet if Hamas had expected to
trump the PLO with edicts they were to be disappointed because, once
Arafat and his people gained control of the Palestinian Authority's
Ministry of Religious Affairs, they issued their own *fatwa* in defiance of
those issued by the Hamas-affiliated and Gaza-based Palestinian Clerics
Association.

In the prisons, Hamas and Fatah also ended up in seemingly endless
cycles of confrontation over the fate of the Palestinians in negotiations
with Israel. The clashes seemed to intensify throughout 1991–2 until, after
one intensive round of inter-Palestinian dialogue and negotiations, the
two sides agreed to a 'code of honour' which included important recognition of Hamas as a separate political entity that should be accorded due
respect from Fatah leaders and their cadres.

Imprisonment carried no stigma but was instead the reverse: a badge
of honour. The PLO had special departments dedicated to prisoner issues.
Solidarity for the prisoners and support for their families were key activities of those engaged in the uprising.

The prisons were a microcosm of the relationship between Hamas and
the PLO on the outside. Only rarely did prisoners take the lead in resolving major differences between the two sides. One such instance was in
2006, when Hamas and Fatah leaders in prison agreed a document which
laid the foundation for national reconciliation between their main factions
on the outside.

Ending the differences

Khartoum, the Sudanese capital, was the unlikely destination for further
Palestinian dialogue in January 1993. Under the patronage of Sheikh

Hassan Turabi, the Sorbonne-educated Sudanese leader of an Islamic regime, Hamas and the PLO appeared to approach the issues seriously. Hamas agreed to join the PLO and thus recognize it as the sole representative of the Palestinians. But in return it demanded that Arafat give up on a negotiated settlement with Israel and that Hamas would enjoy 40 per cent of the seats in the PLO's main institution, the Palestinian National Council. Arafat refused. As he later recounted, 'In Khartoum they wanted me to hand over the PLO to them without them paying any price. This was not the first or last time that Hamas thought they could take the Palestinian people to the gates of hell with a free pass from the PLO. I was not prepared to accept such a deal.'[20] Hamas was typically more sanguine about its demands. 'We cannot accept a deal that our brothers among us would not accept', said Dr Mahmoud Zahar. 'How can we trust such silly attitudes?'[21]

Throughout 1993 the differences of opinion between Hamas and Fatah over Israel were becoming insurmountable. Hamas could feel the tide of public opinion slip away from it as it maintained its principled and fundamental rejection of Israel and the idea of Palestinians ceding land for peace. Fatah continued to support the two-state solution. It would renounce violence, while Hamas wedded itself to the principle of jihad until liberation. The ideological rift between the two movements appeared to widen, with Hamas losing ground to Fatah.

When the peace process culminated in the Oslo Accords of 1993, it left Hamas even further from the centre of Palestinian power. Only a year earlier the majority of its leadership had been deported to Lebanon, and the PLO looked like it had triumphed over the Islamists again. As Yasser Arafat prepared to return from decades in exile, Hamas was not prepared to offer much by way of loyalty to the man, or to the organization he headed. Israel was now counting on Arafat to deal with its Hamas problem. 'Why should we chase the Hamas when the PLO can do it for us?', declared Israel's then foreign minister, Ariel Sharon.[22]

Hamas and the Fatah Palestinian Authority

Although a temporary truce of sorts was called between Fatah and Hamas after the Oslo Accords and the return of the PLO from exile in Tunis, relations quickly soured. They descended to outright enmity when the PA orchestrated a series of security crackdowns on Hamas as it attempted to meet Israel and America's demands for counter-terrorism responses and security.

The Hamas leadership has never forgotten how quickly the PA appeared to act on Israel's orders to deal with Hamas, and weaken it. With Israeli attacks continuing, settlements expanding and PA officials enriching themselves, it became easy for Hamas to turn the tables of their rivals and brand the PA as collaborators with Israel. At the same time, it intensified its efforts to consolidate its position within the Palestinian community through its social and welfare projects. It also concentrated on survival, which meant withstanding the security campaigns orchestrated against it by the PA and Israel throughout the 1990s.

Almost from the start Hamas was clashing with Yasser Arafat's security forces. Identifying the 'enemies' of peace was not a difficult task for the heads of Arafat's newly created and myriad intelligence services. Hamas, with many other elements of the Palestinian house, had denounced the Oslo Accords and declared the PA an illegitimate expression of a fatal compromise on the issue of Palestinian aspirations for independence from Israel. The heads of these new security agencies, including Mohammed Dahlan in Gaza and Jibril Rajoub in the West Bank, knew they faced a formidable obstacle in Hamas, whose members and supporters were in their families and among their friends. Hamas leaders and supporters were their long-standing neighbours. Hamas was an intimate source of tension ever present for these men.

Hamas continued to hold an obsessive distrust of the Oslo process because it perceived it to be both capitulation to Israel's security demands and Arafat's desperation for some kind of political deal at a point of crisis for the PLO. Bassam Jarrar, a West Bank cleric known to be a 'pragmatic' supporter of Hamas, outlined the prevailing mood: 'The Palestinian people in general feel that this current agreement does not meet the basic needs of the people. This is not a real peace.'[23]

Yasser Arafat and many others in the ranks of the senior leadership of Fatah were determined to let Hamas paint itself into a corner by opposing Oslo, and spared no effort to damage its credentials. Time and again Hamas was publicly accused by Yasser Arafat of being a stooge of Iran. This accusation had important repercussions for Hamas, both at home and abroad. No Palestinian faction wanted to be tarred by association with outside elements, as it undermined its national credentials at home. Abroad, Hamas could not afford to let such accusations go unchallenged because it needed the support of powerful Sunni Arab allies in the Gulf, such as Saudi Arabia.

Black Friday

Hamas had much to prove on its home territory, but the Fatah-dominated PA and Yasser Arafat were in their way. Hamas was determined, however, to carry on its struggle by its own means. In 1994, the year of Arafat's return to Gaza, it embarked on the first of a series of deadly suicide bombings in Israel. When Arafat had made his triumphal return to Gaza amid a carnival atmosphere, Israel was not prepared to join the party. Almost immediately Israel began to hold Arafat accountable, saying it was his job to stop the attacks from Palestinian territory under his control.

The first real test came in October 1994, when Hamas kidnapped an Israeli soldier, Corporal Nachshon Waxman, and demanded the release of Sheikh Yassin from an Israeli jail. Then came a suicide bomb attack, killing twenty-one Israelis, which Hamas claimed was revenge for three of its members killed in the IDF's attempt to free Waxman. Israel demanded that Arafat stop Hamas. Arafat acted quickly, and over 400 activists and leaders were arrested in the first Palestinian security swoop against the movement. Hamas supporters were outraged. On 17 November 1994, 20,000 supporters gathered after Friday prayers at the Palestine mosque in Gaza to protest against the detentions. Arafat's police officers opened fire on the demonstrators, wounding 270 and killing fourteen.

In April the following year Hamas accused the PA of playing a part in orchestrating a fatal attack against one of Hamas's top operatives, Kamal Kahil. Israel had accused Kahil of preparing Hamas bombers for their deadly suicide missions and despatching them against Israeli targets, and wanted him dead.[24] Hamas responded with more bomb attacks, and the PA with more arrests and a demand for Hamas to disarm. The PA and Fatah were calculating that Hamas would become weaker and weaker, but Hamas had other ideas. 'Suppression of the opposition', said Dr Zahar, with a dismissive wave of his hand, 'this has only strengthened us. They hoped Hamas would be weakened and isolated by Oslo, but in fact we are strengthened. It has allowed for the blossoming and rise of a younger, more militant, Islamic leadership in the Gaza Strip and West Bank. It also generated considerable popular support for Hamas even from those quarters who were not previously our supporters.'[25]

But Hamas was bloodied by this latest bout of Palestinian infighting and entered into further rounds of inter-factional dialogue, agreeing to a period of calm (*tahdiyah*) in late 1995 and until Palestinian elections had been contested in early 1996. Yahya 'the Engineer' Ayyash, was considered by Israel to be responsible for numerous suicide attacks. A fugitive from Israel's military and intelligence operatives, by January 1996 he was hiding out in the PA-controlled territories of the Gaza Strip. On 5 January Israel finally caught up with him, and he was assassinated. This overrode any pretensions that Arafat might have had concerning security control over his tiny autonomous territory.

Once again Hamas vowed revenge. Fifty days after the assassination, suicide bombers, declaring themselves to be the 'Students of Ayyash', launched four attacks in Israel which killed fifty-eight people and wounded hundreds. In the wake of the final attack a Hamas-issued communiqué said the bombings would abate now that it had taken revenge for Ayyash's assassination. The Hamas leadership immediately went into crisis talks with the PA. But it was too late.

Torture

In the following days and weeks, thousands of Palestinian security forces were deployed in the move against Hamas. Over 2,000 leaders, members, activists and supporters were arrested and thrown into Palestinian jails and so-called detention centres. Hundreds of mosques, where Hamas had reigned supreme, were placed under the direct authority of the PA. Many institutions in Hamas's network of social, welfare, political, educational, research and medical institutions were raided and closed down. It wasn't so much the rounding up of Hamas supporters that caused the greatest bitterness – one that would only be avenged a decade later. It was what happened in detention.

From the thousands of Hamas activists thrown into jail and inter-rogated during the 1996 crackdown there emerged stories of brutality, humiliations, blackmail and abuse at the hands of security forces. 'You know they shaved the beards off our imams and sodomized them with bottles . . . We will never forget the men of Fatah who did this to us',[26] said Dr Abdel Aziz Rantissi years later. Rantissi was talking about the forces working for his neighbour, the PA intelligence chief Mohammed Dahlan. The Dahlan and Rantissi families were part of the same neighbourhood in Khan Younis refugee camp. Rantissi had known Dahlan a long time, and yet what unfolded between the two men – each gravitating to the oppo-site ideological side – symbolized a growing political rift in Palestinian society.

Mohammed Dahlan contends he was doing his job: fighting terrorism and dangerous opponents of peace. 'We played our part and met our security commitments according to the Oslo Accords', he said, in a short but tense meeting with British security and other officials in 2003. Dahlan even acknowledged that there may have been isolated incidents where Palestinian intelligence operatives overstepped the rules, but he claimed that his service was accountable to the law and no one had died in deten-tion or suffered systematic ill-treatment.[27] Some in Hamas had altogether different accounts. 'They took my father-in-law', said one life-long Hamas supporter. 'They came in the night. Dragged him from his bed and took him into detention. The following day we went to the detention centre to visit him, take him some clothes, food and his medicines because he is a diabetic.'

At the jail it became apparent that the detention came with conditions: 'They were treating my father-in-law well. He was the chairman of one of the Islamic charities here in Gaza. But then we were told that he would only be released if we paid the people holding him $10,000. This was a huge amount of money, and we were in shock.' The family of the detained man decided to raise the money. 'It was a high price to pay, but it was worth it. They knew he was sick with diabetes and that they could just let him die and it would be "medical causes". From that point my family knew not to be too strongly associated with Hamas, but it put us at the mercy of God alone.'[28]

Hamas was temporarily thwarted in its ambition to become a meaningful alternative to the PLO. Throughout the late 1990s the organization experienced all-time lows in its popularity as Palestinians enjoyed the dividends – albeit short-lived – of the emerging peace deal with Israel. When peace seemed possible, support dropped for those opposed to it.

Second Intifada

A decade later, amid growing disillusionment about the peace process, Hamas recovered its credibility as the 'resistance' arm of the Palestinian movement during the post-September 2000 Second Intifada. Over this period, when Arafat was periodically forced by Israeli and international pressure to curb Hamas's attacks on Israelis, Hamas's forces came into conflict with Fatah once again. In 2001 Gaza saw the deadliest bout of infighting for years, as PA forces tried to halt Hamas and other militant groups firing rockets and mortars into Israel.

During one such anti-mortar operation in December 2001, PA forces killed a seventeen-year-old youth. Palestinian on Palestinian violence broke out at his funeral in Jabalia when angry Hamas and Islamic Jihad supporters attacked a PA police station and the police fired into the crowd, killing six people. Such outbreaks of internecine strife gave glimpses of the real hatred that had festered since the 1990s, and was to erupt again to far more deadly effect in later years.

Throughout this period Hamas devised two approaches to defeat Fatah. The first was to undermine the PLO's claim to be the sole representative of the Palestinian people. It was for this reason that Hamas from 2000 onwards participated in endless sessions of dialogue to achieve 'national unity'. It believed that it was moving ever closer to that goal in 2005, when President Mahmoud Abbas agreed to its demands for 'reform' of the PLO in talks in Cairo. Yet, despite the interminable rhetoric, neither side was willing to trust the other and this became an insurmountable obstacle in the wake of Hamas's election victory in January 2006.

The second approach was to achieve – at the very least – parity of strength with the PA's security forces. Hamas had come to view the PA as the handmaiden of Israel and, as such, a danger to its own strategy of ongoing armed resistance against the Israeli occupation. It felt that the guns of the PA were more likely to be used against the Palestinians than against Israel. So Hamas redoubled its efforts to ensure that there would never be a repeat of the events of 1996, when it was at the mercy of the Palestinian security agencies. 'We learnt the lessons of Hezbollah', said one Hamas security official. 'We have to protect our institutions from the rascals in our midst.'[29]

The same clashes, but for a different reason, came once the Second Intifada had petered out and Hamas had replaced its suicide bombings with rocket attacks into Israel. In July 2005, under pressure from Israel to stop the rocket attacks in the build-up to Israel's planned withdrawal from Gaza, Arafat's successor, President Mahmoud Abbas, sent his forces in large numbers into Hamas's Zaytoun stronghold. Abbas was also furious that Hamas had deliberately undermined his authority by timing the attacks on Israel just as his own presidential motorcade was arriving in Gaza for talks intended to restore internal law and order. Nabil Abu Rudeineh, a senior Abbas aide, said: 'Orders were given to the security apparatus to do their duty in full, without any restrictions. All the Palestinians got the message clearly, that there will be one authority, one law.'[30]

Certainly, the PA security forces fought running gun battles with Hamas in Zaytoun in what was intended to be a show of force. But it ended with televised scenes of Hamas gunmen dancing on the burning wreckage of ancient PA armoured riot control vehicles, and dozens of PA and Hamas fighters lying side by side in hospital. 'This is not a good situation', said Ibrahim Abu Thuraya, a twenty-year-old member of the Palestinian Authority's Force 17, wincing at the pain from bullet wounds to the leg. 'Today was nothing. But if it continues like this, it is going to go crazy. It could end in civil war.'[31]

In Zaytoun the contempt among Hamas supporters for Mr Abbas's forces was beyond even what they usually said about their Zionist foe. 'We defeated the Israelis', sneered Mohammed, twenty-five. 'It is much easier to beat these scum.'[32] As they celebrated, Palestinian firefighters lamented that they were increasingly having to clear up the damage from Palestinian on Palestinian bloodshed. And within hours Hamas had come under fire from Israeli helicopter gunships, making it an easy task to portray Fatah as acting in concert with the Israelis to break Hamas.

Civil war?

Despite their rivalry, Hamas and Fatah always pledged to their supporters that, though they would perhaps clash, they would never go to war. For two decades Hamas leaders vowed to avoid *fitna* (civil war), because it was not permissible theologically, and because it would play straight into Israeli hands. 'The Prophet Mohammed said, if you point at your brothers with a piece of iron, the angels will curse you', Hamas's Ismail Haniyeh told his congregation during Friday prayers during one particularly charged moment in the domestic feud.[33]

When Hamas won the parliamentary election in January 2006, the victory, needless to say, did nothing to heal the rift between the two internal enemies. Fatah and other parties refused to join Hamas in a coalition government, leaving it isolated and twisting in the wind at the mercy of an international community which found it far easier to demonize a 100 per cent Hamas government than a coalition in which Hamas sat with moderates. When the rest of the world imposed its boycott on the newly elected government, the Islamists interpreted it as a move by Washington to bring about the early demise of Hamas and restore Fatah to power. But Hamas was not going to let Fatah have the upper hand so easily. 'There is a US conspiracy against the Hamas government. There is complicity by regional powers such as Egypt and Jordan', said Ahmed Yousef, a Hamas spokesman. 'The US is an enemy committing themselves to do everything to hurt the Palestinian cause and collapse the Hamas government . . . they support our enemies.'[34]

Dr Mahmoud Zahar, who was by now foreign minister in the new Hamas government, believed that Fatah was now composed of two 'totally different' groups, one led by Fatah security chief Mohammed Dahlan, seeking confrontation, and the other led by Abbas, seeking cooperation and negotiation. Sitting amid the wreckage of his Israeli-bombed ministry building, he cynically concluded: 'The dominant voice in Fatah, though, is the one that has the money and the guns – the US has already given them $64 million.'[35] Later that day, as he sipped on bitter Arabic coffee served in tiny porcelain cups, a pro-Fatah security chief warned of Hamas's growing military strength and prowess and the need for careful handling by outside agencies. 'In my opinion', said Abu Wassim, 'any declared external support [from the US] will be for Hamas's ultimate benefit. In this current situation Hamas is stronger than Fatah.' Ironically, he blamed others for Fatah's predicament: 'Israel and the US are responsible for weakening Fatah . . . their siege has only strengthened Hamas.'[36]

Assistance

American support for Hamas's enemies was ill-disguised. Within weeks of its election victory, advisers to the administration of President George W. Bush were urging action against Hamas. The neoconservatives of the Bush administration turned to their proxies in Fatah and offered them assistance if they could topple the Islamists.

The growth of the Fatah–US intelligence and security alliance was a by-product of the Oslo era rather than a shared ideological goal of hostility to Islamism. In the late 1990s, under a variety of security arrangements and agreements to keep the peace process on track, the CIA had moved into an important oversight and training support role in the developing security relationship between the PA and Israel. The Tenet Plan, signed in 2001 (and named after the former CIA director George Tenet), pledged that Israeli and Palestinian security chiefs would engage in senior-level meetings once a week with US security officials in Jerusalem. One object of the plan was to tackle the 'terrorism' threat in the West Bank and Gaza Strip. Everyone knew that meant Hamas.

By this point the US was also engaged in a series of regional conflicts which were increasingly perceived abroad as a proxy battle with Iran, its clerical elite and the new hardline Iranian president, Mahmoud Ahmadinejad. As with Hezbollah in Lebanon, it became increasingly apparent that, after Hamas's victory, both Iran and the USA would engage more actively in the Palestinian arena. But this was not a new development. Each had picked its side long ago.

It wasn't just the frequent presence of armoured black GM Suburbans outside the headquarters of the Preventive Security Organization (PSO) that signalled the CIA was in town meeting Palestinian security chiefs, it was that everyone else was bumped down the line, even other intelligence agencies. Indeed, for regular visitors to the heavily fortified PSO compound in Gaza, the presence of the CIA was palpable. PSO officers were often at CIA headquarters in Langley on training courses, or were delayed for meetings because they were going through their paces with CIA operatives who had become regular visitors in Gaza. As America and Israel began increasingly to regard Arafat as someone who had outlived his usefulness, they appeared to have found an heir apparent in PSO intelligence chief Mohammed Dahlan. Hamas was also watching the PSO with a wary eye. It regarded the Tenet Plan as a means to 'allow the CIA to run the Palestinian intelligence forces' and to 'get Dahlan to try and finish the job he started in 1996 against us'.[37] When Hamas launched its 2007 military takeover of Gaza, Dahlan's headquarters was one of its first targets.

Born in Khan Younis refugee camp in 1961, Mohammed Dahlan was a Fatah activist from an early age. A member of the Fatah Youth Organization from 1981, he was imprisoned for political activism by the Israelis in the 1980s, learned fluent Hebrew, and became active in the First Intifada as a student leader and street captain whose competence quickly became legendary. In 1988 he was rounded up by Israel and deported to Jordan. When he arrived at the headquarters of the exiled PLO in Tunis he was promoted by Arafat, allegedly, over the objections of the latter's suspicious deputy, Abu Jihad, and his coronation as a future leader seemed assured. The word on the street was that Dahlan was tough, smart and sophisticated. After the PLO returned from exile in 1994, he went back and was appointed Gaza head of the newly created PSO.

For years, Dahlan's enemies alleged, the American CIA and British MI6 had been grooming the man who had become derided in Hamas circles as 'Prince Charles' – the heir apparent to Arafat. He went to Cambridge to improve his English and was considered the darling of the American and British intelligence community. By 2002 overseas security support to PSO increased as part of the three-way security relationship between the PA, Israel and the CIA.

Hamas leaders had nothing but contempt for Dahlan, arguing that he was a powerful enemy backed by the CIA and, later, by key Bush administration officials such as Elliott Abrams, a senior director at the National Security Council. Even so, the US continued to consider Dahlan as a good candidate to fill Arafat's shoes and remained committed to assistance programmes to the security forces most closely associated with him. Hamas maintained the rhetoric that such foreign help would do Fatah no good in the long run. 'Does it buy loyalty stronger than the loyalty to Allah?', asked Hamas's rising star, Mushir al-Masri.[38] Nevertheless, convinced that American political and intelligence assistance was being used by Fatah to fight Hamas on Israel's behalf, Hamas leaders cast their eye around the region for their own patron to help fend off the assault from Fatah.

Iran

In many respects Iran is not a natural ally for Hamas. The regime in Tehran is governed by a clerical Shi'a elite which has long been on the other side of a deep sectarian divide in the Middle East. The late Ayatollah Ruhollah Khomeini's principle of *vilayat-e-fiqah* – rule of the clergy – is anathema to Sunni traditions. Hamas, by contrast, is a wing of the Muslim Brotherhood, a Sunni Islamist movement. As such, it has also traditionally looked to Saudi Arabia and other Gulf states for support from former Palestinian Muslim Brothers who settled there, and from Gulf rulers who sympathize with the Palestinian cause and support Hamas's social and welfare projects. Israel's former Ambassador at the UN, Dore Gold, also contends that the Saudis finance Hamas: 'The Saudis' . . . terrorist financing . . . has underwritten 60 to 70 per cent of the Hamas budget.'[39]

Hamas established contacts with Tehran in the mid- to late 1990s. Some Hamas leaders had spent time there, and also engaged with the regime through their connections in Damascus and Beirut. At this time the links were not considered to be high-level, but the Iranian authorities had offered the hand of friendship to Hamas, inviting them to events at the Iranian Foreign Ministry. From 2000 onwards, one element of Hamas's resistance strategy was the 'Hezbollah model', looking to Iran's Lebanese proxy. Some Hamas leaders are willing to acknowledge that throughout the 1990s the relationship with Iran grew, at the expense of Yasser Arafat's own ties with Tehran when the PLO signed up for the peace process with Israel.

Usama Hamdan, one of Hamas's first representatives in Tehran, said that the Iranians, like other Islamist actors, were keen to demonstrate their solidarity with the Palestinians. Hamdan claims that Iran assisted Hamas with funds 'to support the families of the prisoners and martyrs', but denied that – up until this point at least – it was providing money for Hamas to fight Fatah. 'The Iranians thought it was important to support the case of the Intifada – which was to end the occupation and not sur-render to the enemy', he said.[40] In December 2005 Hamas's political chief Khaled Meshaal visited the Iranian capital and was offered support against Israel. Iranian support, finances and arms rose exponentially after Hamas's 2006 election victory, when Western aid and development money dried up. Hamas leaders openly acknowledged during this imme-diate post-election period that they were getting financial help from Iran and others, and that it was being used to pay the salaries of public sector employees such as teachers, police officers and doctors.

Israeli intelligence officials warned of the dangers of allowing such a relationship to be perpetuated. For the most part their assessments centred on undermining Iran's growing regional influence. Avi Dichter, Israel's hard-nosed minister of internal security, warned in 2007 that Israel's Middle East strategy was under serious threat from Iran. 'Iran [is] the biggest terror state in the world today', he told an audience of diplo-mats and journalists. He then accused Hamas of 'trying to implement the Iranian strategy toward Israel' from Gaza.[41]

Other regional players found themselves sucked into ever deeper disagreements over Hamas's demand for a greater share of power as a legitimate representative of the Palestinian people. Egypt, Jordan, Syria, Qatar, Saudi Arabia, Iran, Sudan and Libya all engaged in the high-stakes game, siding – often alternately – with one of the two Palestinian factions, or urging them to reconcile and make peace.

Hamas was increasingly challenging Fatah's traditional dominance of the PLO, and its task was being made easier by Israel's actions. When Israel bombed PA ministries in 2002 during Operation Defensive Shield, Hamas organized relief and welfare efforts to fill the vacuum that was left. When persistent rumours of corruption tainted the PA, Hamas pointed to its own untainted record and asked the Palestinians to reach their own conclusions about who was fit to govern them. Years of rivalry were culminating in bitter grievances that soon pulled the Gaza Strip and parts of the West Bank into lawlessness, anarchy and feuds between clan, family and faction. Far worse was still to come.

Revenge

Hamas's first eighteen months in power were marked by a vicious inter-necine feud as Fatah sought to undermine the new regime in Gaza, and Hamas began to demonstrate that it would employ brutal means to deal with the growing chaos and lawlessness. One veteran Mossad analyst termed this looming conflict the 'showdown' – a reckoning that had been festering since the dawn of the Oslo process.[42]

No one understood Fatah better in late 2006 than Khaled Abu Hilal, a former Fatah official and wisp of a man who, surrounded in his front room by thickset Hamas bodyguards, was relentlessly cheery for someone branded a traitor by his former colleagues. Like so many others in Hamas's ranks, Abu Hilal had become disillusioned at Fatah's corruption and stance towards Israel. Unlike the others, he changed sides and joined the Islamists. He insisted on making tea for his visitors while he expounded on the war that lay ahead. Refusing to let his bodyguards help – 'they need to save their energy for protecting me' – he hinted at what lay ahead: 'There is a particular group that seeks to provoke us. They have a foreign agenda, foreign funding, and they want to bring Hamas down.' Hilal was referring to Mohammed Dahlan and the belief of many within Hamas that, now Fatah was out of power, Dahlan and his supporters were being pushed even more by outside forces to bring about Hamas's downfall.

Amid much talk of a 'coup', full-scale armed confrontation was avoided – postponed, it later transpired – by a new internal ceasefire on 28 October 2006. But tensions remained high, as national unity government talks broke down again. Hamas appeared to adhere to the ceasefire. Its forces were pulled from the streets and pro-Fatah security forces were allowed to deploy in Gaza again. A tenuous sense of order appeared to prevail, but in reality there were daily tensions, armed incidents and conflict between official and unofficial armed units. Hamas's interior minister Said Siam was by now being advised on strategy and tactics by a 'Security Affairs Committee' composed of Hamas loyalists. Hamas acknowledged that by now its Executive Forces consisted of 6,000 armed men, and the Izz ad-Din al-Qassam Brigades were also busy. In northern Gaza, where the border with Israel represented both threat and opportunity, the Qassam Brigades spokesman said that it had established a forward position and operations room.[43] Egyptian security officials believed that the balance of arms was changing.

By the end of 2006 weapons were on public display throughout Gaza. All the political factions, and powerful clans and families, used weapons to signal their status and strength. Egyptian security officials spent much of their time brokering ceasefires between factions and clans. But the balance of power was inexorably tipping in Hamas's favour. 'Hamas for sure have five times the armaments of the others', said one Egyptian official.[44] Commanders within Gaza's pro-Fatah intelligence services were also getting alarmed. 'We consider the situation to be an emergency where two extremisms are being nurtured', said the head of one agency, who warned of further chaos. 'Hamas is planning a coup d'état, but they need to understand that anyone doing this would hurt himself.'[45]

December 2006 proved to be a bleak month. PA coffers were empty because of the siege, and thousands of its employees grew increasingly angry at their Fatah overlords who, despite their promises, were not paying their salaries. Meanwhile the Hamas government was sharing whatever largesse it enjoyed and making a virtue out of sacrifice under siege. Ismail Haniyeh had defiantly told the world, 'We'll eat salt and *za'atar'* rather than capitulate. In Gaza, however, the air was growing thick with hatred between Hamas and Fatah.

Death on a school day

Civilians have always been casualties in the conflict between Israel and the Palestinians. The unarmed, the defenceless, the young, the vulnerable, the old and women have often paid a high price. And, even as inter-factional fighting escalated between Hamas and Fatah, both sides insisted that there were 'red lines' that neither would cross. That changed on the morning of 11 December 2006.

As a senior Fatah intelligence chief, Baha Baloush was unpopular with his rivals in the Gaza Strip. He and his family had previously been targeted for assassination, yet even he did not expect what was to come when gunmen shot dead his three sons – Salameh, three, Ahmad, five, and Usama, eight – on their way to school. A big but broken man, Baloush recounted the events of the morning from the rented apartment in Ramallah, where he sat in exile more than 50 miles from his Gaza home. That morning a car had arrived at his home, as usual, he recalled, to ferry the boys and their cousin to school. They duly set off, with the sandwiches he had prepared for them.

> Just as the car moved, I heard shooting, and immediately I told my wife the kids were killed. I pulled my Kalashnikov and started shooting in the direction of the masked men – more than fifteen of them. My wife kept screaming: 'They killed the children'. The terrorists killed my innocent children in cold blood while on their way to school. This incident was a message to the PA . . . The message was that no one was safe anymore in Gaza, not even children are safe.

Eighteen months on from the murder of his sons, Baloush holds every-one responsible. He stopped short of accusing Hamas of the murders, saying his wife only wants to go back to Gaza to be near the graves of her children.[46] Samira Tayeh is less reticent. Her husband, Jad, was a senior Palestinian intelligence officer gunned down with his four bodyguards in Gaza City in September 2006. 'I will never forgive Hamas for what they have done to me and my beloved husband', she says, her hands shaking visibly as she recounts her story. Sitting in Ramallah's Café de la Paix, she expresses her grief: 'My life without my husband is finished. I will take revenge. I will sue them sooner or later. These are criminals of war who should be punished.'[47]

The killing went on. If Fatah was attacked, it retaliated against Hamas, and vice versa. On 14 December 2006 the Hamas prime minister, Ismail

Haniyeh, was caught in a gun battle at the Rafah border as he tried to get back into Gaza from a trip abroad, but was denied entry to Gaza by the Fatah-controlled Presidential Guard forces who manned the crossing. Hamas accused Fatah of trying to kill the democratically elected Prime Minister. Haniyeh's adviser Ahmad Yousef, who lost a finger in the incident, warned: 'There will always be some with an interest in disunity . . . but their files will be opened one day and exposed.'[48]

Hamas consistently blamed the Fatah-supporting security forces in Gaza for the chaos and violence. The Izz-ad-Din al-Qassam Brigades issued warnings against the Preventive Security 'Death Squads' and Haniyeh complained publicly about the 'proliferation of Fatah forces' in Gaza. Nearly a year into Hamas's period of rule, any talk of the two sides forming a national unity government was irrelevant in the face of bloodshed on the streets.

Things can only get worse

By the end of 2006 there had been a progressive decline in law and order in Gaza and the West Bank, accompanied by a reassertion of family and clan authority. This phenomenon appeared more prevalent in Fatah circles than with Hamas. 'Abu Wassim', the head of one intelligence unit loyal to Fatah, was protected exclusively by members of his extended family. Towns such as Beit Hanoun were widely considered to be completely outside the control of official security institutions and answerable only to powerful local families.

Hamas remained suspicious that the United States was helping President Abbas to launch a 'coup' against the democratically elected Hamas government, partly to strike at an Iranian proxy as part of its broader regional standoff with Tehran. Fatah and others saw Tehran's support for Hamas as one component of Iran's drive to establish a Shi'a crescent across the Levant.

By January 2007 Gaza and the West Bank were strewn with the debris of the most serious infighting in more than twenty years. Gun battles, clashes and security chaos were an everyday fact of life on the streets of Palestinian cities. In Nablus, a hard-faced Al Aqsa Martyrs' Brigades commander led the way to his front parlour surrounded by heavily armed supporters. Explaining why he and his men were behind recent attacks and kidnappings of prominent Hamas figures in the city, he said, in a steely voice that brooked no argument: 'Hamas is killing children in Gaza, so what is happening in Nablus is the punishment. It is a natural reaction. We fight the occupation, yeah, but we're also here to defend ourselves against Hamas.'[49]

Ordinary Palestinians had become enveloped in the chaos. There were negotiations to restore a national unity government based on an agreement drawn up by Palestinian prisoners from both factions. The intention of the prisoners' document was to break the deadlock, thereby removing international sanctions and restoring the peace process onto the track laid down by the Roadmap. In the meantime, internal pressures and public protest, strikes, demonstrations and unrest grew, amid desperation from thousands of Palestinian employees who had been without salaries for months because of the international embargo on direct aid to a Hamas-controlled PA. Public ire was directed against both political factions, who in turn sought to manipulate it in their ongoing contest with each other.

The eventual formation of a national unity government under an agreement brokered by Saudi Arabia in February 2007 appeared to offer hope that Hamas and Fatah could put aside their differences and work together in government. Yet it was already clear from the begrudging hand-shakes and the body language of Fatah's Mahmoud Abbas and Hamas's Khaled Meshaal that the breach between the two sides was growing ever wider. Some wondered whether there would ever again be unity in the Palestinian house.

12

Bullet and Ballot

Israel and America Say No to Hamas. What Do You Say?
> Hamas election banner, January 2006

There is no ballot box on Hamas's crest, only crossed swords and Jerusalem's glittering Dome of the Rock. But, as the Islamist movement neared its twentieth anniversary, the grass roots and leadership believed the time was right to end its carefully cultivated outsider status and move into the political mainstream. The vehicle was the January 2006 elections for the parliament of Gaza and the West Bank – the Palestinian Legislative Council – an assembly without power over its borders, sea, airspace, military or would-be capital, all of which are under Israel's control – but the nearest the Palestinians have to a Westminster-style parliament.

Hamas had boycotted the first and only previous round of elections, in 1996 (when Fatah won 70 per cent of the seats), scorning the fledgling Palestinian Authority's legislative branch as little more than a rubber stamp for Yasser Arafat and the Oslo peace process. Publicly Hamas insisted that it boycotted that poll out of principle – because it rejected any institution set up under the Oslo Peace Accords. It even had clerics issue a *fatwa* initially declaring the elections *haraam* (forbidden).[1] But sceptics believe, and some Hamas officials concede, that the faction's motives were altogether more self-serving.

In the optimistic days of the mid-1990s, with memories still fresh of Yasser Arafat, Bill Clinton and Yitzhak Rabin shaking hands on the White House lawn, Hamas was swimming against a tide of popular support for the peace process and faced certain electoral defeat. For it to take part, lose and spend the next few years sitting impotently on the backbenches of a Fatah-controlled parliament would have been the worst of both worlds. It would have alienated its hardliners by associating itself with its Zionist enemy, but have received no reward for doing so because it would be powerless to overturn Fatah's built-in parliamentary majority.

Hamas did debate whether it should participate. Some, such as Ahmad

Sa'ati, argued in favour of the political route. 'Let us have free elections', he said, 'and we will abide by the rules and results whatever the outcome.'[2] Others were less enthusiastic. 'We reject the Oslo framework and we reject the elections',[3] said Musa Abu Marzouq, a member of the Political Bureau in Damascus.

Experiment

The leadership decided against participation, and set out throughout the rest of the 1990s to make sure that Oslo would fail. However, as its military wing tried to bomb the peace process into oblivion, Hamas allowed 2,000 to 3,000 of its followers to experiment by creating a semi-detached political wing, which they named the National and Islamic Salvation Party. The Salvation Party was given permission to join the PLO, where three of its members sat on the Central Committee, thereby creating the anomaly that, as Hamas members, they refused to recognize Israel while, as PLO officials, they sat within a body that had already done so.

Explaining the rationale behind the creation of the Salvation Party the most prominent of its founding members, Yehya Moussa Abbadsa, said:

> When the Oslo agreement was signed there were two groups in the Islamic movement. Some people considered Oslo a variable that we should deal with, and deal with whatever came out of it. They believed that we should participate in the election and go from underground to overground, working to change the priorities of our agenda to make human rights and civil rights and development an immediate priority, and to delay the priority of liberation because the new reality after Oslo would not allow us to march toward liberation without putting us in conflict within the Palestinian homeland. They thought we could move back the agenda of liberation until conditions permit. There was another school saying, 'We can't sacrifice anything in the path of liberation, because the essence of the struggle is the land'. They are two different attitudes within the movement. We agreed that we should have some sort of agreement between us, so those who believed in the first path could form a political party and the others could continue in their way. This way we wouldn't have two contradictory movements, but two working in different streams.[4]

One of the opponents to electoral participation was Dr Mahmoud Zahar, a hardliner. 'Elections . . . what is the point of these elections? What we will have is an "Arab election" with a 99.9 per cent vote in favour of Arafat', he said. 'We will participate in rebuilding our society, but not in this way.'[5]

The Salvation Party gave its members political experience which proved invaluable a decade later. Indeed many of the Hamas MPs elected to the Palestinian parliament in January 2006 were Salvation Party veterans, including Abbadsa himself, Salah al-Bardaweel and Jamila al-Shanti. While the Salvation Party maintained the public fiction of independence from Hamas, it remained within the Hamas fold, with what Abbadsa described as 'under the table coordination'. The arm's length experiment reached its limit when Yasser Arafat offered them cabinet seats, which they refused because it would have been embracing too many internal contradictions. The experiment was finally halted in September 2000, when the Second Intifada broke out. Amid polarization and hardening positions, Hamas's fledgling politicians returned to the fold. Abbadsa admits to feeling 'regret' when the decision was made. He believes that some of Hamas's later difficulties could have been avoided if the Salvation Party had remained on the shelf as a political entity to be entered instead of Hamas itself for the 2006 elections, allowing the movement to distance itself from the elected government if the need arose.

Hamas ascendant

As the Oslo process ran into difficulties, Hamas's military and political strength grew, and it wanted to capitalize on that strength in parliament as well as on the street. One turning point was the July 2000 summit between Ehud Barak, Yasser Arafat and Bill Clinton at Camp David, the US presidential retreat where two decades earlier Clinton's predecessor Jimmy Carter mediated the historic peace agreement between Israel and Egypt. Seeking to repeat Carter's feat in the final days of his scandal-ridden presidency, Clinton tried to wring an equally historic breakthrough between the Israeli and Palestinian leaders, but to no avail.

After the initiative failed it became an Israeli article of faith that Arafat turned down the best deal the Palestinians would ever be offered, while the Arafat camp protested that no Palestinian leader could have signed up to the concessions he was asked to make. Camp David convinced Israelis that Arafat was a man who was not serious about doing a deal. But, watching from Damascus and Gaza City, Hamas's leadership came to exactly the opposite conclusion: that Arafat came far too close to giving away the Palestinian birthright, and must be stopped before he could do so in future. 'People started thinking deeply, "Where are those brothers in Fatah heading?", recalls Ahmad Yousef, a senior Hamas official. 'They felt our higher national interests were becoming threatened because there were people ready to compromise, or sell out. That "No" wasn't strong enough to convince people that they weren't saying "Yes, maybe".'

Fearing that the armed struggle would quickly be neutered if the PLO signed a comprehensive peace agreement with Israel, Hamas decided that it must enter the Palestinian parliament to block any such future deal. 'Our legitimate resistance was going to be at risk. To protect these things we would have to be part of the Palestinian Legislative Council', said Yousef.[6] Confirming Yousef's analysis, Jamila al-Shanti, Hamas's most prominent woman activist, said Hamas's strategy was the reverse of that in Northern Ireland, where the Provisional IRA eventually agreed to decommission its weapons to allow its political wing to enter the government. 'The difference between us and Sinn Fein is that when we entered the election we entered it with the intention of sheltering the resistance', she said. 'It wasn't a choice between resistance and politics, it was to protect the resistance.'[7] In other words, Hamas went into politics to keep its guns, not to lay them down.

Reconsidering

After the failure of Camp David, and the eruption of the Second Intifada in September 2000, Palestinian politics entered a period of enforced paralysis. Arafat and the PA argued that it was impossible to hold elections of any kind while Israeli tanks sat on the streets of Ramallah, Nablus and Jenin and candidates and voters could not move through Israeli checkpoints. Throughout this period Fatah's ageing clique of PLO veterans ignored repeated calls to restore their credibility by standing for long overdue internal Fatah and PLO elections. This created tensions with the ambitious younger Fatah generation – notably the West Bank political firebrand Marwan Barghouti and Gaza security chief Mohammed Dahlan – who were keen to shove the old generation aside. The political paralysis was increasingly seen on the Palestinian street as a self-serving ploy. Blaming Israel for the frozen status quo, although an easy political sell, could not deflect all of the criticism all of the time.

The pressure for change was magnified by dissatisfaction at Arafat's handling of the crisis. By mid-2002 Palestinians were furious at the destruction of Palestinian city centres as Ariel Sharon's troops sought to hunt down the 'terrorist' apparatus responsible for carrying out a wave of suicide bombings and shootings. As the attacks and counter-attacks intensified, so did feelings on both sides, with some polls showing more than 70 per cent of Palestinians supporting suicide bombings.[8]

The extent of the hardening became apparent when Arafat secured two controversial deals – the first to end an Israeli siege of his Ramallah headquarters by jailing six wanted men in Jericho, and the second to end the month-long siege of the Church of the Nativity in Bethlehem by deporting thirteen Fatah and Hamas militants to Europe. For Palestinians reared on tales of how entire families were driven into exile in 1948, deportation held a special dread. Even Fatah officials acknowledged that acquiescing in the forced exile of any Palestinian – even gunmen – had damaged Mr Arafat's standing. 'Arafat's popularity decreased', said Hussain ash-Sheikh, a prominent Fatah leader in Ramallah. 'The PA can't legalize the expulsion of Palestinians. This has political and legal implications. I can find an excuse for sending people to Jericho, but no Palestinian can find any reason to send thirteen away.'[9]

But behind the cacophony of Israeli and Palestinian anger were subtler notes, often lost in the background noise. Even as Israelis were clamouring for tighter security measures, 63 per cent told the Hebrew-language daily newspaper *Yedioth Ahronoth* in mid-May that they supported the creation of a Palestinian state if accompanied by a peace agreement (a phenomenon that Israeli political analysts call 'short-term hawks, long-term doves'). Likewise, Palestinian opinion was more nuanced. Even as Palestinians united behind the attacks there was widespread dissatisfaction at the way their own internal affairs were being handled. By May 2002 Arafat was forced to respond to the growing domestic and international calls for reform by promising new presidential and parliamentary elections and a 'comprehensive review' of the PA. Even then, in the midst of its deadliest ever bombing campaign, and a full three years before Hamas publicly committed itself to contesting elections, Hamas officials kept their options open. 'We have the right to have reform, elections and democracy, but now our priority is resistance', said Sheikh Hassan Yousef.[10]

Hamas's signals did not go unnoticed. Ghassan Khatib, a political analyst and former Palestinian cabinet minister, noted that the extremist group had benefited from the violence. 'They took advantage of the Intifada to more than double their public support. It used to be 10 per cent and now it is 22 per cent, even without Islamic Jihad. This is very significant in terms of public opinion. A very significant political growth, very unusual.' While he believed that Hamas would likely maintain its rejectionist stance, it was no longer a foregone conclusion: 'If they accept the election, they will have a minority role and will have to work from within the system and have to work in the role of minority activists, which is not good for them. Now they can do what they want: they don't need to abide by the rules because they don't recognize the system.'[11]

At this stage Fatah tended to minimize the threat, predicting that the Islamists would contest grass-roots municipal elections, but that their rejection of Oslo would not allow them to contest parliamentary and presidential polls. Nevertheless some Fatah officials closest to the street took the threat seriously enough to begin counting up Hamas's likely strongholds, even in the West Bank.

As early as June 2002 Hussain ash-Sheikh ticked off Hamas's likely electoral gains – Gaza, Nablus and Hebron, because of their social conservatism – as against Fatah's 'safe' areas of Ramallah, Jenin and Jerusalem. 'I wish Hamas would take part in the institutions and build civic society in a democratic way', he said. 'This would influence the way it functions. I believe that when Hamas takes part side by side this will be good for an effective and serious development of the democratic way. It won't be about hatred of Israel, it will be about building a better society.'[12]

Such statements were somewhat disingenuous, hiding the fact that for the better part of twenty years Hamas and its political predecessors had played an active part in elections for student councils, professional associations and civil society organizations. The problem was that neither Hamas nor its main opponent was keen on sharing power. Each sought to trump the other.

In the event it proved academic. Arafat set no timetable for presidential and parliamentary elections – neither was to be held until after his death – and his announcement was widely seen as an attempt to stall critics. 'He knows very well what reforms are needed, but he is hoping the pressure will vanish, as it has done before', said Dr Khalil Shikaki, director of the Palestinian Centre for Policy and Survey Research. 'He doesn't want to share power, and any attempt at reform will involve that.'[13]

Fifty miles away from Ramallah, Dr Abdel Aziz Rantissi, Hamas's deputy leader, watched with barely concealed satisfaction from Gaza as *'al-Khetiyar'* (the Old Man) twisted in the political wind. For Rantissi, politics was a zero-sum game. When Arafat was up, Hamas was down. And when Arafat was manifestly down, as now, Hamas was up. 'When the ruling party fails, it is natural that the opposition benefits', said one of Israel's most hated men, as he served tea in his home in Gaza City's Sheikh Radwan district. 'The option of the PA is negotiations. When that fails, those who have other options benefit.' Having watched the Palestinian street become more radicalized during the Second Intifada, Rantissi exuded confidence that this shift in public opinion insulated Hamas against a repeat of Arafat's 1990s Oslo-era crackdown on Islamist dissenters:

> In 1996 Fatah terrorized many in Hamas, but when they did so there was political hope for the Palestinian people. Hamas was the only organization on the ground fighting against the Oslo agreement and all the Palestinian people were with the PA . . . so the reaction against the arrests of Hamas was not that strong. Today we have a different situation. Firstly, there is no political horizon. The Israelis are massacring our people, they have reoccupied the West Bank, and all the other factions are carrying out resistance, including Fatah – which means the Palestinian people would never accept the return to arrests of Hamas, or anyone else.[14]

Hamas was ready to put pressure on Arafat to harden his stance in the face of Israel's demands. It also calculated that Arafat would now yield to its demands on elections and a share of authority in the real powerhouse of Palestinian nationalism: the Palestine Liberation Organization. While Hamas is always prone to maximizing its own importance and centrality to events, its analysis was nevertheless shared by other more neutral observers. 'Arafat is in control, and not in control at the same time', said Ghassan Khatib.

He has to have a peace process in his hands in order to use it as a tool. When the Israelis are killing civilians it is difficult for him to swim against the stream. If Arafat had a peace process he would be able to convince a majority of people to stop it because it jeopardizes the peace process, but the reason the majority remain in favour despite the closures and clampdowns is because they see no alternative.[15]

But Hamas leaders were also facing their own challenge. Most unusually, they openly acknowledged a split in their ranks over whether the movement should follow a political as well as a military path. 'We have inside the Hamas movement a dispute about this issue. Rantissi represents one side, which refuses any interference in the Palestinian Legislative Council. I represent the other side of the issue, which bases parties of Hamas in the PLC elections', said Ismail Abu Shanab, one of Yassin's inner circle. 'If the PLC is not authorized to abide by Oslo, there is no problem for us to take part in the elections.'[16]

But even Rantissi the hardliner was willing to entertain publicly the notion that Hamas could open a new front in its struggle. Assessing that the Islamic movement 'has strategic depth in all West Bank cities', he confirmed that it would certainly contest municipal elections 'if they happen, because this has nothing to do with politics'. He noted that Hamas had amassed considerable experience in other elections, winning control of professional bodies representing engineers, doctors and lawyers, as well as professional associations and student unions in universities from Gaza to Birzeit, Hebron and Nablus. What is significant is that, in so doing, Rantissi was finely calibrating Hamas's position from one based on principled rejectionism to the altogether more pragmatic – and easily finessed – objection that the Palestinian parliament had little power because it was subordinate to Arafat's 'appointed' cronies who wielded real power on the decision-making bodies of the PLO. 'We will participate in any elections based on clear democratic principles', he said, adding enigmatically: 'We are out of the seats of the Palestinian Legislative Council, but we are not out of the political picture.'[17]

While Hamas repositioned itself, the Israelis appeared more focused on the political power struggle within Fatah. In March 2002 one senior Israeli military official in Tel Aviv said Fatah was undergoing an unseemly internal succession struggle even before Arafat's death, as the political wing – principally Marwan Barghouti – tried to wrest power from its security chiefs Mohammed Dahlan and Jibril Rajoub. The analysis was astute. But, as so often, the Israelis seemed much less sure-footed about the Islamists. 'Although Hamas and Islamic Jihad are considered the opposition to Fatah, they are not really', the official stated blithely. 'They are opposed to Oslo. But they don't have any ambition to become the next Palestinian regime.'[18]

Less than four years later, Hamas was the next Palestinian regime.

First cracks in Fatah

The catalyst for reform within the Palestinian political arena was a raft of changes which was intended to marginalize radicals and strengthen moderates, but achieved quite the reverse. In September 2002 Arafat faced one of his first serious challenges from the hitherto supine Palestinian parliament, and in an embarrassing last-minute manoeuvre was forced to dismiss his entire cabinet rather than have his elderly, jaded and deeply unpopular cronies rejected by a vote of no confidence. 'For the first time the Palestinian political system has shown an attempt to have genuine separation of powers', said Ali al-Jarbawi, professor of political science at Birzeit University.[19]

The internal clamour for reform was matched by irresistible external pressure. The United States insisted that Arafat appoint the internationally respected former World Bank and IMF official Salam Fayyad as Finance Minister to increase accountability and transparency over the murky PA finances. The White House also demanded that Arafat share powers with a Prime Minister, which led to the short-lived appointment of his veteran deputy – and future Presidential successor – Mahmoud Abbas. Seeking to fend off the new pressures, Arafat also sought to bring Hamas into the picture, on his own terms. PLO and Hamas officials began a series of talks on national unity and internal reform, mediated by Arab and European interlocutors who sought to build trust between the Palestinian antagonists.

By November 2002 the issues were brought to a series of meetings in Cairo, where Arafat hoped that offering Hamas a quota of seats on the PNC would persuade the Islamists to stop suicide bombings against Israel. 'He had to look at Hamas again', said one former Arafat loyalist, 'and show his authority to all the people by being seen to bring them to heel.'[20] But the Islamists had far wider ambitions than, as one Hamas official put it, 'helping save Fatah from itself'.[21]

Hamas's inclusion in the talks was a public acknowledgement that it was now taken seriously by Egypt, and also demonstrated that Fatah and the PLO could no longer claim to be the sole, undisputed leaders or representatives of the Palestinian people. While in public the Hamas leadership paid respect to Arafat, in private it had concluded that he was a spent force politically. In Cairo, Hamas refused to capitulate to Arafat's terms, telling Fatah it would take its chances in elections, would continue to press for the reform of the PLO, and would deal with the issue of a ceasefire with Israel itself. Arafat's men were incensed but powerless. The American-backed reforms were intended to marginalize Arafat and suited everyone – Israel, Hamas and Fatah's young guard, who were keen to see their elders give way. But, in the rush to prise power from Arafat's grip, few considered who might fill the vacuum. 'Everybody wanted to take powers from Arafat as quickly as possible and wanted to put that power in the hands of somebody else', said the Palestinian analyst and pollster Dr Khalil Shikaki. 'Democrats wanted to put it in the hands of the parliament because then change in the situation became possible. The Americans and Israelis and old guard didn't care who would control the system once it was taken away from Arafat.'[22]

The unveiling in April 2003 of a detailed Roadmap to a Permanent Two-State Solution – under the auspices of the Quartet of mediators comprising the United States, Russia, the European Union and the United Nations – further weakened Arafat in Hamas's eyes. Although it was intended to be a starting point for the creation of a Palestinian state, by 2005 the Roadmap also appeared to offer opportunities for political reform and elections that Hamas could exploit.

Meanwhile, Fatah officials were noting Hamas's growing support on the Palestinian street. In Nablus's Balata refugee camp, one of the most militant areas in the West Bank, the maverick Fatah activist Husam Khader told anyone who would listen that, while Arafat's position was still beyond serious challenge, Fatah's reputation for sleaze and ineffi-ciency was quickly causing it to lose ground:

> I am not like Arafat in an isolated castle, seeing through liars' eyes and hearing through liars' ears. I live with the people. Hamas's popularity has really increased over time. I don't believe statistics and polls. They own social institutions, they are well organized and very fair. There is corruption, but not in front of the people. They don't have palaces like the PLO. Most of them are still living in the camps and they fight against Israel. I think they should stand in the elections or they will be real criminals to their people, and it will be an historic mistake.[23]

Hamas also believed it was on an upward spiral and could capitalize on growing disillusionment within Fatah. 'We are clean, we actually fight the occupation when they raid our homes and those of our neighbours . . . we are the true defenders', stated one West Bank Hamas activist.[24]

As the peace talks continued, Fatah grew increasingly frustrated, finding itself squeezed between two sides. Israel was insisting that it crack down on extremists, and Hamas was demanding that it persuade Israel to stop its assassinations, incursions and settlement expansion. 'We have got to get an agreement with Hamas in order to get an agreement with Israel, and we have to get an agreement with Israel in order to get an agreement with Hamas. We are caught between', said a strained Michael Tarazi, a PLO spokesman. 'When we have the support of the Palestinian popula-tion on the street we can take much stronger measures against extremists, if it is necessary. But so far nobody thinks they have anything to lose any more.'[25]

The next generation

From 2002 to 2005 the political and geographical landscape changed completely, as a generation of leadership passed from the scene. The first to go was a phalanx of Hamas's senior figures – Salah Shehadeh, Ibrahim al-Maqadmeh, Ismail Abu Shanab, Sheikh Yassin and Dr Abdel Aziz Rantissi – all assassinated by Israel. Israel's apparent aim was twofold: to punish those they considered directly responsible for organizing terror against Israel and to weaken the movement to the point of collapse. It certainly brought about a changing of the guard and the first real chance for a new generation of Hamas leaders to emerge. But it did not break Hamas.

Instead Ismail Haniyeh, widely seen as a pragmatist, became the face of the movement. Before Haniyeh became prime minister in 2006, his home was simply another nondescript refugee shelter in Gaza City's Shatti camp, built to house more than 78,000 registered Palestinian refugees. He had been born in the camp in 1961 to parents who were refugees of the war of 1948. Of the camp and from the camp, he joined Hamas around the same time that he graduated from the Islamic University of Gaza with his degree in Arabic literature. Visitors to the home were usually greeted by Haniyeh himself dressed in a white *galabiya* and prayer cap. The dark serge suits, white shirt and tie would come only later. Haniyeh is always calmly spoken. In his sermons he never shouts and amid a crowd is never flurried or impolite. For years he headed Yassin's office and was a near permanent companion to the wheelchair-bound sheikh. Some might say he learned at the feet of the most important man in Palestinian Islamism. For Israel, Haniyeh is a terrorist leader, arrested in the late 1980s, deported to Marj al-Zahour in 1992, and targeted for assassination on several occasions since.

The emergence of the telegenic and popular Haniyeh in Gaza was a counterbalance to the hawkish Dr Mahmoud Zahar. But even Zahar had changed his tune about politics. As early as February 2003 he declared that Hamas was 'absolutely' ready to replace Yasser Arafat and lead the Palestinian people. 'Hamas has an infrastructure; it has its cadres that can lead in all directions politically, financially, socially. And with respect to an army, we can create one with all capabilities',[26] he said.

Outside the Palestinian Territories, Khaled Meshaal, the exiled leader of its Political Bureau in Damascus, assumed a greater role in the movement, particularly after the assassination of Yassin and Rantissi. Meshaal's public and international profile grew from his Syrian base. For the increasing number of foreign journalists and former diplomatic heavyweights and statesmen who wanted to visit him, securing an interview with the man at the top of Israel's 'most wanted list' required tenacity, patience and a willingness to accept strict security precautions. Meshaal would often 'gift' his guests with candied fruits or Palestinian handicrafts. But such simple gestures belied the serious political calculations behind his willingness to meet with each and every foreign visitor. 'There is no political horizon if Hamas is not included as a legitimate element of the Palestinian people', he said during one interview, two months after Hamas had seized control of Gaza. Even at a time when Hamas had just made itself even more of a pariah to the international community, it was noticeable that a confident Meshaal, speaking in a clear and direct manner, used terminology akin to that of a national leader. Talking about Hamas's centrality to 'the national agenda' and 'the national objective', he reiterated the movement's position on eventual statehood and peace with Israel: 'There can be no peace process without Hamas included in the equation.'[27] Hamas has never been characterized by a theological hierarchy; therefore even the loss of its founder and spiritual figurehead, Yassin, did not fatally undermine the movement.

Unlike the founding generation, the younger leaders who were emerging and rising through the ranks in Gaza and the West Bank had often not worked or studied abroad. For them, unlike the Egyptian-educated Rantissi and Zahar, the world effectively began and ended at the Israeli checkpoints surrounding the Palestinian Territories. Many were graduates of the Islamic University of Gaza, combining technological competence and public relations awareness with the core conservative Islamic and family values they had imbibed from their families, lecturers and preachers. They had been raised on pedagogy and a curriculum of Islamism informed by the agenda of Hamas and the Muslim Brotherhood. They had also gained years of experience in the participative structures of Palestinian society, in student council and professional elections, and by sitting on the committees of Hamas's Islamic charities and associations. Through these they were familiar with the concerns of different Palestinian constituencies: the young, the old, women, men, the urban poor and the rural communities subsisting on declining agricultural revenues.

One such emerging leader is Mushir al-Masri. Al-Masri, born in the north Gazan town of Beit Lahyia in 1978, wore a black leather bomber jacket beneath his brown *abaya* as he led hundreds in Friday prayers outside the ruins of a mosque bombed by Israel during Operation Cast Lead in January 2009. The sartorial combination sums up the new generation. This thirty-something leader was the youngest candidate to be elected to the Palestinian parliament in 2006. Before that he was a member of the municipal council in Beit Lahiya. Educated at the Islamic University in Gaza – first obtaining a degree in Islamic law (*shari'a*) and then a masters in *fiqh* (jurisprudence) – he is a product of generation Hamas. Al-Masri was an activist on campus, became a deputy leader on the student council, and was involved as a board member of the Gaza-based charity al-Nour. His dark black beard and hair betray a youthful energy to help shape, direct and steer Hamas into the future. At his office in the Palestinian parliament his assistants are savvy, both at accessing the latest technology and in calibrating the different strengths of the tea to be served to foreign or local visitors.

Recognizing the new context, Salah al-Bardaweel, a senior Hamas leader, cited an ancient proverb:

> One of the Greek philosophers said, 'Man does not cross the river twice'.[28] History does not repeat itself. Hamas in 2005 is different from Hamas in 1996. I don't mean in terms of arms but in terms of our place in the fabric of Palestinian society . . . Before Hamas was a sitting duck, but now Hamas has major insurance. If you target Hamas, then you target the whole society.[29]

But the leadership change that presented the biggest opportunity was outside Hamas. On 11 November 2004, Yasser Arafat died in a Paris hospital after a lengthy and mysterious illness. It followed an even lengthier period of marginalization and public decline while he sat confined under virtual house arrest in his hilltop Muqata compound in Ramallah, too afraid to leave lest Israel refuse to let him back into the Palestinian Territories. He had passed his last days before illness living a spartan existence. He would greet visitors with a ceremonious kiss on the hand and the offer of tea served in mismatched crockery on a camping table set in a bare corridor. In the late afternoon some of his aides and functionaries would join him, grown men clamped into headlock 'hugs' as the President greeted his loyal fellows. Arafat's view from the confines of the Muqata was framed by the Israeli destruction to his headquarters two years earlier.

Although Arafat had become a shadow of the presence he once was, his death meant that Fatah had lost an iconic leader, whose personal charisma and legacy of struggle was unique within his now squabbling and fractious movement. 'Until the death of Yasser Arafat everything was in his hands. Everyone worked for Arafat; they were puppets on his fingers. After Arafat, there was no one to work for and they didn't want to work for each other', said Ambassador Dr Abdelrahman Bsaiso, a senior Foreign Ministry official.[30]

Arafat's successor, Mahmoud Abbas, widely known as Abu Mazen, had never emerged from Arafat's shadow and had little personal standing in the opinion polls. Nevertheless, he easily won the January 2005 Presidential election – helped by Hamas's decision not to contest the ballot. Although Hamas was then actively considering engaging in politics, the election was deemed the wrong point of entry. Part of the President's role was to negotiate with Israel, and the position would therefore have placed Hamas in an impossible position. The timing was also wrong. 'We couldn't go all at once into the Presidential elections and the Palestinian Legislative Council elections, it would be too great a leap', said Yehya Moussa Abbadsa. 'We wanted a margin or a space for all these contradictions that we could pass through in the transition to the

Presidency.'[31] Note the statement of long-term intent: the parliament was a step along the road to the ultimate destination.

Abbas was far more willing than his predecessor to countenance new elections, including municipal-level polls, which Hamas had long signalled that it was willing to contest. Whereas Arafat resisted new elections at every turn, Abbas – against the advice of many of his senior Fatah lieutenants – appeared to calculate that the only way to revitalize his sclerotic movement was to open it up to a challenge at the ballot box. Abbas also argued that, rather than risk military confrontation with Hamas, it would be better to wean it off violence by bringing it into the political process, thereby blunting its radicalism and being better able to control it. 'This is the difference between the era of Arafat and Abu Mazen. Arafat was stalling the legislative and presidential elections, not because he wanted one-man power but because he was afraid that, if he allowed them, Hamas would win. If that happened it would mean that he had thrown away forty years of dedication to secular politics', said Brigadier-General Nizar Ammar, a senior planner within the PA's General Security force in Gaza. 'Now there has been a strategic change in Fatah, an acceptance that, okay, if Hamas win the municipal elections, why not? This is the only way to revive Fatah, to confront the movement with the reality that we have a strong competitor and that we have to unite.'[32]

The flaw in Mr Abbas's plan – as it was in Hamas's own reasoning – was that it assumed that Hamas would participate, and lose. However, Mr Abbas faced conflicting opinions within his movement. Many veterans dragged their feet, unwilling to lose their sinecures. Others pushed for even faster internal reform, with even Fatah leaders outside the Palestinian Territories pronouncing themselves dissatisfied with the pace of internal reform. In Ein Hilweh refugee camp, in southern Lebanon, Munir Miqdar, a senior Fatah leader, said:

> Mr Abbas made a mistake. He delayed too long in rebuilding Fatah. After he won the election he should have made it his priority to reform the organization. Fatah was not working well before the election, it made many mistakes. Every time I talk to him I tell him this. There are a lot of leaders on the [Fatah] central committee who have not faced elections since 1979. We need new elections to build a new central committee and rebuild Fatah's structure according to democratic rules. We have to rebuild the entire parliamentary party with a new generation of Fatah, with new blood.[33]

Hamas leaders say that its decision to enter parliamentary polls was taken in early 2005 after extensive consultations of the grass roots and *shura* consultative councils throughout the movement, and that it had the blessing of the exiled political leadership in Damascus led by Khaled Meshaal. The clearest indication that Hamas would run, and run hard, for political office came in April 2005 from the one-time sceptic Dr Mahmoud

Zahar, by then the elder statesman of Hamas following the assassinations of Yassin and Rantissi. While many still doubted whether Hamas would even participate, Zahar confirmed that it would, and that, if it won seats in parliament or the government, it would fill them.

> If we are a majority, we are going to establish the government or will form the cabinet. But if we are a minority we have to reach with others for a national project in politics, economy, social and other areas. Now we are preparing everybody, not just our people, through the media . . . We have three options, either to be the majority and to ask others to participate according to our programme; second, to be a minority and participate in government, or to be a strong political opponent in the parliament.[34]

Municipal elections

Even as Dr Zahar spoke, Palestinians were preparing to vent their frustration at Fatah in municipal elections, both inside and outside Hamas's Gaza stronghold. In early May 2005 Hamas swept the electoral slate in the West Bank town of Qalqilya, deposing the once dominant Fatah and taking all fifteen municipal seats, even though its candidate for mayor, Sheikh Wajih Nazal, was elected from inside the Israeli prison where he had spent the last three years. Expressing their disgust with the incumbents, many of the town's 40,000 residents said they voted for the Islamists to send a clear message to the Fatah-dominated Palestinian Authority. 'After the death of Mr Arafat people hoped that some changes would take place with the election of Mahmoud Abbas, but we have not had changes', said Nidal Jaloud, a town hall official. 'People have not tasted the fruits of peace.'[35] Standing outside a grocery store, Umm Wael, a 45-year-old teacher, complained that the corruption and nepotism was at the expense of even the poorest townsfolk. 'Even the petrol coupons, telephone cards and food aid that were sent as donations to poor families never reached them', she said. 'It all went to clan and family members. This has nothing to do with religion. It is about our daily needs.'[36]

The seriousness of Hamas's intent was evident from the alacrity with which it had responded when the dates for municipal elections were announced. It mobilized hundreds of supporters to stand as candidates, printed electoral literature, organized rallies, polled voters and campaigned in the communities. The efforts paid off. In the first rounds Hamas won enough of the popular vote to secure a majority in a number of major towns in the Gaza Strip. In the May 2005 local elections, it won 270,000 more votes than Fatah. Throughout the Gaza Strip and the West Bank it was able to win power from Fatah and even dislodge its secular rival from its traditional West Bank strongholds such as Nablus, where in December 2005 it won the municipal poll.

Senior Fatah figures, incredulous at losing power, lodged complaints of electoral violations. In northern Gaza, Mohammed al-Masri, the Fatah-appointed mayor of Beit Lahiya, stood in the garden of his family compound in shock. 'The criticism against Fatah is not about our perform-ance as elected officials though, it's politics', he opined. 'To be clear on this issue, we on the Fatah lists were made to pay for the mistakes not of the PA but certain officials in the PA, and the opposition took advantage of this.'[37] Not even family allegiance to the powerful al-Masri clan was enough to stop his defeat. His victorious Hamas opponent was his cousin, Mushir al-Masri.

By the end of the second round of municipal elections in the summer of 2005, Hamas controlled forty-eight local councils, compared with Fatah's fifty-six. Hamas optimists extrapolated a similar electoral outcome at the parliamentary polls, while others dismissed the munici-pal elections as uniquely suited to Hamas's grass-roots approach. The Hamas victories alarmed Israeli ministers, some of whom called for the parliamentary election to be delayed and for Israel's proposed pullout from Gaza to be cancelled. Meanwhile, two major obstacles to Hamas's participation had disappeared, through a combination of Fatah weak-ness, and oversight.

Firstly, President Abbas balked at insisting that election contest-ants disarm, correctly surmising that he would have as much trouble getting his own Fatah-based Al Aqsa Martyrs' Brigades to lay down their weapons as he would with Hamas. Secondly – and with hindsight many conceded this was a major error – no one insisted that parties taking part in the elections should recognize Israel or sign up to the Oslo agenda. The loophole did not go unnoticed by Hamas. 'There was no actual restric-tion', recalls Ahmad Yousef, a Hamas leader. 'Nobody told them "You should run under the Oslo restrictions, and this is one, two and three." No, it was open. It was an encouraging sign for them, that there were no conditions for participation.' The results had also contained encouraging signs for the leadership, he said:

> The people in Damascus became convinced, after the results from some elections in the universities and unions and some local syndicates, that whenever they run for any engineering union or medical union they always get a high percentage. So, if we get that kind of popularity and support from Palestinian academics and the street, why shouldn't we actually be part of the legislative council?[38]

Disengagement

One final act remained, and it played perfectly to Hamas's strengths. In the summer of 2005, Israel's prime minister, Ariel Sharon, pulled all the

Jewish state's settlers and soldiers out of the 140 square mile Gaza Strip, thirty-eight years after Israel seized it from Egypt in the Six Day War. Mr Sharon insisted on carrying out the evacuation unilaterally, presenting it to the Palestinians as a fait accompli, rather than negotiating it with President Abbas. A frustrated Abbas was thereby unable to claim it as a victory for his chosen path, that of negotiations. Although the PA made elaborate preparations for securing the sites of the evacuated settlements, the plans fell apart within minutes of the Israelis' departure. Palestinian looters rampaged through the abandoned Zionist homes, shops and synagogues as Palestinian police stood by.

In the wake of disengagement, the 'liberation' of Gaza led to competing claims of victory from Hamas and Fatah, and old rivalries resurfaced. Law and order began to break down on the streets as the PA's security forces, facing a rampant and increasingly confident Hamas, proved unable or unwilling to cope with score-settling among well-armed factions and powerful clans.

Hamas lost no opportunity to proclaim Israel's pullout as a victory for Palestinian arms. It was an argument that gained widespread credence among Palestinians and helped propel Hamas to power, even if it deliberately glossed over the complex demographic, security and internal political considerations that prompted Sharon to order the withdrawal. No Gazan who watched the demolition of Israeli settlements felt anything but a sense of victory at the destruction of outposts whose watchtowers, snipers and Israeli-only highways had blighted their lives for decades. 'Hamas said that resistance is the solution, and events have proved it was correct. No one can claim the disengagement was a unilateral step and a gift from Sharon. It was a crushing defeat to the dignity of the Jewish State', proclaimed Dr Mahmoud Zahar.[39] To ram home the point – and create momentum for the coming parliamentary election – within days of Israel's withdrawal Hamas's propaganda unit erected green street banners in Gaza, proclaiming: 'Jerusalem and West Bank after Gaza – Hamas.'

End of Oslo

By late 2005 Hamas was convinced that the ideological obstacles which a decade previously had stopped it participating in the parliamentary elections were no longer relevant, with Oslo a distant memory. Israel and secular Palestinians regarded Hamas's ambitions with deep suspicion, fearing its embrace of democracy to be a ploy to bring about theocracy and authoritarianism on a one-way ticket to 'Hamastan'. But Hamas's political leadership had spent years highlighting Fatah corruption in running the Palestinian Authority. Hamas was proclaiming itself the new guardian of the 'resistance' against Israel, and increased the welfare and

Photo 12.1   A Hamas banner in Gaza in September 2005, shortly after the Israeli withdrawal from the Gaza Strip

social activities for which it was famous. With Israeli troops out of Gaza since the summer, it felt increasingly secure on the streets as autumn gave way to winter and election day approached.

On the day itself, 25 January 2006, Hamas fighters quietly deployed near polling stations to ensure that the Fatah-dominated Palestinian security forces did not try to rig the ballots. They even had torches and battery-powered lamps ready to rush to polling stations if Fatah cut the lights to stuff ballots amid the confusion. Hamas was everywhere. According to Yehya Moussa Abbadsa:

> The withdrawal of Israel from Gaza created a new fact on the ground. We were stronger. Democracy could not be protected in 1996, but by 2006 Hamas was stronger on the ground than the PA. That is what created the balance. They couldn't tamper with the election because we could protect the process. Politics and democracy aren't protected purely by values. In Algeria the Islamic Society won the elections but didn't have the power to save itself. In Egypt, if they held a real election the Islamists would win, also in Jordan. But since they don't have a balance of power, it allows democracy to be weak.[40]

Secular political observers had a more sceptical perspective on Hamas's decision, saying it acted more out of desperation and fear of being marginalized. 'For two years now Hamas has been feeling that the jihadi approach was reaching a dead end, especially with the opposition of the regional and international community to this approach. It was classified as a terrorist movement by the US and some other countries', said Ibrahim Ibrach, a Gaza political analyst.

> From this point it decided to log into the Palestinian political system. It felt besieged by the outside world. They froze all their money and stopped all its institutions. So they started seeking new legitimacy through the ballot box and decided to enter the electoral process. Not, I think, because they believe in democracy, but because they want legitimacy, to say to the world

that they are a party or a movement that represents the Palestinian people through democratic elections.[41]

Whatever its motivations, Hamas had long ago concluded that Fatah's corruption and bad management were not only electoral liabilities that Hamas could exploit, but were now undermining Palestinian society to the point where its own armed activities were being jeopardized. 'It placed the internal front on very weak foundations with all the corruption and mismanagement, and when you have weak foundations you can't build a strong resistance', said Ismail al-Ashqar, a senior Hamas strategist.

> We wished to obtain popular legitimacy for the resistance and legal legitimacy. We knew we would be much stronger when we had legitimacy backing you up, because no one can accuse you of breaking the law. In 1996 thousands of Hamas had been jailed as terrorists. The authority was new, so it was very hard to take such a decision. In 2006 we had experienced the Second Intifada and the popularity of Hamas was very high, and the ability to capitalize on this politically was very obvious.[42]

Fear

For external actors such as Israel, the European Union and the United States of America, the prospect of Hamas domination at the polls was problematic. When President Abbas announced a delay in the parliamentary elections, and Washington called – in vain – for Hamas to be excluded, the Islamists were quick to point out the irony. 'The US and EU called for elections to get rid of Arafat and others – well, they got an election but they didn't get the result they wanted, because we in Hamas won. Now there is the demand by the US to exclude us from the political arena',[43] said Mushir al-Masri. Musa Abu Marzouq, one of Hamas's most senior political leaders in exile, felt confident enough to boast about Hamas's prospects in the parliamentary elections, and unwittingly give a foretaste of events to come: 'When we win those elections it will be great problems for the Americans, I am sure. Is the international community prepared to ignore these elections and their results if they go in our favour?'[44]

But few seriously believed that Hamas would, or could, win. Its principal opponent – President Abbas – was by now a welcome guest in foreign capitals – most notably in Washington, where in May 2005 he was entertained by President George W. Bush, who had steadfastly refused to have any dealings with Arafat. Standing beside Abbas in the White House Rose Garden, President Bush made clear his support by voicing a misplaced public confidence that secular Fatah would prevail over its Islamist opponents:

Our position on Hamas is very clear, it's a well-known position and it hasn't changed about Hamas: Hamas is a terrorist group, it's on a terrorist list for a reason. President [Abbas] ran on a peace platform; you know, maybe somebody will run on a war platform – you know, vote for me, I promise violence. I don't think they're going to get elected, because I think Palestinian moms want their children to grow up in peace just like American moms want their children to grow up in peace. As a matter of fact, I think the people that campaign for peace will win.[45]

Polling

Ultimately the decision to enter the electoral fray had been a victory for the pragmatists, who persuaded the hardliners that Hamas could push forward the Islamization of Palestinian society far faster if it was running ministries and budgets. 'We always knew our main strength was resistance, not to be preoccupied with the burden of ruling', said Jamila al-Shanti. 'There were studies about if we win how should we behave, should we participate and why. Should we not, and why.'[46] But, once it had decided to run, Hamas united behind the new strategy. It deployed thousands of highly educated Islamist managers, media professionals, opinion-formers, teachers, engineers, doctors, political scientists – male and female – who gave it an organizational sharpness and sophistication far superior to its more politically experienced, but fatally complacent, rivals. For its venture into the mainstream, Hamas deliberately and calculatedly toned down its rhetoric.

Even Hamas's opponents conceded that its choice of electoral label – 'Change and Reform' – was inspired, capturing the pent-up desire among Palestinians for a new broom. The election manifesto also downplayed Hamas's implacable external agenda, making no mention of its ultimate goal of eradicating Israel. Instead it spoke of 'resistance to the occupation' and 'balanced' relations with the West. It was a wolf in sheep's clothing. In fact, Hamas's new cadre of articulate spokesmen did continue to insist that the movement retained its claim to all of Palestine – Israel as well as the occupied Palestinian Territories. But they said it was still committed to Yassin's 1997 offer of a long-term *hudna* based on a Palestinian state in the West Bank, East Jerusalem and Gaza. Hamas's customary insistence on proclaiming its commitment to the armed struggle was sidelined behind management consultancy talk of priorities, competence, transparency and delivery of services.

'We have our electoral programme on politics, agriculture, health, education, and so on', said Sheikh Mohammed Abu Teir, Hamas's Jerusalem figurehead, who has spent more than twenty-five years in Israeli jails. Just after being released from a night in the cells for defying an Israeli ban on campaigning in Jerusalem, the henna-bearded no. 2 on

Hamas's electoral list took advantage of a brief gap between incarcerations to deliver the on-message Hamas electoral line: 'Even with modest means we have succeeded in gaining the trust of the people. We will fight the corrupt and serve the Palestinian people.'[47] Sami Abu Zuhri, a Hamas spokesman in Gaza, summarized the party's election manifesto: 'The emphasis was on resistance as a main tool. Now we are more interested in political participation without making any concessions on our principles.'[48]

Compared with Hamas's energy and drive, the Fatah campaign seemed listless and complacent. Fatah's ageing old guard – Arafat's generation – had spent three decades outside Palestine, from 1967 until 1994, and had lost touch with the Palestinian street, a criticism that was heard as often from their own ranks as from outsiders. Inside Fatah's pristine election headquarters near the counterfeit 'Stars and Bucks' coffee shop in the West Bank city of Ramallah, clean-shaven youths and affluent young women wearing fake designer labels handed out leaflets advertising the party's website: www.vote4fatah.plo.ps. But the election headquarters seemed stuck in another era. In the front lobby the sound system played the 1960s Beatles song 'Revolution' – from an era long before many Palestinian voters were born – and the walls bore twenty-eight posters of the dead Yasser Arafat but just two of its current leader, President Mahmoud Abbas.

In a back room elderly officials in tweed jackets and improbably black hair seemed bemused by questions about where Fatah was strong or weak in the West Bank. 'We don't have any indication of where Fatah or Hamas have strongholds or majorities', said one, after going into a huddle for several minutes to confer with his colleagues.[49] Collectively, they assured journalists that voters would stick with the movement because of its self-proclaimed status as 'guardians of the national project' – an ancient PLO cliché devoid of specifics, inspiration or direction. Summarizing the mood of inevitability and entitlement, one elderly apparatchik pronounced, to general nods of assent: 'Fatah's history is evidence enough to testify that people will support it at the ballot box.'

Not all Fatah officials were so complacent. A younger generation had fought alongside Hamas, Islamic Jihad and the other factions during the First and Second Intifada and appeared to recognize the threat from their religious contemporaries, whose rise they had seen up close from inside Israeli jails and on the barricades. Mohammed Dahlan, by then a key aide to President Abbas, warned that those in Hamas were fanatics on their best behaviour for the elections. 'We pledge that the mistakes of the past will not be repeated', Dahlan told one rally in Ramallah, apparently calculating that it was better to be frank and contrite about past mistakes than to pretend they never happened. He urged Fatah's listless supporters not to take victory for granted and cautioned – in vain – against a protest vote mentality. 'Let us be clear: if anyone thinks that he can vent his anger upon Fatah by making them lose, he is making a mistake. You will not be able to practise what you are experiencing today. It will be the policy of mouth-shutting, those who take religion at the expense of freedom of speech.'[50]

Others were equally alarmed. Diana Buttu, a former communications director in President Abbas's office, said that, in the year leading up to the ballot, Abbas and his senior lieutenants on Fatah's principal decision-making committees were so focused on Israel's pullout from Gaza that they paid no attention to much needed internal Fatah reforms. 'One of the things that Abu Mazen failed to do from the time of his election in January 2005 was to capitalize on the momentum that it gave him', she said.

> Post-disengagement, from September onwards, at a time when he should have been focused on primaries, he just wasn't. He was focusing on everything else but whether it was how to revitalize the economy, what was to be done with the infighting in Gaza, to the Qassams, to whatever it was. He just wasn't focused on Fatah as an institution. He let it slide because he was focused on other things – he just didn't think that Fatah was an issue. He didn't put his political office together until two months into the Presidency. He was really lax at all of this stuff. And I think it was because his direction came from the central committee, and sometimes from the revolutionary council.

She said many party workers were dismayed by the lack of proper Fatah primary elections to decide candidates, an oversight which resulted in two competing lists being drawn up: one by the Fatah establishment and the other by the younger generation. A late compromise to merge the two lists left out many Fatah notables. This in turn prompted the rejects to stand as independent Fatah candidates, with electorally fatal results.

Unlike the 1996 parliamentary elections and the 2005 Presidential election, for the first time Fatah was now up against a significant challenge. 'Hamas already had its posters done, it was already organized, it had submitted its list, it knew how it was going to proceed, and Fatah didn't even have a list. And at this point we are just two weeks away from the start of the campaign', said Buttu. 'Hamas had its election platform and a very clever name, Change and Reform. Fatah had nothing other than a slogan: "We have been with you forty-one years".' Money was spent 'needlessly', she said. There was no week by week strategy about what Fatah's message should be, or how they were they going to get people out to vote. 'Hamas were arm wrestling with a baby. It wasn't so much that Hamas were so superior, Fatah gave it to them.'[51]

Amani Abu Ramadan, who worked with the Fatah campaign dealing

Photo 12.2   Hamas executive forces training in the abandoned Israeli settlement of Neve Dekalim after Israel's pullout from Gaza in 2005

with the international media in Gaza, said she quit early because the campaign was so badly run. She recalls driving Miguel Moratinos, the former EU Special Representative for the Middle East Peace Process, around Gaza four days before the election.

> We went from Erez to Rafah, one and a half hours in the car, talking about the elections. I remember counting the election posters, and there were one, two, three, four billboards for Hamas, maybe two for Fatah and then another for Hamas. I told him the result of the election would be the same. It was complete chaos. The Third Way or Change and Reform had someone at reception giving you campaign materials. At Fatah there was basically a bunch of boys sitting at the desk pretending to be a campaign.[52]

But the lack of preparation and wasted money could still have seen Fatah to victory, had it not been a house divided against itself. Fatah's campaign chief, Nabil Shaath, conceded that his biggest concern was the party's rejected independent candidates, who stood against the official Fatah candidates out of genuine if misguided hope of winning, in order to punish the party for rejecting them, or to use the threat of candidacy as leverage to obtain some other benefit. Nevertheless, on the eve of the election he voiced confidence that Fatah would still win:

Yes absolutely, I have no doubt. There is something about the Fatah movement which defies any prediction. Fatah people look like they are quarrelling and fighting over trivia, and jockeying for position. But when it comes to a real challenge with someone else, whether it is the Israelis, some Arab regime or a Palestinian opponent such as Hamas, there is something electrical that just fuses them again and pushes them forward. This is exactly what happened this time. It looks very late because we were very late in starting the campaign. Everybody believed that the elections were going to be delayed indefinitely, so people were very complacent.

Shaath brushed aside allegations of Fatah corruption, dismissing them as 'election rubbish'. The real cause of Palestinian hardship, he insisted, was 'the Israeli siege, the Israeli wall, the Israeli settlement policy, continued Israeli attacks and destruction . . . It is the Israeli siege that has killed this economy and turned it into rubbish, and also caused the lawlessness.' About Hamas's role in that breakdown of law and order he was bitter, saying that, although Hamas 'tries to act prim and proper', it had in fact been a 'major factor' in the lawlessness by continuing to carry out rocket and mortar attacks against Israel in defiance of the PA, which left the Palestinian police looking impotent because they were unable to take action against powerful Islamist cells. The police were also, he complained, unable to arrest Hamas's 'protected people when they have committed crimes, as has happened several times'. But, while conceding that the PA was partly responsible for its plight, Shaath sought to put the Palestinian experience into wider perspective, pointing out that there were few examples of societies freeing themselves painlessly from external hegemony.

> Yes, part of this is our responsibility as a people, and not only as an authority. But look at it from a historical context of post-trauma societies such as Bosnia, Kosovo, Ireland, Lebanon, Somalia and Iraq. It took Lebanon twenty-five years, and they are not really out of the post-trauma period. Whenever you are in a conflict with a far superior occupation army, this immediately leads to the proliferation of small arms, which are used by guerrillas and other types of violent resistance to ambush and fight far superior forces. The problem is when that superior force either vanishes, withdraws or starts to reduce significantly its own campaign against the occupied territories, then those who fought with small arms look around and substitute the goals with other local, provincial, personal or sectarian objectives to survive after the end of the conflict, to obtain assurances about their own future or to engage in local politics or power.[53]

Meanwhile Hamas's campaign was in full swing. It was a winter election, but only one party's posters were covered in plastic to protect them from the rain. Beneath the sheeting was the face of Hamas's founder,

Photo 12.3 A Hamas election poster

Sheikh Yassin, invariably with a broad smile on his face. The Hamas art and design department clearly went into overdrive to produce variations of campaign posters, literature and propaganda for the Change and Reform candidates.

The momentum for the victory that Dr Zahar accurately predicted had been set in motion by Hamas's electoral plan. Its slogan, 'Change and Reform', was adapted from its successful earlier municipal campaigns and refined by a sophisticated campaign team. Dr Nashat Aqtash, a Nablus-born public relations expert, was among the professional image consultants hired to sharpen its image. They ensured that Hamas had a three-member election committee in each town – the head, the fund-raiser and the person in charge of mobilizing activists – each on call twenty-four hours a day. They also gave candidates training in public speaking, on how to appear on camera, and on how to address the national and international media.

'We organized rallies, meetings at clubs, in public places and individual meetings. Personal communication is number one in Palestine because there is historic mistrust of the media and because Fatah wasn't scheduling its candidates to meet people. Their candidates were ministers and public figures, so they had no time to go to the public. That was a plus for Hamas', said Dr Aqtash. He said he adapted a three-week formula devised by the 1960s American advertising guru Rosser Reeves, which stipulated a different plan for each week of the campaign. Newspapers, radio and local terrestrial television channel campaigns were also directed at Hamas's target audience: the 40 per cent of Palestinians who could not afford Arabic satellite channels such as al-Jazeera. The advertisements addressed four frequent voter questions identified by their research: Why was Hamas participating in 2006 when it boycotted elections in 1996? What would a Hamas government do for ordinary Palestinians? How would it deal with other parties and the peace process? and Would it form government alone, or join a national unity coalition?

Ismail Haniyeh, who was a compelling public speaker, appeared in one sixty-second advertisement which addressed all four issues and was released through ten local TV stations over five days, six times every evening. 'He said that they participated in the election under one slogan: "We need to lift the oppression and suffering of our people". When Hamas participated in the election it was because of you, because we needed to improve your situation, not because of our interests', explained Dr Aqtash.

In the final week they also had five single-issue radio spots, addressing corruption, women's rights, education, opposition to the Oslo Accords, and Change and Reform. Candidates were advised not to campaign negatively against rival parties, not to use Mahmoud Abbas as a campaign issue, 'because he is the President and we have to respect that', and to emphasize religion by suggesting that, if voters selected those who were weak in their practice of Islam, they would be punished by God. 'The failure of peace talks for the last ten years helped Hamas. People had started to believe the rhetoric that peace was a waste of time and that resistance was the answer. So the message was addressing internal Palestinian issues. It had nothing to do with the occupation, nothing to do with the Israelis. All internal issues.'[54]

Much as Barack Obama's careful attention to the complex electoral arithmetic in the 2008 US Presidential primary campaign saw him to victory over his longer-established rival Hillary Clinton, so Hamas had a far sharper grasp of the complex electoral system in place for the 2006 Palestinian elections. The vote for the parliament's 132 seats was divided into two lists: half for a party and half for individual candidates in sixteen districts. While Fatah put its strongest people on the national list, Hamas did the opposite, because it calculated, correctly, that people would vote along party lines for the party list but would be swayed by personal considerations when choosing a local MP. 'When you vote for Hamas on the national list you are voting for the party, not for individuals. In the districts you select individuals, so if people are corrupt, not credible, people will not vote for them. Fatah wasted their strong candidates', said Aqtash. Hamas's one major mistake, he pointed out, was to try too hard, ignoring the cold realpolitik about what international obstacles they would face if it won.

> They didn't listen to advice. I told them not to run more than 50 per cent of candidates in the election because, if they actually won, they would find themselves in an impossible position. They wouldn't be acceptable to the international community and they would be embarrassed in front of their people. But [Khaled] Meshaal insisted on running with a full list. I warned them they would fall into a Fatah trap, that the Fatah people and US wouldn't give them a chance to succeed. I told them, 'Assign a technocratic government, assign a Christian Prime Minister. You can embarrass the US and Israel with that.'

Israel was increasingly alarmed by Hamas, which one poll showed at 31 per cent in Gaza, just four points behind Fatah. Tzipi Livni, the Israeli foreign minister, expressed her dismay. 'Can you imagine any European country or the United States allowing a terrorist organisation to take part in elections?'[55]

The international community was also alarmed. In December 2005, Javier Solana, the European Union's foreign policy and security chief, warned of a freeze in European aid to the PA if the Palestinians embraced a party which refused to abandon violence and continued to urge the destruction of Israel. This was a grave prospect for the Palestinians, as the EU was their single largest donor, contributing one-third of the PA's international funding in 2005, more than $340 million. Two days before the election, the British prime minister, Tony Blair, stepped up the pressure. 'It is very difficult for us to be in the position of negotiating or talking to Hamas unless there's a very clear renunciation of terrorism', he said. 'In the end all organisations have to choose whether they want a path of violence or a path of politics, and there's no way they will get anywhere with a path of violence.'[56]

The foreign interventions proved pointless, even counterproductive. To neutralize them Hamas held back its closing message until the final days of the campaign – huge banners across the main streets of Palestinian cities which proclaimed: 'Israel and America say no to Hamas. What do you say?'

It is not an original selling point. The Iraqi dictator Saddam Hussein enjoyed huge support across the Arab world – not least among Palestinians – because of his successful campaign to sell himself as the one Arab leader prepared to stand up to Israel and America. More recently, Iran's controversial – and controversially re-elected –- President Mahmoud Ahmadinejad carved out a similar niche, delighting in the opprobrium of the Western world because this sold well among his poor, Islamic revolutionary base. In the Middle East it is a pitch which comes as naturally to opposition parties as Western politicians promising to stand up for 'us' – i.e. John Bull, Main Street, ordinary working people, the misunderstood middle classes, motherhood, apple pie, the silent majority or the flag – against the (invariably venal, corrupt and self-interested) 'them' – inside Westminster, Brussels, the Washington Beltway or wherever. It is not an original tactic, but a tried, trusted and highly effective one.

Two days before the election, the opinion pollsters, Fatah and most voters were still expecting a slim majority, and most senior Hamas leaders later conceded that they did not expect outright victory either. Publicly, Dr Mahmoud Zahar was one of the few who continued to proclaim the possibility of a major upset. 'Please don't trust the research centres in Gaza or the West Bank, because all the time they indicate that Hamas represent 18 per cent or 20 per cent, or something like that', he said on the eve of the election. 'It may be 25 per cent, it may be 50 per cent, it may be more than that. Nobody can tell, because this is the first time we are going to participate in political elections.'[57]

One reason that the opinion pollsters were thrown off was that Hamas told its people to mislead them. Two years after the victory, Mushir al-Masri, a Hamas MP, conceded that this was one of the Machiavellian tricks used to conceal the true strength of the Islamist movement, but said it was a small factor compared with the pro-Fatah leanings of many of the polling institutions which were caught out by the final result. 'It wasn't a comprehensive vision. It was wily politics', he said. 'This deception was a small part of it, but the opinion polls were politicized because these [polling] centres belonged to Fatah. They were deceiving themselves.'[58]

Photo 12.4   A Hamas youth rally in Gaza in December 2006

Photo 12.5 An image of the newly elected Hamas leader, Ismail Haniyeh, beamed from Gaza to the Palestinian parliament building in Ramallah in the West Bank, March 2006

Victory

The outcome was emphatic. Hamas won seventy-four seats in the 132-seat parliament and Fatah won just forty-five. The turnout was high, around 77 per cent. But most startling was the disparity between the percentage of the vote and the seats won. Hamas won 56 per cent of the seats with just 44 per cent of the national vote, whereas Fatah had 41 per cent of the vote but gained only 36 per cent of the seats. The main factor was the Fatah independents, who took thousands of votes from their own party's official candidates and allowed Hamas to rout Fatah by forty-five seats to seventeen in the district lists. Political analysts calculated that the unofficial candidates might have lost Fatah up to eighteen parliamentary seats.[59]

The biggest defeats were in Hebron, where Hamas won all of the nine seats; in Nablus, where it won five to Fatah's one; and in secular, liberal Ramallah, which should have been Fatah's power base but where it won four seats and Fatah only one. A good indication of how Fatah fatally divided its vote was in Hebron, where Hamas gained 49.9 per cent (61,433 votes) and Fatah 35.98 per cent (44,668). But Hamas won all nine of the seats because it only fielded nine candidates, whereas Fatah split the field with nine official and other independent candidates. Fatah did better in areas where it put big name candidates in their home towns, such as Mohammed Dahlan in Khan Younis and Saeb Erekat in Jericho. In the party list vote the race was much closer: Hamas won twenty-nine seats with 44 per cent of the vote, and Fatah twenty-eight seats with 41 per cent.

Far behind were the PFLP, with three seats, the DFLP, with two, and The Third Way, which returned Salam Fayyad and Hanan Ashrawi. Mustafa Bargouthi's Independent Palestine gained two seats. With an absolute majority in the parliament, Hamas had won political power.

13

Hamastan

There is a long history of Islamic movements everywhere – in Libya, Algeria, Morocco and Syria. But the victory came here in Palestine. The people of the Islamic nation are not interested in the Islamic movements in these countries. They are interested in here.

Prime Minister Ismail Haniyeh, Hamas[1]

It was immediately obvious that Hamas's election victory was seismic in proportion. It forced governments, generals, intelligence agencies, bankers, humanitarian organizations and ordinary Palestinian and Israeli citizens into a radical rethink of decade-old assumptions and working practices. In the West Bank and Gaza, Fatah had begun overnight celebrations, prematurely. These fell quickly silent after midnight, as initial results indicated first that Fatah would fall short of an absolute majority, then that it would lose, and finally that Hamas had won its own controlling majority of a Parliament in which it had never sat. There was to be no long political transition from opposition to power. Hamas was propelled straight from political wilderness to political power in a development that was to be disastrous for the Palestinian people.

Gaza woke up with an alcohol-free hangover. The streets were emptier of traffic than normal, and even pedestrians moved slower, stopping every few yards to talk through the whys and what nows with everyone else. Power leaked rapidly from Fatah – cocky soldiers who only a few hours earlier had hurtled through the streets in armoured SUVs now sat in headquarters, unsure of the chain of command which had sustained them, in one form or another, back through the Palestinian Authority (PA), PLO and Fatah, since the late 1960s.

The scale of Hamas's victory shocked even the majority of its leadership. Ismail Haniyeh, the new prime minister designate, was mobbed in Shatti refugee camp as scores of journalists and well-wishers crammed into his home. But, outside, the stillness was funereal rather than celebratory. The leadership had quickly sent out orders banning celebratory gunfire in the air or partying in the streets, and its intended message was clear: from minute one, the new regime would be one of discipline, not chaos.

Publicly Hamas leaders tried to claim that they expected victory all along. But privately many conceded that they had wanted – and needed – a period in opposition to help the movement adjust. 'The result was a shock for us . . . we decided to go for elections, but we were not expecting that any great significance would come from it', conceded Usama Hamdan, Hamas's senior representative in Lebanon.[2]

Hamas inherited a lawless Gaza. In 2002, Israel's missile strikes and F16 bombing raids had all but destroyed the Fatah-dominated PA's security infrastructure, leaving it weak and vulnerable. However, it had already laid the foundations for power in the most important arena: security. It had spent two decades relentlessly recruiting, training and arming its military wing, and had redoubled its efforts since Israel's pullout from Gaza six months earlier. Hamas, armed with its democratic mandate, walked into the Palestinian Ministry of the Interior ready to take charge of the security forces, preparing for the inevitable battles against Israel, and Fatah. It was to get both within two years.

As Palestinians absorbed the shock, the question being shouted down the phone to every diplomat and foreign correspondent in Jerusalem was: 'What does this mean for the peace process?' Most outsiders could not understand how Palestinians would embrace a group so wedded to violence, having voted in President Mahmoud Abbas – a man openly critical of the path of the gun – just twelve months before. One of the most succinct analyses came from Michael Tarazi, a former legal adviser to the PLO, who had watched the descent from Intifada in 2000 to full-out war in 2002–3.

> Anyone who says this is going to destroy the peace process has not been paying attention to the fact that there isn't a peace process to destroy. This is part of the problem that Fatah faced. They had nothing to show for their many years of negotiation with Israel. They had nothing to show for their recognition of Israel. For all of the handshakes and all of the meetings, the situation of Palestinians actually got worse during the so-called peace process.[3]

Israel's acting prime minister, Ehud Olmert, immediately announced that his government 'will not negotiate with a Palestinian administration if its members include an armed terrorist organization that calls for the destruction of the State of Israel'.[4] He all but placed the blame at the door of the PA and the international community, accusing them of having been gullible by allowing Hamas to renege on an agreement that it would disarm if allowed to participate in the elections. Mr Olmert's government also quickly signalled that it would refuse to hand over to a Hamas-led authority around $60 million in customs revenues that it collected each month on the PA's behalf.

President George W. Bush was characteristically firm in his support of Israel, proclaiming: 'The United States does not support a political party that wants to destroy our ally Israel . . . it means you're not a partner in peace and we are interested in peace.'[5] In Jerusalem, Jacob Walles, the US consul general, stated that Washington would discontinue its $368 million (£208 million) annual direct aid to the PA. 'I don't see how we would do that if those ministries were controlled by Hamas', he said.[6] Moving quickly, the United States, the United Nations, the European Union and Russia – the four international powers known as the Quartet – said they would refuse to deal with a Hamas-led government unless it accepted three conditions: renounce violence, recognize Israel and respect previous agreements signed by Hamas's predecessors. But Ismail Haniyeh set an equally defiant tone, making clear that Hamas would not soften its position: 'The Americans and the Europeans say to Hamas: either you have weapons or you enter the legislative council. We say weapons *and* the legislative council. There is no contradiction between the two.'[7]

Money quickly emerged as the first tool of international pressure on Hamas, but one that had to be used carefully. While no world leader wanted to fund Hamas's arms-acquisition programme, neither did they want the inevitable humanitarian, domestic and regional security consequences of pushing Palestinians into penury. James Wolfensohn, a former head of the World Bank, whose financial expertise was invaluable in his new role as Middle East envoy for the Quartet, warned that the PA could face a cash crisis within days if Israel and international donors withdrew funding. 'The Palestinians are basically bankrupt. If you do not have money to pay 135,000 Palestinians, you are going to have chaos.'[8] He frankly conceded that Hamas's victory had surprised him and his team of diplomats and security advisers as much as everyone else. Giving evidence to the US Senate Committee on Foreign Relations, he was asked by Senator Barbara Boxer: 'How blindsided were you – I don't mean just you, personally – you and the diplomats who follow this?' Wolfensohn replied: 'I think almost universally, Senator, although in retrospect, we shouldn't have been when we saw multiple candidates from Fatah for seats confronting a single candidate from Hamas, which was clearly an important element in the result.'[9]

Wounded

Hamas found itself all but alone. Early talk of a national unity coalition foundered as defeated Fatah saw the scale of the international opposition to Hamas, and left it isolated. Hamas's preachers and politicians tried to nuance its position, Dr Mahmoud Zahar first saying that it was ready to enter talks with the international community over the prospect of Israeli and Palestinian states coexisting, and then trying – in vain – to remove itself from the equation by deferring major decisions on relationships with Israel to a referendum of the Palestinian people. 'We may need to ask the general attitudes of our people. This is the land of the people. It is not the land of the government. We are not the owners of Palestine.'[10]

Three months into its term, Hamas was performing even more verbal gymnastics. 'We accept a state on the 1967 borders without recognizing the legitimacy of occupation. They can have their state on the 1948 lands, but I don't recognize it', said Usama al-Mazini, a member of Hamas's dialogue committee. 'That is not a recognition of Israel, and there is no acceptance of the two-state solution. We will not recognize its legitimacy. We will deal with them on daily matters, but not at a practical level.'[11] But Hamas had little chance of finessing its way to legitimacy on issues of such existential importance. Israel and the West made it clear they were not interested in wordplay, and heard only 'No, no, no' on the three Quartet demands.

Fatah, needless to say, had no intention of surrendering real power, whatever had transpired at the ballot box. As Hamas and the international community laid down their front lines, Fatah began working to undermine its rival from within. Soon after the defeat one very senior Fatah official in Gaza disclosed that Fatah had teams of legal experts studying the law to see how far it could circumvent Hamas's control over the parliament and concentrate power in the hands of Mahmoud Abbas. The analysis was that, as he was both President of the Palestinian Authority inside the Palestinian Territories and head of the Palestine Liberation Organization, representing 4.6 million registered Palestinian refugees in the Middle East and other Palestinians worldwide, Abbas, not the parliament or government, was responsible for negotiations with Israel. 'There is no need for Abu Mazen to go back to the Palestinian Legislative Council to approve any agreement with Israel', said the official, at his comfortable Gaza City home. 'Legally speaking, the Palestinian Legislative Council has nothing to do with Israel.'[12]

There was desperation in the air as Fatah sought to convince the international media that, at the very moment of its defeat, it had conveniently discovered that the parliament – which it had controlled for a decade – had all along been a meaningless entity imbued with no more authority than a municipal council. Fatah was a bad loser with lawyers, and within hours of its defeat was already more intent on frustrating the outcome of an inconvenient expression of democratic will than addressing the deep-seated structural, democratic, financial and ethical failings within its own organization that should have been its first priority.

The plotting achieved little. Just over a year later, in June 2007, the same Fatah officials were ejected from Gaza in their underpants during Hamas's armed takeover of the Gaza Strip. This takeover, an increasingly inevitable outcome of the power games set in train during these first days, represented the military consolidation of Hamas's political victory.

Seeking some consolation from the loss of its unreliable proxy, American diplomats highlighted the fact that Fatah's Mahmoud Abbas was still in place as President and was committed to a negotiated two-state solution with Israel. David Welch, Assistant Secretary in the US State Department's Bureau of Near Eastern Affairs, told one congressional hearing that the result was a quirk of a complex electoral process that had allowed Hamas to turn a 'narrow plurality of popular votes into a larger number of seats due to superior organization during the election, and idiosyncrasies of the bloc-voting system'. He said he believed, nevertheless, that 'the Palestinian people's aspirations to live in peace remain strong' and that 'opinion polls and analysis of the balloting suggest the vote for Hamas was more a protest against Fatah's governance record than a vote of support for Hamas's political agenda. We continue to believe that the Palestinian people support the policies of President Abbas, whom they also elected on a platform of peace just over a year ago.'[13]

It's the economy, stupid

The moves by Fatah and the international community to emphasize the role of the Fatah presidency at the expense of the Hamas-dominated legislature provoked an angry broadside from Dr Mahmoud Zahar, Hamas's Foreign Minister-designate, who condemned 'international interference in the elections'.[14] More disturbingly, Zahar signalled a radical new post-election strategy. He was scathing about previous agreements with Israel signed by the Fatah-led PA, indicating that the new Hamas-led PA wanted and expected little from Israel, America, Europe and the West. 'We have to open the door to the Arab and Muslim world. We have to separate our relationship on all levels with Israel for our national interest', he said.

It is a common Hamas charge that PLO negotiators such as Arafat, Ahmed Qureia (Abu Ala'a), Mahmoud Abbas and Saeb Erekat were, throughout the Madrid and Oslo era, consistently out-negotiated by the Israelis into accepting deals harmful to Palestinian interests. Dr Zahar said that Hamas did not consider talking to Israel to be *haraam*, merely a waste of time, because the Israelis could not be trusted. 'The people before us, the Palestinian Authority, negotiated with them for many, many years and reached lastly a deadlock. So why should we be a new copy like Fatah, wasting time and money of the people negotiating with Israel for nothing?' he asked. 'What is the project of Israel for the Palestinians? Up to this moment no projects, no offers, no intention of giving the Palestinian people their legitimate demands.' Fatah would have replied angrily that, far from being innocent bystanders lamenting the failure of past negotiations, Hamas had done more than anyone to wreck such initiatives. Nevertheless, there was widespread pessimism among Palestinians that talks with Israel would ever prove fruitful, and Hamas capitalized on this.

But Dr Zahar went far beyond the customary Hamas critique of Fatah – that it had reduced the PA to little more than a security sub-contractor for Israel. He also gave notice of Hamas's continued antipathy to other basic cornerstones of Israeli–Palestinian relations, including the 1994 Paris Economic Agreement which governed trade and tax issues. 'We destroyed our economical status by the linkage of our economy with the Israelis through what is called the Paris Agreement', he said. 'We have ten commercial agreements with the Arabic and Islamic world without taxes. Israel takes from us seventeen taxes, and they are destroying our industry.'[15] The reams of data he provided were intended to buttress his argument that Palestinians should be released from restrictive agreements that limited them to Israeli suppliers. Their significance was not that the information was necessarily verifiable or accurate, but that, for Zahar to have had such a long list of specific examples immediately to hand, Hamas's research and media units must have spent considerable time preparing the ground in advance to present this case to the Palestinian public.

This impression was buttressed by the on-message unanimity with which Hamas officials claimed that the besieged movement could find extra money for the PA by cutting back on the corruption and inefficiency of the Fatah era. And, as the scale of the international embargo became clearer, it became equally clear that Hamas was serious about its 'Look East' strategy. Hamas leaders in Damascus went on fund-raising tours of the Arabic and Islamic world. Hamas claimed that Saudi Arabia and Qatar had promised $33 million (£19 million) to fix the PA's impending budget crisis, and on 1 February 2006 a Hamas delegation from Gaza passed through the Rafah crossing into Egypt on the first stage of their own money chase.

Early post-election jokes that Hamas would soon be reduced to bringing millions of dollars back into Gaza in ministerial briefcases quickly became a reality, and Israel began pressing Egyptian officials and international monitors from the European Union at the border to close the Rafah crossing because Ismail Haniyeh and other government officials were doing exactly that. Haniyeh and his officials were more than happy to declare the money to customs officers.

Throughout this period it became clear that the Egyptian-controlled Rafah crossing was to become a focal point of future confrontation. Rafah is Gaza's only official lifeline to the outside world beyond Israel. Israel exercises complete military control along 90 per cent of the rectangular coastal strip's 70 mile perimeter – the coastal, northern and eastern sides – as well as from the sky, since Israel bombed and bulldozed the Palestinians' only airport early in the Second Intifada. Only to the south does Gaza border another country: Egypt. If this 8 mile Egyptian frontier remains closed, Gaza is sealed from all 360 degrees of the compass. If Hamas can keep the Egyptian side open, it doesn't have to rely on the illicit tunnels to flood goods into its domain.

After Israel pulled all its soldiers and settlers out of Gaza in 2005, the border arrangements at Rafah became Byzantine in their complexity. Under the agreement worked out by all sides and the international monitors, Palestinian and Egyptian officials would control their own sides of the crossing while Israeli officials – although not physically present – would monitor it on cameras from Israel's nearby military base at Kerem Shalom. The border would remain open only while the European monitors (EUBAM) were present. These terms had been agreed under the 2005 Access and Movement Arrangement (AMA). Technically Israel did not control what or who went through the Rafah crossing, but it quickly became apparent that, because the European monitors lived in Israel, Israel could shut the crossing at any time simply by closing the access road for 'security reasons' and denying them passage to the border. With no European monitors the crossing could not – and increasingly did not – open, leading to a worsening economic situation.

In Egypt, Omar Suleiman, the powerful head of the intelligence services and one of the leading candidates to take over from the ageing President Hosni Mubarak, cautioned that, if the West cut off Hamas, 'Iran will give them the money.'[16] His concern reflected that of other Sunni Arab states – Egypt, Saudi Arabia, Jordan and the Gulf Emirates. None wanted to see their ancient Shi'a rival, Iran, hijack the Palestinian cause by public support for its long-time proxy Hamas. That concern was exacerbated when Hamas began referring to the political landscape of the Middle East in quasi-military terms. Mushir al-Masri addressed the isolation issue by saying: 'I think if the international position continues as unyielding there will always be an alternative through controlling our resources and resorting to our Arabic and Islamic strategic depths. Many of the leaders and the prime ministers and princes and investors have made calls and confirmed that they will stand by the Palestinian people.'[17]

Hamas remained defiant in the face of the donors' threats, and warned the West not to penalize the democratic choice of the Palestinian people. At one huge rally in Gaza's Khan Younis, the voice of Hamas leader Khaled Meshaal, was relayed to 10,000 supporters. 'We're telling the world that it's in your interests to support the Palestinian people because we will reach our goals with or without you', he said in a recorded message broadcast through huge loudspeakers.[18]

Washington

Summoned back to Washington to give their assessment of the new status quo, American envoys and security advisers quickly gained a sense of how determined American lawmakers were to isolate Hamas. Calling its covenant a 'hate-filled screed', California's ranking Democratic representative Tom Lantos told one Washington policy hearing:

> Hamas leaders have not changed their rhetoric one iota since winning the election, far from it. Hamas leaders are now holding out their hands and asking US taxpayers to continue the flow of dollars, but the blood of dozens of Americans and hundreds of Israeli men, women, and children is on those hands. It has long been US policy not to support terrorists in any way. We must make absolutely clear that we will not deal with the terrorist thugs who now lead the Palestinian Authority. Not a single penny of US taxpayer money should end up in Hamas coffers.

Establishing the tone which was to be the keynote of US policy over the coming months, he continued:

> I also want to make it clear that simply ending direct assistance to the Palestinian Authority does not cut it. There must be an end to all non-humanitarian assistance that could benefit Hamas. The last thing in the world we in Congress want to do is to let a Hamas government reap the credit for development projects that are funded by the American taxpayer. Of course, I support the continuation of humanitarian assistance to the Palestinians, but we must be clear about how we define such aid. The phrase 'humanitarian assistance' means just what it says, and it is clearly defined in our legislation: food, water, and medicine.[19]

Called to brief the legislators James Wolfensohn, the Quartet's envoy, spelled out the financial black hole facing Hamas. He testified to a Senate committee that the PA had a $2 billion annual budget, so needed $165 million income each month just to cover its expenditure. With the Palestinians raising just $35 million each month from internal taxes, and Israel threatening not to hand over around $60 million monthly PA customs and other revenues, that left a deficit of around $130 million in the finances every month. 'The current fiscal situation in the Palestinian territories is dire and unsustainable and may have wide-ranging consequences for the Palestinian economy, and for security and stability for the Palestinians and the Israelis', he testified. Singling out troublesome specifics, he pointed out that, without money, the PA could not pay its roughly 150,000 employees – 37 per cent of the Palestinian workforce in Gaza and 14 per cent in the West Bank. As a quarter of the population, more than 940,000 Palestinians, were directly dependent on a PA wage-earner, there were obvious humanitarian and law and order implications, he said. 'Non-payment of salaries to some 73,000 security staff risks rising criminality, kidnapping and protection rackets . . . the already highly charged environment needs no additional fuel for a spark to ignite.'[20]

Robert Malley, Middle East and North Africa Program Director for the International Crisis Group, cautioned that obvious attempts to make Hamas fail could backfire, and only increase its domestic support. Acknowledging the 'temptation' to ensure Hamas's 'quick and painful failure' to teach the Palestinian electorate a lesson, he said:

> I think it's a very appealing logic. I also think it may be short-sighted and ultimately self-defeating. If the US and Israel and others are perceived as trying to engineer Hamas's downfall and quick disruption of the government, the Palestinian people are not going to take from that the lesson that Hamas failed them, but that others failed them. And in that sense, Hamas's failure may not necessarily be America's success. It depends very much how it fails.

He also spelled out the distinction between Hamas, which was prepared to participate in elections, and more extreme jihadist organizations, which were not. 'There's a broader regional picture', he told the policymakers.

> However we may dislike it, the debate today in the Muslim world is not between secularists and Islamists . . . right now the real debate . . . is between political Islamists, who, however radical their views may be, are evolving toward greater acceptance of democracy, of elections, of the nation-state as a framework within which to wage their struggle, and the jihadi Islamists, al-Qaeda being the best example.[21]

Hamas leaders themselves also warned that, by failing to deal with them as the face of political Islam, the West would only have itself to blame if they were then pushed out of the way by even more radical jihadi organizations such as al-Qaeda.

Al-Qaeda's rejectionist stance towards Hamas was apparent from statements condemning 'brothers in Palestine', issued through Usama bin Laden's deputy, the Egyptian-born surgeon Ayman al-Zawahiri: 'Those trying to liberate the land of Islam through elections based on secular constitutions or on decisions to surrender Palestine to the Jews will not liberate a grain of sand of Palestine.'[22] Khaled Meshaal instantly rejected al-Qaeda's criticism, insisting that Hamas was 'determined to wed power and resistance'.[23]

Meanwhile, in Gaza, Hamas was likewise being criticized by its largest domestic Islamist rival. 'We as Islamic Jihad don't believe that the step Hamas has taken to democracy and elections will take us to the end of the struggle', said Abu Ahmad, the leader of one Palestinian Islamic Jihad cell in Gaza City. 'What distinguishes us from Hamas is that we are a revolutionary Islamic movement, and they are attempting Islamic political thinking . . . For Hamas, jihad is an interim phase. Our whole strategy is jihad.'[24] Although such criticisms were irritating to Hamas – not least because they found an echo among hardliners within its own movement who were not reconciled to the way of the ballot – it used the al-Qaeda and Islamic Jihad interventions as evidence to reinforce its own argument – that, unless the West dealt with Hamas, it would soon find itself facing more implacable foes. 'Compare', said one senior Hamas leader, 'the rhetoric with the firebrands of al-Qaeda and what our leadership offers and then ask again where does the real threat lie?'[25]

Looking beyond the Palestinian arena, other regional analysts pointed to wider damaging consequences, arguing that, by allowing Hamas to compete in the election, the Bush White House had further demonstrated its capacity for poor judgement in the Middle East. Cautioning that this had only accelerated the decline in American influence in the region, Jon B. Alterman, of the Center for Strategic and International Studies, told US lawmakers that US standing in the Middle East grew when governments felt threatened by other states, and they looked to American military might to protect them. But times and needs had changed, he cautioned:

> Now the United States is able to offer far fewer protections from the things that governments most fear – internal threats against which a close US relationship is more of a mixed blessing. Governments welcome the tools of US counterterrorism – the communications intercepts, the paramilitary training, and the equipment – but they doubt the wisdom of the US prescription of more open politics, respect for human rights, and the like. Instead, many have the sense that the United States is dangerously naive; they see US insistence pushing forward with Palestinian parliamentary elections in 2006 despite the disarray of Fatah and the gathering strength of Hamas as a prime example of that naivete.[26]

While most Palestinian and other observers judged that the election results were an aberration attributable largely to Fatah's underperformance and candidate selection idiocy, others gave a different assessment. Brigadier General Shalom Harari, a retired senior adviser on Palestinian affairs to the Israeli Defence Ministry, said it bore out his long-held but minority view that the Palestinian Islamists had a significantly larger underlying base of support than the 20 to 30 per cent usually cited by political analysts. 'For the last twenty years I have shouted that the Islamic bloc has for many years – not in the last year or two, not because of the Intifada, for the last twenty or thirty years – had 40% per cent support inside the Palestinian territories', he said a year after Hamas's election. 'When the Islamic bloc was ready to go to elections they showed that they had 40 per cent. They don't have the 62 per cent that came out from the results of the parliamentary elections, but they no doubt have 40 per cent.'[27]

Descent

Experienced Palestinian politicians outside Hamas and Fatah watched aghast as it quickly became clear that the democratic process was beginning a long, slow slide into a power struggle to be fought with any tools available: guns, lawyers, bankers, diplomats, lobbyists, tunnels, rockets and assassinations.

From her office near President Abbas's headquarters in the West Bank capital, Ramallah, Dr Hanan Ashrawi, legislator and veteran negotiator from the Madrid era, said the election outcome demonstrated the failure of the gamble by Fatah and the international community to bring Hamas into the political fold, with the expectation that it would lose, sit on the opposition benches, and take time to mature into a political organization. 'They really miscalculated, to bring them in as the majority', she said. 'Hamas had to learn very quickly how to be in power and Fatah had to learn how to be out of power. Both of them haven't learned, really. Fatah is not used to being in opposition, it doesn't know how to, and Hamas is not used to being in government, and it behaved like an opposition.'[28]

Having been too optimistic about his own party's chances before the result, Fatah's campaign chief, Nabil Shaath, proved remarkably prescient afterwards about the difficulties Hamas was about to face. 'What are we going to do about the peace process?', a despairing Shaath asked in Gaza. 'Hamas thought it could get away with muddied double-talk: "Yes, we will negotiate", "No, we will never negotiate", "Yes, we may negotiate", "No, we can't negotiate because it's useless", "Yes, we can negotiate only humanitarian matters." As if it is more important to negotiate a room in [Israel's] Hadassah Hospital for my sick grandmother than for a Palestinian state. Rubbish.' The best reason Israel could have for not returning to a peace process, he said, was 'if we have a government with Hamas eternally debating questions about violence, negotiation and dealing with Israel that Fatah settled under Arafat decades ago.'[29]

As Hamas prepared to name its first government, it did so without the line-up of technocrats and independents which it had hoped to use as a fig leaf of respectability; most were scared away by the prospect of becoming international pariahs. It also did so in the full knowledge that now it was Fatah's turn to sit on the sidelines – as Hamas had done in 1993 – and begin the sabotage.

By March 2006 the Israeli border closures were causing severe shortages in Gaza. Crops were spoiling because they could not be moved out through the Israeli-controlled Karni crossing into Israel and to international markets. Gaza clothing factories – a cheap source of labour for Israeli fashion stores in Tel Aviv – were shuttered, and Palestinian bakeries began rationing bread. Israel cited security concerns for its refusal to open Karni, saying Palestinian militant groups frequently tried to infiltrate and attack it. But Palestinians accused Israel of collective punishment of an entire population, as international humanitarian agencies were forced to cancel food handouts to thousands of needy people. A United Nations report in March 2006 said that Israel had already closed Karni for forty days since the start of the year – 60 per cent of the time – compared with 18 per cent for the whole of 2005 and 19 per cent in 2004.[30] It was to get much worse over the next few years.

When Hamas did announce its cabinet line-up on 20 March, it was headed by Ismail Haniyeh, with Dr Mahmoud Zahar as foreign minister, the hardliner Said Siam as interior minister, and the American-educated West Bank economist Dr Omar Abdel-Razeq as finance minister. The government was shunned by the West from its first day, particularly by an international financial system terrified of stringent US legislation banning dealings with terrorist organization

After his first look at the Palestinian Authority accounts, Dr Abdel-Razeq said it had inherited from its Fatah predecessor $1.2 billion (£687 million) in debts to banks and unpaid bills to suppliers, including Israeli utilities companies. It also found itself unable to pay the PA workforce of 160,000 – 20,000 more than previously estimated. 'The government ran out of money before the Hamas government. Now the problem is becoming larger and larger because of the action taken by the donors and the Israeli government', he said. Warning that the Palestinian territories could become 'another Somalia' if they were allowed to fester, he continued:

> If there is chaos in this area it is going to affect the whole security of the region. The relationship with Israel is not going to stay this calm, I'm sure of that. I'm not saying that we will, as a government, push things in that way, but starvation and economic problems and not paying salaries is going to result in probably more resistance acts and security problems.[31]

What was unclear was whether the situation was genuinely becoming unstable, or whether Hamas was being deliberately alarmist, using the threat of chaos as a means of leverage.

But it was certainly facing genuine opposition from Fatah loyalists at home. A common complaint by Hamas ministers was about the political leanings of the civil service and military apparatus that it inherited. 'No one would work with us . . . they are 99.9 per cent Fatah loyalists', complained Said Siam, the new Interior Minister.[32] One of his lieutenants opined that the security situation they faced was 'very bad'. Abu Ramleh, an incongruous George Clooney lookalike from Hamas, claimed he and his ministry were trying to take the factions out of the security equation, 'We want to make them neutral. But here's the point: the percentage of those who work for Hamas doesn't exceed more than 3 per cent. The rest is Fatah.'[33]

The civil servants, in turn, complained that ministries were thrown into paralysis because Hamas ministers issued instructions at odds with long-standing Palestinian policy, and that most ministry buildings in Gaza were flooded with bearded Hamas supporters sitting two or three to a desk alongside the existing civil service staff. 'The conflict between the government and the president took over everything. The Ministry of Foreign Affairs had its own plans drafted and discussed at all levels, but they were not implemented . . . because of the disagreements between the president and the government', said the ministry's chief of staff, Dr Abdelrahman Bsaiso. 'It was a terrible situation, with daily conflicts. Senior staff trying to work as professionals who can't only work with the government because we also have to work with the president, and foreign affairs is the responsibility of the president according to the constitution. So it was not easy.'[34]

He who has the gun

This was particularly the case in the myriad Palestinian Authority security forces created by Yasser Arafat. Stunned at the sudden change in leadership, the pro-Fatah security chiefs and the men they commanded were not prepared to raise the salute to Dr Mahmoud Zahar or Said Siam. Fatah quickly established a powerful but alternative security structure called the Directorate of Internal Security (DIS), headed by Rashid Abu Shabak, and also strengthened its existing security forces by recruiting extra numbers to the Presidential Guard, the Preventive Security, the National Security Forces, and General Intelligence. Hamas had a powerful opponent in Rashid Abu Shabak, who was known as tough and unyielding He was born in Jabalia refugee camp in Gaza in 1954. In the early 1970s, after completing his university education, he joined Fatah and progressed quickly through the ranks of the movement. He spent more than fifteen years in Israeli jails, but after the PLO established power in Gaza and Jericho in 1994 he emerged as an important player in the intelligence and security sector. A close ally of Mohammed Dahlan, Abu Shabak was deputy head of Preventive Security from 2002 to 2006 and then headed the DIS structure, which he built as a foil to the Hamas administration.

With Gaza living under a Hamas political leadership and Fatah security leadership, the inevitable result was conflict. Along Gaza City's inaptly named Unity Street, Hamas and Fatah forces mounted rival sandbagged checkpoints, the two sets of guards eyeing each other warily. The population was often left cowering inside its homes as armed gangs took advantage of the deteriorating security situation and shot at each other from cars and balconies, carried out abductions and killings. Month after month, throughout the autumn and winter of 2006 and the spring and early summer of 2007, armed clashes, assassinations, assaults, attacks and brutal bloody violence broke out between Hamas and its rivals. Added to this violent mix were lawless but powerful clan-based militias, who kidnapped locals and foreigners and extorted from the terrified local population.

Each side would put up its spokesman, denounce bloodshed, and call for calm. Egyptian officials and other local actors would embark on ceaseless locally negotiated ceasefires between the warring factions. Many Palestinians in Gaza, however, concluded that they were heading inexorably for some kind of Mogadishu-style breakdown. Analysts believed that this was a deliberate strategy designed to make Gaza ungovernable for Hamas.

As the power struggle continued, Hamas worked to consolidate its military strength, and gradually took the upper hand. However, it also found itself in confrontation with Israel, which began pounding northern Gaza with thousands of artillery shells to try and stop militant groups launching rockets into Israel.

Gilad Schalit and war with Hezbollah

The Israeli attacks and border closures increased dramatically in June 2006 when Hamas took part in a tunnel raid on Kerem Shalom military base, from which Israel monitors the southern tip of Gaza. Burrowing through a 600 metre tunnel, three cells – Hamas, the Popular Resistance Committees and the Army of Islam – killed two Israeli soldiers with bombs and grenades and snatched a third, Corporal Gilad Schalit. Israel launched a furious series of attacks in a vain effort to recover the nineteen-year-old Schalit, who rapidly became a cause célèbre in Israel. Israel retaliated with airstrikes, which shattered bridges and threw much of Gaza into darkness as they destroyed transformers at the only power station, and fired missiles into Hamas government offices.

But the furore over Schalit in Israel found little echo among Palestinians, many of whom regarded the action as a legitimate raid on a military target. They were also angered that the fate of one Israeli soldier drew far more international attention than that of thousands of Palestinians held by Israel. In a telling insight into the different mindsets, one Rafah-based tunneller with the Hamas-affiliated Popular Resistance Committees reacted with scorn when Israel sought to engage sympathy for Schalit by disclosing that he also held a French passport. 'He has dual citizenship? This guy has two choices, one to live in Israel and one to live in France. For us, we have no other place to go. He cannot be as motivated as us', he sneered.[35]

Pointing to the curious timing of the Kerem Shalom raid – soon after Hamas tried to form a government – the Israeli intelligence establishment claimed that it had been ordered by Hamas's exiled leadership in Damascus, with support from Syria and Iran. Khaled Meshaal, the Israelis said, was becoming nervous that the new Haniyeh government in Gaza would increasingly moderate Hamas's positions because it was now answerable to all Palestinians in Gaza and the West Bank, not just Hamas's hard-line membership. According to an Israeli Foreign Ministry analyst in Jerusalem,

> The outside leadership was quite afraid of the new emerging focal point inside [the Palestinian Territories]. The Hamas leadership inside was tending to get closer to Mahmoud Abbas. I suspect the outside leadership was afraid the Hamas government would leave the main road of Hamas and have its own independent policy. I think it's common knowledge that Haniyeh was not involved, though it seems Mahmoud Zahar was involved right from the beginning.[36]

However, Usama Hamdan, Hamas's leader in Lebanon, insisted that the exiled political leadership did not involve itself in such military issues and instead dealt mainly with fund-raising and propaganda. 'The Qassam Brigades have their own leadership and make their own decisions according to the field situation', he said at a Hamas safe house in Beirut's southern suburbs.[37]

The impact of the Gaza closures began to tell, and three weeks after Schalit's capture Gaza was hit hard by Israel when the Lebanese militant group Hezbollah attacked Israel from southern Lebanon, launching a cross-border raid and firing scores of Katyushas into the Galilee, and farther south into Haifa. Pictures of Hezbollah's leader, Sheikh Hassan Nasrallah, sprang up all around a gleeful Gaza, and Hamas was visibly emboldened by the sight of thousands of Israelis fleeing Hezbollah's rockets. 'I regret to say that many of the Arab regimes and international leaders were living under the illusion that the Israeli army was unbeatable', said Abu Bakr Nofal, a Hamas negotiator.'This war has had a huge negative effect on the Israeli street, and it has sent a message that the occupation can never stand against the resistance if you have a really good resistance.'[38]

Internal criticism

Hamas was increasingly isolated as time went by. Educated Palestinians, especially those with foreign passports, became more and more hesitant to participate in any government job associated with a regime so toxic to the West, while ordinary Palestinians began muttering that they simply wanted food and access to the outside world.

In his weekly sermons, Ismail Haniyeh, a gifted public speaker, constantly sought to reassure the movement's followers by comparing them to the early followers of the Prophet Mohammed – reviled and outcast, yet ultimately victorious. 'When things became so hard for him in many of his battles he had with the infidels, all of the Arab tribes united against him. That was described in the Koran', he told listeners at the Sheikh

Ahmed Yassin mosque in Gaza. Then, pointedly seeking historical precedent to support Hamas's refusal to comply with the West, he added: 'And people asked why God did not help them. There were dialogues and negotiations at that time. All of the negotiations were to make the prophet fail.'[39] But the size of the congregations for Haniyeh's sermons dwindled from month to month. Hamas also faced serious internal criticism from Gazans for the political and economic paralysis. 'Of course we don't accept being dictated to by foreigners. But we should also not be closed off to the rest of the world', said Mahmoud Khalefa, a civil servant, at one anti-government demonstration. 'Any government, whether Hamas or Fatah or PFLP, has obligations and duties. For the past six months there has been no political horizon towards a solution.'[40]

On the streets there was a tension between ideological purity and pragmatism, with Fatah and the West hoping that pragmatism would win out. Many, motivated by pride and resentment at perceived foreign interference, continued to side with Hamas. In Beit Lahiya, Ibrahim, a 23-year-old policeman, said he was not a natural Hamas supporter, but he did not want to see it bow to pressure from outsiders. 'I am Fatah, but I don't want this government to fall. We would vote for Hamas again', he said:

> I have been employed by the Palestinian Authority for five years, and all I've seen was members of the security forces stealing in front of my eyes. All they want are their bottles of wine, to steal the wealth of the Palestinians. Before this government there was no siege, and now we starve more, but at least we really feel they are standing up for our dignity as Palestinians.[41]

Hamas's supposed incorruptibility was also a major factor for those sickened by the sight of Fatah officials building huge mansions on the hilltops of Ramallah, complete with ornate double staircases and driveways holding several limousines and SUVs. Umm Osama, forty-five, the wife of a civil servant in Gaza, said she was impressed with Hamas's apparent lack of interest in amassing personal wealth. 'They sold their women's gold for money, like the rest of the population has had to do. That is good enough for us.'[42] But there was also desperation on the streets, with many simply wanting an ordinary life, and Gaza was increasingly being referred to by its 1.5 million inhabitants as a *sijen kbiir* (large prison). Amal Saleem, twenty-six, a Welfare Ministry employee, said:

> I don't want Hamas to recognize Israel, but at the end of the day I want to live. My son has a virus which costs me 100 shekels for a ten-injection course of treatment. But I don't have a job. I want to take him to Egypt, but there is no crossing. This government was for Change and Reform. This is not Change and Reform. This government is not accepted internationally and nobody is dealing with them. We are not selling our land or rights or recognizing Israel. But we want a government that can govern.[43]

However, Hamas also had to be mindful of its other constituency in Palestinian refugee camps beyond the borders, in Lebanon and Jordan. They looked on aghast as members of Hamas and Fatah shot, kidnapped and assassinated one another, but many continued to insist that there should be no compromise on territory and on their right to return to Palestine. In Ein Hilweh refugee camp in southern Lebanon, Maher Sukkar, twenty-seven, said his family fled the now Israeli coastal town of Jaffa in 1948, but still regarded it – not Lebanon – as their home. Significantly, even though he was born in Lebanon and had never visited Palestine, he spoke Arabic with a Palestinian, not a Lebanese, accent, denoting how little the Palestinian refugee population has been diluted by, or absorbed into, Lebanese society. Mr Sukkar said that, if the Palestinians inside Palestine accepted the 'lands of 1967', he could not stand against 'the words of the nation', but made it clear that he would accept that interim position only in order to solve the 'Right of Return' issue later. It was Hamas he deemed best suited to defend that long-term goal – 'Hamas will never give up on these principles' – and Hamas that he, and many others, saw as being the current victim of an American-led goal to crush Islam: 'There is a project to disarm Hamas and all the Islamic resistance movements around the world, but Hamas especially. This project is called the New Middle East, which is based on the lack of resistance and strengthening Zionism in Palestine and in the Arab World. These are American aims: to proclaim control from the Gulf to the Sea.'[44]

Brief thaw

Inside Palestine, however, Hamas was losing support. In December 2006 the Palestinian Center for Policy and Survey Research found that if early parliamentary elections were held Hamas would receive 36 per cent of the vote and Fatah 42 per cent, with Fatah doubling its narrow lead from three months earlier. In a two-way Presidential election Mahmoud Abbas would receive 46 per cent and Ismail Haniyeh 45 per cent.[45]

As Western countries increasingly channelled aid directly through Mr Abbas's presidential office to bolster support for him – the most visible sign of this being teams of roadsweepers deployed on the street wearing caps and vests bearing presidential office and international aid agency logos – twelve United Nations agencies identified a 'massive increase in poverty', caused mainly, they said, by Israeli closures and international sanctions.[46]

Hamas and Fatah were finally persuaded by Saudi Arabia on 8 February 2007 into a power-sharing agreement, in which Hamas held nine Cabinet seats and Fatah six. Hamas said it went into the agreement with open eyes about the hazards of sitting down with the very people who were working to undermine it, but maintained that the priority was to alleviate the siege on Gaza. 'There are spoiler factors that we are aware of, but we will still sit with them . . . to save the situation for ordinary Palestinians', said Usama Hamdan.[47]

The new national unity government was sworn in a month later. But it was immediately apparent that there would be difficulties of transition in an administration half-filled with international pariahs yet also including internationally respected figures such as the new finance minister, Salam Fayyad, the former World Bank and IMF official who was welcome in Western capitals. Even as he left the swearing-in ceremony in Ramallah and rushed to study the state of the PA's books after a year of Hamas rule, Mr Fayyad was expressing a fervent hope that the international community would now deal with the Palestinian government. He promised to use the international credibility which he had, and which Hamas so sorely lacked, to work for the benefit of ordinary Palestinians. But he cautioned that the 'biggest challenge' remained the inflated civil service and security forces payroll which he had inherited from Hamas and previous administrations, and said that, although he hoped 'to put the finances of the PA on a more sustainable path' to reduce the need for foreign money, Palestinians 'are going to need financial assistance for development needs for a long time'.[48]

Desperately hoping for a 'unity dividend' from Israel and the West in the light of the injection of at least one-high profile technocrat into the hitherto ideological government and Hamas's agreement to drop prominent hard-line figures such as Dr Mahmoud Zahar and Said Siam, President Abbas immediately called for a resumption of Western aid and for the hundreds of millions of dollars of PA revenues confiscated by Israel. Israel remained firm on its demands that any government including members of Hamas agree to the three international demands – recognize Israel, renounce violence and abide by past agreements. However, the installation of Fayyad and others began an immediate thaw in relations with other countries. Norway announced that it would lift sanctions, and Britain indicated that it might begin contacts with non-Hamas ministers. Without mentioning Fayyad by name, a spokeswoman at the US Consulate in Jerusalem said: 'It is a new situation for everyone, but we are not going to cut off contacts with individuals who may now hold official positions and with whom we have worked on a regular basis on other issues. We are going to continue to have contact with them as individuals.'[49]

Some believed that Hamas's agreement to enter a national unity government meant that it was 'moving toward the mainstream, very clearly'.[50] 'I think Hamas wants international acceptance and legitimacy and recognition, wants to be part of the international community and wants to stay in power', said Dr Hanan Ashrawi.

> The only way it can stay in power is to be accepted internationally and, if the price is a political flexibility and a political platform, I think they will pay that. They have already started . . . It is not just a question of suicide bombings or

resistance slogans. They themselves are building their own institutions, so they are taking the decision to enter into the democratic process. To run for elections is the first dramatic expression of this transformation.[51]

Others were less complimentary. On 11 March al-Qaeda's deputy leader, Ayman al-Zawahiri, again criticized Hamas, this time for making a deal with Fatah. In order to keep heading the Palestinian government, he sneered, 'The leadership of Hamas surrendered to the Jews most of Palestine . . . It has fallen in the quagmire of surrender.'[52]

Some in Hamas saw a hidden agenda behind al-Qaeda's message – believing that Zawahiri's real goal was to create a fissure within Hamas by appealing to its *salafi* jihadi-inclined military hardliners. Creating a breakaway splinter group would provide a foothold for al-Qaeda in Palestine, they feared. Certainly there was criticism of Hamas's political leadership from within the military wing. 'The sons of Qassam are unable to decide what they will do. They are still struggling to spearhead [the resistance], and others [are] going in the other direction', said one commander.[53] Hamas sought to use this spectre as a lever on its new partner in government, Fatah. 'I am worried by the presence of al-Qaeda in Palestine', said Younes al-Astal, a Hamas hardliner. 'I cannot say for certain that al-Qaeda has a presence in Gaza, but I can say the current political conditions provide fertile ground for planting al-Qaeda ideas, whether affiliated or not.'[54]

The perceptions – and the reality – of hawk versus pragmatist and Damascus versus Gaza internal divisions prompted Hamas to draft in senior leaders to rebut the increasingly public rumours. Always obsessed with maintaining an image of unity, it used Sheikh Hamid Beitawi to counter the reports by insisting that, although it had entered a coalition with Fatah, it had not abandoned its 'constant principles', including the right of return of refugees, control over Jerusalem, the release of prisoners and the removal of settlements.

Arming

But, in the final analysis, Mecca and the national unity government was a doomed attempt to graft two antagonistic heads onto one body, and proved short-lived. Israel's domestic security agency, Shin Bet, Egypt's intelligence services, and others assessed that Hamas was now far stronger than Fatah in the Gaza Strip. One Egyptian security official estimated that Hamas had 'five times the amount of armaments than the PA forces'. He spoke of millions of bullets at a local market rate of $2 per round as a result of smuggling armaments into the Gaza Strip.[55]

Soon, the violence resumed. In mid-April an American international school in Gaza was attacked, and behind the scenes the armed wings were acquiring arms and ammunition at a rapid rate. Major General Yoav

Galant, a former operational commander for the Israeli army's Southern Command, assessed in March 2007 that Hamas was organized into different brigades for each area of the Gaza Strip. He said that each area had a commander, battalions, companies, platoons and special forces to deal with observation, sniping, infantry, explosives and anti-tank weapons. 'Everything is well organized. This is in a way more similar to an anti-tank commando division than to a terror organization', he remarked. 'The know-how is brought by Palestinians from abroad, most likely from Iran, but also from Syria and Hezbollah.'[56]

The Israeli rhetoric was very similar to that it used about Hezbollah a year earlier, that it was no longer dealing with a militant – terrorist in Israel's vocabulary – group, but something more akin to a small army. Few were convinced that Hamas's infrastructure was anything approaching that of Hezbollah, which could fly supplies in by the container-load from Tehran or bring them across the border from Syria instead of having to smuggle them in piece by piece through tunnels. Nevertheless, if Hamas could not outgun Israel, there was growing concern that it could outgun Fatah. Hamas was manifestly better armed, better drilled and better organized than the PA's Fatah partisans in the security forces.

Most observers also judged Hamas to have emerged politically as the big winner from Mecca. Hamas kept the prime minister's office and Interior Ministry security forces, while the other most prestigious ministry – Finance – had gone not to Fatah but to Salam Fayyad, who belonged to the Third Way party, which he had co-founded with Dr Hanan Ashrawi. Yuval Diskin, the head of Shin Bet, said that Hamas had succeeded in all its goals: gaining legitimacy by bringing Fatah into the government while retaining control not only of the Interior Ministry, but also of the other government departments most important to it: those dealing with cultural, social welfare and education issues. Fatah appeared to have no 'clear policy or strategy for internal matters', he assessed, while Hamas was clearly intent on eventually assuming leadership in the Palestinian diaspora as well as inside the Palestinian Territories. 'It thinks it can control the PLO. Hamas is not in a hurry.'[57]

Diskin's analysis of the government as one arm of the wider Hamas movement is shared by the movement itself. 'In serious political decisions, like the recognition of Israel, it is not the decision of the government, it is the decision of the organization', said Mustafa Sawwaf, an Islamist political analyst in Gaza. 'Recently the ministers have had nothing to do with the political leadership. Hamas learned from previous Fatah governments, which mixed members of the government and party and couldn't differentiate between the political party and the government. That's why Fatah collapsed.'[58]

The national unity government quickly ran into trouble. In April, after just six weeks, the battle for control over the security forces intensified when the new minister for the interior, Hani al-Qawasmi, resigned after finding himself obstructed at every turn by senior Fatah chiefs within the security forces. An independent chosen to replace Said Siam, he had lost the confidence of Fatah, which regarded him as a puppet of Hamas and which had no intention of surrendering control of the main security arms of the PA. Haniyeh assumed the security portfolio a month later.

In March 2007 Hamas was infuriated when it was announced that its number one opponent, the former Fatah security chief Mohammed Dahlan, had been appointed national security adviser by President Abbas. As one Hamas minister remarked: 'We can never forget that this was the man who burnt our beards and tortured us.'[59] Some in Hamas became increasingly convinced that Dahlan was preparing his loyalists for an armed showdown to seize power in Gaza. Others warned that the Mecca Agreement was demanding too much from Hamas and not enough of Fatah. 'What's requested of Hamas is too close to surrender', said one senior Egyptian diplomat. He also warned that Hamas was being offered no incentive to share power with Fatah: 'It took them nearly twenty years to get power, and they won't give it up without a fight.'[60] Within a month of uttering this statement, this same diplomat was forced to flee Gaza in the dead of night as Hamas forces vanquished their opponents in the Fatah-affiliated security forces.

One enemy at a time

The relentless acquisition of arms continued. Hamas's response to Fatah's reluctance to cede control of Gaza had been to form the Executive Forces and to strengthen its Izz ad-Din al-Qassam Brigades and other armed elements. The purpose of the Executive Forces was to assert armed domination over Gaza should circumstances warrant. They were headed by an ex-Qassam Brigades commander named Abu Obeidah al-Jarrah. 'We're here to protect the public, and whatever we have achieved in the last few months', said al-Jarrah, 'is more than the others have done in years.'[61] Within six months of the formation of the Executive Forces, al-Jarrah and his janissaries had expanded from a single office with two desks, a phone and a chair into a formidable organization with the logistic resources of a self-standing militia. Officially designated a 'new police force' for the Hamas era, al-Jarrah's men would prove highly effective auxiliaries in the military takeover. These men initially answered to Hamas's first interior minister, Said Siam.

Before his elevation, Siam had had a lengthy career as a schoolteacher but had always been involved in the Hamas movement. He emerged in leadership circles in 2004 as a hardliner and was elected an MP in January 2006, polling the highest number of votes in Gaza. With his short steel-grey crew-cut hairstyle, closely trimmed beard, penetrating brown eyes and self-contained composure, he demanded respect from his Hamas aides and cadres. He was a man who always portrayed an air of utmost seriousness and bore himself with an upright military manner. 'When you have nothing to lose', he had warned during an interview at his ministerial headquarters, 'you are prepared to sacrifice everything for the people.' His appointment as minister of the interior allowed him to emerge as one of the most hard-line players in the post-Rantissi era. In January 2009 Israel would kill him in a missile attack.

Siam claimed Hamas was not going to train its guns on its fellow Palestinians: 'We are not coming here to create a coup d'état against Fatah . . . our forces are all created to fight occupation, not a civil war.'[62] But in reality he and others in the leadership were preparing Hamas's forces for a showdown as it sought to consolidate its power in the Gaza Strip. One sign of what was to come was the audacious attack on a Presidential Guard (PG) position at an Israeli border crossing in mid-May 2007, in which Hamas forces quickly overwhelmed a position guarded by the US-backed and -trained soldiers. The Karni crossing project had hitherto been regarded as the jewel in the crown of the US security assistance mission. The PG's rapid collapse despite the American support left US security coordinator General Keith Dayton having to explain to a congressional committee a few days later how the vital security position on Israel's border had been so comprehensively breached by Hamas. Dayton claimed that the unit 'stood its ground during the attack' and 'fought Hamas off'.

Such spin may have been necessary to win congressional support, but the general did acknowledge that it was a 'worrisome' development. 'I fear Hamas is in this fight for keeps', he told the committee.[63] Back in Gaza, however, the survivors admitted that they had fled their posts, but said that while doing so they had run into a hail of bullets from the Israeli side of the border. Hamas spokesman Ayman Taha insisted that Hamas had come under attack first, and that its fighters had merely responded to the PG soldiers, who were 'using American weapons and are aided by the Americans against us'.[64] The fact that Hamas could so quickly overwhelm a well-armed and trained PG position so close to the border with Israel was a dangerous portent of what was to come. Hamas commanders certainly considered the attack a strategic success and an indication of its military preparedness for any threat from Fatah, despite the public backlash against the killing of fellow Palestinians.

There was also a growing sense among the hard-line elements of the Hamas leadership that, once Fatah was dealt with, decisively, the fight against Israel would be easier. 'Sometimes we are fighting Israel with one hand tied behind our back', said one Hamas military commander. 'It is Fatah that tied it for Israel, and now we have to undo these bindings even if it means taking the knife against Fatah itself.'[65]

Worse was yet to come.

14

Inferno

The past era has ended and will not return. The era of justice and Islamic rule has arrived.

Islam Shahwan, Hamas[1]

From a distance it looks like a grey hill that materialized overnight in a southern corner of Gaza, where few have the curiosity to go and look. It is not a hill, it is a graveyard – a settlement graveyard: a 30 foot high pile of rubble whose broken chunks of stone were once the walls, ceilings and garden patios of Israel's settlements. Those settlements are gone, along with the thousands of settlers and soldiers who were evacuated in August 2005 as part of Ariel Sharon's Disengagement Plan. At a stroke that pullout transformed the internal dynamics of the Gaza Strip. With Israeli soldiers gone, Palestinian armed factions moved into the once-hated outposts. Hamas used one of the largest, Neve Dekalim, as a training ground.

In the former settlement's industrial estate, Hamas's lean, black-uniformed weapons experts in the Executive Forces trained new recruits in unarmed combat and on shooting ranges, operating in broad daylight. 'This is a beautiful irony', said Islam Shahwan, a spokesman for the Executive Forces, as he poured sugary orange squash for visitors. 'We are proud to be able to use this. I spend more time here than I spend in my house. We were deprived of this land for 30 years.'[2]

Hamas commanders were initially less than forthcoming about the source of money to buy the AK47 semi-automatic weapons, bullets and hundreds of brand-new black boiler suits. However, they eventually admitted that Iran and Arab countries were supporting them. After returning from a fund-raising trip to Iran, one Hamas commander even encouraged his guests to oversee the distribution of money to rank-and-file Hamas armed forces. Sitting in a building whose wall bore the defiant settler graffiti 'We Will Be Back!', Shahwan said Hamas had been forced to create the Executive Forces because the new Hamas government was facing a deliberate attempt by its opponents to undermine its authority.

'You can see everybody is trying to strengthen themselves – the formation of armed groups, the deployment of them on the streets. Fatah is trying to recruit groups and deploy them.' Such a training base was possible only in post-disengagement Gaza. In the West Bank, Fatah outnumbers Hamas, and Israel's ever-present troops, tanks, helicopters and snatch squads would never tolerate an overt Hamas armed presence.

Amid growing alarm at Hamas's burgeoning military strength, in 2006 reports began to leak out from meetings of the Quartet powers in London and Cairo that Washington was pushing to contain the Islamists by supplying more guns and soldiers to its rival, Fatah. Non-American members of the Quartet were apparently deeply uneasy as senior US officials appeared to push Fatah's leader, President Mahmoud Abbas, to confront Hamas militarily. 'As far as we are concerned, what the Americans are proposing to do is back one side in an emerging civil war', said one Western diplomat who was familiar with the discussions. 'A lot of what the Americans are saying is: "If this is going to be a fight, we might as well make sure that the right person wins".'

Some of those familiar with the talks believed that the Americans were divided about the plan, their security advisers apparently reluctant to pump more guns and support to Fatah troops in Gaza, while others were being encouraged by neighbouring Arab regimes. These secular, autocratic and sclerotic regimes feared that a strong Hamas would strengthen its Muslim Brotherhood cousins in their own countries, and wanted a Palestinian proxy to crush it. 'It is the Arabs who are giving the Americans the ideas. It's quite an Arab way of doing things', said the Western diplomat.[3]

One Western military official acknowledged that senior Fatah security official Mohammed Dahlan, with the help of the government of Israel, was bringing in weapons, ammunition, vehicles, camp stores and other equipment through Israeli crossings at Kerem Shalom and Erez. Indeed, at one point in the spring of 2007, parts of the crossing at Erez looked like a second-hand car lot, as vehicles awaited processing from one side to the other. Dahlan, it was alleged, was also encouraged to form his own Special Force, cherry-picking men from the existing Fatah security organizations and preparing them through intensive training for a showdown.

Rumours about the role of Fatah security officials exploded into the open eighteen months later, when the American magazine *Vanity Fair* claimed to have obtained confidential documents 'which lay bare a covert initiative, approved by Bush and implemented by Secretary of State Condoleezza Rice and Deputy National Security Adviser Elliott Abrams, to provoke a Palestinian civil war'. It said the plan 'was for forces led by [Mohammed] Dahlan, and armed with new weapons supplied at America's behest, to give Fatah the muscle it needed to remove the democratically elected Hamas-led government from power.'[4] When the *Vanity Fair* article broke, Rice refused to comment directly but did not deny it.

'It is very clear that Hamas is being armed and it's very clear that they're being armed, in part, by the Iranians. So if the answer is that Hamas gets armed by the Iranians and nobody helps to improve the security capabilities of the legitimate Palestinian Authority security forces, that's not a very good situation', she said, elliptically.[5]

Some officials, however, believed that the weapons were intended not to topple the regime, but to provide a balance of power. Mutual deterrence, it was hoped, would dissuade Hamas from taking total control of Gaza and imposing its Islamist will by diktat. In the event, the plan was rejected by President Abbas, but even before he did so many Israeli officials had already been very wary about seeing more weapons flooding into Gaza. They feared, with good reason, that guns intended to augment pro-Fatah forces would end up in Hamas's hands.

This was precisely what a confident Hamas was already predicting. 'Disregard the intention', said Khaled Abu Hillal, a spokesman for Hamas's minister of the interior, Said Siam. Pointing out how many of the PLO fighters who returned with Yasser Arafat from exile in 1994 later fought against Israel, he said: 'The weapons they brought and the bullets, where are they now? They were used against the Israelis. Let them remember the lessons of history.' Abu Hillal was contemptuous of what he referred to as the 'American currents' within Fatah. 'Despite all the channels of financial and military support, this is a weak, isolated and outcast current', he sneered. 'They are like balloons.'[6]

Build up

The balloon burst in 2007. After one particularly bloody round of infighting, one veteran Qassam fighter gloated that a series of Hamas raids on Fatah headquarters in northern Gaza had taken their enemy by surprise, and resulted in quick victories. 'We, the sons of Hamas, showed that our movement is much stronger and bigger', he boasted. 'They underestimated us. They weren't prepared for this day: they didn't know that we were holding back from confrontation not because we were weak, but because we were preparing.'[7] It was a harbinger of what was to come and a proud declaration of what Israel had long observed about Hamas, that it used ceasefires and quiet periods to regroup, not to reform.

Hamas also used the first eighteen months after its election victory to bring in the necessary arms, munitions and money for a final showdown with Fatah. Restricted by almost perpetual border closures, the burgeoning business of illicit tunnels and smuggling, Hamas, like everyone else in Gaza, turned to this counter-economy to get their weapons of war into the Strip. Hamas, according to Israeli intelligence sources, used the hundreds of tunnels in 2006 to smuggle in 28 tons of explosives, 14,000 guns and 5 million ammunition parts, 40 rockets, 150 rocket-propelled grenades, 65 launchers, 20 'improved' anti-tank missiles and 10 anti-aircraft missiles.[8] Fatah was also bringing in its own weapons, but the decisive factor would prove to be motivation.

Gaza's tunnel operators readily confirmed many of the Israelis' claims. They were happy to show off the smaller commercial tunnels – waist-high, 3 feet wide and fitted with winches to drag goods through from Egypt using hollowed-out petrol barrels as sleds. But the tunnels dug and guarded by Hamas were far larger, more sophisticated and less public. Big enough for a man and beast to walk through, they are often shored up with wood or concrete. One Rafah tunnel operator, Abu Qusay, said that each hole took three to six months to dig by hand and machine, and stretched for half a mile. It was a profitable but risky enterprise, he said, with profits of up to $100,000 in a single day, divided sometimes ten ways, between the tunnel's owners, diggers, guards and the smugglers who delivered the goods through Sinai. Abu Qusay said that much of what the tunnellers brought in was weapons. The most profitable were bullets, bought for $1 each in Egypt and sold for $6.5 in Gaza, and Kalashnikovs bought for $800 in Egypt and sold for twice that in Gaza.[9]

In this way everyone, including Hamas, gained access to weapons and ammunition while the official Palestinian armed forces loyal to President Abbas jokingly warned that, if they ordered their men to fire their weapons, they would send one officer ahead to catch the bullets so that they could be used again. According to Brigadier General Yossi Kuperwasser, a retired director of intelligence analysis for the Israeli military, Hamas was also able to smuggle in larger and longer-range rockets. He said they came from East Africa and were then shipped up the Red Sea to the Sinai peninsula and smuggled in by long-established trading and criminal networks. Bemoaning Egypt's apparent inability to stop the smugglers, he said the Egyptian government could do a 'much, much, much better job' to prevent the weapons reaching Gaza. 'Rafah is not New York City. This is something I just cannot understand: why they don't close them down.'[10]

In the light of Hamas's growing strength in Gaza, many observers questioned how committed Fatah's security forces were likely to prove, manned as they were by people generally more interested in salaries than jihad. One Palestinian police major even observed of his own men, 'They are weak in comparison to Hamas because Hamas guys fight for Allah and not a monthly salary.'[11] 'I'm not optimistic about Fatah', said a prescient Yuval Diskin, the director of Shin Bet, in March 2007.[12] He assessed that Hamas was 'much stronger than Fatah in the Gaza Strip' and that Fatah had done little to rebuild itself politically or militarily since its 2006 election defeat. 'If you speak to Fatah, they tell you about all their plans. But when you check, there is not much happening.'[13]

Colonel Michael Pearson, the Canadian Task Force commander assigned to work with General Dayton, disagreed with this assessment.

'You could say that the training was insufficient, or that there was insufficient weapons or ammunition, or that there were not enough troops . . . but to say not much was happening is somewhat of an understatement. There was a great deal happening.'[14] He cited 700 men recruited to Abbas's Presidential Guard, naval police training in Egypt, specialist borders and crossings training, National Security Force training and equipping, Preventive Security Organization training, and the 'recruiting, training and equipping of Mohammed Dahlan's Special Force'. Moreover, there were a series of regular meetings between Egypt, Israel, the PA and US government representatives where the security challenges posed by Hamas including smuggled weapons and rocket fire, were discussed and strategized.

Despite the overwhelming numerical superiority of the estimated 70,000 pro-Fatah forces against Hamas's 6,000-plus Executive Forces and more than 10,000 members of the Izz ad-Din al-Qassam Brigades, it appeared that Hamas was preparing for a much larger confrontation.

Military takeover

The confrontation came on Monday 11 June 2007, when Hamas launched the five-day military operation in which it took over Gaza, forcing hundreds of Fatah members to flee Gaza, fearing for their lives. In a carefully coordinated plan, Hamas's forces swept through the streets from southern to northern Gaza, besieging, attacking and capturing one Fatah stronghold at a time before moving on, inexorably, to the next. Among the first to die was Jamal Abu al-Jediyan, the most senior Fatah official in northern Gaza, killed when Hamas gunmen attacked his house in Beit Lahiya. Fatah claimed he was executed at gunpoint. The ruthlessness appalled onlookers, and both sides blamed each other, with Hamas accusing Fatah of having killed one of its preachers, Mohammed Rifat.

There were claims from both sides of supporters being thrown to their deaths from high buildings, including Mohammed Sweirki of Fatah, hurled from the fifteenth floor of one tower block, followed by Abu Kainas of Hamas, from the twelfth floor of another building. Firefights broke out on the streets, moving through the city as Hamas quickly pushed Fatah back into its most heavily secured headquarters. Snipers took up positions on high buildings to control the ground below. Gunmen commandeered vehicles, and impromptu checkpoints were set up. The vast majority of Gazans stayed in their homes, too afraid to go out onto the streets.

The Fatah-dominated PA forces – the Presidential Guard, Force 17, the National Security Forces, the General Intelligence, the Preventive Security Organization, the Borders and Crossings Administration, and the civil police – fled the Gaza Strip, or hid at home. Some Hamas leaders issued reassurances that they would not target Fatah people indiscriminately.

'We will not antagonize any elements in the Palestinian forces so long as they don't target us', said one Hamas leader. However, another warned: 'The elimination will spare no effort to continue until there is victory and we provide security and safety.'[15]

On Tuesday 12 June, Hamas forces captured the headquarters of the Fatah-led General Intelligence services in northern Gaza – known locally as The Ship – after a day-long battle between 500 Fatah activists inside the building and an estimated 200 Hamas attackers. The commander of the Intelligence, along with senior leaders of other Fatah-led branches of the security services such as the NSF, Preventive Security, the Presidential Guard and Force 17, fled to the temporary sanctuary of the Egyptian diplomatic mission and residential building in Gaza's seafront Beirut Towers. Ahmed Hilles, a senior Fatah leader, explained their actions: 'These members of the Palestinian forces, along with other officials such as Tawfiq Abu Khusa, Majed Abu Shammaleh, Hajj Mosbah and others who were hiding at the Egyptian delegations headquarters, were taken and sent safely through coordination to Erez. The reason some of these personalities needed to get out of Gaza is because they would have been arrested or killed by Hamas.'[16] By nightfall Fatah had abandoned and surrendered The Ship, and Hamas's fighters were 'requisitioning' anything they could lay their hands on. They also ensured that Hamas's propaganda operation was in full swing, with pro-Hamas websites abuzz with 'reports' of wine bottles and pornography found in Palestinian Authority filing cabinets, alongside intelligence reports that would – Hamas threatened – later be used as evidence against Fatah officials accused of collaborating with Israel.

Some in Fatah fought back, firing a rocket-propelled grenade that blew a hole in the wall of Ismail Haniyeh's house in Shatti refugee camp. But as President Abbas was urged to dismiss the Hamas-led government, junior officers complained that they were given no clear orders and had no central command structure. By this point most of the senior military leadership had been secreted out of Gaza. President Abbas described the fighting as 'madness', even as he and his chief negotiators were making panicked calls to Washington, already admitting that they had 'lost Gaza'.

As Hamas gunmen, many wearing black masks, took more and more Fatah offices, General Keith Dayton, the US government-appointed security coordinator in the Middle East, had his staff on the phone from Jerusalem urging Fatah's security chiefs to organize their men and defeat the masked Hamas attackers. But Fatah appeared to be in a state of paralysis. 'There was no overall PSF commander in Gaza for the fight', observed Colonel Pearson. 'In the end each Palestinian Security Force [member] fought and died or fled on their own. They did not support each other. They gave all power of movement and manoeuvre to Hamas, and so comprehensively lost.'[17]

In the south, Ali Qaisi, a Presidential Guard spokesman, claimed that Hamas overran a Preventive Security compound in Khan Younis by burrowing a tunnel beneath the building and setting off an explosion beneath it, after broadcasting warnings over loudspeakers that they were about to blow it up. Two days later Khan Younis was fully under Hamas control.

Hamas's radio station, Al Aqsa, explicitly outlined the endgame. An announcer declared that Hamas's offensive would push north through the Gaza Strip to Mahmoud Abbas's presidential compound and security headquarters in Gaza City. As each security installation fell into Hamas hands, the organization broadcast accompanying photographs revealing barrels of drugs, requisitioned vehicles plastered with posters of Hamas martyrs, and hundreds of seized security files. Hamas gave Fatah holdouts until Friday 15 June to surrender. Farther south, in Gaza City, it seized the Awdah building, an apartment complex which was home to many senior Fatah leaders, killing at least eight Fatah men during the battle, according to witnesses. Hamas surrounded the huge city-centre national security headquarters known as the Saraya – a Turkish name for 'palace' – which dated back to the Ottoman era.

Many Gazans were furious at both sides for allowing the descent into civil war, and protesters marched through Gaza City, chanting 'Stop the killing'. But the situation was out of control, and the crowd drew gunfire, which killed two of the demonstrators and wounded four.

A confidential report written by one of the Fatah commanders in the wake of the Hamas takeover contended that Fatah's internal differences and Israel's spoiler tactics hobbled their efforts to hold the line in Gaza, now inexorably broken. Fatah security chiefs fled, and their luxurious Gaza City homes lay as abandoned, looted and graffiti-scrawled as the Israeli settlers' homes less than two years before.

By the time Friday prayers were over on 15 June, Hamas was in charge of the Gaza Strip. President Abbas accused it of a coup, as masked Hamas gunmen posed for victory pictures in his beachside Presidential palace, the Saraya, the Rafah crossing terminal and other headquarters. The triumphant masked men carrying their guns and wearing ammunition belts were photographed in a variety of poses in the President's office, amid his personal possessions and sitting at his desk. The images were a searing humiliation for the Palestinian president.

Aftermath

The attack drew widespread international condemnation and served to isolate Hamas even further from the international community. The US secretary of state, Condoleezza Rice, referred to it as an 'illegal seizure of Gaza, including throwing aside the legitimate Palestinian institutions that were governing there'. Throughout, Hamas insisted that its onslaught was not a coup, but a counter-coup against Fatah conspirators within the PA security forces who were planning to implement Israeli and American plans to bring down the elected government. 'We are here to defend the legitimately elected government of Hamas and bring public order', said one Hamas official.[18] However, the charge of serving Israel's interests was thrown back in Hamas's face by Maher Miqdad, a Fatah commander, who after fleeing with his family said the takeover would make it easier for Israel to divide and rule the Palestinians. 'This is an Israeli plan', he said. 'They want to connect the West Bank to Jordan and make Gaza a separate jail. This will be the end of an independent Palestinian state.' [19]

Other Hamas leaders were more frank about the realpolitik which underpinned Hamas's offensive. When it came to power in January 2006, Hamas had promised Gazans that it would be strong and they would be safe. But, for the first eighteen months of its rule, continued infighting left people feeling unsafe. That made it look weak, said Hamas MP Ismail al-Ashqar, and it could not afford to look weak:

> We didn't want it to end like this. There was no political agenda in Gaza for that to happen. But when your back is put to the wall you don't have any choice. When people are being killed and houses being burned you are afraid that your own grass roots will turn against you and call you soft. The movement as a movement had to protect its own children and members. It wasn't our choice, but there was no other choice.'[20]

One reason for the swiftness of Hamas's takeover was that it had carefully, and thoroughly, infiltrated Fatah's security forces. Some of its plants inside the PA forces helped it out of conviction, others through fear, yet others because they could see what was coming and wanted to make sure they were on the eventual victors' side. The inevitability of such infiltration – in a society where brothers, cousins and uncles belong to different factions and many change their allegiances over years – was one of the reasons that sceptics of the 'strengthen Abbas' plan were so concerned not to give too many weapons to the Fatah forces.

Nine months later, Captain Abu Yazi, the newly appointed head of a Hamas border police station on the Egyptian border at Rafah, confirmed that until the takeover he had served in Mahmoud Abbas's PA in nearby Khan Younis as a member of the coastal police. But he had effectively switched sides long before that, after being approached by Hamas activists who told him that – when the day came – he could either run away and live, or fight and die. 'I used to work secretly with the Qassam. Nobody knew I was Qassam', he said. 'Not all the PA security forces participated in the fight. When the fighting started Qassam came with megaphones and said, "If you want to preserve your lives abandon your positions and go home." Ninety per cent went home.' The first to run, he said, were 500 of the coastal police who only a year or two earlier had been taken to

Egypt, America and Yemen to be trained as an elite Fatah force to counter Hamas's Executive Forces: 'The Fatah Special Forces were the first ones to desert their positions. The day of the takeover nobody stayed at their post. They were only there for the salaries, and they knew who was right and who was wrong. Everyone did.'[21]

'The Preventive Security were so thoroughly corrupt that they melted away and lost their heart', said one Western official closely involved in events. He also spoke of a National Security Force commander of one Gaza-based brigade which 'actually changed sides on the first day' of the fighting and others who had betrayed security force strategies to Hamas.[22]

Few doubted that Hamas would deliver on its threats, and so it proved. One of the most damaging legacies of the takeover was that Hamas demonstrated, time and again, its willingness to kill in cold blood to get rid of its enemies. There were numerous accounts during and after the fighting, from eyewitnesses, survivors and officials, testifying that Hamas not only killed its enemies during the fighting, but also executed them afterwards. In the southern town of Rafah one police officer was targeted: 'The Hamas members attacked me, shot at my leg and confiscated my phone. They also took my money and started screaming at me and my other colleagues, "You are all the dogs of Dahlan" . . . the people rushed to help me and took me to hospital.' Eventually evacuated from Gaza for hospital treatment in Jerusalem, the police officer was too afraid to return to his home and family while Hamas remained in charge. 'As long as Hamas is in Gaza it will be impossible for me to return. I am a Fatah member, who will be immediately targeted by Hamas if I were to return.'[23]

The most notorious case was that of Samih Madhoun, an Al Aqsa Martyrs' Brigades leader in northern Gaza and close ally of security chief Mohammed Dahlan. Madhoun had alienated the Islamists by boasting in a radio interview that he had executed some Hamas activists and threatened: 'I swear to God I will kill every last member of Hamas.'[24] On 14 June a prominent Hamas preacher issued a religious edict, or *fatwa*, saying Hamas was entitled to kill Madhoun,[25] and his brother later recounted the events that followed: 'My brother Samih was stuck at home during that time for fear of being killed by Hamas. It became obvious that Samih was in danger and he threatened to burn Hamas houses. After Hamas killed Baha Abu Jarad and Jamal Abu al-Jediyan we advised him to take refuge in the Presidential compound.' But, while making his escape, Madhoun ran into trouble: 'Hamas spotted Samih approaching one of their checkpoints and opened fire on his car.' Samih retaliated, his brother said, and in the ensuing gunfight killed a Hamas operative, Jamal Abu Swaileh. Hamas promptly seized Madhoun and took him to the home of the dead Hamas man. 'They told his parents to kill Samih for killing their son, and, when they refused to do so, Hamas killed Samih [themselves] in front of the people and then they mutilated him.'[26] After the lynching, Hamas posted a photograph on its website showing a crowd standing over Madhoun's body as it lay face down on the ground. A video of Madhoun's death and mutilation appeared on the internet, including YouTube. The Izz ad-Din al-Qassam Brigades later released a statement confirming that it had 'executed the collaborator Samih al-Madhoun'.[27]

When challenged later about the ruthlessness of the takeover, some Hamas leaders sought to minimize the numbers killed or to concede – in general but vague terms – that some individuals 'overreacted'. Not so some among the hardliners, who made no excuses. Asked if he regretted the deaths of Fatah supporters, Abu Thaer, an implacable Qassam border commander in Rafah, irritatedly waved away any criticism, saying that the deaths were not personal, but strictly business. 'If it had been a score-settling day we would have killed all the Fatah people, because everyone here has debts', said the heavily bearded Abu Thaer, whose name translates as 'Father of Wrath'.

> In the few days before the takeover between twenty and thirty people were killed, no one was safe . . . The decision was taken that, instead of losing people over a long period of time, we should go in and fight and suffer 200 people killed at once, but after that there would be no more deaths. The majority were killed in battle but, maybe, yes, there were some people who deserved to be killed. I'm not going to hide it. For instance, Samih al-Madhoun. He killed twenty-five Hamas people, so there was no way he would be caught and not killed. He killed a guy ten minutes before he was killed, so feelings were high.[28]

Back in Ramallah, President Abbas dissolved the ill-named national unity government, outlawed Hamas's militias and swore in an emergency government, elevating Salam Fayyad from finance minister to prime minister. The new emergency cabinet was packed with independents, the only senior Fatah member being Abdel Razak Yehyeh as interior minister, in charge of security forces. Fayyad was a well-respected figure on the international stage, but he was appointed, not elected, and his Third Way party had only two parliamentary seats. In Gaza, the democratically elected prime minister, Ismail Haniyeh, insisted that Hamas was still the proper government mandated by Palestinian electors through a majority vote at the ballot box.

Israel indicated it could work with the Fayyad government and also signalled its intention to tighten the siege on Gaza, cutting off fuel to all depots except those which supplied the power station. Washington, too, swung its support behind the alternative regime in Ramallah. Arab leaders appeared dazed by the speed of events, with Saudi Arabia – brokers of the short-lived Mecca unity government deal – embarrassed and clearly irritated. Addressing an emergency meeting of the Arab League, the Saudi foreign minister, Saud al-Faisal, said: 'The Palestinians have come close to putting by themselves the last nail in the coffin of the Palestinian cause.'[29]

Consolidation in Gaza

In the wake of the takeover, Hamas – for the first time ever – had complete control of Gaza. It had seized all the guns, cars, motorcycles, communications equipment and infrastructure of the PA's foreign-funded security forces and was unchallenged in its stronghold. But, although it had achieved a tactical victory, the strategy remained in doubt. It was in charge of the castle, but the drawbridge and moat were controlled by Israel, and the intermediaries between the two sides had just been shot, had fled or had been thrown off buildings.

The international reaction was as swift after Hamas's military victory as it had been after its political victory eighteen months earlier. Egypt closed down its Palestinian mission in Gaza and opened a new one in the Abbas-controlled West Bank. As Israel increasingly tightened the squeeze on Hamas, Gaza became more and more isolated. Fatah activists sought direct revenge, reacting to the Gaza debacle by ransacking, burning and destroying many Hamas institutions in the West Bank. They feared, with some justification, that after its successes in Gaza Hamas would now target the West Bank. But Hamas appeared to be gambling, as it has done consistently, on the likelihood that Palestinians would blame the country besieging them, not the government under siege.

The political wrangling continued. A month after the takeover, Abbas offered and Hamas flatly rejected a proposal to send an international force into Gaza to enable early elections to be held. The Qassam Brigades warned that any such troops would be regarded as an occupying force, and immediately fired upon.

Also within a month, Hamas secured the release of the BBC correspondent Alan Johnston, who had spent four months in captivity in Gaza after being kidnapped by a maverick Fatah-affiliated Gaza clan calling itself the Army of Islam. But the release did Hamas no good: Israel was far more concerned with another prisoner – the Israeli soldier Gilad Schalit, whom Hamas and others had held captive since seizing him in a tunnel raid on an Israeli border post in 2006. The West was also lining up behind Fatah in the West Bank. Soon basic supplies – such as construction materials – ran out in Gaza, and increasing numbers of Gazans became dependent on United Nations handouts. Israel repeatedly insisted that reports of a humanitarian crisis in Gaza were exaggerated. But United Nations officials cautioned that a collapsed economy and further privations would only fuel anger and instability. John Ging, the Gaza director of the UN refugee agency, said: 'If present closures continue, we anticipate that Gaza will become nearly a totally aid-dependent society, a society robbed of the possibility of self-sufficiency and the dignity of work.'[30]

Meanwhile, Hamas moved to consolidate its hold over Gaza. It fired long-standing Fatah loyalists from senior positions, including the head of the main Shifa hospital, and opened corruption investigations against some of them. It also closed Fatah's radio station, prompting Fatah to make similar moves against Hamas-backed newspapers in the West Bank. It raided weddings where Fatah partygoers sang songs in praise of Yasser Arafat. Public protests were subject to Hamas permit. At a Fatah rally to commemorate the death of Arafat in November 2007, Hamas forces killed six people and wounded 100. Fatah rallies were finally banned. Fatah worshippers who had used the occasion of their Friday prayer services to protest against Hamas were prohibited by a Hamas order – backed by the Gaza clerics' federation – from holding further prayer sessions outdoors. The move followed clashes in which Hamas police officers beat worshippers and journalists. Hamas said the ban was necessary because the prayers were being used for political ends.

Fatah activists claimed that they were being shot at, that offices and institutions were being raided and closed down, and that funds were being requisitioned by Hamas. They also complained of death threats to their families and that all forms of Fatah-based activity had been effectively terminated by Hamas decree. From the safety of exile in the West Bank, Khalil Saidi, a Fatah supporter, recounted one alleged Hamas attack against him in September 2007.

> I was attacked by ten Hamas men while walking near my house. One of the masked men approached me, grabbed my arm and said: 'You are one of the dogs of Samih Madhoun. You are one of the dogs of Dahlan . . . Where have you been hiding all this time?' Then they jumped on me and pointed a gun at me . . . They shot me. I passed out and was taken to hospital.[31]

In Gaza's Shejaiyah neighbourhood, two brothers gave testimony to the high price paid for supporting Fatah under the new Hamas regime. Hobbling from a first-floor room down to the street below, Samir and Munzer al-Halouli pointed to the arc of bullet holes that rose across the front of a shop beneath their home and up to the height of the salon, where the family was sitting when gunmen fired more than 120 bullets, they claim, down their alleyway in December 2007. One was injured and the other escaped the bullets, only to be captured by Hamas security forces, detained, tortured and interrogated for fifteen days: 'They tied my hands, blindfolded me, pistol-whipped me, stood on me and subjected me to sleep deprivation for five days. They accused me of working for Ramallah against their interests. But we are not afraid of them, we didn't do anything wrong.'[32]

Hamas denied torture and beatings and insisted that its measures, such as banning the firing of weapons in the air, were taken to restore order to a Gaza which had long been starved of it. One Hamas leaflet circulated in Gaza read: 'Those who disseminate filth and vices such as licentiousness, drug and alcohol trafficking, lustful parties and outings, it is our religious duty to uproot. They poison the soul of society.'[33] Sheikh Nizar Rayan, an Izz ad-Din al-Qassam commander, menacingly declared: 'We exposed the security services in order that they repent to Allah and know that there is no room [in Gaza] for apostates and heretics. We are right and they are wrong. Remember that Abu Bakr [a companion of the Prophet Mohammed] fought apostates to prevent violation.' He and his followers saw Fatah as a threat to the religious fabric of the society that they were intent on creating. This was retribution against people he referred to as 'those who attacked and burned our mosque, and stepped on the Koran, and executed our mujahidin, and are only interested in "dialogue" with us that takes place through the barrel of a gun.'[34]

The other enemy

Hamas also continued to strike at Israel. Throughout 2007, according to Israel's domestic security agency, Shin Bet, Hamas fired or allowed others to fire more than 1,200 rockets from Gaza, of which more than 800 landed in Israel. Two Israelis were killed.[35] Shin Bet warned that one consequence of the Gaza takeover was that Hamas could now increase the number and range of the rockets it was firing into Israel. But the development that really appeared to concern the Israelis was what officials described as a 'leap forward' in Hamas to the stage of being 'an organized military apparatus'. They claimed that Hamas was receiving training in Iran and transmitting the skills back to the Izz ad-Din al-Qassam Brigades in Gaza. The Iranian link was also seized upon by Fatah, which increasingly taunted its fellow Sunni Muslims in Hamas for being Shi'a puppets of Tehran. The insult was calculated to capitalize on growing anti-Shi'a sentiment across the Sunni world in the aftermath of the post-2003 sectarian slaughter between Shi'a and Sunni Muslims in Iraq.

As President Abbas held a series of meetings with Israel's prime minister, Ehud Olmert, Gaza continued to decline. At one point, when Israeli commercial banks stopped all transactions with Palestinian banks in Gaza, its banks even ran out of money. To relieve the situation, Hamas increasingly appeared to be focused on opening the Rafah border crossing into Egypt, but insisted that there must be no Israeli eyes or ears at the terminal, as under the arrangement before its takeover. 'If we accept that mechanism, then Israel still has the veto', said Mushir al-Masri. 'And if we accept the old mechanism, the border is effectively closed too. Look at how many times it was actually opened under the old mechanism: a few days here and there, but not continuously open – this was the problem.'[36]

Israel understood how important Gaza's crossings and borders were to Hamas, and these became a crucial instrument of leverage between the two sides. Israel's policy was to impose a siege to make clear to Palestinians the consequences of supporting Hamas, while Hamas sought to bypass the closures through tunnels and – in January 2008 – by bull-dozing the old Israeli wall which ran along the border, opening up the Egyptian Sinai to tens of thousands of Palestinians, who streamed through the gap until it was once again sealed.

In November 2007 President George W. Bush's administration con-vened the Annapolis conference to shore up President Abbas, but it was in the final year of a lame duck American presidency and excited little interest. Hamas called for a boycott and organized large protest rallies in Gaza.

The long prelude

In the aftermath of Annapolis, Palestinian analysts took stock of Hamas's situation two years after its ascent to power. Opinion was divided. In Gaza experts such as Dr Adnan Abu Amer contended that it had been made to pay a 'heavy price for taking power' and that it now faced a 'complicated equation in terms of the balance between government and resistance'.[37]

Professor Ali al-Jarbawi, at Birzeit University, said that Hamas made two major misjudgements. Firstly, that, once Israel withdrew its forces from inside Gaza, Hamas would have free rein to rule, not fully appreciat-ing the limitations upon it that would be imposed by the fact that Israel's military still ringed the narrow coastal strip:

> I think Hamas got delusions that Gaza was liberated when Sharon left . . .
> and that they could act as a fully fledged 'state' or liberated territory . . .
> And I think that was a factor that played a key role in how they dealt with
> winning the election. If Gaza had still been under direct Israeli occupation, I
> think the response would have been different.

Secondly, Jarbawi contended that, for all its decades of sneering at Arafat, Hamas made exactly the same mistake as Arafat by thinking that it could get away with flip-flopping between being an armed group and a legiti-mate government, and failing to appreciate that this would simply not be tolerated by the international community. 'Either you want to remain a liberation movement struggling against occupation, or you want a quasi-state and accept the limitations that this will put on you, either by the international community or by your opponent, Israel.'[38]

Opinion polls also demonstrated that support for Hamas was beginning to slip, particularly after the breakdown of the national unity government.

Many ordinary people held both Hamas and Fatah responsible for the bloody civil war in Gaza. Palestinians were still sceptical about promises of progress in the peace process or of easing the occupation.

Meanwhile, throughout 2008 Hamas's continuing rocket fire increasingly dominated Israel's domestic news agenda. Having been mauled by critics for mishandling the war against Hezbollah in 2006, Prime Minister Olmert's government was further weakened by scandal after scandal, and was now under pressure over Hamas's sustained rocket attacks on Israel's southern border towns such as Sderot. In March 2008 the number of Palestinian deaths reached its highest daily toll since the 1980s, and Israeli forces stormed into Gaza to strike at Hamas's Jabalia refugee camp stronghold, killing more than sixty Palestinians.

President Abbas was forced to suspend peace talks with Israel as the Palestinian death toll passed 100, many of them civilians. Israel laid the blame at Hamas's door, Israel's defence minister, Ehud Barak, saying: 'Hamas is responsible and will pay the price. They fire at innocent civilians. They leave us no choice. We will deploy force to change the situation – and we will change it.'[39] The level of Israeli force and the justifications offered – in particular the emphasis on bringing about a 'change' in the situation around Gaza – was a foreshadow of what was to come.

Around this time Hamas began to indicate a change in its position on negotiating a settlement to the embargo on Gaza, and a possible form of *tahdiyah*, or temporary cessation of hostilities. In the aftermath of the Jabalia raids, Mushir al-Masri said that Hamas would permit Abbas's Presidential Guards back into Gaza to man the crossing. He claimed that Hamas's objection to them rested on the unit's 'widespread corruption and bribery against the people when they were the only ones in charge of the crossings', a problem that could be resolved if they 'can be there with us, and not on their own'. Theorizing that the US wanted calm in the Middle East ahead of its own Presidential elections later that year, al-Masri said Hamas believed that it had ridden out the storm and proved it could not be broken. 'There has been considerable movement because of the realization that Hamas is a big number in the equation, whether militarily or politically, which they cannot ignore.'[40]

The proposed 'ceasefire' suited both sides. Israel wanted an end to the rocket fire, and Hamas wanted to lift the siege and end Israeli raids into Gaza. Brokered by Egypt as a middleman – because Hamas and Israel would not hold public face-to-face talks – it came into force on 19 June 2008, the first such reciprocal agreement. Hamas hoped the ceasefire would lead to Israel lifting its stringent border closures, and Israel that Hamas would make progress towards the release of its kidnapped soldier, Gilad Schalit.

On both sides there was disagreement between sceptics and pragmatists about the fundamental principle of doing a deal – albeit at arm's length – with apparently implacable enemies. For Israel it was about the survival of an enemy opposed to its very existence. For Hamas it was about halting resistance against an illegitimate occupation force. The pragmatists on both sides would prove the sceptics wrong only if the borders were open and Schalit was freed. Israeli sceptics believed Hamas would use the cessation to rearm and prepare for the next round of the war against Israel, and Hamas's military commanders conceded the point. 'Listen, our men have been fighting daily for the last years now', said one Hamas commander. 'Of course we will use the calm to benefit from it and do training . . . it's a ceasefire, not the end of the war.'[41] Yet even the military commanders averred that they would respect the political decision of their leadership and allow them to pursue the route of indirect negotiation with Israel. Hamas fighters, moreover, were deployed to the border areas to 'police' the cessation and ensure that rogue elements did not launch missiles into Israel and undermine the tenuous calm. As one embittered resident on Gaza's frontline complained: 'Hamas is now preserving the security of Israel! Hamas has been exposed now, and we see them doing the same job that all the others in Fatah did before them . . . Hamas doesn't control the situation . . . Israel does.'[42]

As the ceasefire dragged on and the siege of Gaza continued, Hamas's strategy appeared to be failing. In the West Bank its members, supporters, and organizations were targeted by a sustained campaign of harassment and suppression by the government forces of Salam Fayyad. Hamas supporters complained that their institutions were being raided and closed by both Israeli and Palestinian armed forces. International diplomats confirmed in private that, in some instances in northern governorates of the West Bank, officials from the PA had 'coordinated with the Israelis on raids against Hamas charities'.[43]

Within Gaza, Hamas spent the summer and autumn of 2008 extending its total control, including a crackdown on powerful clans such as the Hilles and Dogmush families, both linked to Fatah. Radical Islamist elements, such as *salafi* organizations, were also targeted as Hamas sought to exert authority in an environment that was an increasingly fertile recruiting ground for discontented, radical youths frustrated by a lack of political progress, Hamas's failure to secure the opening of border crossings, and zero prospects of national unity with Fatah. 'Frankly speaking, since Hamas took over in Gaza, nothing got better in terms of achieving our goal of liberation from this illegal occupation', lamented one armed fighter. 'Today I am hunted by Hamas and Israel. We are the Palestinian resistance between a hammer and an anvil.'[44]

In Gaza the situation was desperate. Fuel shortages had compelled Gazans either to drive cars on cooking oil, ruining the engines and poisoning the atmosphere in the streets, or to abandon them entirely and travel on foot or by donkey cart. Shortages of food, building materials, manufacturing parts, school books and paper, as a direct result of the Israeli siege, was creating desperation. Increasingly Hamas maintained order through fear. 'The economical situation is getting worse', said Ayman Kafarneh, a resident of the northern Gaza town of Beit Hanoun. 'The people need political leadership – whether it is Hamas or Fatah – to relieve us from this pressure. This means they have to deal with Israel.'

By November 2008, eighteen months after its 'coup', Hamas had slumped in the polls. Just 19.5 per cent of Palestinians said they would vote for it, as against 36.8 per cent for Fatah, according to a survey by the Jerusalem Media & Communications Centre. Palestinians were also pessimistic about the chances of a national unity government, with twice as many blaming Hamas as Fatah for the failure of talks: 35 per cent overall, rising to 42 per cent in Gaza.[45]

By December the ceasefire had entered its final month, and neither Israel nor Hamas had achieved its goal. Gilad Schalit was still a hostage and Gaza's 1.5 million residents were still trapped. 'The majority of people are worn out . . . Whether it's Hamas or Fatah that controls us, internally Israel controls the crossings and thus it controls our fate', concluded Mr Kafarneh, the Beit Hanoun resident.[46] Few Gazans had any idea of how high a price they would pay for the failure of the political game involving Hamas, Fatah and Israel.

Operation Cast Lead

Hamas was becoming frustrated that it could see few tangible benefits from its ceasefire. In Damascus, Khaled Meshaal said that it had yielded little in the way of freed prisoners or an end to the Israeli closures in Gaza, and for Hamas – particularly – it was anathema to repeat what it had long preached was the experience of Yasser Arafat and Fatah before it: to sign up to a deal with Israel and get nothing out of it. So, on 19 December 2008, six months to the day after it began its ceasefire, Hamas ended it. Rockets immediately began flying across the border fence into Israeli towns, sixty in one day alone. The Hamas leadership went into hiding, apparently expecting a stern but limited Israeli response, swiftly followed by renegotiation of the ceasefire on more favourable terms. But Israel's government hit back far harder than Hamas had expected.

On 27 December 2008 Israel launched air strikes the length and breadth of the Gaza Strip which destroyed or damaged nearly every Palestinian security installation. Palestinian medical officials said that at least 155 people were killed and 200 wounded in the first strikes, which began without warning shortly before noon as the opening wave of an offensive named 'Operation Cast Lead, the IDF's Fight against Terror in Gaza'. The airstrikes targeted Hamas security headquarters, training compounds and weapons storage facilities, the Israeli military and witnesses said.[47] At least fifteen traffic police were killed in one courtyard, where they were attending a graduation ceremony. Satellite television news channels

Photo 14.1 Israeli damage to the Palestinian neighbourhood of Izbit Abed Rabbo in Gaza, January 2009, after Operation Cast Lead

showed non-stop footage of piles of Palestinian policemen's charred bodies lying on the parade ground. Most were dead; one or two were still twitching. At Shifa Hospital in Gaza City, scores of dead bodies were laid out in front of the morgue waiting for family members to identify them. Many were dismembered. The Palestinian newspaper *al-Hayat al-Jadida* printed a black front page with white letters spelling out the headline: '1,000 Martyrs and Wounded in Saturday Slaughter'.[48]

In Israel there was near universal support for the war. Having learned the lesson of 2006 – when it was widely perceived to have lost both the military and public relations campaigns – Israel launched an intensive and sustained *hasbara* (propaganda) effort driving home its key talking points: that Hamas had broken the ceasefire, that Hamas was 'hiding' behind civilians, and that no country would accept rockets being fired into its territory. Two days into the operation, Prime Minister Ehud Olmert's spokesman, Mark Regev, held a telephone conference call with more than 600 journalists worldwide in which he accused Hamas of holding hostage a quarter of a million Israelis and the entire civilian population of Gaza. Israel, he said, had no choice but to strike hard to halt the rocket fire which was terrorizing border towns such as Sderot, and increasingly cities as far north as Ashkelon and east to Beersheba. 'Our aim is to create a new reality, a new security environment in which no longer will hundreds of thousands of Israelis have to live in fear. Hamas took over the Gaza Strip almost two years ago and have tried to become a Taliban-type regime . . .'[49]

Israel's domestic audience was supportive, even though many conceded that an invasion of Gaza was not a long-term answer. They appeared to believe that their government had no choice but to act as it had. Standing in the road where a Hamas Grad rocket landed in Beersheba, narrowly missing his nine-year-old daughter and his wife and son, Yona Pavtulov said his army should press home the assault. The Ukrainian-born Mr Pavtulov's argument fused two common Israeli themes: that Israel is the world's front line against Hamas and other Islamist militants, and that Western countries unfairly judge it by different standards from those they apply to their own armies in conflicts such as Iraq and Afghanistan. The lesson to be drawn from the American experience of Iraq, he believed, was that regime change works. 'I hope the same thing that happened in Iraq will happen here. They should just change the [Palestinian] leadership. We will have quiet for a few years and after that, well, God is big. He will solve the problem. In a country like ours we do not know what will happen in a year, or two or five years. We don't plan for the long run.'[50]

The international media was unable to report from inside Gaza because the Israeli army sealed off the Gaza Strip to foreign journalists from the first hours of the strike. Palestinian cameramen and journalists also said the gunfire and bombings meant it was often too dangerous to do anything but run from their office to the hospital and back again, to get a sense of the death toll. The result was that the bloody details of the offensive quickly became a daily propaganda game of allegation, rebuttal and counter-allegation. Both sides accused each other of using human shields – Israel denouncing Hamas for operating among civilians, and Hamas alleging that Israeli troops operated from within buildings in which Palestinian families were still trapped, and shot dead innocent men, women and children – sometimes as they fled. As the death toll mounted to 300 in two days, Khaled Meshaal in Damascus called for a Third Intifada. But Hamas had miscalculated the ferocity of Israel's onslaught, and did not have anything like the arsenal available to Hezbollah in 2006 to strike back at Israel.

Although huge crowds turned out around the Arab world to protest against Israel's offensive, the reaction was short-lived in the West Bank. By day two, protests in and around Ramallah were confined to a few dozen youths burning tyres and hurling stones at Israeli soldiers, who fired back plastic bullets and tear gas. The Fayyad government had ordered Palestinian police and forces to clamp down on protests about Gaza and to prohibit any public demonstration of support for Hamas, including the display of Hamas flags. One security chief conceded: 'We will not let them go to Manara Square and shout for Hamas.'[51]

With emotions high, many were furious at Hamas for bringing down such fire upon their own people. But this was counterbalanced by growing anger among Palestinians at what was perceived to be the tepid response of President Mahmoud Abbas. His officials refused to answer questions about why flags on Palestinian Authority buildings were not at half mast to mourn the loss of life. Two commonly expressed sentiments in the West Bank, from Hamas and Fatah supporters alike, were that Abbas should be pressing Israel harder to stop the assault, and that 'at least Hamas are doing something'. This was borne out on the street and by opinion polls. 'I am originally Fatah and my voice will always be Fatah', said Mustafa Saleh, a 37-year-old clothing store worker, as he hurried his two young daughters past a protest demonstration in the West Bank city of Ramallah. 'But Hamas is resisting and we are a nation under occupation. I support the resistance, even here in the West Bank.'[52]

As he watched the processions go by, another Palestinian businessman sighed and said that emotions were high, but would calm down. Explaining Hamas's 2006 election victory and continuing support for the Islamists, Mohanad Salah, forty-two, said Israel's overwhelming use of force would only provoke more Palestinian violence, not deter it. 'The more military operations by Israel, either here or in Gaza, the more it will make people go away from wanting agreements', he said. 'If they were going to stop the Palestinian people from reacting, the Palestinians would have stopped in 1948 and 1967. But these military operations don't stop the Palestinians fighting for our rights.'[53]

While the Israelis consistently denied that there was any humanitarian crisis, United Nations officials contradicted them. Robert H. Serry, the UN envoy for the Middle East peace process, lamented both sides' behaviour, saying: 'The protection of civilians, the fabric of Gaza, the future of the peace process and regional stability – they all are trapped between the irresponsibility of Hamas rocket attacks and the excessiveness of Israel's response.'[54]

During the campaign Israel inflicted two major blows on the Hamas leadership: on 1 January 2009, the military commander and radical Sheikh Nizar Rayan was killed, along with his four wives and nine of his children, when his five-storey home was bombed by Israeli jets. Then, in the closing days of the war, Israel bombed the hideout of Hamas's hard-line security chief Said Siam, killing him. Operation Cast Lead killed more than 1,300 Palestinians, among them more than 900 civilians, and destroyed thousands of homes, commercial buildings and government institutions, according to Palestinian human rights groups. But, despite short-term anger against Hamas, it was by no means clear that the offensive immediately succeeded in turning Palestinians away from the Islamists in significant numbers.

Once again Hamas was playing to the core conviction among many Palestinians that they can achieve more through arms and negotiations than through negotiations alone – a phenomenon explained by critics as an addiction to violence and by supporters as the only realistic way of squeezing concessions from a more powerful enemy. Questioned about the possibility of embracing less violent means of dealing with Israel, Ismail Ashqar, a Hamas MP, replied scornfully: 'If we threw roses at Israeli tanks and slept under them, would we have the sympathy of the world? Would they give us our rights back?'[55] Following the war, one Palestinian poll found that Palestinians gave Hamas the highest positive rating for its performance at that time, at 51 per cent, followed by Haniyeh's government at 46 per cent, Iran, 41 per cent, Syria, 34 per cent, Fatah, 34 per cent, President Abbas, 25 per cent, and Salam Fayyad's government, 23 per cent.[56]

Aftermath

Nevertheless Hamas fared badly from the Gaza war. Gaza's civilian infrastructure had been destroyed or damaged by Israel to such an extent that United Nations human rights investigators considered it a deliberate use of disproportionate force intended to punish the entire population of Gaza,[57] an accusation denied by Israel. Hamas's military infrastructure was also significantly reduced. It had promised that it would fight Israel face to face once a ground incursion commenced, but afterwards it claimed to have lost only forty-eight Qassam fighters.

Numerous Gaza residents in the worst-affected areas said that they had heard little evidence of Qassam Brigades fighters taking the battle to the Israeli forces.

When Israel ended the war it left entire districts razed, and post-war estimates indicated that it would take more than $2 billion to reconstruct Gaza. Much of the economic infrastructure, including electricity supplies, water, sewerage, roads, factories and warehouse facilities was also damaged.

When the war ended on 18 January 2009 – and once nationalist loyalties and heightened emotions subsided a little – there was widespread criticism of Hamas for bringing down such destruction on their heads. As Gazans began to internalize the scale of the wreckage the mood was of anger, sometimes open, sometimes coded. In scores of interviews, from the southern tip to the northernmost towns in the Gaza Strip, fear and anger rose to the surface, and not all directed at Israel. 'I want to change the situation', said Hazem Abu Shaaban. 'I will vote for those who deserve it, and I will vote in order to change the situation in Gaza.' He voted for Hamas in 2006, but barely three years after the slogan 'Change and Reform' propelled Hamas into power, the word 'change' had become a code word for a desire to end the Hamas experiment:

> The policy of this government is not suitable for international policy. I voted Hamas for change. The PA was corrupt and there were problems in Gaza. I tried to change that. It was a mistake. I expected them to be an important bloc in parliament and to be the opposition, not to lead the government. When they won I knew this destruction would come.[58]

Across Gaza, Hamas still had a large reservoir of loyal support. Beside the Saraya, the main Gaza City security headquarters which once saw daily gun battles between Hamas and Fatah, the memory of that infighting prompted others to adhere to the Islamists. 'Security is more important than trade or business', said Nasser, a shop owner. 'I am Fatah, but they are corrupt.'[59] He, and others, accepted Hamas's argument that Israel was simply using Hamas as a pretext to destroy Palestinian life and society, as it had with Yasser Arafat and the PLO before.

Only a few days after the end of the offensive, in the southern town of Rafah, industrial generators and full-size Caterpillar bulldozers were already working in broad daylight to repair smuggling tunnels damaged by Israeli airstrikes. There Abu Ahmed, a 50-year-old tunnel operator, said 90 per cent of the tunnels had been put out of action, but teams were already back at work repairing the damage – easily visible to Israel's spy drones and Egyptian watchtowers 100 yards away across the border. 'I am Fatah, but I will vote Hamas because they are the good guys, they stand by us', he said.[60]

But amid mutterings of discontent there were already signs that Hamas was becoming more open about enforcing its writ. When the Israelis reopened the northern Erez crossing to foreign journalists after the offensive, Hamas 'morality police' were standing just inside it to monitor what came through. At a makeshift checkpoint a few hundred yards from the heavily fortified Israeli crossing, bearded Hamas officials questioned drivers and searched cars for alcohol.

Even more crudely, one Rafah tunneller who dared to criticize Hamas was dragged away by bearded enforcers even as he was being interviewed by one of the authors on 28 January 2009. 'Under Hamas the border crossings are closed and everything is damaged', he began to say. His colleagues grew visibly uneasy at his words, and one tried to silence him, but he continued, saying: 'They say that Fatah were corrupt and thieves, and they were, but the border crossings were open . . .'[61] He got no further. As one of the listeners muttered, 'Stop him speaking', a car filled with burly bearded men drove up behind him – having evidently received a signal from one of the group – and one of the men inside jumped out and grabbed the dissenter around the throat, dragging him away in mid-sentence. When the dissenter reappeared and tried to talk once more, he was again stopped by those around him. 'He is a big liar, a big liar', the burly man interjected, and dragged him away. When he was approached for a third time a few minutes later, this time away from the sight of the crowd, the man refused to talk, saying: 'I don't want to get into any fights. I don't want to get shot.'[62]

It was no idle fear, in a climate reminiscent of the Mujamma's intimidation of secularist and leftist opponents during the rise of the Islamists three decades earlier. Even amid the mayhem of the Israeli offensive there had been reports – confirmed even by Hamas sympathizers – of Hamas opponents being executed or wounded in summary 'punishment' shootings of Gazans deemed to be collaborators, or seemingly pleased at the damage inflicted on Hamas by Israel. In the Sheikh Radwan district of northern Gaza, A'ed Sa'ado Abed, a Fatah loyalist, showed the bloodstained bandages on his left leg where, he said, Hamas had shot him twice on 26 January, 'only because I am a Fatah activist, to scare me and the Palestinian people. They are afraid of any gathering of Fatah. They are afraid Fatah may jump on them at any time. They know that Fatah represents the majority of the Palestinians.'[63]

Supportive

The Israeli operation curtailed, but did not stop, Hamas's missiles. In the four months from the end of January until May 2009, more than 200 were fired from Gaza. When Israel headed into a general election less than two weeks after the offensive, Hamas appeared intent on keeping the pressure up right to the wire. On election day, 10 February 2009, it fired a rocket into the Israeli border town of Sderot half an hour before the polls closed.[64]

Whether intentionally or otherwise, it succeeded in shifting Israeli public opinion to the right. Although the centre-right Kadima Party inherited by Tzipi Livni from the comatose Ariel Sharon and scandal-plagued Ehud Olmert won marginally more seats than Binyamin Netanyahu's right-wing Likud, Livni was unable to put together a coalition with the left. So, a decade after he first held the position, Netanyahu once again became Israel's prime minister.

On the Palestinian side, opinion polls were ominous for Fatah. One survey in January by the Jerusalem Media and Communications Centre (JMCC) found that perceptions of Hamas's performance were far more positive among Palestinians who did not have to live in Gaza – 53.3 per cent of respondents in the West Bank said Hamas won the war, compared with 35.2 per cent of those who lived through the operation in Gaza. Despite the split, when asked who they would vote for if parliamentary elections were held immediately, the percentage voting for Hamas rose nearly 10 points, from 19.3 per cent in April 2008 to 28.6 per cent. Fatah fell from 34 per cent to 27.9 per cent over the same period. The pollsters again added a caveat: 'It is clear from the poll that the rise in Hamas's popularity is due to an increase in popularity in the West Bank – it rose from 12.8 per cent last November to 26.5 per cent in this poll.' Individuals' performance reflected the party trend – trust in Ismail Haniyeh went up from 12.8 per cent to 21.1 per cent, while trust in President Abbas fell from 15.5 per cent to 13.4 per cent.

A direct comparison between the two governments was also disappointing for Salam Fayyad, those who thought his government was doing better falling from 36 per cent to 26.9 per cent and those who thought Hamas was doing better rising from 29.1 per cent to 40.7 per cent. Crucially, more than half – 50.8 per cent – of Palestinians said rockets fired from Gaza helped 'achieve the Palestinian national goals', up from 39.3 per cent nine months earlier.[65] By March, once the physical and political dust had settled, a rival poll by the Palestinian Center for Policy and Survey Research (PSR) showed 'a significant increase in the popularity of Ismail Haniyeh and Hamas and decrease in the popularity of President Mahmud Abbas and Fatah. They also indicate a significant decline in the status and legitimacy of Salam Fayyad.' Hamas rose from 28 per cent in December 2008 to 33 per cent, while Fatah fell from 42 per cent to 40 per cent – very different figures and rates of movement from the JMCC poll.

If a presidential race were to be held, the PSR found Haniyeh and Abbas virtually head to head, with the Hamas leader on 47 per cent and the incumbent president on 45 per cent, but the position was radically different if the jailed West Bank leader Marwan Barghouti were Fatah's candidate – Barghouti beating Haniyeh by 61 per cent to 34 per cent. Another like-for-like comparison of the two governments found the

Fayyad government's ratings declining from 34 per cent to 32 per cent while Haniyeh's rose from 36 per cent to 43 per cent. Although Hamas increased in popularity, from 28 per cent in December 2008 to 33 per cent, and Fatah fell, from 42 per cent to 40 per cent, Fatah was 12 points ahead in Gaza but only 3 points in the West Bank. Haniyeh's popularity was higher in the West Bank (50 per cent), than in the Gaza Strip (44 per cent), supposedly Hamas's stronghold. The opposite is true for Abbas, who was more popular in the Gaza Strip (50 per cent) than in the West Bank (41 per cent). Underlying all this, the pollsters found, was 'a decline in public support for the peace process'. After the Gaza war, more than half (54 per cent) of Palestinians supported armed attacks against Israeli civilians inside Israel, up from 48 per cent before the Israeli offensive, and 73 per cent believed that the chances for the creation of an independent Palestinian state in the next five years were 'slim to non-existent . . . indicating an increase in the level of pessimism'.[66]

Both Hamas and Fatah were eager to be seen taking the lead in rebuilding Gaza, and the stakes for doing so increased dramatically in March 2009, when, at an Egyptian conference, international donors pledged $4.5 billion – much of it for reconstruction – to President Abbas's Palestinian Authority. As both sides manoeuvred to control the levers of money and patronage, they also continued to hold rounds of unity talks in Cairo. But these became bogged down in arguments over security and political issues, including the programme of any joint Hamas–Fatah government.

After the fifth round of talks broke up in May, senior Fatah officials disclosed that one stumbling block was that Fatah wanted to see Hamas's security force in Gaza replaced by a joint force, 10,000 to 15,000 strong, made up of both factions. Hamas insisted on keeping its own forces and having a tiny joint force of around 300 people, only to oversee borders. The two sides also disagreed about which bodies a coordinating committee should coordinate with. Hamas wanted it to liaise between the two governments in Gaza and the West Bank. But Fatah insisted that there was only one government, in Ramallah, which would liaise with the Hamas movement in Gaza. Hamas leader Khalil al-Hayeh scoffed at the very idea of allowing Fatah forces back into Gaza. 'The security situation has improved tremendously since they went', he said. 'As an interim measure we could maybe agree to having some of them at the Rafah crossing.'[67]

On 19 May 2009, President Abbas reappointed Fayyad as prime minister, this time at the head of a twenty-four-member cabinet, more than a third of whose members were Fatah. Hamas immediately greeted the new government with scorn, pointing out that, unlike its own organization, it was unelected and had no popular mandate. 'This government is illegal, unconstitutional and came with the blessing of the Zionist and American administrations', said Hamas MP Mushir al-Masri.[68] The other side was no less adamant. Granting his first meeting with a foreigner, the new Fatah-affiliated minister of the interior, Dr Said Abu Ali, contended that change had to come from Hamas. 'Everything is deadlocked until we get a new Hamas . . . Dialogue serves the interest of the nation, but unless a new Hamas that is dedicated to the same national project and not the regional agenda of the wider Muslim Brotherhood evolves, then this is a problem.'[69]

Throughout the autumn and winter of 2009 Palestinian unity talks limped on, but even with Egyptian and other Arab inputs there seemed little chance that Fatah and Hamas would reconcile. President Abbas announced presidential and legislative elections for early 2010, but Hamas announced that it would not allow such elections to take place in Gaza and threatened dire punishments if anyone defied them. All the steam appeared to run out of the Obama administration's attempts at peacemaking when Binyamin Netanyahu's government resisted American pressure for a halt to settlement-building. Stasis, stalemate, intransigence and enmity clouded the political landscape.

The future

Husam Khader relishes freedom. He has spent many years in Israeli jails, imprisoned for his role in the Palestinian resistance against military occupation. As a Fatah leader and self-declared nationalist revolutionary, his political credentials are among the most solid in the Palestinian Territories. Something of a local hero, he has long spoken out against PLO corruption and cronyism.

In 2009 the reality he saw from the sparsely furnished salon of his refugee camp home in Nablus was a depressing one for his own organization. 'This is the Hamas era', he said starkly. 'We failed in Fatah to take the chance to lead society and politics again.' Khader believes that Hamas's stance in championing the cause of Palestinian resistance against Israel, combined with the ineffectiveness of its rivals, will allow Hamas to emerge only marginally diminished after the battering it received in Gaza. 'On its decision to resist . . . this alone was a victory for Hamas. Even if Gaza is destroyed, Hamas still wins. Yes, Hamas will win the battle, but the people of Gaza will lose the war.'[70]

Certainly it appeared that, as it emerged from the rubble, Hamas had survived yet again. Israel – the strongest military power in the Middle East – did not succeed in breaking the Islamists, nor did its generals and political leaders seriously expect one military offensive to achieve such a far-reaching objective. Indeed, the longevity of this Islamic movement seems assured. From the earliest roots of anti-colonial and anti-Zionist resistance, represented by Sheikh Izz ad-Din al-Qassam's call to jihad in the 1930s, Islamism has flourished on Palestinian soil. But unlike other Islamic movements in the Middle East, the Muslim Brotherhood, the Mujamma and later Hamas were all to be forged not only by their conflict with secular Arab nationalist rivals but also by their proximity to the phenomenon of Zionism, and its manifestation in the state of Israel created in 1948.

Israel is backed by a powerful ally, the United States. Hamas has become increasingly dependent on Iran. This does not augur well for the regional balance of power as the Obama administration seeks to alter its policy in the Middle East. Hamas is still perceived as part of the problem, not just to Israeli–Palestinian peace but because of its influence on ascendant Islamist movements in Egypt, Jordan, Lebanon and Iraq, where the Muslim Brotherhood remains a powerful opponent to incumbent Arab leaders of undemocratic regimes.

All of this leaves President Abbas, the government of Israel, the US, the Quartet and other regional actors with a dilemma. This centres on whether peace between Israel and the Palestinians can be achieved while Hamas enjoys a democratic mandate, and rules Gaza. In short, is peace possible if Hamas is not part of the equation?

Many Israelis believe that Hamas can never be trusted to make peace and that its objective is to achieve the opposite: to foment holy war against the Jews and to expel them from Palestine. They continue to argue – along with their Western supporters – that Hamas must be crushed. But, if Hamas is broken, will a more radical Islamist threat arise in its place? Some Israelis perceive Hamas in less existential terms. They caution that for Israel to achieve security it must reconcile itself to the Hamas phenomenon. But any dealings between the two parties would require Hamas to recognize Israel, and the Hamas leadership has continued to shroud its public statements on this issue with ambiguity. Additionally, it has made no effort to water down its founding 1988 covenant, and it remains unclear whether this implacably anti-Israel document continues to define the movement, or if it could be rewritten to reflect twenty-first-century realities.

Many secular Palestinians are also deeply suspicious of Hamas's intentions, fearing that its agenda is to turn the Palestinian Territories into a Taliban-style fiefdom of Islamic fundamentalist rule. They claim that its democratic credentials are increasingly thin on the ground in Gaza, pointing to escalating restrictions on freedoms. However, some Palestinians, particularly those who support its Islamist agenda, believe that Hamas and Hamas alone is capable of delivering independence and statehood. They feel secure under a system of rule that inspires conservative social order, and reflects mainstream Islamist discourse in the realm of society, politics and economy.

For the Obama administration and other Western countries there is a quandary. In private diplomats and politicians recognize that dialogue with Hamas is ultimately necessary, but in public they continue to recite the mantra that Hamas must make all the concessions.

Hamas's message is that it is now a fact on the ground in the Middle

East, and must be acknowledged as such. 'They failed to get rid of Hamas in Gaza', said Dr Nasser Eddin al-Shaer, a Hamas leader in Nablus. 'This is a message for the politicians. There is no solution if it doesn't include Hamas.'[71]

Chronology

1516–1917	Palestine ruled by the Turks as one of the Arab territories of the Ottoman Empire.
1896–7	Publication of Theodor Herzl's *Der Judenstaat* [The Jewish state]. First Zionist Congress convenes in Basel, Switzerland.
1914–18	First World War: Turkey allies with Germany.
1916	Sykes–Picot agreement by Britain, France and Russia to divide the crumbling Ottoman Empire between them, including Palestine.
1917, November 2	The Balfour Declaration declares British government support for 'the establishment in Palestine of a national home for the Jewish people'.
1917, December 9	General Sir Edmund [later Viscount] Allenby captures Jerusalem from Turkish forces.
1920	At San Remo the victorious Allies divide the former Ottoman Empire; Britain is awarded the mandate for Palestine. Later approved by the League of Nations.
1921	Syrian-born Sheikh Izz ad-Din al-Qassam arrives in Haifa and begins work as a preacher. The British appoint Hajj Amin al-Husseini the mufti of Jerusalem.
1929	'Western Wall riots' in Jerusalem; Palestinian Arabs kill dozens of Jews in Hebron.
1935	Qassam's 'Black Hand gang' attacks British and Zionist targets.
1935, November 19	Qassam killed in a shoot-out with British police near Jenin.
1936–9	Palestinian Arabs stage a general strike and revolt; 'Qassamite' rebels involved.
1945–6	The Muslim Brotherhood, founded in Egypt in 1928 by Hassan al-Banna, opens its first branches in Palestine.
1947, November	United Nations Partition Plan: the General Assembly of the UN adopts UN Resolution 181 proposing the division

	of post-mandate Palestine into two separate Jewish and Arab states, with Jerusalem internationalized.
1948, May 14	Israel declares independence.
1948, May 15	The date set by Britain for ending the mandate.
1948, May 15	The first Arab–Israeli war begins.
1949, May 11	Israel becomes a member state of the United Nations.
February to July	Armistice agreements signed between Israel and neighbouring Arab states.
1954	President Gamal Abdel Nasser of Egypt cracks down on the activities of the Muslim Brotherhood in the Gaza Strip.
1964–6	Nasser orders another crackdown on leftists and the Muslim Brotherhood in Egypt and Gaza, leading to the imprisonment of activists.
1967, June	The Six Day War: Israel is victorious, capturing and occupying the West Bank, the Gaza Strip and East Jerusalem, including the Temple Mount/Al-Haram al-Sharif.
1973, October	Yom Kippur War between Israel, Egypt and Syria. Sheikh Ahmed Yassin forms the Mujamma in the Gaza Strip.
1978	Israeli civil authorities in Gaza register the Mujamma as a charity.
1980	Violent clashes in Gaza between Islamist supporters of the Mujamma and secular PLO loyalists.
1981	First cells of Palestinian Islamic Jihad established in the Gaza Strip.
1984	Israeli authorities arrest Yassin and his colleagues and imprison them for membership of an illegal organization, weapons possession and receiving funds.
1985	Yassin released from jail in Israel/PFLP–GC prisoner exchange.
1987, December	First Intifada breaks out. Hamas, the Islamic Resistance Movement, is formed.
1988, August	Hamas publishes its covenant.
1989	Hamas's first attacks against Israeli military targets, including the kidnap and murder of two Israeli soldiers. Israeli authorities outlaw Hamas and imprison Yassin.
1990–1	Gulf War: the PLO alienates its wealthy Gulf backers by siding with Saddam Hussein after his invasion of Kuwait. Hamas refuses to align itself with Hussein.
1991	Madrid Peace Conference between Israel, Syria and Jordan with a Palestinian delegation. Hamas denounces the peace initiative. Hamas announces its new armed wing: the Izz ad-Din al-Qassam Brigades.
1992	Israeli prime minister, Yitzhak Rabin, orders the deportation of more than 400 Islamists, including Hamas leaders, to south Lebanon after an Israeli police officer is kidnapped and murdered.
1993, September 13	After secret peace talks in Norway, Israel and the PLO sign the Oslo Accords, outlining an agenda for peace, final

	status negotiations and interim Palestinian autonomy in the West Bank and Gaza Strip. Hamas rejects the accords and escalates attacks on Israel.
1994, February 25	Baruch Goldstein, a far-right Jewish settler, kills twenty-nine Muslims at prayer in Hebron's Ibrahimi mosque during Ramadan.
1994, April 4	First Israeli troop redeployments from Jericho and Gaza.
1994, April 6	Hamas revenge for Hebron massacre, killing eight Israelis with a suicide bomb in Afula.
1994, April 13	Hamas suicide bomb in Hadera kills five Israelis.
1994, May 4	Israel and the PLO sign the Gaza–Jericho Agreement.
1994, July 1	Yasser Arafat returns to Gaza after three decades in exile.
1994, October 14	Israeli soldier Nachshon Waxman abducted and killed by Hamas.
1994, October 19	Twenty-two people killed in Hamas suicide bomb on a bus in Dizengoff Street, Tel Aviv.
1994, December 10	Yasser Arafat, Yitzhak Rabin and Shimon Peres awarded the Nobel Peace Prize in Oslo.
1995	Israeli authorities conduct arrest campaigns against Hamas in the West Bank.
	The Palestinian Authority conducts an arrest campaign against Hamas in the Gaza Strip and Jericho. Israeli troops redeploy from most major Palestinian towns in the West Bank.
1995, November 4	Yitzhak Rabin assassinated by an Israeli extremist. Shimon Peres takes over.
1996, January	Yahya Ayyash, the Hamas bomb-maker known as 'the Engineer', assassinated by Israel.
1996, January 20	First Palestinian parliamentary and presidential elections are held. They are boycotted by Hamas.
1996, February 25	Hamas suicide bombing kills twenty-six on a bus in Jerusalem.
1996, May	Binyamin Netanyahu elected prime minister of Israel. Hamas and Islamic Jihad engage in further suicide bombing attacks to derail the peace process.
1997, September 25	Mossad agents try to assassinate Khaled Meshaal in Amman, but fail and are captured. Israel releases Sheikh Yassin to secure their return from Jordan.
1998, October 23	Wye River Agreement between Israel and the PA.
1999, May 4	Expiry of five-year deadline for final status negotiations.
2000, May	Israel withdraws from south Lebanon.
2000, July 11–25	Israeli Prime Minister Ehud Barak, Palestinian President Yasser Arafat and US President Bill Clinton fail to reach agreement at Camp David summit.
2000, September 28	Israeli opposition leader Ariel Sharon tours Temple Mount, prompting Palestinian riots which escalate into the Second, Intifada.

2000, September 30	Mohammed al-Dura, aged twelve, killed during cross-fire between Israeli soldiers and Palestinian militants at Netzarim in the Gaza Strip.
2000, October 12	Two Israeli reservists, Yosef Avrahami and Vadim Norzhich, lynched in Ramallah.
2001, February 6	Ariel Sharon wins Israeli general election, becomes prime minister.
2001, April 16	First Palestinian rocket into Israel from the Gaza Strip.
2001, June 1	Hamas suicide bomber kills twenty-one Israelis, mainly teenagers, outside a Tel Aviv disco.
2001, August 9	Sbarro Pizzeria bombing in Jerusalem, fifteen dead. Hamas and Islamic Jihad claim responsibility.
2001, December 1	Hamas double suicide bombing kills eleven people on Jerusalem's Ben Yehuda pedestrian mall.
2001, December 2	Hamas kills fifteen Israelis in a bus bomb in Haifa.
2001, December 16	Yasser Arafat orders a cessation of attacks on Israel.
2001, December 28	European Union adds Izz ad-Din al-Qassam Brigades to its list of terrorist organizations.
2002, January 3	Israeli commandos seize *Karine A* vessel, loaded with 50 tons of weapons believed to be for the Palestinian Territories.
2002, January 14	Israelis assassinate Fatah Al Aqsa Martyrs' Brigades militant Raed al-Karmi in Tulkarem.
2002, January 27	Wafa Idris, the first ever Palestinian woman suicide bomber, kills one Israeli and wounds 150 in Jaffa Street, Jerusalem. Al Aqsa Martyrs' Brigades claim responsibility.
2002, March 2	Eleven people killed in Al Aqsa Martyrs' Brigades suicide bombing in ultra-orthodox Jerusalem neighbourhood Beit Yisrael.
2002, March 27	Hamas suicide bomber kills thirty Jewish celebrants at a Passover seder dinner at the Park Hotel in Netanya.
2002, March 29	Israel launches Operation Defensive Shield military reoccupation of the West Bank and besieges Arafat's HQ in Ramallah.
2002, July 7	The Palestinian Basic Law comes into force, intended to form the basis for a constitution.
2002, July 22	Salah Shehadeh, Hamas's military leader, is among more than a dozen people killed when Israel drops a one ton bomb on the building where he is staying in Gaza.
2003, March 5	Seventeen people killed in suicide bombing of an Egged bus in Haifa. Hamas claims responsibility for the attack.
2003, May 19	Suicide bombing at a shopping mall in Afula kills three people.
2003, June 11	Seventeen people killed in a Hamas suicide bombing on a bus in Jerusalem's Jaffa Road.
2003, June 23	Hamas declares a ceasefire.
2003, August 19	Twenty-three people killed in a suicide bus bomb in Jerusalem. Hamas claims responsibility.

2003, August 21	Ismail Abu Shanab, one of Hamas's chief negotiators, killed in an Israeli missile attack on Gaza. Israel also tries to assassinate Yassin.
2003, September 10	Hamas leader Dr Mahmoud Zahar survives an Israeli missile attack on his house in Gaza City. His wife's back is broken and his son is killed.
2003, October 4	Suicide bombing at Maxim's restaurant in Haifa, in which twenty-one Israelis are killed.
2003, October 15	A bomb is detonated against a US embassy convoy in the Gaza Strip; three American security guards are killed.
2004, March 22	Hamas's leader and founder, Sheikh Yassin, is assassinated in an Israeli air strike. Dr Abdel Aziz Rantissi is declared his successor.
2004, April 17	Less than a month after taking over in Gaza, Rantissi is also assassinated in an Israeli air strike. The Hamas leadership goes into hiding and the identity of Rantissi's successor is kept secret. Khaled Meshaal, based in Damascus, is widely believed to be the new leader.
2004, August 31	Sixteen people killed in two suicide bombings on buses in Beersheba. Hamas claims responsibility.
2004, November 11	The Palestinian president, Fatah founder and PLO leader, Yasser Arafat, dies in a Paris hospital.
2004, November 12	Arafat buried in Ramallah.
2005, January 9	Mahmoud Abbas elected president of the Palestinian Authority to succeed Arafat. Hamas does not contest the election.
2005, January 15	Abbas sworn in to office.
2005, April	Cairo declaration: Hamas and Fatah agree to reform of the PLO. Hamas announces that it will contest forthcoming legislative elections for the first time.
2005, May	Hamas contests local municipal elections and wins the majority of seats in many constituencies.
2005, August	Israel evacuates all its settlers and soldiers from the Gaza Strip. Hamas declares the Israeli withdrawal its 'victory'.
2006, January 25	Hamas wins overall majority in the first parliamentary elections since 1996. The Quartet says 'all members of a future Palestinian government must be committed to non-violence, recognition of Israel, and acceptance of previous agreements and obligations'.
2006, March 17	Said Siam, Hamas's minister of the interior, announces the founding of a new Hamas police force in the Gaza Strip, the Executive Forces.
2006, March 29	The newly appointed, Hamas-nominated, twenty-four-member cabinet of the Palestinian National Authority sworn in, led by Prime Minister Ismail Haniyeh.
2006, May 15	Hamas deploys first Executive Forces to restore law and order in the Gaza Strip, creating tension with civil police still loyal to Fatah.

2006, June 25	Hamas, the Popular Resistance Committees and the Army of Islam carry out a tunnel raid near Kerem Shalom military base on Israel's side of the Gaza border, killing two Israeli soldiers and abducting Corporal Gilad Schalit. Israel arrests and imprisons Hamas legislators and leaders.
2006, July 12	Hezbollah kills eight Israeli soldiers and kidnaps two in a cross-border attack from southern Lebanon. It fires nearly 4,000 Katyusha rockets into Israel, which retaliates with air strikes, artillery shelling and a ground invasion.
2006, August 14	Ceasefire. On the Israeli side, forty-four civilians and 121 soldiers killed (including the two kidnapped soldiers, whose bodies were returned on 16 July 2008). More than 1,000 Lebanese killed, mostly civilians.
2006, September– December	Fighting between Hamas and Fatah breaks out in Gaza and the West Bank, leaving many dead, including three children murdered on their way to school.
2007, January	Fighting between Hamas and Fatah paralyses the streets of Gaza. Women and children are among the dead.
2007, February 8	Hamas joins Fatah in signing up to the Mecca Agreement on power-sharing and the formation of a National Unity Government.
2007, March 17	The new government is sworn in.
2007, June 10	New outbreaks of violence in Gaza.
2007, June 15	Hamas seizes control of Gaza after five days of fighting. Hundreds of Fatah security personnel flee the Gaza Strip. President Abbas declares a state of emergency and dismisses the Hamas-led government.
2007, June 17	Abbas announces an emergency Palestinian government based in Ramallah in the West Bank, headed by Salam Fayyad. The government is made up of independent and Fatah ministers.
2007, June 27	The former British prime minister Tony Blair appointed the Quartet's special envoy to the Middle East.
2007, July 4	The kidnapped BBC journalist Alan Johnston released in Gaza and handed to Hamas officials.
2007, September 2	Abbas changes the electoral law to eliminate district voting in place of a party list system. All presidential and parliamentary candidates are required to recognize the PLO as the sole legitimate representative of the Palestinian people.
2007, September 19	The Israeli security cabinet votes to declare Gaza an 'enemy entity'.
2007, November 2	President Abbas meets Hamas officials for the first time since the June takeover of Gaza.
2007, November 12	Hamas police kill at least six people at a Fatah rally in Gaza to mark the anniversary of Arafat's death.
2007, November 27	US-sponsored peace conference at Annapolis involving Israel and President Abbas.

2008, January 23	Hamas encourages thousands of Palestinians to break the siege of Gaza by smashing the border with Egypt at Rafah.
2008, February 4	Suicide bomb attack in Dimona, Israel.
2008, March 7	Hamas and Israel enter into an informal ceasefire.
2008, April	Former US President Jimmy Carter meets with exiled Hamas leader Khaled Meshaal in Damascus.
2008, June 18	Hamas and Israel enter into first mutual six-month ceasefire agreement.
2008, July 25	A bomb at a Gaza City beachside café kills five Hamas militants and a little girl. Hamas blames Fatah and shuts down its remaining offices. Abbas responds with a similar crackdown on Hamas in the West Bank.
2008, December 19	Hamas and Israel ceasefire ends without renewal.
2008, December 24	Palestinian militants in Gaza fire more than sixty rockets into Israel.
2008, December 27	Israel launches Operation Lead Cast in Gaza. In the first week 400 Palestinians are killed. Palestinian rockets kill four Israelis.
2009, January 1	Sheikh Nizar Rayan, a senior Hamas leader, killed in his home in Jabalia by an Israeli air strike.
2009, January 3	Israel launches three-pronged ground offensive into Gaza.
2009, January 15	Said Siam, Hamas's interior minister, killed by Israel.
2009, January 18	Israel declares a unilateral ceasefire in Gaza. More than 1,300 Gazans and thirteen Israelis killed. Hamas announces a unilateral one-week ceasefire, calling for a complete Israeli withdrawal. Israeli troops commence withdrawal.
2009, February 10	Israeli general elections held. Right-wing and centrist parties gain nearly the same number of seats. Likud's Binyamin Netanyahu becomes prime minister.
2009, February	Hamas and Fatah enter national unity talks hosted in Cairo.
2009, March	Hamas and Israel engage in Egyptian-mediated indirect negotiations on the release of prisoners, including Israeli soldier Gilad Schalit.
2009, May	Six killed in clashes between Hamas and Palestinian security forces during a raid in the West Bank town of Qalqilya.
2009, June 1	UN Human Rights Council investigative panel led by Judge Richard Goldstone enters the Gaza Strip to investigate alleged war crimes during Operation Cast Lead. Israel refuses to cooperate with the investigation.
2009, July	Hamas and Fatah both complain of tit-for-tat arrest campaigns organized in Hamas-controlled Gaza Strip and Fatah-controlled West Bank. Hamas declares that any further rounds of national unity talks are conditional on the release of Hamas prisoners from PA jails in the West Bank.

2009, August	Fatah holds sixth congress in Bethlehem, its first for twenty years, to elect new leaders and debate reform. Israel permits activists from Lebanon and Syria to attend. Hamas stops Fatah delegates leaving the Gaza Strip.
2009, September 15	UN Human Rights Council report into Israel's Operation Cast Lead is released. It concludes that there is evidence indicating serious violations of international human rights and humanitarian law, actions amounting to war crimes, and possibly crimes against humanity committed by Israel during the Gaza conflict. The report also finds evidence that Palestinian armed groups – principally Hamas – committed war crimes, as well as possibly crimes against humanity, in their repeated launching of rockets and mortars into Southern Israel.
2009, October	Abbas calls for presidential and parliamentary elections in January 2010. Hamas announces a boycott in the Gaza Strip.
2009, November	Abbas announces that he will not seek renomination as a candidate in the presidential elections.

Notes

Chapter 1   We Deal with Allah Directly

1 Abu Bakr Nofal, author interview, Gaza City, 6 September 2006.
2 Israeli Ministry of Foreign Affairs, *Victims of Palestinian Violence and Terrorism since September 2000*, www.israel-mfa.gov.il.
3 Ghazi Hamad, author interview, Gaza City, 15 July 2008.
4 Address by PM Netanyahu at the memorial service for victims of terror at Mount Herzl, 28 April 2009, Israel Prime Minister's Office, www.pmo.gov.il.
5 Reuters, 'Abbas says won't recognise Israel as Jewish state,' Ramallah, 27 April 2009.
6 Member States of the United Nations, www.un.org/en/members/index.shtml; Permanent Mission of Israel to the United Nations, http://israel-un.mfa.gov.il.
7 'Entity having received a standing invitation to participate as observer in the sessions and the work of the General Assembly and maintaining permanent observer mission at Headquarters: Palestine – Permanent Observer Mission of Palestine to the United Nations'; www.un.org/members/entities. shtml.
8 Dr Abdel Aziz Rantissi, author interview, Gaza City, 8 July 2002.
9 Khaled Abdel Shafi, author interview, Gaza City, 10 November 2006.
10 Hamas Covenant, Article 2: 'The Islamic Resistance Movement's relation with the Muslim Brotherhood Group', August 1988, the Avalon Project, Documents in Law, History and Diplomacy, Lillian Goldman Law Library, Yale Law School, http://avalon.law.yale.edu/20th_century/hamas.asp.
11 Ismail Haniyeh, author interview, Gaza City, 26 January 2006.
12 Ghazi Hamad, author interview, Gaza City, 15 July 2008.
13 Taghreed el-Khodary and Ethan Bronner, 'Addressing U.S., Hamas Says it Grounded its Rockets to Israel', *New York Times*, 4 May 2009.
14 Yuval Diskin, director, Israel Security Agency (Shin Bet), media briefing, 5 March 2007.
15 Prime Minister's Office, Government of Israel: www.pmo.gov.il/PMOEng/ Archive/Press+Releases/2006/01/spokemes260106g.htm.

16 Dr Ron Pundak, interview, *Australian Jewish News*, 8 December 2006.
17 Dr Yossi Beilin, 'Needed: A Cease-Fire with Hamas, Now', *Washington Post*, 23 November 2007, p. A39.
18 Binyamin Netanyahu, *The Times*, 27 January 2006, p. 35.
19 Dr Ibrahim Ibrach, author interview, Gaza City, 20 December 2006.
20 Professor Ali al-Jarbawi, author interview, Ramallah, 18 May 2009.
21 Hamas Covenant, Article 20, August 1988, http://avalon.law.yale.edu/20th_century/hamas.asp.
22 Hamas Covenant, Article 22, August 1988, http://avalon.law.yale.edu/20th_century/hamas.asp.
23 Dr Mahmoud Zahar, author interview, Gaza City, 29 May 1995.
24 Yehya Moussa Abbadsa, author interview, Gaza City, 19 March 2008.
25 Dr Omar Abdel Razeq, author interview, Ramallah, 11 April 2006.
26 Sheikh Saleh al-Arouri, author interview, Aroura, 26 March 2007.
27 Colonel Yossi, author interview, Jerusalem, 12 July 2004.
28 Haim Jelin, author interview, Magen, 7 May 2009.
29 Joint Israeli–Palestinian poll by the Harry S. Truman Research Institute for the Advancement of Peace at the Hebrew University of Jerusalem and the Palestinian Center for Policy and Survey Research in Ramallah, 1–7 March 2009, www.pcpsr.org/survey/polls/2009/.
30 Dr Eyad Sarraj, author interview, Gaza City, 13 March 2007.
31 Dr Abdel Aziz Rantissi, author interview, Gaza City, 22 June 2002.
32 Abu Bakr Nofal, author interview, Gaza City, 6 September 2006.

Chapter 2   In the Path of al-Qassam

1 *Al-Jamia'a al-Islamiyya*, editorial, 25 November 1935.
2 Anonymous, author interview, Galilee, northern Israel, 11 June 2008.
3 Hamas Covenant, Article 7: 'The universality of Hamas', August 1988, the Avalon Project, Documents in Law, History and Diplomacy, Lillian Goldman Law Library, Yale Law School; http://avalon.law.yale.edu/20th_century/hamas.asp.
4 The Balfour Declaration, 2 November 1917, http://avalon.law.yale.edu/20th_century/balfour.asp.
5 PRO, file CO733/257/12, 'Situation in Palestine', 1935.
6 See S. A. Schleifer, 'The life and thought of Izz ad-Din al-Qassam', *Islamic Quarterly*, 30/2 (1979), pp. 60–81.
7 Middle East Centre, St Antony's College, Oxford, Tegart Papers, Box 1, File 3C, from 'Report on Terrorism 1936–37', p. 7.
8 'Alleged terrorists' case continued', *Palestine Post*, 2 March 1936, p. 1.
9 Ibid.
10 Ibid.
11 'Between the lines', *Palestine Post*, 22 November 1935, p. 8.
12 Anonymous, author interview, Galilee, northern Israel, 11 June 2008.

13 'First sentence of death passed by military court', *Palestine Post*, 25 November 1937, p. 1.
14 'Echoes of the terrorist gang', *Palestine Post*, 19 January 1936, p. 5.
15 'Between the lines', *Palestine Post*, 22 November 1935, p. 8.
16 *Al-Jami'a al-Islamiyya*, editorial, 25 November 1935.
17 PRO, file CO 75156/4/35, report from Sir Arthur Wauchope on the situation in Palestine, 1935.
18 'Large crowds at burial of three Arab terrorists – police on guard at funeral procession', *Palestine Post*, 22 November 1935, p. 1.
19 Rawiya Shawwa, author interview, Gaza City, 14 March 2007.
20 'Arab leaders admit losing influence', *Palestine Post*, 27 November 1935.
21 'A new orientation needed', *Palestine Post*, 25 November 1935, p. 3.
22 'Arabs decry council', *Palestine Post*, 6 January 1936, p. 5.
23 Ibid.
24 S. K. Farsoun and C. E. Zakaria, *Palestine and the Palestinians* (Boulder, CO: Westview Press, 1997), p. 106.
25 PRO, file CO 75156/4/35, report from Sir Arthur Wauchope on the situation in Palestine, 1935.

Chapter 3   Sowing

1 Dr Haider Abdel Shafi, author interview, Gaza City, 14 November 1989.
2 'Nablus bandits seen as Izz-ed Din's followers,' *Palestine Post*, 17 April 1936, p. 1.
3 Hajj Mohammad Abu Attar, author interview, Deir al-Balah, Gaza Strip, 5 September 1993.
4 Subhi Anabtawi, author interview, Nablus, 12 August 1989.
5 *The Origins and Evolution of the Palestine Problem: 1917–1988* (New York: United Nations, 1990).
6 Mohammed Habash, author interview, Nusseirat refugee camp, Gaza Strip, 6 September 1993.
7 Abu Mohammed, author interview, Nusseirat refugee camp, Gaza Strip, 5 September 1993.
8 Sheikh Ahmed Yassin, author interview, Gaza City, 11 July 2002.
9 Dr Atef Adwan, author interview, Gaza City, 8 September 2002.
10 Abu Mohammed, author interview, Nusseirat refugee camp, Gaza Strip, 5 September 1993.
11 Sheikh Ahmed Yassin, author interview, Gaza City, 11 July 2002.
12 Abu Zaki Mohammed al-Radwan, author interview, Gaza City, 17 November 1989.
13 Ibid., 13 November 1989.
14 Dr Mahmoud Zahar, author interview, Gaza City, 27 November 1989.
15 Rawiya Shawwa, author interview, Gaza City, 13 March 2007.
16 Dr Mariam Abu Dagga, author interview, Gaza City, 14 March 2007.

17 Dr Yousef al-Athm, author interview, Amman, 20 June 1989.

18 A. Azzam, *Hamas: al-judhour al-tarikhiyya wal-mithaq* [Hamas: History and Charter] (Peshawar: n.p., 1989).

19 Dr Mahmoud Zahar, author interview, Gaza City, 27 November 1989.

20 Sheikh Ahmed Yassin, author interview, Gaza City, 11 July 2002.

21 Dr Atef Adwan, author interview, Gaza City, 8 September 2002.

22 Dr Mahmoud Zahar, author interview, Gaza City, 29 May 1995.

23 A. Idwan, *Shaykh Ahmad Yassin, hayatah wa jihad* [Sheikh Ahmad Yassin, his Life and Jihad] (Gaza, n.d.), p. 40.

24 This also happened at Birzeit University in the West Bank. See W. Claiborne, 'Brotherhood blooms on the West Bank', *Washington Post*, 15 March 1982.

25 Dr Riad al-Agha, author interview, Gaza City, 28 November 1989.

26 Professor Ali al-Jarbawi, author interview, Ramallah, 5 May 2009.

27 Ismaen Fagawi, author interview, Khan Younis, Gaza Strip, 7 November 1989.

28 Brigadier General Yossi Kuperwasser, author note, Israel Newsmakers Forum, Mishkenot Shananim, Jerusalem, 11 November 2007.

29 Brigadier General Itshak Segev (retired), author interview, Ramat Gan, 18 May 2009.

30 Dr Rabbah Muhanna, author interview, Gaza City, 28 November 1989.

31 Dr Haider Abdel Shafi, author interview, Gaza City, 14 November 1989.

32 Dr Riad al-Agha, author interview, Gaza City, 28 November 1989.

33 Dr Haider Abdel Shafi, author interview, Gaza City, 14 November 1989.

34 D. Rubinstein, 'Rising Hamas is undaunted by loss of leader Yassin', *Independent on Sunday*, 28 March 2004, p. 10.

35 Dr Eyad Sarraj, author interview, Gaza City, 13 March 2007.

36 Dr Rabbah Muhanna, author interview, Gaza City, 28 November 1989.

37 Basim, author interview, Khan Yunis, Gaza, 19 October 1989.

38 'Islamic bloc enlist thugs to break employee strike at Islamic University', *Al-Fajr*, 3 June 1983, p. 3, and 'Muslim fanatics attacks Bir Zeit and Gaza University', *Al-Fajr*, 10 June 1983.

39 Dr Abdel Aziz Rantissi, author interview, Khan Younis, 24 September 1990.

40 Hamdi, author interview, Shatti refugee camp, Gaza, 11 November 1989.

41 Ibrahim Hamad, author interview, Qalandia refugee camp, West Bank, 17 February 1988.

42 Avner Cohen, author interview, Moshav Tekuma, 7 May 2009.

43 Ibid.

44 Rafat Najar, author interview, Khan Younis, 14 November 1989.

45 Ibid., 7 November 1989.

46 Avner Cohen, author interview, Moshav Tekuma, 7 May 2009.

Chapter 4   The First Intifada

1 Sheikh Ahmed Yassin, author interview, Gaza City, 11 July 2002.

2 'Statement in the Knesset by Defense Minister Rabin, 23 December 1987', Israel

Foreign Ministry, historical documents 1984–1988, no. 312, www.mfa.gov.il/
MFA.

3 'Interview with Vice Premier and Foreign Minister Peres on Israel Radio, 23
December 1987', Israel Foreign Ministry, historical documents 1984–1988, no.
313, www.mfa.gov.il/MFA.

4 'Interview with Defense Minister Rabin on Israel Television, 14 January 1988,'
Israel Foreign Ministry, historical documents 1984–1988, no. 322, www.mfa.
gov.il/MFA.

5 Yitzhak Rabin, 'Israel's new violent tactic takes toll on both sides', *New York
Times*, 22 January 1988.

6 'Statement in the Knesset by Defense Minister Rabin, 23 December 1987', Israel
Foreign Ministry, historical documents 1984–1988, no. 312, www.mfa.gov.il/
MFA.

7 *New York Times*, also quoting *Haaretz*, 22 and 25 January 1988.

8 'Cabinet Statement on the Uprising, 20 December 1987', Israel Foreign
Ministry, historical documents 1984–1988, no. 307, www.mfa.gov.il/MFA.

9 'Statement in the Knesset by Defense Minister Rabin, 23 December 1987', Israel
Foreign Ministry, historical documents 1984–1988, no. 312, www.mfa.gov.il/
MFA.

10 Avner Cohen, author interview, Moshav Tekuma, 7 May 2009.

11 Hamas communiqué no. 3, February 1988.

12 Mohammed Barghouti, author interview, Ramallah, 7 October 1989.

13 Musa Abu Marzouq, author interview, Beirut, 22 March 2005.

14 Hamas communiqué, 'In memory of the massacres of Qibyah and Kufr
Qassam', 5 October 1988.

15 Mahmoud Musleh, author interview, Ramallah, 12 January 2009.

16 Hamas communiqué, 'In memory of the massacres of Qibyah and Kufr
Qassam', 5 October 1988.

17 Bashir Barghouti, author interview, Ramallah, 26 March 1990.

18 Dr Riad al-Agha, author interview, Gaza City, 28 November 1989.

19 Marwan Gheneim, author interview, Ramallah, 27 March 1990.

20 'News reports', *Crescent International*, September 1988, pp. 5–6.

21 UNLU communiqué, 'Appeal on the Feast of Independence', 20 November
1988.

22 'Grassroots forcing change in Hamas?', *Muslimedia*, 16–31 December 1989.

23 Ibid.

24 Dr Mahmoud Zahar, author interview, Islamic University of Gaza, 12 February
1990.

25 'Interview with Defense Minister Rabin on Israel Television (Arabic Service),
27 July 1989', Israel Foreign Ministry, historical documents 1988–1992, no. 85,
www.mfa.gov.il/MFA.

26 Dr Raanan Gissin, author interview, Jerusalem, 7 March 2007.

27 Avner Cohen, author interview, Moshav Tekuma, 7 May 2009.

28 Brigadier General Shalom Harari, author note, Jerusalem Institute for
Contemporary Affairs lecture, Jerusalem, 9 January 2007.

29 'Sheikh tried for army deaths', *The Times*, 4 January 1990.
30 Abu Issa, author interview, Gaza City, 11 March 1990.
31 Abu Zaki Mohammed al-Radwan, author interview, Gaza City, 11 March 1990.
32 'Marxists and Moslem fundamentalists in areas join in move against Fatah', *Jerusalem Post*, 2 April 1990, p. 1.
33 Dr Mahmoud Zahar, author interview, Gaza City, 1 September 1992.
34 Hamas communiqué, 'Toledano kidnapping', 12 December 1992.
35 Dr Atef Adwan, author interview, Gaza City, 11 September 2002.
36 Yitzhak Rabin, speech to the Israeli Knesset, Israel Government Press Office, 21 December 1992.
37 Dr Abdel Aziz Rantissi, author interview, Gaza City, 10 September 2002.
38 See A. Gowers and T. Walker, *Arafat: the biography* (London: Virgin, 1994), p. 162.
39 Dr Mahmoud Zahar, author interview, Gaza City, 29 May 1995.

Chapter 5   Oslo and 'Vain Endeavours'

1 H. Salman, 'Interview with Musa Abu Marzouq', *al-Safir*, 25 August 1994, p. 1.
2 'Mideast accord: statements by leaders at the signing of the Middle East pact', *New York Times*, 14 September 1993.
3 Hamas communiqué, issued 30 August 1993.
4 Dr Mahmoud Zahar, author interview, Gaza City, 29 May 1995.
5 Hamas communiqué, issued 7 September 1993.
6 F. Al-Shubayl, 'Hamas spokesman on strategy', *al-Wasat*, 25 October 1993, p. 5.
7 Hamas communiqué, issued 8 October 1993.
8 H. Salman, 'Interview with Musa Abu Marzouq', *al-Safir*, 25 August 1994, p. 1.
9 Anonymous, author interview, Beirut, 22 March 2005.
10 M. Abu Marzook, 'Hamas is ready to talk', *The Guardian*, 16 August 2007.
11 Hamas Covenant, Article 13: August 1988, http://avalon.law.yale.edu/20th_century/hamas.asp.
12 Hamas Covenant, Article 34: 'Across history in confronting the invaders', August 1988, http://avalon.law.yale.edu/20th_century/hamas.asp.
13 Ibid.
14 Hamas communiqué, 'The Gaza–Jericho Accord', issued 29 August 1993.
15 Mohammad Issa, author interview, Aida refugee camp, West Bank, 30 June 1994.
16 'PNA plan for confrontation', document, February 1995.
17 President Yasser Arafat, author interview, Muqata, Ramallah, 12 July 2004.
18 Dr Mahmoud Zahar, author interview, Gaza City, 29 May 1995.

19 Mohammed Nazzal, 'Hamas is planning to inherit the PLO', *al-Wasat*, 5 October 1993, pp. 3–4.
20 Dr Abdelrahman Bsaiso, author interview, Gaza City, 14 March 2007.
21 Ismail Abu Shanab, author interview, Gaza City, 13 September 2002.
22 Abu Islam, Izz ad-Din al-Qassam Brigades, author interview, Gaza City, 18 March 1995.
23 'Rabin's speech extracts', *New York Times*, 1 March 1994.
24 Hamas communiqué, 'The settlers will pay for the massacre with the blood of their hearts', February 1994.
25 *Daily Mail*, 14 April 1994.
26 Musa Abu Marzouq, author interview, Beirut, 22 March 2005.
27 Dr Abdel Aziz Rantissi, author interview, Gaza City, 14 September 2002.
28 Usama Hamdan, author interview, Beirut, 22 March 2005.
29 Hamas communiqué, 'Rabin's attempt to cover up his failing criminal policies', 16 April 1994.
30 *Palestine Report*, 23 October 1994, p. 1.
31 Jibril Rajoub, author interview, Jericho, 27 March 2000.
32 Colonel Nasr Yusuf, author interview, Gaza City, 14 July 1995.
33 Jibril Rajoub, author interview, Jericho, 20 October 1999.
34 Hamas statement, issued 1 July 1994.
35 Ibrahim Ghosheh, *Al-Sharq al-Awsat*, 16 August 1994, p. 18.
36 Mohammed Abu Warda, in Serge Schmemann, 'Target was Israeli government, says Arab linked to 3 bombings', *New York Times*, 7 March 1996.
37 Youssef M. Ibrahim, 'Hamas political chief says group can't curb terrorists', *New York Times*, 9 March 1996.
38 Bassam Jarrar, author interview, El-Bireh, 22 May 1995.
39 Bassam Attiyah, author interview, Ramallah, 13 March 1996.
40 Sheikh Ahmed Yassin, press conference, Gaza City, 6 October 1997.

Chapter 6   The Second Intifada

1 Jamila al-Shanti, Hamas MP, author interview, Gaza City, 19 March 2008.
2 Senior Israeli intelligence official, author interview, Jerusalem, 3 November 2002.
3 Palestinian Human Rights Monitoring Group, East Jerusalem, www.phrmg.org.
4 Israeli Ministry of Foreign Affairs, www.mfa.gov.il.
5 Sheikh Nizar Rayan, in James Bennet, 'Mideast balance sheet', *New York Times*, 22 March 2002.
6 Dr Abdel Aziz Rantissi, author interview, Gaza City, 22 June 2002.
7 Stephen Farrell, 'Palestine militants deny suspicions of involvement; terror in America', *The Times*, 12 September 2001.
8 Israeli Prime Minister's Office, author interview, Jerusalem, 13 September 2001.

9 Phil Reeves, 'Sharon appeals to America not to "appease" Arabs', *The Independent*, 5 October 2001.

10 Charles Grassley, in Stephen Farrell and Nicholas Blanford, 'Sharon brands Arafat as another bin Laden', *The Times*, 14 September 2001.

11 Yoram Schweitzer, Ehud Sprinzak, author interviews, Jerusalem, 13 September 2001.

12 'Terrorist attack on bus at Immanuel, December 12, 2001', Israeli Ministry of Foreign Affairs, www.mfa.gov.il.

13 Prime Minister Ariel Sharon, author interview, Jerusalem, 3 November 2002.

14 Senior Israeli intelligence official, author interview, Ashkelon, 3 November 2002.

15 Abu Ahmed, author interview, Gaza City, 26 July 2003.

16 Abu Yousef, NSF commander, author interview, Gaza City, 29 July 2003.

17 Palestinian Center for Policy and Survey Research, Ramallah, 19–24 December 2001, www.pcpsr.org.

18 Development Studies Programme, Bir Zeit University, Poll no. 8, 12 August 2002.

19 Ismail Abu Shanab, author interview, Gaza City, 20 June 2002.

20 Dr Mahmoud Zahar, author interview, Gaza City, 19 June 2002.

21 Senior Israeli military official, author interview, 5 March 2002.

22 Palestine Red Crescent Society, www.palestinercs.org/humanitarian_Arch. aspx?cat_id=20, accessed 15 Nov 2009; Israeli Ministry of Foreign Affairs, *Victims of Palestinian Violence and Terrorism since September 2000*, www.israel-mfa.gov.il (accessed 10 October 2008).

23 Hussein Abu Kweik, author interview, Ramallah, 4 March 2002.

24 Danny Ben Simon, author interview, Jerusalem, 1 March 2002.

25 Danny Ayalon, author interview, Jerusalem, 27 February 2002.

26 Dr Abdel Aziz Rantissi, *New York Times*, 9 February 2002.

27 Sheikh Hassan Yousef, author interview, El Bireh, 4 March 2002.

28 Senior Israeli military official, author interview, Tel Aviv, 5 March 2002.

29 Al Aqsa Martyrs' Brigades leader, author interview, Ramallah, 22 March 2002.

30 Qadura Fares, author interview, Ramallah, 3 May 2002.

31 Hussein ash-Sheikh, author interview, Ramallah, 22 June 2002.

32 Senior Israeli military official, author interview, Jerusalem, 5 March 2002.

33 Efrat, author interview, Jerusalem, 9 March 2002.

34 Hamas communiqué, issued 27 March 2002.

35 Paulette Cohen, author interview, Netanya, 17 April 2002.

36 Arye Mekel, author interview, Jerusalem, 28 March 2002.

37 Amram Mitzna, in Ross Dunn and Stephen Farrell, 'Sharon orders assault on Palestinian terrorism as bomber kills 14 Israelis', *The Times*, 1 April 2002.

38 Meir Sheetrit, Reuters, 1 April 2002

39 Abed Rahman, author interview, Nablus, 10 April 2002.

40 Mustafa, author interview, Nablus, 10 April 2002.

41 Mahmoud al-Aloul, author interview, Nablus, 10 April 2002.

42 Jamila al-Shanti, author interview, Gaza City, 19 March 2008.
43 Israeli Ministry of Foreign Affairs, 'What happened in Jenin?', www.mfa.gov.
   il/MFA/MFAArchive/2000_2009/2002/8/Answers+to+Frequently+Asked+
   Questions-+Palestinian.htm#force.
44 UNISPAL, April 2002, citing AFP and Reuters.
45 'Anti-Israeli terrorism, 2006: data, analysis and trends', Intelligence and
   Terrorism Information Center at the Center for Special Studies, March 2007.
46 'Shin Bet, 2004 terrorism data', www.mfa.gov.il/MFA/MFAArchive/ 2000_
   2009/2005/Summary+of+Terrorist+Activity+2004.htm.
47 The Palestinian Human Rights Monitoring Group, East Jerusalem, www.
   phrmg.org/aqsa/fatalities_list.htm.
48 'Suicide bombing terrorism during the current Israeli–Palestinian confrontation (September 2000 – December 2005)', 1 January 2006, Intelligence
   and Terrorism Information Center; www.terrorism-info.org.il/malam_
   multimedia/English/eng_n/pdf/suicide_terrorism_ae.pdf.
49 The Palestinian Human Rights Monitoring Group, East Jerusalem, www.
   phrmg.org/aqsa/fatalities_list.htm.
50 Ismail Abu Shanab, author interview, Gaza City, 15 September 2002.
51 'Defence minister: Israel prepared to "liquidate" Hamas terrorists', *Israel Insider*,
   30 January 2006; http://web.israelinsider.com/Articles/Security/7676.htm.

Chapter 7   The Qassam Brigades

1 Dr Abdel Aziz Rantissi, author interview, Gaza City, 22 June 2002.
2 www.alqassam.ps/english/.
3 Abu Mohammed, author interview, Gaza City, 16 July 2008.
4 Maher Shaban, author interview, Shatti refugee camp, Gaza Strip, 9 March
   2006.
5 Dr Abdel Aziz Rantissi, author interview, Gaza City, 22 June 2002.
6 Israel Defence Forces spokesman, 22 March 2004, www.mfa.gov.il/MFA/
   Terrorism.
7 Israeli Ministry of Foreign Affairs, 22 March 2004, www.mfa.gov.il.
8 Israeli Ministry of Foreign Affairs, 18 April 2004, www.israelemb.org/arti-
   cles/2004/April/2004041700.htm.
9 Israeli government official, interview for *The Times*, Jerusalem, 27 September
   2006.
10 Usama Hamdan, author interview, Sidon, 6 October 2006.
11 Mohammed, author interview, Gaza Strip, 15 March 2007.
12 Abu Khalil, author interview, Gaza Strip, 15 March 2007.
13 Mohammed, author interview, Gaza Strip, 15 March 2007.
14 Sheikh Saleh al-Arouri, author interview, Aroura, 25 March 2007.
15 Mohammed, author interview, Gaza Strip, 15 March 2007.
16 *The Times*, 4 January 1990.
17 Abu Khalil, author interview, Gaza Strip, 15 March 2007.

18 Ministry of Foreign Affairs, 'Ahmed Yassin, leader of Hamas terrorist organiza-
     tion', 22 March 2004, www.mfa.gov.il/MFA/Terrorism+Obstacle+to+Peace/
     Terror+Groups/Ahmed+Yassin.htm.
19 Mohammed, author interview, Gaza Strip, 15 March 2007.
20 www.alqassam.ps/english/?action=aboutus.
21 Abu Khalil, author interview, Gaza Strip, 15 March 2007.
22 'Videotape transcript – killing collaborators: a Hamas how-to', *Harpers
     Magazine*, May 1993, p. 10.
23 Yizhar Be'er and Saleh Abdel-Jawad, *Collaborators in the Occupied Territories:
     Human Rights Abuses and Violations* (Jerusalem: B'Tselem, 1994), p. 128.
24 Dr Eyad Sarraj, author interview, Gaza City, 14 March 2007.
25 Sheikh Ahmed Yassin, interview by Saleh Abdel-Jawad and Yizhar Be'er,
     Ashmoret jail, Israel, 28 September 1993.
26 Sheikh Saleh al-Arouri, author interview, Aroura, 25 March 2007.
27 Ibid.
28 Ibid.
29 Mohammed Abu Teir, author interview, Jerusalem, 16 January 2006.
30 'The snake's head is smashed for now', *Ma'ariv*, 27 November 1998, p. B14.
31 R. Shaked, 'Abu Teir', *Yedioth Ahronoth*, 30 January 2006.
32 Mohammed Abu Teir, author interview, Jerusalem, 16 January 2006.
33 'Hamas operations: The glory record', 2001, www.jewishvirtuallibrary.org/
     jsource/Terrorism/Hamas2.html.
34 Abu Khalil, author interview, Gaza Strip, 15 March 2007.
35 Hamas communiqué, 'Rabin's attempt to cover up his failing criminal poli-
     cies', 16 April 1994.
36 Mushir al-Masri, author interview, Beit Hanoun, 19 March 2008.
37 Abu Mohammed, author interview, Gaza City, 16 July 2008.
38 Sheikh Hamid Beitawi, author interview, Nablus, 26 October 2006.
39 Yuval Diskin, Shin Bet director, press briefing, Jerusalem, 5 March 2007.
40 Mohammed Abu Teir, author interview, Jerusalem, 16 January 2006.
41 Knel Deeb, author interview, Gaza City, 23 July 2002.
42 Shimon Peres, comments to author, Jerusalem, 18 July 2002.
43 'Spain investigates claims of Israeli crimes against humanity in Gaza', *The
     Guardian*, 29 January 2009.
44 Gideon Meir, author interview, Jerusalem, 21 July 2002.
45 'The hospitality of the gun', Al Jazeera documentary, July 2006.
46 Israeli government official, author interview, Jerusalem, 27 September 2006.
47 Dr Abdel Aziz Rantissi, author interview, Gaza City, 9 July 2002.
48 Sayed Salem Abu Musameh, author interview, Gaza City, 4 July 2006.
49 Jamal Abu Hashem, author interview, Gaza City, 23 January 2007.
50 Abu Khaled, author interview, Gaza Strip, 20 March 2008.
51 US Department of State transcript, Jerusalem, 5 March 2008.
52 Abu Bakr Nofal, author interview, Gaza City, 6 September 2006.
53 Yuval Diskin, press briefing, Tel Aviv, 5 March 2007.
54 Abu Khaled, author interview, Gaza Strip, 20 March 2008.

55 Abu Mohammed, author interview, Gaza City, 16 July 2008.
56 Dr Eyad Sarraj, author interview, Gaza City, 13 March 2007.
57 Avi Dichter, speech at Jerusalem Centre for Public Affairs, 12 March 2007.

Chapter 8   The Martyr Syndrome

1 Khaled Meshaal, Hamas leader, statement on Gaza crisis, 28 December 2008.
2 Mohammed, author interview, Gaza Strip, 15 March 2007.
3 Anonymous, author interview, Jenin refugee camp, 11 September 2001.
4 Ibid.
5 Ibid.
6 Hamas Covenant, Article 8, http://avalon.law.yale.edu/20th_century/hamas.asp.
7 Sheikh Ahmed Yassin, author interview, Gaza City, 13 June 2003.
8 Ibid.
9 Dr Eyad Sarraj, author interview, Gaza City, 13 March 2007.
10 Ibid.
11 Ibid.
12 Yaghi Yaghi, author interview, Gaza, 13 November 2006.
13 Mohammed, author interview, Gaza City, 15 March 2007.
14 Hamas Covenant, Article 35, August 1988, http://avalon.law.yale.edu/20th_century/hamas.asp.
15 Dr Atef Adwan, author interview, Islamic University of Gaza, Gaza City, 8 September 2002.
16 Anonymous, to Reem Makhoul, Nablus, 7 July 2007.
17 Anonymous, senior Israeli military official, press briefing, Tel Aviv, 9 October 2002.
18 Abu Ashraf, author interview, Beit Lahiya, Gaza, 21 July 2003.
19 Sheikh Ahmed Yassin, author interview, Gaza City, 20 July 2003.
20 'Suicide bombing terrorism during the current Israeli–Palestinian confrontation (September 2000 – December 2005)', 1 January 2006, Intelligence and Terrorism Information Center; www.terrorism-info.org.il/malam_multimedia/English/eng_n/pdf/suicide_terrorism_ae.pdf.
21 Israeli Ministry of Foreign Affairs, *Victims of Palestinian Violence and Terrorism since September 2000*, www.israel-mfa.gov.il (accessed 10 October 2008).
22 Palestine Red Crescent Society, www.palestinercs.org.
23 Ghassan Khatib, author interview, Ramallah, 22 June 2002.
24 Dr Abdel Aziz Rantissi, author interview, Gaza City, 17 March 2004.
25 Ibid., 22 June 2002.
26 Anonymous, author interview, Gaza City, 17 March 2004.
27 Umm Mohammed [Rantissi], author interview, Beit Hanoun, Gaza Strip, 13 July 2005.
28 Dr Abdel Aziz Rantissi, author interview, Gaza City, 22 June 2002.

29 Sheikh Ahmed Yassin, author interview, Gaza City, 13 June 2003.
30 Dr Abdel Aziz Rantissi, author interview, Gaza City, 22 June 2002.
31 Ibid.
32 C. Price Jones, 'Speaker says terrorists are normal people', *Michigan Daily*, 2 December 2002.
33 *Al Quds*, 19 June 2002.
34 Colonel Noam, Israel Defence Forces, author interview, Nablus, 2 October 2002.
35 Ghassan Shakah, author interview, Nablus, 2 October 2002.
36 Husam Khader, author interview, Nablus, 2 October 2002.
37 'Bomber's family hits out at Islamic Jihad', *The Guardian*, 16 January 2004.
38 *New York Times*, 24 September 2001.
39 Usama Hamdan, author interview, Beirut, 22 March 2005.
40 Mohammed, author interview, Gaza, 15 March 2007.
41 Dr Abdel Aziz Rantissi, author interview, Gaza, 17 March 2004.
42 Mushir al-Masri, author interview, Gaza City, 9 July 2005.
43 Stephen Farrell, *The Times*, 11 April 2006.
44 Abu Ali, author interview, Beit Lahiya, 16 July 2008.
45 Israel Defence Forces spokesman, author interview, 8 November 2006.
46 Ghazi Hamad, in Stephen Farrell, 'Israel braced for revenge attack after dawn barrage kills family', *The Times*, 9 November 2006.
47 Mohammed Yasji, author interview, Beit Hanoun, 5 November 2006.
48 Abu Sharif Basyouni, author interview, Beit Hanoun, 5 November 2006.
49 Major Rafi Laderman, author interview, Jerusalem, 19 April 2002.
50 Israeli Ministry of Foreign Affairs, 'The exploitation of children for terrorist purposes', 15 January 2003, www.mfa.gov.il.
51 Isaac Herzog, Israeli minister of social welfare, 8 January 2009, www.radione-therlands.nl/currentaffairs/region/middleeast/090108-israel-herzog-mc.
52 Ilan Tal, Israel Defence Forces spokesman, www.hurriyet.com.tr/english/domestic/10735803.asp?scr=1.
53 Malcolm Smart, Amnesty International statement, 8 January 2009.
54 Umm Subhi, interviewed by Hassan Jabr, Gaza City, 11 January 2009.
55 Israeli Prime Minister's Office, PM Netanyahu's remarks at the start of the cabinet meeting, www.pmo.gov.il/PMOEng/Communication/Spokesman/2009/10/spokestart011009.htm.
56 Mohammed Odeh, author interview, Tulkarem, 25 March 2007.
57 Mohammed and Ala'a Zakout, author interview, Gaza City, 3 November 2006.
58 Mohammed Abu al-Jidyan, author interview, Gaza City, 3 November 2006.
59 Umm Suheib, 'Hamas women vow martyrdom', statement to Al Aqsa TV, broadcast 30 December 2008; www.youtube.com/watch?v=5iGyc9gvD-U.
60 Israel Defence Forces, http://dover.idf.il/IDF/English/News/the_Front/.
61 *Associated Press*, 1 January 2009.
62 Ahmed Mohammed Dardona, author interview, east Jabalia, 29 January 2009.

63 Issaber Aziz, author interview, east Jabalia, 29 January 2009.
64 Shahab ad-Din Abul el-Aish, author interview, Izbit Abed Rabbo, Gaza Strip, 29 January 2009.
65 Giora Eiland, *New York Times*, 18 January 2008.
66 Anonymous, author interview, Ramallah, 28 December 2008.

Chapter 9   Harvesting

1   Mushir al-Masri, author interview, Gaza City, 6 September 2006.
2   Ghassan Khatib, author interview, Jerusalem, 22 June 2002.
3   Amjad Shawa, author interview, Gaza City, 14 July 2008.
4   Yuval Diskin, Shin Bet director, briefing to foreign journalists, Tel Aviv, 5 March 2007.
5   Abdullah, author interview, Gaza City, 15 July 2008.
6   Fayez, author interview, Gaza City, 15 July 2008.
7   Israeli Ministry of Foreign Affairs, 'The exploitation of children for terrorist purposes', 15 January 2003, www.mfa.gov.il.
8   Riham al-Wakil, author interview, Gaza City, 15 July 2008.
9   Anonymous, author interview, Gaza City, 15 July 2008.
10 Hamas Covenant, Article 16, http://avalon.law.yale.edu/20th_century/hamas.asp.
11 Hamas Covenant, Article 21, http://avalon.law.yale.edu/20th_century/hamas.asp.
12 Anonymous senior PA official, author interview, Nablus, 26 May 2009.
13 Anonymous senior Israeli intelligence official, author interview, Ashkelon, 3 November 2002.
14 Israeli Foreign Ministry, 'The financial sources of the Hamas terror organization', 30 July 2003, www.mfa.gov.il.
15 Ibid.
16 White House executive order 12947, 'Prohibiting transactions with terrorists who threaten to disrupt the Middle East peace process', 23 January 1995, www.treas.gov/offices/enforcement/ofac/legal/eo/12947.pdf.
17 US Department of the Treasury, Office of Terrorism and Financial Intelligence, additional background information on charities designated under executive order 13224, www.treas.gov/offices/enforcement/key-issues/protecting/charities_execorder_13224-e.shtml.
18 US Department of the Treasury, Office of Public Affairs, 'US designates five charities funding Hamas and six senior Hamas leaders as terrorist entities', 22 August 2003, www.treas.gov/press/releases/js672.htm.
19 US Department of the Treasury, additional background information on charities designated under executive order 13224, www.treas.gov/offices/enforcement/keyissues/protecting/charities_execorder_13224-a.shtml.
20 Usama Hamdan, author interview, Sidon, Lebanon, 6 October 2006.
21 Usama Hamdan, author interview, Beirut, 6 February 2007.

22 HM Treasury, 'Consolidated list of financial sanctions targets in the UK', http://www.hm-treasury.gov.uk/d/sanctionsconlist.htm.

23 Summaries of EU legislation, 'Freezing funds: list of terrorists and terrorist groups', http://europa.eu/legislation_summaries/justice_freedom_security/fight_against_terrorism/l33208_en.htm.

24 Foreign and Commonwealth Office spokesperson, 27 June 2009.

25 Ibid.

26 Tom Lantos, Committee on International Relations, US House of Representatives, http://commdocs.house.gov/committees/intlrel/hfa26332.000/hfa26332_0f.htm.

27 Robert Malley, US Senate Committee on Foreign Relations, Hearing on the Middle East after the Palestinian elections, 15 March 2006.

28 Yuval Diskin, Shin Bet director, briefing to foreign journalists, Tel Aviv, 5 March 2007.

29 Brigadier Tawfiq Jabr, chief of police, author interview, Gaza City, 15 July 2008.

30 Office of Foreign Assets Control, US Department of the Treasury, 'Terrorist assets report', calendar year 2007.

31 Ismail Haniyeh, author interview, Shatti refugee camp, Gaza City, 22 July 2002.

32 Abu George, author interview, Gaza City, 12 November 2006.

33 Ismail Haniyeh, quoted in R. Ben Efrat, 'Hamas encounters reality', *Challenge Magazine*, May/June 2006.

34 Ghassan Mohammed, author interview, Hebron, 7 July 2008.

35 Israeli Ministry of Foreign Affairs, 'IDF operates against institutes associated with Hamas in Hebron', 26 February 2008, www.mfa.gov.il.

36 Ghassan Mohammed, author interview, Hebron, 7 July 2008.

37 Mohammed Daraghmeh and Dalia Nammari, 'Hamas orders book of Palestinian folk tales pulled from schools', *The Independent*, 6 March 2007.

38 BBC News, Middle East, 8 March 2007, http://news.bbc.co.uk/2/hi/middle_east/6426441.stm.

39 Dr Naser Eddin al-Shaer, author interview, Nablus, 12 January 2009.

40 ANSA news agency, Ramallah, 6 July 2005.

41 Hamas Covenant, Article 19: 'The role of Islamic art in the battle of liberation', August 1988, http://avalon.law.yale.edu/20th_century/hamas.asp.

42 Dr Mahmoud Zahar, in Stephen Farrell, 'No dancing and no gays if Hamas gets its way', *The Times*, 7 October 2005.

43 Naima al-Sheikh Ali, author interview, Gaza City, 13 March 2007.

44 Riham al-Wakil, author interview, Gaza City, 15 July 2008.

45 Mehdi Lebouachera, 'The cursed gypsies of conservative Gaza Strip', Agence France Presse, 27 October 2006.

46 Nabil Kafarneh, author interview, Beit Hanoun, 14 March 2007.

47 Swords of Islamic Righteousness communiqué, Gaza City, 20 December 2006.

48 Fawzi Barhoum, author interview, Gaza City, 21 December 2006.

49 Anonymous internet café owner #1, author interview, Gaza Strip, 16 July 2008.
50 Anonymous internet café owner #2, author interview, Gaza Strip, 16 July 2008.
51 Mohammed Shahab, author interview, Jabalia Town, 9 June 2002.
52 Mohammad Azaliya, author interview, Jabalia Town, 9 June 2002.
53 Release from Israeli prime minister's media adviser, 22 November 2006.
54 Sakkar Abu Hein, author interview, Gaza City, 27 November 2006.
55 UN–OCHA Special Focus report, November 2006, www.ochaopt.org/documents/OCHA_Special_focus_8_Nov_2006_Eng.pdf.
56 Saher Jarbouah, author interview, Rafah, 15 September 2006.
57 Nasser Barhoum, author interview, Rafah, 15 September 2006.
58 Ghazi Hamad, author interview, Rafah, 15 September 2006.
59 United Nations Conference on Trade and Development (UNCTAD) report: *Intensified Aid and Urgent Action Needed to Avert Palestinian Economic Collapse*, 12 September 2006.
60 Shlomo Dror, author telephone interview, 15 September 2006.
61 Riham al-Wakil, author interview, Gaza City, 15 July 2008.
62 Mushir al-Masri, author interview, Gaza City, 6 September 2006.
63 Dr Ismail al-Ashqar, author interview, Gaza City, 28 January 2009.

Chapter 10   Women

1 Hamas Covenant, Articles 17 and 18: 'The role of the Moslem woman', August 1988, http://avalon.law.yale.edu/20th_century/hamas.asp.
2 Jamila al-Shanti, author interview, Beit Hanoun, Gaza, 4 November 2006.
3 Hamas Covenant, Articles 17 and 18: 'The role of the Moslem woman', August 1988, http://avalon.law.yale.edu/20th_century/hamas.asp.
4 A. Schleifer, 'The life and thought of of Izz ad-Din al-Qassam', *Islamic Quarterly*, 23:2 (1979), p. 63.
5 Dr Mariam Abu Dagga, author interview, Gaza City, 14 March 2007.
6 Randa, author interview, Gaza City, 12 March 2007.
7 Umm Mohammed, author interview, Aida refugee camp, West Bank, 12 February 1989.
8 Umm Mohammed Rantissi, author interview, Beit Hanoun, 13 July 2005.
9 Naima al-Sheikh Ali, author interview, Gaza City, 14 March 2007.
10 Hamas Covenant, Article 17: 'The role of the Moslem woman', August 1988, http://avalon.law.yale.edu/20th_century/hamas.asp.
11 Ibid.
12 Dr Mahmoud Zahar, author interview, 29 May 1995.
13 Zeinab el-Ghunaimi, author interview, Gaza City, 14 March 2007.
14 Naima al-Sheikh Ali, author interview, Gaza City, 14 March 2007.
15 Al-Azzam family, author interview, Beit Lahiya, Gaza, 6 September 2006.
16 Reem, author interview, Gaza City, 19 March 2008.

17 Hanan, author interview, Khan Younis refugee camp, Gaza, 12 November 1989.
18 Dr Mahmoud Zahar, author interview, Gaza City, 23 January 2006.
19 Iman Abu Jazar, author interview, Islamic University of Gaza, 13 March 2007.
20 Dr Hanan Ashrawi, author interview, Ramallah, 20 March 2007.
21 Naima al-Sheikh Ali, author interview, Gaza City, 14 March 2007.
22 'Suicide bombing terrorism during the current Israeli–Palestinian confrontation (September 2000 – December 2005)', 1 January 2006, Intelligence and Terrorism Information Center; www.terrorism-info.org.il/malam_multimedia/English/eng_n/pdf/suicide_terrorism_ae.pdf.
23 Israeli Ministry of Foreign Affairs, *Victims of Palestinian Violence and Terrorism since September 2000*, www.israel-mfa.gov.il.
24 'We don't need women suicide bombers: Hamas spiritual leader', Agence France Presse, 2 February 2002.
25 Ibid.
26 Dr Ismail al-Ashqar, author interview, Gaza City, 19 March 2008.
27 Abu Aisheh family, author interview, Nablus, 28 February 2002.
28 Ibid.
29 Sheikh Hassan Yousef, author interview, el-Bireh, 4 March 2002.
30 Israeli Foreign Ministry, 'The role of Palestinian women in suicide terrorism', January 2003, www.mfa.gov.il/MFA/MFAArchive.
31 Israeli Ministry of Foreign Affairs, 'Terror victims 2004', www.mfa.gov.il.
32 Mohammed, author interview, Gaza City, 15 March 2007.
33 Jamila al-Shanti, author interview, Gaza City, 19 March 2008.
34 Al Aqsa television, 8 March 2007.
35 Tim McGirk, 'Palestinian moms becoming martyrs', *Time*, 3 May 2007.
36 Israeli Ministry of Foreign Affairs, 'The role of Palestinian women in suicide terrorism', January 2003, www.mfa.gov.il/MFA/MFAArchive.
37 Israeli Ministry of Foreign Affairs, 'Summary of terrorist activity 2004', 5 January 2005, www.mfa.gov.il.
38 Jamila al-Shanti, author interview, Gaza City, 19 March 2008.
39 Family of Fatima al-Najjar, author interview, Beit Hanoun, 27 November 2006.
40 Majdi Hamouda, author interview, Beit Hanoun, 27 November 2006.
41 Israel Defence Forces spokeswoman, author interview by telephone, 3 November 2006.
42 Abu Obaida, author interview, Gaza Strip, 3 November 2006.
43 Interview with commander of Hamas women's armed wing, *al-Risala*, 18 August 2005.
44 Aziza Abu Ghabin, author interview, Beit Lahiya, 13 September 2005.
45 Anonymous, author interview, Gaza City, 14 March 2007.
46 Mohammed el-Kafarneh, author interview, Beit Hanoun, 13 September 2005.
47 Anonymous, author interview, Beit Hanoun, 13 September 2005.
48 Umm Nidal [Maryam Farahat], Hamas video, March 2002.
49 Umm Nidal [Maryam Farahat], author interview, Gaza City, 28 January 2006.

50 Dr Hanan Ashrawi, author interview, Ramallah, 20 March 2007.
51 Naima al-Sheikh Ali, author interview, Gaza City, 14 March 2007.
52 Salah Bardaweel, 'The woman . . . who is she', *al-Resalah*, March 2007.
53 Umm Usama, author interview, Gaza City, 6 September 2006.
54 Zainab, author interview, Gaza City, 6 September 2006.
55 Suha, author interview, Gaza City, 14 March 2007.
56 Naima al-Sheikh Ali, author interview, Gaza City, 14 March 2007.
57 Mona Shawa, author interview, Gaza City, 14 March 2007.
58 Huda Naim, author interview, Gaza, 12 February 2006.
59 Iman Abu Jazar, author interview, Islamic University of Gaza, 13 March 2007.
60 Dr Hanan Ashrawi, author interview, Ramallah, 20 March 2007.
61 Umm Mohammed Rantissi, author interview, Beit Hanoun, 13 July 2005.
62 Abed Hamdan, author interview, Islamic University of Gaza, 13 March 2007.

Chapter 11   A House Divided

1 Dr Mahmoud Zahar, author interview, Gaza City, 23 January 2007.
2 Dr Mariam Abu Dagga, author interview, Gaza City, 14 March 2007.
3 Abu Mohammed, author interview, Nusseirat refugee camp, Gaza Strip, 6 September 1993.
4 Assad Saftawi, author interview, Gaza City, 20 December 1989. An Islamist, a member of the Muslim Brotherhood and a Fatah leader, Saftawi was assassinated by unknown assailants in the Gaza Strip on 21 October 1993.
5 Ibid.
6 Rafat Najar, author interview, Khan Younis refugee camp, 19 December 1989.
7 Assad Saftawi, author interview, Gaza City, 20 December 1989.
8 Abu Mahmoud, author interview, Khan Younis refugee camp, 7 November 1989.
9 Sheikh Mahmoud Musleh, author interview, Ramallah, 12 January 2009.
10 W. Claiborne, 'Brotherhood blooms on the West Bank', *Washington Post*, 15 March 1982, p. 12.
11 Dr Abu Dajani, author interview, Nablus, 14 March 1990.
12 Dr Mahmoud Zahar, author interview, Islamic University of Gaza, 12 February 1990.
13 Ashraf al-Masri, author interview, Gaza City, 13 September 2006.
14 Hamas communiqué, 'In memory of the massacres of Qibyah and Qufr Qassam', 5 October 1988.
15 Dr Mahmoud Zahar, author interview, Gaza City, 1 September 1992.
16 Dr Abdel Aziz Rantissi, author interview, Gaza City, 14 July 2002.
17 Dr Mahmoud Zahar, author interview, Gaza City, 1 September 1992.
18 Sheikh Ahmed Yassin, author interview, Gaza City, 12 July 2002.
19 Hamas communiqué, no. 28, 1 September 1988.
20 President Yasser Arafat, author interview, Muqata, Ramallah, 4 August 2004.
21 Dr Mahmoud Zahar, author interview, Gaza City, 8 September 1994.

22 Ariel Sharon, *Jerusalem Post*, 13 September 1995.

23 Bassam Jarrar, author interview, el-Bireh, 22 May 1995.

24 Roni Ben-Yeshai, 'Anatomy of suicide', *Yedioth Ahronoth*, 27 January 1995, p. 7.

25 Dr Mahmoud Zahar, author interview, Gaza City, 29 May 1995.

26 Dr Abdel Aziz Rantissi, author interview, Gaza City, 10 September 2002.

27 Mohammed Dahlan, author interview, Gaza City, 30 July 2003.

28 Abu Mohammed-Mohammed, author interview, Gaza City, 9 September 2002.

29 Abu Bilal, author interview, Ministry of Interior, Gaza City, 13 September 2006.

30 Nabil Abu Rudeineh, author interview, Gaza City, 16 July 2005.

31 Ibrahim Abu Thuraya, author interview, Gaza City, 16 July 2005.

32 Mohammed, author interview, Gaza City, 16 July 2005.

33 Ismail Haniyeh, author note, Friday sermon, Sheikh Ahmed Yassin mosque, Gaza, 23 June 2006.

34 Ahmad Yousef, author interview, Gaza City, 23 January 2007.

35 Dr Mahmoud Zahar, author interview, Gaza City, 23 January 2007.

36 Abu Wassim, author interview, The Ship, Gaza Strip, 23 January 2007.

37 Dr Abdel Aziz Rantissi, author interview, Gaza, 10 September 2002.

38 Mushir al-Masri, author interview, Beit Lahiya, Gaza Strip, 13 September 2005.

39 Dore Gold, 'Saudi Arabia's dubious denials of involvement in international terrorism', Jerusalem Center for Public Affairs, 1 October 2003.

40 Usama Hamdan, author interview, Beirut, 6 June 2004.

41 Avi Dichter, author note, Jerusalem, 12 March 2007.

42 Mossad analyst, author interview, Jerusalem, 17 September 2006.

43 Abu Obaida, author interview, Gaza Strip, 30 October 2006.

44 A. A., Egyptian security official, author interview, Gaza City, 29 October 2006.

45 Y. I., Preventive Security Organization, author interview, Gaza City, 29 October 2006.

46 Baha Baloush, author interview, Ramallah, 30 June 2008.

47 Samira Tayeh, author interview, Ramallah, 4 April 2008.

48 Dr Ahmad Yousef, author interview, Gaza City, 24 January 2007.

49 Da'as Qanna, author interview, Nablus, 22 January 2007.

Chapter 12   Bullet and Ballot

1 H. el-Barghouti, *Al-Hayat Al-Jadida*, 21 October 2008.

2 Dr Ahmad Sa'ati, author interview, Gaza City, 8 September 1994.

3 Musa Abu Marzouq, *al-Safir*, 25 August 1994, p. 1.

4 Yehya Moussa Abbadsa, author interview, Gaza City, March 19 2008.

5 Dr Mahmoud Zahar, author interview, Gaza City, 29 May 1995.

6 Dr Ahmad Yousef, author interview, Gaza City, 18 March 2008.

7 Jamila al-Shanti, author interview, Gaza City, 19 March 2008.

8 Jerusalem Media and Communication Centre, public opinion poll no. 44, March 2002.

9 Hussain ash-Sheikh, author interview, Ramallah, 22 June 2002.
10 Sheikh Hassan Yousef, author interview, Ramallah, 15 May 2002.
11 Dr Ghassan Khatib, author interview, Ramallah, 22 June 2002.
12 Hussain ash-Sheikh, author interview, Ramallah, 22 June 2002.
13 Dr Khalil Shikaki, author interview, Ramallah, 16 May 2002.
14 Dr Abdel Aziz Rantissi, author interview, Gaza, 22 June 2002.
15 Dr Ghassan Khatib, author interview, Ramallah, 22 June 2002.
16 Ismail Abu Shanab, author interview, Gaza, 7 November 2002.
17 Dr Abdel Aziz Rantissi, author interview, Gaza, 22 June 2002.
18 Senior Israeli military official, author interview, Tel Aviv, 5 March 2002.
19 Professor Ali al-Jarbawi, author interview, 12 September 2002
20 Abu Fadi, author interview, Ramallah, 26 March 2003.
21 Usama Hamdan, author interview, Beirut, 22 March 2005.
22 Dr Khalil Shikaki, author interview, Yale University, 25 October 2006.
23 Husam Khader, author interview, Balata refugee camp, Nablus, 2 November 2002.
24 Fares Mohammed, author interview, Ramallah, 12 July 2003.
25 Michael Tarazi, author interview, Gaza, 16 June 2003.
26 Dr Mahmoud Zahar, Associated Press, 7 February 2003.
27 Khaled Meshaal, author interview, Damascus, 2 August 2007.
28 Heraclitus, 'You can't step twice into the same river', quoted in Plato, *Cratylus* (*The Yale Book of Quotations*, Yale University Press, 2006).
29 Salah al-Bardaweel, author interview, Gaza, 7 July 2005.
30 Ambassador Dr Abdelrahman Bsaiso, author interview, Gaza City, 14 March 2007.
31 Yehya Moussa Abbadsa, author interview, Gaza City, 19 March 2008.
32 Brigadier General Nizar Ammar, author interview, Gaza, 19 January 2005.
33 Munir Miqdar, author interview, Ein Hilweh refugee camp, Lebanon, 8 October 2006.
34 Dr Mahmoud Zahar, author interview, Gaza City, 5 April 2005
35 Nidal Jaloud, author interview, Qalqilya, 8 May 2005.
36 Umm Wael, author interview, Qalqilya, 8 May 2005.
37 Mohammed al-Masri, author interview, Beit Lahiya, Gaza, 10 July 2005.
38 Dr Ahmad Yousef, author interview, Gaza City, 18 March 2008.
39 Dr Mahmoud Zahar, *Asharq al-Awsat*, 18 August 2005.
40 Yehya Moussa Abbadsa, author interview, Gaza, 19 March 2008.
41 Dr Ibrahim Ibrach, author interview, Gaza, 19 December 2006.
42 Dr Ismail al-Ashqar, author interview, Gaza City, 19 March 2006.
43 Mushir al-Masri, author interview, Gaza Strip, 9 July 2005.
44 Musa Abu Marzouq, author interview, Beirut, 22 March 2005.
45 White House, Office of the Press Secretary, 26 May 2005.
46 Jamila al-Shanti, author interview, Gaza City, 19 March 2008.
47 Sheikh Mohammed Abu Teir, author interview, Jerusalem, 16 January 2006.
48 Sami Abu Zuhri, *The Times*, 20 January 2006.
49 Fatah election headquarters, author interview, Ramallah, 15 January 2006.

50 Mohammed Dahlan, author notes, Ramallah, 15 January 2006.
51 Diana Buttu, author interview, Ramallah, 20 March 2007.
52 Amani Abu Ramadan, author interview, Gaza City, 14 March 2007.
53 Nabil Shaath, author interview, Gaza City, 13 January 2006.
54 Dr Nashat Aqtash, author interview, Ramallah, 14 November 2006.
55 Tzipi Livni, in Stephen Farrell, 'Extremists who pose a new threat – at ballot box', *The Times*, 20 January 2006.
56 Tony Blair, in Stephen Farrell, 'Hamas tries to exploit its pariah status at ballot box', *The Times*, 24 January 2006.
57 Dr Mahmoud Zahar, author interview, Gaza City, 23 January 2006.
58 Mushir al-Masri, author interview, Gaza City, 16 July 2008.
59 Jarrett Blanc, 'Palestinian election analysis: how Hamas won the majority', International Foundation for Electoral Systems, 20 February 2006, www.ifes. org/features.html?title=How%20Hamas%20Won%20the%20Majority.

Chapter 13   Hamastan

1 Ismail Haniyeh, author note, Friday sermon at Sheikh Ahmed Yassin mosque, Gaza City, 23 June 2006.
2 Usama Hamdan, author interview, Beirut, 6 February 2007.
3 Michael Tarazi, Associated Press Report, 27 January 2006.
4 Israel Prime Minister's Office, 'Acting PM Olmert held a security discussion in the wake of the results of the Palestinian Authority (PA) elections', 26 January 2006.
5 President George W. Bush, *The Times*, 27 January 2006.
6 Jacob Walles, in Stephen Farrell and Ian MacKinnon, 'Show restraint or lose money, say donors', *The Times*, 28 January 2006.
7 Ismail Haniyeh, author interview, Shatti refugee camp, 25 January 2006.
8 Stephen Farrell and Ian MacKinnon, 'Show restraint or lose money, say donors', *The Times*, 28 January 2006.
9 James Wolfensohn, Senate Committee on Foreign Relations hearing on the Middle East after the Palestinian elections, 15 March 2006, CQ Transcriptions, Inc.
10 Dr Mahmoud Zahar, author interview, Gaza City, 6 April 2006.
11 Usama al-Mazini, author interview, Gaza City, 23 June 2006.
12 Senior Fatah official, author interview, Gaza City, 1 February 2006.
13 Honorable C. David Welch, assistant secretary, Bureau of Near Eastern Affairs, Department of State, US House of Representatives, 2 March 2006,www.house. gov/international_relations.
14 Dr Mahmoud Zahar, author interview, Gaza City, 23 January 2006.
15 Ibid.
16 Omar Suleiman, in Stephen Farrell, 'Hamas starts fundraising tour of the Arab world', *The Times*, 3 February 2006.
17 Ibid.

18 Khaled Meshaal, author note, Khan Younis, 26 January 2006.

19 Tom Lantos, 'United States policy toward the Palestinians in the aftermath of Parliamentary elections', Committee on International Relations, US House of Representatives, 2 March 2006, www.house.gov/international_relations.

20 Testimony of James D. Wolfensohn, quartet special envoy for disengagement, to the Foreign Relations Committee, United States Senate, 15 March 2006.

21 Robert Malley, Senate Committee on Foreign Relations hearing on the Middle East after the Palestinian elections, 15 March 2006, CQ Transcriptions, Inc.

22 Ayman al-Zawahiri, Agence France Presse, Dubai, 20 December 2006.

23 Khaled Meshaal, Agence France Presse, Doha, 21 December 2006.

24 Abu Ahmad, author interview, Gaza City, 18 April 2006.

25 Usama Hamdan, author interview, Beirut, 19 September 2007.

26 Jon B. Alterman, director and senior fellow, Middle East Program of the Center for Strategic and International Studies, statement to House of Representatives Committee on Foreign Affairs, subcommittee on the Middle East and South Asia, 5 June 2008.

27 Brigadier General Shalom Harari, author note, Jerusalem Institute for Contemporary Affairs lecture, Jerusalem, 9 January 2007.

28 Dr Hanan Ashrawi, author interview, Ramallah, 20 March 2007.

29 Nabil Shaath, author interview, Gaza City, 24 January 2006.

30 UN-OCHA, 'The Gaza Strip: February access report: closure at Karni crossing', 8 March 2006, www.ochaopt.org/documents.ochaSR_GazaAccess_Feb06.pdf.

31 Dr Omar Abdel-Razeq, author interview, Ramallah, 11 April 2006.

32 Said Siam, author interview, Gaza City, 16 November 2006.

33 Maher Abu Ramleh, author interview, Gaza City, 22 February 2007.

34 Dr Abdelrahman Bsaiso, author interview, Gaza City, 14 March 2007.

35 Popular Resistance Committees tunneller, author interview, Rafah, 27 June 2006.

36 Israeli Foreign Ministry analyst, in Stephen Farrell and Nicholas Blanford, 'Who controls Hamas – Haniya or Mashaal?', *The Times*, 10 July 2006.

37 Usama Hamdan, author interview, Beirut, 19 September 2007.

38 Abu Bakr Nofal, author interview, Gaza City, 6 September 2006.

39 Ismail Haniyeh, author note, Friday sermon at Sheikh Ahmed Yassin mosque, Gaza City, 23 June 2006.

40 Mahmoud Khalefa, author interview, Gaza City, 12 September 2006.

41 Ibrahim, author interview, Beit Lahiya, 6 September 2006.

42 Umm Osama, author interview, Gaza City, 6 September 2006.

43 Amal Saleem, author interview, Gaza City, 6 September 2006.

44 Maher Sukkar, author interview, Ein Hilweh refugee camp, Lebanon, 8 October 2006.

45 Palestinian Center for Policy and Survey Research in the West Bank and the Gaza Strip, 14–16 December 2006.

46 *The Times*, 10 December 2006.

47 Usama Hamdan, author interview, Beirut, 6 February 2007.

48 Dr Salam Fayyad, author interview, Ramallah, 17 March 2007.

49 US Consulate spokeswoman, author interview, Jerusalem, 17 March 2007.
50 Dr Hanan Ashrawi, author interview, Ramallah, 17 March 2007.
51 Ibid., 20 March 2007.
52 Ayman al-Zawahiri, *Al Jazeera*, 11 March 2007.
53 Anonymous, Izz ad-Din al-Qassam Brigades commander, author interview, Gaza Strip, 10 May 2007.
54 Younes al-Astal, Hamas leader, author interview, Gaza Strip, 10 May 2007.
55 A. A., Egyptian intelligence official, author interview, Gaza Strip, 28 October 2006.
56 Major General Yoav Galant, author note, Institute for Contemporary Affairs, Jerusalem Center for Public Affairs, 7 March 2007.
57 Yuval Diskin, Shin Bet director, briefing to journalists, Tel Aviv, 5 March 2007.
58 Mustafa Sawwaf, author interview, Gaza City, 4 July 2006.
59 Dr Mahmoud Zahar, author interview, Gaza City, 26 March 2007.
60 Anonymous, senior Egyptian diplomat, author interview, Gaza City, 11 May 2007.
61 Abu Obeidah al-Jarrah, author interview, Gaza City, 13 September 2006.
62 Said Siam, Hamas minister of interior, author interview, Gaza City, 29 October 2006.
63 General Keith Dayton, USSC, testimony to House Committee on International Relations, 23 May 2007.
64 Ayman Taha, Hamas spokesman, statement, 15 May 2007.
65 Izz ad-Din al-Qassam commander, author interview, Gaza Strip, 11 May 2007.

Chapter 14   Inferno

1 Islam Shahwan, author interview, Gaza City, 19 June 2007.
2 Islam Shahwan, author interview, Neve Dekalim, Gaza Strip, 2 November 2006.
3 Anonymous Western diplomat, author interview, 15 November 2006.
4 David Rose, 'Gaza bombshell', *Vanity Fair*, April 2008.
5 Condoleezza Rice, Cairo, 4 March 2008, US Department of State, www.state.gov/secretary/rm/2008/03/101745.htm.
6 Khaled Abu Hillal, author interview, Neve Dekalim, Gaza Strip, 2 November 2006.
7 Mohammed, author interview, Gaza City, 15 March 2007.
8 Shin Bet, 'Palestinian terrorism in 2007: statistics and trends', http://bern.mfa.gov.il/mfm/Data/131697.pdf.
9 Abu Qusay, author interview, Gaza City, 20 March 2008.
10 Brigadier General Yossi Kuperwasser (retired), author interview, 9 January 2009.
11 Mustafa Yaghi, author interview, Khan Younis, 12 November 2006.
12 Yuval Diskin, Shin Bet director, briefing to journalists, Tel Aviv, 5 March 2007.

13 Ibid.
14 Colonel Michael Pearson, USSC, author interview, Jerusalem, 11 August 2008.
15 Sami Abu Zuhri, author interview, Gaza City, 13 June 2007.
16 Ahmed Hilles, author interview, Gaza City, 23 April 2008.
17 Colonel Michael Pearson, USSC, author interview, Jerusalem, 11 August 2008.
18 Islam Shahwan, author interview, Gaza City, 19 June 2007.
19 Maher Miqdad, *New York Times*, 14 June 2007.
20 Dr Ismail al-Ashqar, author interview, Gaza City, 19 March 2008.
21 Captain Abu Yazi, author interview, Rafah, 20 March 2008.
22 Anonymous Western security official, author interview, Jerusalem, 13 August 2008.
23 Abu Suheil, author interview, Ramallah, 20 April 2008.
24 Reuters, 'Hamas hunts "collaborators" after Gaza rout', 14 June 2007.
25 Anonymous, Associated Press, 14 June 2007.
26 Ibrahim Madhoun, author interview, Ramallah, 20 May 2008.
27 Reuters, 'Hamas says "executed" top Fatah militant in Gaza', 14 June 2007.
28 Abu Thaer, author interview, Rafah, 20 March 2008.
29 Saud al-Faisal, *New York Times*, 16 June 2007.
30 John Ging, *New York Times*, 19 July 2007.
31 Khalil Saidi, author interview, Ramallah, 10 June 2008.
32 Samir and Munzer al-Halouli, author interview, Gaza City, 14 July 2008.
33 Hamas leaflet, Gaza City, June 2008.
34 Sheikh Nizar Rayan, statement to author, Gaza City, 15 June 2007.
35 Shin Bet, 'Palestinian terrorism in 2007: statistics and trends', http://bern.mfa.gov.il/mfm/Data/131697.pdf.
36 Mushir al-Masri, author interview, Beit Lahiya, 18 March 2008.
37 Dr Adnan Abu Amer, author interview, Gaza City, 16 July 2008.
38 Professor Ali al-Jarbawi, author interview, Ramallah, 18 May 2009.
39 Reuters, 'Israeli defence minister says to push on in Gaza', 2 March 2008.
40 Mushir al-Masri, author interview, Beit Lahiya, 13 March 2008.
41 Mohammed, author interview, Gaza City, 16 July 2008.
42 Ali, author interview, Beit Lahiya, 16 July 2008.
43 Anonymous, author interview, Jerusalem, 9 July 2008.
44 Abu Ahmad, author interview, Shejaiyah, Gaza Strip, 14 July 2008.
45 Jerusalem Media and Communication Centre, poll no. 66, November 2008, www.jmcc.org/publicpoll/results.html.
46 Ayman Kafarneh, author interview, Beit Hanoun, 16 July 2008.
47 *New York Times*, 27 December 2008.
48 *Al-Hayat al-Jadida*, 28 December 2008.
49 Mark Regev, author telephone note, 28 December 2008.
50 Yona Pavtulov, author interview, Beersheba, 4 January 2009.
51 Preventive Security official, author interview, Ramallah, 12 January 2009.
52 Mustafa Saleh, author interview, Ramallah, 28 December 2008.
53 Mohanad Salah, author interview, Ramallah, 28 December 2008.
54 Robert H. Serry, author interview, Jerusalem, 2 January 2009.

55 Dr Ismail al-Ashqar, author interview, Gaza City, 19 March 2008.

56 Palestinian Center for Policy and Survey Research, Ramallah, 31 May 2009

57 UN Human Rights Council, *Report of the United Nations Fact Finding Mission on the Gaza Conflict*, 29 September 2009, http://www2.ohchr.org/english/bodies/hrcouncil/specialsession/9/FactFindingMission.htm.

58 Hazem Abu Shaaban, author interview, Gaza City, 28 January 2009.

59 Nasser, author interview, Gaza City, 29 January 2009.

60 Abu Ahmed, author interview, Rafah, 28 January 2009.

61 Anonymous, author interview, Rafah, 28 January 2009.

62 Ibid.

63 A'ed Sa'ado Abed, author interview, Sheikh Radwan, 29 January 2009.

64 'Qassam strikes near Sderot, half an hour before election polls close', *Haaretz*, 10 February 2009.

65 Jerusalem Media and Communication Centre, poll no. 67, January 2009, www.jmcc.org/publicpoll/results.html.

66 Palestinian Center for Policy and Survey Research, Ramallah, public opinion poll no. 31, 5–7 March 2009.

67 Khalil al-Hayeh, author interview, Gaza City, 24 May 2009.

68 Mushir al-Masri, *Associated Press*, Ramallah, 19 May 2009.

69 Dr Said Abu Ali, minister of the interior, author interview, Ramallah, 25 May 2009.

70 Husam Khader, author interview, Nablus, 13 January 2009.

71 Dr Nasser Eddin al-Shaer, author interview, Nablus, 13 January 2009.

Index